BITTER FRUIT

War Worker, *The Crisis*, May 1943

BITTER FRUIT

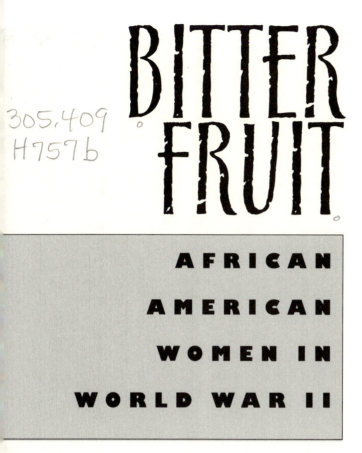

AFRICAN AMERICAN WOMEN IN WORLD WAR II

EDITED WITH AN
INTRODUCTION BY
Maureen Honey

University of Missouri Press
Columbia and London

Library of Congress Cataloging-in-Publication Data

Bitter fruit : African American women in World War II / edited with an
    introduction by Maureen Honey.
        p.   cm.
    Chiefly material reprinted from The crisis, Opportunity, Negro
    digest, and Negro story.
    Includes bibliographical references (p.   ) and index.
    ISBN 0-8262-1242-5 (alk. paper).—ISBN 0-8262-1265-4 (pbk. : alk. paper)
    1. World War, 1939-1945—Women—United States.   2. Afro-American
    women—United States—History—20th century.   I. Honey, Maureen,
    1945-   .
    D810.N4B4   1999   99-36106
    940.54'03—dc21   CIP

Text design: Elizabeth K. Young
Jacket design: Stephanie Foley
Typesetter: BookComp, Inc.
Printer and binder: Edwards Brothers, Inc.
Typefaces: Garamond Book, Gill Sans Condensed & Extra Bold

For credits, see page 399.

To Keith and Betty Honey,
my parents and members of
"the greatest generation."

I do not wear run-down shoes

Nor stand serene—nor pause to muse

Nor once relax my vigilance

Nor think in terms of recompense!

I stride on—alert and bold,

Vibrating with the bond I hold.

I do not play wild or free

Nor cast my eyes coquettishly

Toward him—to be thrown in contempt

Away! Of this I am exempt.

I square my shoulders, for on my breast

The weight of a race drops down to rest.

My humble being is glorified;

My beauty cannot be denied.

Look you upon me—fool or sage—

NEGRO WOMAN HAS COME OF AGE!

—CONSTANCE C. NICHOLS, "CONFIDENCE"
 (*Negro Story*, December–January 1944–1945)

Contents

Illustrations

Acknowledgments

There are many people who helped me put this project together and whom I would like to thank. I am most indebted to the NAACP and the National Urban League for their permission to reprint material from *The Crisis* and *Opportunity*. Without their generous support, I would not have been able to proceed. I would also like to thank them for persevering throughout the bulk of the twentieth century with their efforts to bring African American issues to the fore with their magazines and with courageous legal and journalistic actions challenging segregation and racism. Both organizations have been important as well in fostering the arts through publishing black writers who would otherwise not have found a national venue. African American literature would be much the poorer without their vision and commitment.

Scholars of African American women's literature and the history of World War II have been instrumental in laying the groundwork for this project. Among the most central to my wartime research for this volume have been Jacqueline Jones, Paula Giddings, Gretchen Lemke-Santangelo, Darlene Clark Hine, Ruth Milkman, Sherna Gluck, Susan Hartmann, Sonya Michel, Susan Schweik, Neil Wynn, and Karen Anderson (whose friendship over the years has helped sustain me as well). I am indebted to the recovery work of Lorraine Roses, Ruth Randolph, Elizabeth Ammons, Mary Helen Washington, Ann Allen Shockley, Gloria Hull, Claudia Tate, Hazel Carby, and Erlene Stetson, who have edited important anthologies of black women's writings in the early twentieth century. Deborah McDowell, Barbara Christian, Cheryl Wall, Amaritjit Singh, Nathan Huggins, Arnold Rampersad, David Levering Lewis, Henry Louis Gates, Jr., and others have helped lay the foundation for such scholarship. They have inspired my own recovery work in this important medium. Ronald and Abby Arthur Johnson made it possible for me to contextualize the wartime fiction included here, as well as to find out important information about *Negro Story*, in their groundbreaking analysis of the literary politics in these magazines. Similarly, Stanley Nelson's powerful new film on the black press gave me a sense of the key role played by African American journalists in their communities. A crucial reference work in this regard was Walter Daniel's exhaustive compilation of circulation figures, editorial history, and publication dates for every African American journal ever created in *Black Journals of the United States*. Finally, the research of Thomas Cripps and Donald Bogle on black film stars of the 1940s made it possible for me to understand the significance of Lena Horne, Dorothy Dandridge, Hazel Scott, and others in pioneering a new role for African American women in film after the war, a much neglected but badly needed topic of scholarship.

There are other key scholars and writers informing this anthology. Gwendolyn Brooks's warm and generous correspondence around this project has meant everything to me. Similarly, I have drawn strength from the gift of friendship extended by Joyce A. Joyce, June Jordan, Cheryl Clarke, Myriam Chancy, Angela Davis, and Hortense Spillers. I need to make special mention of my colleague Venetria Patton, whose feedback on the introduction was immensely valuable to me and whose daily friendship sustains me. I also want to thank Jim Knippling for his generous sharing of information on Chester Himes and his enthusiasm for the project. My colleagues Oyekan Owomoyela and Wheeler Winston Dixon were helpful at key points in directing me to appropriate publishers for this book, while Alpana Sharma, Sharon Harris, Linda Pratt, Domino Perez, Barbara DiBernard, Fran Kaye, Sue Rosowski, Grace Bauer, Judy Slater, Gerry Shapiro, Ellen and Paul Eggers, Joy Ritchie, George Wolf, Ray Ronci, and Gwendolyn Foster provided much-needed encouragement along the way. Especially meaningful to me is the support for my work on women and World War II provided by my colleague and close friend Marly Swick, whose writing talents have given me many hours of pleasure. I am also immensely grateful to Harry Reed and Darlene Clark Hine, who provided detailed and positive reviews of the manuscript, which helped me believe in the worth of the project.

I would like to thank as well the director of the University of Missouri Press, Beverly Jarrett, for her enthusiasm and guidance through early negotiations for the manuscript, and Jane Lago, managing editor, along with Julie Schroeder, editor. These women helped make the final product far better. My research assistants, Dawn Vernooy Epp, Michael Schueth, and Stephanie Gustafson, were indispensable in gathering the primary material and scanning it onto discs. Without their ingenuity and diligence, I could not have completed the work. To my great good fortune, they cared about the project and devoted time to it when needed. I wish to thank Martha Allen for her help with the cover of this book and for her sustaining friendship. I am grateful too for the financial support provided by the Research Council at the University of Nebraska in helping me pay the permissions fees attendant upon this publication and to the English Department for covering the cost of the illustrations. I wish to thank the office staff of the English Department for helping me with various phases of this project: Doris Smith, Leann Messing, and Kathie Johnson.

Finally, I want to thank my family for bearing with me while I put this manuscript together over the course of the last two years. I am especially thankful for the love, wise counsel, and academic expertise of my brother, Michael Honey, who read an early draft of the primary materials and pointed me in crucially central directions. He is a stalwart friend, colleague, and soul mate whose outstanding scholarship on black workers and civil rights provides endless inspiration. Last but by no means least, I want to thank my partner, Tom Kiefer, who has shown me bottomless amounts of understanding as I stole time away from our home life to complete this manuscript. Without his love, patience, and forbearance, I could never have brought it to life.

A Note on the Text

All material is reproduced here as it was originally published except for typographical errors, which have been corrected. In a few cases, extraneous passages have been excised from articles, with the missing sections indicated by ellipses. Also, I have occasionally added or deleted paragraph breaks where it seemed logical and helpful to do so. I have added notes to clarify allusions to events, personages, and slang of the period. Certain terms used by these writers no longer carry the connotation they did during the war period. The use of *colored* or *Negro* to signify African Americans, for example, was acceptable at the time, but not today. *Jim Crow* was a common reference to segregation, but it too has fallen out of the lexicon. The term was taken from a nineteenth-century white minstrel character in blackface who danced, sang, and made jokes about African American culture in demeaning ways.

The volume is arranged in four thematic sections, with pieces arranged such that reading them in sequence enhances their impact. Although it does not reflect publishing chronology, this arrangement makes clearer the correspondences between essays, fiction, and poetry illuminating women's roles. African American–authored poetry and fiction begin and end each section. The section introductions provide the reader with background information placing each piece into perspective. The volume begins with "War Work," since that was the subject under which women were given the most prominence. "Racism on the Home Front" concentrates on the military, the race riots of 1943, and segregation in housing and transportation, while giving a sense of how racist American society was during World War II. "The Double Victory Campaign" focuses on African American pride in black soldiers, resistance to racism, and hope for the future, while showcasing women as political activists. The collection ends with "Popular Culture and the Arts" because women were at the heart of African American discourse about culture during the war, and this material leaves the reader with positive images of female strength.

While the anthology favors African American women writers, I have included male and white writers when the subject matter illuminated issues of concern to or helped contextualize the status of black women. Stories reprinted here by Chester Himes, an African American man, for example, either feature black female characters or fictionalize racist situations with which African American women had to contend, such as racism in employment or the military. Likewise, the essay by black composer William Grant Still, while it does not deal with African American women directly, concerns popular culture issues that framed their images and roles as artists. In a few cases, white writers, particularly of fiction about women, were able to create progressive narratives that illustrate common rhetorical tropes about black women's wartime roles. The white writer James Light's "The Job," for instance, focuses on the inability of an African American waitress to keep her job in a white-owned restaurant.

Another reason I included nonblack and male writers is that, although one of the main purposes of this project is to bring to light forgotten female voices from the African American community, another is to make available images of and pertaining to the black woman in periodicals edited *by* African Americans *for* African Americans. I was interested not only in what black women had to say during World War II, but in what they read and in what was relayed about them in magazines with wide distribution in their communities. One part of the recovery of nonwhite female images from the war period, in other words, is studying what African American editors selected for an African American audience. Perhaps one thing to be learned from reading writers of both genders and various ethnicities published by these magazines is that gender issues are inextricably bound to those of race for African American women during World War II, and it was a time when white progressive perspectives on these questions had a place in black venues.

Selection criteria included black female authorship, aesthetic quality, subject matter relevance to black women's lives, and representativeness of themes found in these magazines. The weight given to each of these factors was variable, however. I excluded some well-written literature, for instance, in which women were neither featured prominently nor contextualized to any significant degree, such as important fiction by Ralph Ellison and Richard Wright, or poems by Frank Marshall Davis, Countee Cullen, and others. Alternatively, I did include nearly all of the fiction and poetry by African American women, of varying literary quality and whether it centered on women or not, in order to recover their voices and to examine their artistic choices. At the same time, I decided against reprinting some of the essays written by black women (Estelle Massey Riddle, Mabel Keaton Staupers, and Elizabeth C. Hampton among them) because they were of little heuristic value to the contemporary reader. Their essays on the need for nurses, WACs, and civilian employees, for instance, were neutrally phrased calls for readers to seek work in these areas and simply provided locations where it could be found.

There are six poems and one short story in the anthology that were not published in the four periodicals covered by this study. One of the poems appeared in a collection by the African American poet Owen Dodson, *Powerful Long Ladder* (1946), and was included because its subject is Pearl Primus, a black modern dancer whose choreography encoded a prominent theme of the war period: the political nature of women's contribution to African American art. Another Dodson poem, "Black Mother Praying in the Summer of 1943," was published in *Common Ground* (1944), and it too covers a major subject in wartime discourse about African American women: the mother as race activist. The four other poems are all by women and were drawn from a collection of African American poetry edited by Beatrice Murphy entitled *Ebony Rhythm* (1948). Because these were African American women writers who addressed issues central to the volume, I felt it was appropriate and instructive to include them ("A Woman at War," by Hazel L. Washington; "Black Recruit," by Georgia Douglas Johnson; "Guilty" and "We Launched A Ship," by Ruby Berkley Goodwin). None of these poems has been reprinted, and they are important reminders that African American women adopted militant wartime voices. Ann Petry's "In Darkness and Confusion" was submitted to *The Crisis* in 1943, but the editors rejected it because it was longer than their format allowed. Because this excellent story focused on a major wartime theme and was intended for one of the periodicals in this project, I decided to include it.

The task of gathering material for this volume was made harder by the practice of all four periodicals to include white writers and to avoid identifying contributors by race or ethnicity. Also, biographical encyclopedias do not always include African American women. It is possible, therefore, that I misidentified the ethnic background of some writers, yet I felt it was important to categorize them, since restoration of black women's voices is so important to the literary and historical record (see appendix). Criteria for identifying a writer as African American included information provided by the magazines' contributors notes, scholarship on the writer, the writer's inclusion in collections of African American literature or biographies, and self-identification by the author. There are forty women anthologized here (out of eighty writers) who are identifiably African American using these criteria. There are another twelve women writers who were neither clearly white nor black, and some of these may very well be African American, but there is as yet insufficient information to say who they might be.

BITTER
FRUIT

Introduction

Early one morning in 1944, Major Charity Adams, the first African American to be inducted into the Women's Army Corps, stood at attention for forty-five minutes while her superior officer, a colonel, castigated her for having entered the Fort Des Moines, Iowa, officers club the night before. She had been invited to do so by another officer, a white male colonel, to share a drink. "So you are the Major Adams, the 'negra' officer who went into the officers club last night," the colonel charged. "I don't think any colored person has ever been a guest there before. What were you doing there? Who had the nerve to invite you there? I don't believe in race mixing, and I don't intend to be party to it. . . . Don't let being an officer go to your head; you are still colored and I want you to remember that. You people have to stay in your place. Why, your folks might have been slaves to my people . . . and here you are acting like you are the same as white folks." Bewildered, angry, hurt, Charity Adams never went to the officers club again.[1]

The humiliating treatment WAC Adams endured in this incident represents the racism that fueled African American anger at American society during World War II, a time when segregation not only ruled the armed forces but governed a large part of civilian life. In her 1989 memoir, Charity Adams Earley describes several instances of racial harassment directed at her and other African American WACs by whites who could not tolerate seeing a black woman in uniform, even though she also experienced many examples of white civility and benefited more than she suffered from her military service. Earley's dichotomous wartime experience explains in large part why segregation of the armed forces became the single most volatile issue between African Americans and government leaders while providing the flashpoint for bitter denunciations of racism on the home front. If the country needed its black citizens to win the war, so the reasoning went, they could demand equal treatment in return, especially in a war for democracy.

Charity Adams Earley and others like her witnessed desegregation of the armed forces in 1948 as well as significant inroads into dismantling discriminatory practices in housing, education, jobs, transportation, and media representation after the war, but their wartime challenges to Jim Crow went largely unmentioned in the dominant culture of the 1940s.

---

1. Charity Adams Earley, *One Woman's Army: A Black Officer Remembers the WAC,* 108.

Racist stereotypes in film, radio, popular magazines, and other forms of white entertainment distorted African American life, when blacks were not ignored altogether. This was especially true of black women, who suffered gender as well as race prejudice. Virtually invisible in mainstream media were the 600,000 women out of one million African Americans who were in the wartime labor force; the 4,000 African American WACs; the 330 African Americans in the Army Nurse Corps; the women on social action committees who held communities together; the civil rights activists pressing for integration of public facilities and better housing; the students studying to be lawyers, doctors, teachers, or scientists; and the performing artists who gained critical acclaim during the war years.

Despite this participation of African American women in all aspects of home-front activity, advertising, recruitment posters, and newsreels nearly always portrayed white women as WACs, WAVEs, SPARs, Army nurses, defense-plant workers, service wives, concerned mothers, sales clerks, clerical workers, telephone operators, gas-station attendants, and the like in the national effort to get women into wartime activities. Radio soap-opera stars, actresses in Hollywood melodramas and comedies, singers with white bands, and female tap dancers in film musicals were white, with rare exceptions. This sea of white faces erased the contributions African American women made to the home-front war on racism, while it left for posterity white images of Rosie the Riveter, the glamorous pinup, the female soldier, the compassionate nurse, and the brave mother. This erasure is reflected in the absence of feature articles or fictional stories on African American women in *The Reader's Guide to Periodical Literature* from the war years.[2] Unmentioned in that reference are the many pieces about black women that were published in African American magazines, since most of them were not indexed, including the periodicals in this anthology.

This volume is intended to help correct that distorted picture of women's

---

2. Only one entry on African American women from a mass-circulation magazine is listed in *The Reader's Guide to Periodical Literature* from 1942–1945 under the heading "Negro." It is a profile of a middle-class army wife and her two daughters living in Philadelphia. Wealthy enough to afford a maid and travel by Pullman (sleeper) car when visiting her husband, Cordelia Hinkson was a full-time homemaker, and her children attended the University of Wisconsin and Cornell University when the article was written ("Meet the Hinksons," *Ladies' Home Journal* 59 [August 1942]: 75–79). An important study of the ongoing stereotyping of African Americans in dominant culture magazines of World War II is Bernard Berelson and Patricia Salter's "Majority and Minority Americans: An Analysis of Magazine Fiction."

role in World War II in that it brings together for the first time since they were originally published photos, essays, fiction, and poetry by and about black women in four African American periodicals of the war period: *The Crisis, Opportunity, Negro Story,* and *Negro Digest.* Unable to locate this material in *The Reader's Guide* or easily find the pieces on women scattered throughout these magazines from 1942–1945, the contemporary reader finds in this anthology a thematically organized presentation of writings by or about black wartime women. Here we see photos of nonwhite women operating riveting guns and other technological machinery, in uniform, as canteen hostesses, in glamorous gowns, on concert stages, in nursing caps, and on college campuses, while articles praise their accomplishments as pioneers paving the way toward racial equality. Here too are fictional black female characters in roles other than cardboard domestic servants, who combine paid work with family life, rear children to be talented professionals, protest racial injustice, love passionately, and dream of a democratic future.

Poetry and fiction written by African American women appearing in these magazines allows their voices to be heard as they express bitterness about the color bar and determination to be soldiers of democracy on the home front. Excluded as writers and subjects from the dominant culture, black women found in these journals images of themselves that formulated their historic wartime role and gave them hope for an improved postwar world. These journals told where and how to find well-paying jobs, gave encouragement that racism in the workplace would not be crushing, and provided models of accomplishment and words of anger. Most importantly, the journals gave African American women a podium for announcing who they were and wanted to become.

Although these periodicals were not the only publication outlets for African American women in the war, they were among the most important.[3]

---

3. Other journals in which African American writers were published during the war were *Phylon* (a scholarly journal begun by W. E. B. Du Bois in 1940), *Aframerican Woman's Journal* (founded by the National Council of Negro Women in 1940), *Common Ground* (an interracial journal), the *American Mercury* (another interracial journal), *Negro Quarterly, Pulse, The Negro, Headlines and Pictures,* and *The African.* These were all more limited venues for black women writers because either their circulations were very low or they did not accept large numbers of African American–authored pieces, particularly by women. Two periodicals with wide circulation in the African American community are not covered here because they did not get started until after the war. They are *Ebony,* which was founded in November 1945, and *Jet,* which got off the ground in 1951. This collection does

Edited by John H. Johnson, *Negro Digest* was a Chicago periodical begun in November 1942 that eventually achieved one of the highest circulations of any black magazine.[4] Modeled after *Reader's Digest,* it condensed pieces published in newspapers and other magazines of interest to its African American audience. *The Crisis* was founded by W. E. B. Du Bois in 1910 and reported activities of the National Association for the Advancement of Colored People (NAACP). The NAACP's wartime activism fueled circulation of *The Crisis,* which increased dramatically during the war years from seven thousand to forty-five thousand under the editorial direction of Roy Wilkins, who would become executive director of the organization and a leader in civil rights campaigns. *Opportunity* began publication in 1923 under the editorship of Charles S. Johnson. As the mouthpiece for the National Urban League, it too enjoyed high circulation (six thousand) at this time under initial editorship of Elmer Carter and then Madeleine Aldridge, who took over in November 1942. Of all the African American magazines published during the war, *The Crisis* and *Opportunity* survived the longest, achieved the highest circulations, and enjoyed national stature for the quality of their editors and writers. Central organs of the Harlem Renaissance coming out of New York, they specialized in the arts as well as investigative reporting, which meant that aspiring creative writers could find an audience denied them by dominant-culture publications. Last, *Negro Story* was a Chicago magazine established by two African American women, Alice C. Browning and Fern Gayden, in the spring of 1944; they were aided by Gwendolyn Brooks, Margaret Walker, Richard Wright, Ralph Ellison, Chester Himes, and Langston Hughes. Although its circulation was only one thousand and it went out of business a short time later, in 1946, after publishing only nine issues, it too was a significant resource for African American creative

---

not cover African American newspapers due to lack of space. In addition, because three of the magazines covered by this study published so many black women poets and fiction writers, they have left to us a sizable body of wartime writing that complements the objective reportage contained in those publications. Some of them enjoyed extremely wide circulation during the war, and they do need to be examined. Among the most important were the *Pittsburgh Courier,* the *Chicago Defender,* the *Kansas City Call,* and the *Michigan Chronicle.*

4. *The Ayers Directory of Newspapers and Periodicals* lists *Negro Digest* as a publication of the war years, but it does not list a circulation figure for it. The magazine was published from November 1942 to November 1951. It was restarted in June 1961 and ceased publication again in April 1970, at which time it became *Black World.* It enjoyed a peak circulation of 120,000 during its lifetime. Walter C. Daniel, *Black Journals of the United States,* 262–64.

writers, and its editorship by black women gives the short stories and poetry they selected special importance for people studying this literature today. Together, these four African American magazines represent a counternarrative to the discourse about women contained in dominant culture media and show us what editors of color considered appropriate material for a black audience at a time when not much was available by African American writers in mass-circulation magazines.[5]

There are 40 women writers included here who are identifiably African American, most of them unknown today.[6] This is out of a total of 80 writers in the collection, 57 of whom are female and 57 of whom are African American. There are another 12 women writers in this anthology whose ethnicity is not clear from the scanty biographical information available. It is likely that some of these are African American, but given the lack of historical information on many women writers of color and the fact that white writers were published by all four journals, it is unclear who they might be.

Although the important role of African American periodicals in the publication lives of black writers is not often recognized, some of the women reprinted here were at the dawn of distinguished careers when they debuted in these magazines (Ann Petry, Gwendolyn Brooks, Margaret Walker, Pauli Murray). Still others had gotten their start in periodicals of the Harlem Renaissance (Georgia Douglas Johnson, Zora Neale Hurston, Octavia Wynbush). What united them was a need to write in the midst of a worldwide military conflict that had dramatic potential for ending

---

5. After the war, white mainstream periodicals widened their doors to African American creative writers, but this was at a time when magazine circulations were in decline due to the impact of television and after they shifted away from publishing fiction. For a history of the rise and fall of the magazine industry, see Theodore Peterson, *Magazines in the Twentieth Century.*

6. The appendix lists the writers included here by probable ethnicity when biographical information or contributors' notes allowed such identification. *The Crisis, Opportunity,* and *Negro Story* all provided limited descriptions of some of the writers in each issue, but only *Negro Story* alluded to race, and that was only occasionally. Identifying the African American writers was made even more difficult by the policy of all four journals to include and even solicit pieces by white writers and to downplay the race of authors. These practices grew out of the period's "aesthetics of integration," described in Abby Arthur Johnson and Ronald Maberry Johnson's study of African American periodicals, *Propaganda and Aesthetics: The Literary Politics of Afro-American Magazines in the Twentieth Century,* 125–60. African American women writers are underrepresented in biographical encyclopedias, making identification impossible in some cases.

segregation and opening doors for women at home. Whether just starting their writing careers or ending them, whether they were destined for literary distinction or not, these women sensed that the war brought opportunities for ending the racial and gender restrictions that had hindered black women from full participation in American life. As they confronted World War II, these writers inform us of the home-front battles they had yet to win—against racial discrimination in employment, transportation, restaurants, and housing, or sexism in the home. Buoyed by the doors that were opening, yet bruised by those that remained shut, their hope for the future was tempered by bitterness about the present.

Most of the writers in this volume are not familiar to contemporary readers, and their work has not been reprinted since it was originally published. There are others, however, who have outlasted their time and whose presence here testifies to the importance of World War II as a galvanizing event for African American writers, one that launched the careers of a whole generation while closing those of a previous one. Although much of this group's writings have been made available elsewhere (particularly that of Gwendolyn Brooks, Margaret Walker, Langston Hughes, Ann Petry, and Chester Himes), this is the first volume to reprint these pieces in their original wartime context, a setting that illuminates their concerns. Anthologies of African American literature tend to jump from the Harlem Renaissance to the 1960s, with little having been done on decades between those periods aside from studies of individual authors, and this anthology brings to light the themes related to gender that animate African American wartime writing.

Of particular note are several poems and short stories that are anthologized here for the first time. Heretofore unreprinted, "On Saturday the Siren Sounds at Noon," by Ann Petry, was her first published story under her own name, and it led to her contract with Houghton Mifflin for *The Street* (1946). Similarly, James Baldwin's poem "Black Girl Shouting" was his first publication but appears in none of his collected works. Other noteworthy pieces include unreprinted work by the Harlem Renaissance writers Octavia Wynbush ("The Black Streak") and Georgia Douglas Johnson ("Black Recruit," "Interracial," and "To Friendship"), as well as a poem ("Salty River") by Marie Brown Frazier, wife of the sociologist E. Franklin Frazier. Though it has appeared elsewhere, another notable work is Shirley Graham's story "Tar," here sourced for the first time. Graham, who married W. E. B. Du Bois in 1951, deftly skewers the racism that denied many African American women the skilled work for which they applied.

Having this material available not only helps balance the picture of white female war workers inherited from the past, but it also aids in understanding how race complicates gender issues in the early 1940s. For one thing, the commonly accepted idea that women were able to cross gender barriers in World War II and find better work than was normally available to them is true largely of *white* women, but African Americans and women from other minority groups did not enjoy these benefits to nearly the same degree. Indeed, most scholars maintain that the war had no appreciable impact on economic opportunities for women who were black, and this material testifies to the pain that discrimination caused.[7] Karen Anderson reports that as late as February 1943, nonwhites held only one thousand of the ninety-six thousand positions filled by women in Detroit war industries, for instance, and that black men and women never accounted for less than 6 percent of all employees in aircraft, whereas white women constituted nearly 40 percent of all aircraft workers. African Americans, she says, made their biggest gains in heavily male-employing industrial fields: foundries, shipbuilding, blast furnaces, and steel mills. Black women went into dangerous munitions factories, did heavy labor for the railroads, or were hired as washroom attendants and cleaning women in war plants. Most clerical work, many public service positions, and sales jobs were unavailable to African American women, according to Anderson. While their share of clerical jobs rose significantly due to federal hiring patterns in Washington, D.C., government offices, they only composed 1.6 percent of all clerical workers, and their proportion in the female sales force actually declined to a low of 1.1 percent during the war. Although they achieved significant breakthroughs, African American women made such negligible occupational progress during the war that their relative position in the labor force remained the same at the height of wartime employment in 1944 as it was in 1940, according to Anderson.[8] Restrictive quotas were often

---

7. The most important of these studies are Jacqueline Jones, *Labor of Love, Labor of Sorrow: Black Women, Work, and the Family from Slavery to the Present;* Karen Anderson, *Wartime Women: Sex Roles, Family Relations, and the Status of Women during World War II;* Karen Anderson, *Changing Woman: A History of Racial Ethnic Women in Modern America;* and Neil A. Wynn, *The Afro-American and the Second World War.* Although they agree that wartime opportunities for black women were limited by racism, scholars who view them more positively are Gretchen Lemke-Santangelo, *Abiding Courage: African American Migrant Women and the East Bay Community;* and Paula Giddings, *When and Where I Enter: The Impact of Black Women on Race and Sex in America.*

8. Karen Anderson, "Last Hired, First Fired: Black Women Workers during World War II," 85.

followed by those employers who did hire African Americans but held their proportion to no more than 10 percent of their workers, and they routinely placed them in unskilled or janitorial positions and on night shifts. Barred from most service occupations like telephone operators or waitresses in white eating establishments, black women mainly found industrial work in munitions plants, where accident rates were high and the work unpleasant.

Testifying to the persistence of a wartime racial bar, even in the midst of severe labor shortages, is the bitterness that runs through much of this material and the many fictional stories with characters who are domestic workers. Although between 1940 and 1944, the proportion of working black women employed in domestic service fell from 60 to 44 percent, for instance, they continued to fill a majority of such jobs in the wartime labor force, and domestic employment remained their primary occupation (40 percent of employed black women were in this job category).[9] Even in the military, black women had trouble escaping low-skilled assignments. Six African American WACs, for example, were court-martialed at Fort Devens, Massachusetts, when they refused to take custodial assignments.[10] In her memoir of the Women's Army Corps, Charity Adams Earley mentions the common army practice of dividing into "white" and "colored" the jobs that WACs were given, with the latter being menial and unskilled.[11]

When looking at the segregated hiring patterns of World War II, it is important to keep in mind that few areas of American life were integrated at that time, and employers could routinely avoid hiring workers they considered inferior (due to racist, sexist stereotypes) or requiring separate facilities (segregated rest rooms or work shifts). Affirmative action had not been heard of, and government mandates forbidding race discrimination in defense industries, such as Executive Order 8802 (created in June 1941), were poorly enforced. As the stories and articles on how racism operated in the wartime workplace illustrate here, African American women found themselves at the bottom of the list when it came time to fill well-paying positions.

Maya Angelou's experience in San Francisco as a young black woman eager to get one of these lucrative wartime jobs is instructive. Angelou was a teenager when the war broke out, and she sensed the excitement of new opportunities for women when her family moved her to the Bay

---

9. Ibid. See also David Katzman, *Seven Days a Week: Women and Domestic Service in Industrializing America.*

10. Jones, *Labor of Love,* 253.

11. Earley, *One Woman's Army,* 24, 34.

Area from Arkansas. In love with the cityscape she eagerly explored, Angelou determined to be a streetcar conductor when she read a newspaper advertisement one morning, but when she tried to apply, a clerk at the Market Street Railway Company discouraged her with evasions and negative responses. As historians Jacqueline Jones and Karen Anderson have noted, Angelou's stubbornness brought her victory—she became the first black San Francisco streetcar conductor—but the treatment she endured was for most other women an effective deterrent. Even with her success story, Angelou tells us, the prejudice with which her job query was met cast a pall over the city's romantic glow, and she later wondered if she were being singled out for bad shifts.[12]

Another good example of the limitations faced by African American women is the case of Fanny Christina Hill, described in Sherna Gluck's study of former aircraft workers in the Los Angeles area. Tina Hill migrated to California from Texas in 1940 to take advantage of burgeoning industrial activity on the West Coast and landed a job at North American Aviation, the largest employer of blacks in aircraft. Certainly her wages were good, and she was fortunate enough to return to North American after the initial layoffs of 1946, where she stayed for forty years, but even in this relatively enlightened war plant, Hill says African Americans were segregated from other workers: "I could see where they made a difference in placing you in certain jobs. They had fifteen or twenty departments, but all the Negroes went to Department 17 because there was nothing but shooting and bucking rivets. . . . I just didn't like it." She acknowledges that North American hired black people, "but they had to fight": "They fought hand, tooth, and nail to get in there. And the first five or six Negroes who went in there, they were well educated, but they started them off as janitors. After they once got their foot in the door and was there for three months— you work for three months before they say you're hired—then they had to start fighting all over again to get off of that broom and get something decent. . . . See, the jobs have already been tested and tried out before they ever get into the department, and they know what's good about them and what's bad about them. They always managed to give the worst one to the Negro. . . . There were some departments, they didn't even allow a black person to walk through there, let alone work in there. Some of the white people did not want to work with the Negro. They had arguments right

---

12. Maya Angelou, *I Know Why the Caged Bird Sings;* Jones, *Labor of Love,* 239; Anderson, *Changing Woman,* 189; Angelou, *Caged Bird,* 228.

there."[13] Tina Hill was persistent in gaining access to the jobs she preferred at North American, but her account makes clear that racism was an ongoing battle even for those who found good jobs.

Another important way race intrudes into contemporary pictures of women at this time concerns the war's aftermath. Considerable scholarship has been done on white women, for example, that suggests World War II was a pivotal event paradoxically rolling back many of the gains secured by a feminist movement grown moribund after winning the vote in 1920.[14] Despite the employment of women in traditionally male occupations, perhaps the war's most curious impact on gender roles, according to this literature, was to reinscribe essentialist notions of woman's nature as biologically determined and best located in the sphere of home. Although individuals in the postwar world continued to enter the workforce in ever greater numbers, press for equal rights, and achieve in professional arenas, dominant culture rhetoric created a narrow maternal mission for women that was not fully deconstructed until the 1960s. This rhetorical outcome was foreshadowed in wartime propaganda that identified the homemaker-centered family as synonymous with American democracy, the reason the war was being fought. Coupled with the baby boom and glorification of a suburban postwar ideal, this reductive image of American life fed easily into massive layoffs of women workers during reconversion, who

---

13. Sherna B. Gluck, *Rosie the Riveter Revisited: Women, the War, and Social Change,* 38, 42–43. Paula Giddings supports Tina Hill's assessment of the racism at North American Aviation, whose president is quoted in her study as saying: "While we are in complete sympathy with the Negro, it is against company policy to employ them as aircraft workers or mechanics . . . regardless of their training. . . . There will be some jobs as janitors" (Giddings, *When and Where,* 235). Three African American former war workers are interviewed in the film *The Life and Times of Rosie the Riveter: The Story of Three Million Working Women during World War II* (Connie Field, Miriam Frank, and Marilyn Ziebarth [Emeryville, Calif.: Clarity Educational Productions, 1982]).

14. See, for example, Maureen Honey, *Creating Rosie the Riveter: Class, Gender, and Propaganda during World War II;* Amy Kesselman, *Fleeting Opportunities: Women Shipyard Workers in Portland and Vancouver during World War II and Reconversion;* Sherrie A. Kossoudji and Laura J. Dresser, "The End of a Riveting Experience: Occupational Shifts at Ford after World War II"; Leila J. Rupp, *Mobilizing Women for War: German and American Propaganda, 1939-1945;* and Eleanor Straub, "U.S. Government Policy toward Civilian Women during World War II." For a slightly different view on the war's impact on women, see William Chafe, *The American Woman: Her Changing Social, Economic, and Political Roles, 1920-1970.*

were characterized as "returning to the home" to begin a home-centered, quintessentially American way of life.[15]

Whereas wartime rhetoric segued into a suburban homemaker ideal in the dominant culture, however, much of the material included here interrogates that very model, while lauding women's roles as activists in the Double Victory campaign ("Victory over Fascism Abroad, Victory over Racism at Home"). This is in part because racial covenants that excluded black people from postwar subdivisions like Levittown and Stuyvesant Town, as well as discriminatory real estate practices, confined African Americans to urban ghettos.[16] Rarely did black homeowners penetrate the invisible barriers to life in the suburbs or even white areas of town in the years immediately following the war, and racial covenants were not outlawed until 1948.

While they enjoyed home ownership on an unprecedented scale, African Americans did not often participate in the move toward subdivisions accelerated by postwar construction of new housing. That would come much later, after civil rights successes in the 1950s challenged discriminatory selling practices. Not only were black women excluded from the mainstream rhetorical picture, they generally were not in an economic position to give up gainful employment for a full-time homemaker role. Although many white working-class women were in a similar position, the double bind of racial discrimination in housing and the labor force made the nonworking suburban housewife ideal of the mid-forties a particularly alienating, largely

---

15. Two studies of the emphasis on maternal figures in wartime films are M. Joyce Baker, *Images of Women in Film: The War Years, 1941-1945;* and Mary Ann Doane, *The Desire to Desire: The Woman's Film of the 1940s.* An important work covering the postwar era on this issue is Elaine Tyler May, *Homeward Bound: American Families in the Cold War.* My study of recruitment propaganda identifies the family as the central location of meaning for women and the nation as a whole (Honey, *Creating Rosie the Riveter*). The first analyst to describe postwar narrowing of the ideal woman's role was Betty Friedan, *The Feminine Mystique.* For a reading of the period counter to Friedan's, see Joanne Meyerowitz, "Beyond the Feminine Mystique: A Reassessment of Postwar Mass Culture, 1946-1958."

16. A good description of housing discrimination during the war is provided in Wynn, *The Afro-American and the Second World War,* 60-78; see also Dominic Capeci Jr. and Martha Wilkerson, *Race Relations in Wartime Detroit: The Sojourner Truth Housing Controversy of 1942.* An article in the present volume describing race prejudice in housing is Constance H. Curtis's "Lily White 'Walled City.'" Commenting on the ironies of a white suburban ideal when looked at from a black urban perspective during the 1940s are Ann Petry's *The Street* and Toni Morrison's *The Bluest Eye.*

unattainable goal for African Americans. Awareness of segregated housing and racist employment patterns permeates the magazine material here and makes hollow the full-time–homemaker ideal so central to wartime propaganda.

One of the most striking differences between treatment of the war in these magazines and in dominant culture periodicals is that the latter developed a traditional, conservative vision of America as a united collection of white, middle-class, suburban families. African American discourse, on the other hand, portrayed that very model as a racist monolith of suffocating proportions. Dominant culture magazine stories and advertising featured white women war workers sacrificing their "normal" homemaking desires for "temporary" industrial jobs to win the war. The male soldier was portrayed as an absent breadwinner without whom the family functioned poorly, making victory abroad essential for establishing prosperous, healthy families at home. Mothers and wives were often shown in static roles, waiting anxiously for the return of these soldiers so that they could "resume" their desired lives as housekeepers.[17]

In contrast, women workers in the four magazines represented by this anthology, while similarly portrayed as motivated to support the black soldier, were not cast as housewives temporarily entering new work roles. Rather, they were shown as trailblazers able to escape low-wage domestic service. Labor recruiters, moreover, noted the war's disruption of this group's historic confinement to domestic work and assumed they would continue working once it was over. Indeed, 40 percent of all black women already were in the labor force when the war broke out, as opposed to only 25 percent of white women.[18] In short, African American WACs, welders, riveters, and government clerical workers were praised in black

---

17. Susan Hartmann, among others, describes this aspect of popular culture in "Prescriptions for Penelope: Literature on Women's Obligations to Returning World War II Veterans"; and in Hartmann, *Home Front and Beyond.* See also Sonya Michel, "American Women and the Discourse of the Democratic Family in World War II," in Margaret Randolph Higonnet, Jane Jenson, Sonya Michel, and Margaret Collins Weitz, eds., *Behind the Lines: Gender and the Two World Wars.*

18. Lemke-Santangelo, *Abiding Courage,* 16. In this study of African American women workers in the Bay Area, Lemke-Santangelo reports that paid work was a normal part of life for them and that 95 percent of nonwhite women employed there during the war years planned to continue working after the war (108). Paula Giddings also asserts that wage work was a normal part of family life for black women and that their employment was seen as central to middle-class status by the African American community in the postwar years (*When and Where,* 247).

magazines for helping to erase the ubiquitous portrait of black women in maid uniforms or on their knees with scrub pails.

Moreover, one of the major themes emerging from the material collected here is that the gung ho patriotism of dominant culture narratives is not typical of African American magazines. Mass-circulation periodicals published vast amounts of propaganda designed to unify the population, played on the notion of guilt to recruit women into the labor force, and supported patriotic drives undertaken by the federal government's Office of War Information (OWI).[19] Their African American counterparts, however, while supportive of the war effort, simultaneously critiqued the patriotism that fueled mass-media rhetorical strategies. They did not ask black women to sacrifice their own interests for the good of the country, for instance, because it was well known to them that the country was racist.

A prominent feature of fiction and poetry in this collection, in fact, is subversive treatment of the OWI campaigns being supported by other magazines. Conservation of scarce materials, Victory mail for soldiers, worker-management harmony in industrial employment, stoic acceptance of wartime conditions, and home-front unity were all themes magazines were asked to publicize, but writers for an African American audience approached them with irony, subtly undercutting patriotic campaigns. Chester Himes's "All He Needs Is Feet," for instance, describes the vicious attack on a black man by Georgians who set fire to his feet with gasoline furnished by a ration card. When prompted as an audience member to stand at attention when the flag appears on a movie screen, therefore, he cannot demonstrate respect for his country. Similarly, Gwendolyn Williams's "Heart against the Wind" ostensibly supports OWI's V-mail campaign for civilians to write uplifting letters to loved ones in uniform, but it focuses on a black service wife who finds herself writing a bitter letter to her husband in which she rails against the racism that will taint the life of their unborn child.[20]

---

19. See Honey, *Creating Rosie the Riveter;* and Rupp, *Mobilizing Women.* See also Allan M. Winkler, *The Politics of Propaganda: The Office of War Information, 1942-1945;* Frank Fox, *Madison Avenue Goes to War: The Strange Military Career of American Advertising, 1941-1945;* David Jones, "The U.S. Office of War Information and American Public Opinion during World War II, 1939-1945"; and Robert Howell, "The Writers' War Board: Writers and World War II."

20. A study that describes the propaganda campaign Williams represents here with such devastating irony is Judy Barrett Litoff and David C. Smith's " 'Will He Get My Letter?': Popular Portrayals of Mail and Morale during World War II."

"Tar," by Shirley Graham is another good example of ironic allusion to OWI propaganda.[21] The African American service wife in this story has responded to a radio recruitment ad by enrolling in a defense training school so that she can help build the planes that will lead her country to victory, but when she applies for aircraft jobs, no factory will hire her. Graham parallels this futile search with that of her character's soldier sweetheart, who has attended civil engineering classes only to find that the army will admit his white classmates to officer training school but not him. Ambitious, patriotic, and idealistic, these two characters stumble against racism in both the wartime labor force and the military.

A would-be Rosie the Riveter, the best Graham's sheet-metal worker can do is find a job pouring tar on the night shift, while her husband is put to work unloading military equipment. Both were typical occupations for black civilian workers and soldiers. A field secretary during the war for the NAACP in New York City, where the story takes place, Graham was well aware of the racism that afflicts her characters, having served as a USO director at the biggest army camp for African American soldiers, Fort Huachuca, Arizona, a post from which she was fired for protesting the conditions there. She also lost her son in 1943 to poor medical treatment at an army induction center. In "Tar," Graham effectively skewers the racist underside of patriotic calls to duty by drawing a scenario of disillusionment for her characters, young southern migrants to a supposedly enlightened urban war center. At the story's end, the soldier's letter describing a tank explosion that has left him covered with tar mirrors the protagonist's futile attempts to remove the tar left on her own body from her defense plant job, and it comes to symbolize the racism that permeates their working lives.

Stories by Ann Petry in this collection also contain subversive allusions to the flag-waving propaganda ubiquitous on the home front. For example, a custodial worker at the center of "In Darkness and Confusion" finds that his patriotic remarks at a Harlem barbershop are followed by news that his

---

21. An incident in Graham's story, in which the main character's soldier sweetheart is covered with tar after an explosion on a dock where he unloads military equipment, is based on an actual explosion at a Navy dock in 1944 that killed over 250 African American sailors. For a description of this event, see Robert L. Allen, "The Port Chicago Disaster and Its Aftermath." The story also alludes to and mocks the OWI recruitment technique of comparing women's work in the home, such as sewing (the main character is a seamstress), to factory work. See Anderson, *Wartime Women*, 128–29. An indictment of Fort Huachuca, where Graham had worked, is provided in an article included in this volume, Thelma Thurston Gorham's "Negro Army Wives."

soldier son has been shot and jailed at a Georgia army camp for refusing to go to the back of the bus. Reinforcing this portrayal of racism in the military is his wife's domestic job in a navy household, which pays so poorly and is such hard work that her health is endangered. Together, their menial jobs allow them to afford only a poorly ventilated top-floor apartment in a run-down neighborhood. Moreover, the teenage niece who lives with them is so fed up with the bad jobs open to black women that she prefers unemployment and hanging out with her friends in bars.

Although Petry's story "Like a Winding Sheet" has been reprinted in many anthologies, reading it in its original wartime context reveals the contestatory themes that link it to other African American treatments of the war. A pushcart operator on the night shift at a defense plant, Petry's protagonist is subjected by his white supervisor to a racist tongue-lashing and forced to be on his feet ten hours at a stretch.[22] As in the story "In Darkness and Confusion," where the red and white stripes of the barber pole mock her characters' second-class status in a very un-united America, Petry makes ironic use of red, white, and blue here as well. The white sheet of her character's bed, of course, is a familiar symbol of prejudice to contemporary readers, along with the porcelain tables and marble counter of the diner where he is refused a cup of coffee, but the whiteness of these items, the red lipstick of his supervisor, and his own blue overalls form a trio of patriotic colors at the ironic heart of this war worker's home-front treatment.

Petry's "On Saturday the Siren Sounds at Noon" concerns another factory worker who is surrounded by patriotic symbols when he jumps to his death in front of a subway train.[23] The gleaming metal tracks he sees on

22. Ann Petry, "In Darkness and Confusion," was anthologized in Edwin Seaver, ed., *Cross Section*, 98-128. Petry submitted this story about the Harlem riot of August 1943 to *The Crisis*, but it was rejected because of its length. It has also appeared in Abraham Chapman, ed., *Black Voices*; and Petry's *Miss Muriel and Other Stories*; among other places. Studies of wartime race riots include Dominic J. Capeci Jr. and Martha Wilkerson, *Layered Violence: The Detroit Rioters of 1943*; Cheryl Greenberg, "The Politics of Disorder: Reexamining Harlem's Riots of 1935–1943"; Janet L. Langlois, "The Belle Isle Bridge Incident: Legend Dialect and Semiotic Systems in the 1943 Detroit Race Riots"; Mauricio Mazon, *The Zoot-Suit Riots: The Psychology of Symbolic Annihilation;* and Wynn, *The Afro-American and the Second World War,* 68-73. An essay on the Detroit riot appearing in this volume is Thurgood Marshall's "The Gestapo in Detroit."

23. In February 1946, *The Crisis* published an interview with Petry in which she spoke to James Ivey, the editor who originally read the manuscript in October 1943 and recommended it be published, which led to her book contract with Houghton

the way to work remind him of the brass fixtures he used to clean as a barroom custodian before getting his defense plant job. Petry connects these metallic images to a Coca-Cola ad displayed at the subway station, typical of the period's propaganda, in which a white family is pictured at a dining-room table graced by brass candlesticks and a silver punch bowl. This quintessentially American ad, with its red and white trademark and white models, frames the worker's horrific memory of his own fire-damaged Harlem apartment in which his youngest child has just been killed. His suicidal leap at the story's end results in the red of his blood mingling with the blue of his overalls to ironically mirror the Coke ad overhead. This bloody scenario has as its background an air-raid siren whose wail echoes the fire engine called to the protagonist's burning home, and it signifies a home-front battleground for black people that is every bit as violent as the war overseas.

These and other stories, along with poetry denouncing racism, take a critical view of the propaganda designed to unite a home front that is actually very much divided by racism. The critical tone of *The Crisis* and *Opportunity,* in fact, drew the ire of some federal officials who tried to persuade the Roosevelt administration to sanction and censor them, along with other publications of the African American press. Patrick Washburn in his study of this question asserts that seven federal agencies investigated black publishers in World War II, including the Justice Department, the FBI, the Office of War Information, and the army. Washburn relates that the black press was in danger of being suppressed until June of 1942 when Attorney General Francis Biddle, urged by *Chicago Defender* publisher John Sengstacke, decided that no black publishers would be indicted for sedition.

The Crisis had been a target of government surveillance since World War I, and even with the protection of Biddle's order, it came under the watchful

---

Mifflin. Here, she talks about the inspiration for the piece, which was a story she covered as a reporter for *The People's Voice,* where she worked during the war. It concerned a Harlem fire in which two children had died when their parents were at work: "I knew that many Harlem parents, like Lilly Belle in the story, often left their children home alone while at work." This suggests that the character Lilly Belle might have been working when she left her children locked in their apartment, not amusing herself in a bar as she is accused of doing in the story. Petry also reveals in the interview that a second inspiration for the story came from hearing a siren suddenly sound while she was standing on the 125th Street platform of the New York subway when she noticed the "interesting" reactions of the bystanders (James Ivey, "Ann Petry Talks about First Novel").

eye of FBI head J. Edgar Hoover in September 1943, as did *Opportunity*. In response to the summer race riots of 1943, the FBI produced a seven-hundred-page report that named *The Crisis* and *Opportunity*, along with forty-one other African American publications, as "inimical to the Nation's war effort." Washburn points out that such threats were met with defiance by black publishers, who were dependent upon African American subscribers rather than advertisers for revenue. In addition, they were wary of repeating the mistake of accommodating themselves to government demands in World War I, when W. E. B. Du Bois of *The Crisis* urged suspension of criticism until the war was won, only to see dozens of postwar hate riots erupt. By the time World War II began, black editors were determined not to be silenced again. In the words of the Associated Negro Press director, Claude Barnett, who called OWI propaganda guidelines "paternalistic pap," "[OWI is giving black newspapers] large doses of pure propaganda designed to lull colored people to sleep and make them forget the discrimination and mistreatment accorded Negro soldiers and civilians."[24]

This critical perspective helped insulate black female readers from the more pernicious elements of wartime propaganda designed to recruit women into the labor force on a temporary basis only, although this benefit was outweighed by the "whiteout" that erased them from the mainstream rhetorical picture. On a more important level, however, black women's central home-front role in challenging segregation reinforced autonomous images of them in African American magazines. The first nationally reported use of the sit-in tactic, which drew national attention in 1960 when students in the South integrated lunch counters, for instance, partially originated in actions taken by female students at Howard University in January of 1943. This movement is described here in the poet-activist Pauli Murray's article "A Blueprint for First-Class Citizenship": three Howard coeds were arrested in downtown Washington, D.C., for refusing to pay an overcharge for their hot chocolate at a cigar-store lunch counter. Herself a Howard student at the time, Murray reports that when initially refused service, the three held their ground until they were served but overcharged, then arrested and thrown in jail for paying the lower advertised price. The article mentions another Howard coed, chair of a student Civil Rights Committee that challenged white-only Washington cafés, who had already been "stool-sitting" at D.C. lunch counters on her own.

---

24. Patrick Washburn, *A Question of Sedition: The Federal Government's Investigation of the Black Press during World War II*, 8, 179–80, 11–28, 164.

The positive attention to female activists in these magazines reflects a larger context of black female leadership in the budding civil rights movement of World War II. Jacqueline Jones asserts that it was a woman who suggested marching on the White House at a convention in 1941 in order to press for fair hiring practices at defense plants, an idea that turned into the March On Washington Movement spearheaded by A. Philip Randolph. Jones also relates the 1943 story of a black army nurse whose boarding of an Alabama bus before whites caused her to be beaten by police and then jailed. A similar incident is recounted in a letter to *Opportunity* included here by Sgt. Aubrey Robinson Jr., who describes a Georgia bus operator's vicious assault on a black passenger for asking the driver to request a sleeping white man to move forward to the bus's white section so that she could sit down. It is another black woman, a hostess at a USO club, who brings Sergeant Robinson enough money to get him out of the chain gang to which he was sentenced for defending the assaulted passenger. Similarly, a letter to *The Crisis* reprinted in this collection ("Letter to the Editor from a Soldier's Wife") is from an African American army wife who complains about standing for six hours at a time at Camp Hood bus stops in Texas while drivers accommodated white passengers.[25]

In a similar vein, Darlene Clark Hine has written of the astute political maneuvering of Mabel Keaton Staupers, leader of the National Association of Colored Graduate Nurses, who pressured the armed forces into integrating the nursing corps throughout the war. Hine also describes the groundbreaking work of Ella Baker, a field secretary for the NAACP in 1941– 1942, who became the first director of the Southern Christian Leadership Conference. She reports that Rosa Parks began rebelling against segregation rules on buses in the 1940s, as does Paula Giddings in her detailed account of Parks's role in the Montgomery bus boycott of 1955. Mary McLeod Bethune (cofounder, with Mary Church Terrell and Estelle Massey Riddle, of the National Council of Negro Women) became the first black woman to hold

---

25. Jones, *Labor of Love,* 233. Paula Giddings documents the long history of black women's resistance to segregated public transport, beginning with the 1866 suit of millionaire Mary Ellen Pleasant against the San Francisco Trolley Company when she was forbidden entrance to one of its cars. Giddings also recounts an altercation between Sojourner Truth and a streetcar conductor in Washington, D.C., who tried to evict her from a trolley only to find himself physically subdued by her. Giddings attributes this resistance to the heavy use of public vehicles by black women who needed to get to the white part of town for their domestic employment and whose ill treatment thereon proved to be the final insult to their dignity in a racist, sexist society (Giddings, *When and Where,* 262).

a federal post when she was appointed director of the Office of Minority Affairs in the National Youth Administration during the war years. Pictured in this volume, Bethune was photographed for *The Crisis* in its wartime series "First Ladies of Colored America" to honor women's contributions to African American life. The words of its September 1942 issue introducing this series suggest an affirmation of gender equality significantly stronger than that of white society: "[T]he colored woman has been a more potent factor in shaping Negro society than the white woman has been in shaping white society because the sexual caste system has been much more fluid and ill-defined than among whites. Colored women have worked *with* their men and helped build and maintain every institution we have. Without their economic aid and counsel we would have made little if any progress."[26]

It is important to recognize that relatively positive rhetorical treatment did not necessarily translate into a harmonious reality for black working women. In fact, there is evidence that considerable strain on some African American intimate relationships accompanied new opportunities for female workers. Gretchen Lemke-Santangelo's interviews with former Bay Area defense workers reveal a great deal of conflict with husbands and lovers over their war jobs, and this reality is mirrored in some of the fiction included here.[27] In "Viney Taylor" by Lila Marshall, an industrial worker is so distraught by her unemployed husband's infidelity that she beats her rival up. Ann Petry's "Like a Winding Sheet" features another disturbing portrait of married life when an unskilled factory worker batters his wife, who is also a factory worker. Although all four magazines welcomed employment upgrades for women in the wartime labor force, such pieces imply that gender change carried a price in some cases. Indeed the violence at the heart of relationships in "Viney Taylor," "Like a Winding Sheet," and Petry's "On Saturday the Siren Sounds at Noon" suggests that even as they made progress in employment, black women could become targets of misplaced rage or suffer personal losses.

---

26. Darlene Clark Hine, *Hinesight: Black Women and the Re-Construction of American History*, 183–200, 22; *The Crisis*, October 1942, 319. Giddings, *When and Where*, 262–69. *The Crisis*, September 1942, 287. An account of Bethune's wartime activities is provided by Joyce B. Ross, "Mary McLeod Bethune and the National Youth Administration: A Case Study of Power Relationships in the Black Cabinet of Franklin D. Roosevelt."

27. Lemke-Santangelo, *Abiding Courage*. Further evidence of male-female discord over working women's roles at this time is provided by Paula Giddings, who recounts numerous instances of criticism in the postwar period of women's economic activity and conflict within the black family (*When and Where*, 252–56).

The autobiographical reflections on their World War II experience of James Baldwin and Chester Himes shed light on this matter. Baldwin complains in his 1955 essay "Notes of a Native Son" that he was upset by the racism he encountered as a young man in the wartime labor force when he was fired from job after job for what he considered minor infractions. His rage building, Baldwin recounts an incident in New Jersey when he was refused service by a white waitress at a diner, echoing the pivotal scene in Petry's "Like a Winding Sheet" when the main character storms out of a café and later beats his wife. Enraged by his real-life encounter with a parallel situation, Baldwin left the diner and charged into an elegant restaurant, where he knew he would be refused service, and barely contained his impulse to choke the waitress who told him to leave: "Somehow, with the repetition of that phrase ['don't serve Negroes here'], which was already ringing in my head like a thousand bells of a nightmare, I realized that she would never come any closer and that I would have to strike from a distance. There was nothing on the table but an ordinary watermug half full of water, and I picked this up and hurled it with all my strength at her."[28]

Chester Himes similarly describes his volcanic anger, both over his Depression experiences and his futile attempts to find skilled work in wartime Los Angeles. Of his WPA job in 1930s Cleveland, he writes: "Each day, a thousand times, I had to exert the greatest self-control to keep from smashing the face of some white personnel director." Himes's period in Los Angeles was even more disturbing. Holding down twenty-three jobs in three years from 1941–1944, he bitterly describes his inability to get anything but laborer jobs, even though he had mechanical and carpentry skills:

> Los Angeles hurt me racially as much as any city I have ever known—much more than any city I remember from the South. It was the lying hypocrisy that hurt me. Black people were treated much the same as they were in an industrial city of the South. They were Jim-Crowed in housing, in employment, in public accommodations, such as hotels and restaurants. . . . I had lived in the South, I had fallen down an elevator shaft, I had been kicked out of college, I had served seven and one half years in prison, I had survived the humiliating last five years of the Depression in Cleveland;

---

28. James Baldwin, "Notes of a Native Son," 81. Although Baldwin's anger was directed at a white woman in this account, black women could also become targets of male rage over racism. Toni Morrison attests to this phenomenon in her fiction but also has spoken about it directly: "For years in this country there was no one for black men to vent their rage on except black women" (Toni Morrison, "What the Black Woman Thinks about Women's Lib").

and still I was entire, complete, functional; my mind was sharp, my reflexes were good, and I was not bitter. But under the mental corrosion of race prejudice in Los Angeles I had become bitter and saturated with hate. And finding myself unable to support my black wife, whom I loved desperately, I had become afraid. My wife deserved the support of her man. She was as beautiful and as feminine as a woman can be.

Exacerbating the hurt, he says, was his wife's job as supervisor of USO entertainment, a much better position than he could find: "That was the beginning of the dissolution of our marriage. I found that I was no longer a husband to my wife; I was her pimp."[29] World War II was for Himes, as it was for Baldwin, a time when he felt, with fearful intensity, the depth of his own rage at racism in the wartime labor force. That women figure centrally in both of these accounts helps illuminate the gender politics intersecting with racism during the war to produce an anger deep enough to spill, at times, into the personal realm.

There are other issues reflected in these materials that problematize the idea of progressive attitudes toward women's work in African American periodical representation. One of these is an emphasis on the male soldier or defense worker, even by women writers. In part this is due to the reality that black women were largely kept out of skilled defense work and they were barred from military combat. In part, however, this interest in the male subject grew out of the larger culture's valorization of the male soldier and its suggestion that women's work, whether in the home or not, supported him and that he was only temporarily absent from his breadwinner position. While traditional notions of gender were revised to permit the employment of women in new roles, hypermasculinized conceptions of the male soldier dominated home-front rhetoric, and that is reflected in African American discourse as well. Woman as mother and man as soldier were dominant representations of gender in black as well as white media during the war. As Susan Schweik observes, African American women's wartime poetry often adopts a maternal persona: "The maternal self-consciousness which 'looking' renders [in the maternal female war poem] is far less transgressive . . . than other forms of . . . feminine self-regard."[30]

Nevertheless, there are aspects of this material's treatment of gender undercutting traditionalism. It would be a mistake, for example, to read

---

29. Chester Himes, *The Quality of Hurt: The Autobiography of Chester Himes*, 72, 73-76, 75.

30. Susan Schweik, *A Gulf So Deeply Cut: American Women Poets and the Second World War*, 130.

the male subject as irrelevant to black women's status. Such a focus may have been in tune with sexist assumptions, but the racism suffered by male characters in the poetry and fiction collected here affected African American women, too. Race, in other words, united black women and men in a white supremacist culture. Susan Schweik explains this concept well when discussing Gwendolyn Brooks's choice of a male persona in "Gay Chaps at the Bar": "Her strategies of representation of that masculine figure may be understood as . . . political practices: tactics designed to expose and protest discrimination not of sex but of race." Schweik points out that African American women's poetry had as its specific agenda inclusion of the black soldier in order to correct racist mythologies of heroism. When we read Lucia Mae Pitts's "A WAC Speaks to a Soldier" and "Brown Moon," or Margaret Walker's "Dark Men Speaks to the Earth," then, we are looking at black women poets validating *African American* courage, not simply male valor. Similarly, the critique of violence against men by such African American writers as Georgia Douglas Johnson ("Black Recruit"), Ruby Berkley Goodwin ("Guilty"), and Grace W. Tompkins ("The Smell of Death") is protest against racism, not just victimization of men.[31]

Historians have concluded that race mattered far more to black women's status during the war than gender, and the material here supports that assessment.[32] The male soldier in particular was a focal point of African American protest against racism because it was his presence on the battle-front that enabled the most effective interrogation of segregation at home. His gender privilege, in other words, could provide a wedge against exclusion practices in a racist state. Disadvantaged by their gender as well as race status, black women were in a weaker position to challenge discrimination. They could, however, benefit from battles waged on behalf of African American men. Furthermore, Hazel Carby and others have described the link between racist images of men and prejudice against African American women. Carby connects stereotypes of black men as rapists, for example, and of black women as promiscuous at the turn-of-the-century. Such notions operated in World War II when African American soldiers were accused of rape and white women defense plant workers protested sharing toilet facilities with black coworkers because they were supposedly carriers of

---

31. Ibid., 112. Georgia Douglas Johnson, "Black Recruit," and Ruby Berkley Goodwin, "Guilty," are both in Beatrice Murphy, ed., *Ebony Rhythm,* 16, 25.

32. See Anderson, *Changing Woman;* Hine, *Hinesight;* Jones, *Labor of Love;* and Lemke-Santangelo, *Abiding Courage.*

venereal disease.[33] These connections between racism directed at men and women's own victimization by it, in a context of traditional gender notions, help account for women writers' attraction to the male subject in World War II.

Portrayals of African American motherhood, similarly, while central to women's images in these black periodicals, were significantly more autonomous than those of white mothers in the dominant culture. Mothers in this collection are shown as actively guiding their children toward a new future with greater occupational opportunities, while their white counterparts assure children that life without father, although troubled, is temporary and will soon end. White periodicals gave prominent attention to the campaign against juvenile delinquency that swept the country in late 1944 and early 1945,[34] for instance, whereas these magazines ignored it or attributed teen misbehavior to racism. Two of the stories in this volume link teenage antisocial behavior to alienation from a racist system that fails to provide them with good jobs—Ann Petry's "In Darkness and Confusion," and Pearl Fisher's "Riot Gold." Working mothers are portrayed as a common feature of black life, and they are appreciated for the sacrifices they make to insure a better future for their children. Domestic workers are heroic

---

33. Hazel Carby, *Reconstructing Womanhood: The Emergence of the Afro-American Woman Novelist*, 20–39. One of the best-publicized cases of black soldiers being charged with rape was that of three men at a camp in Alexandria, Louisiana, who were arrested in the summer of 1942 and defended by Thurgood Marshall with backing from the NAACP. Another example is the father of Emmett Till, who was killed a decade later for whistling at a white woman, when he was hanged by the army on a charge of rape while stationed in Italy during World War II, a case that was held up by racists in Mississippi as proof that the son was a potential rapist himself. For a description of one of the most notorious lynchings of the war period in which a black man was accused of assaulting a white woman in January of 1942, see Dominic Capeci Jr., "The Lynching of Cleo Wright: Federal Protection of Constitutional Rights during World War II." The other example comes from a hate strike by white women who walked off the job when Western Electric refused to build separate toilet facilities for African American women on the line in a Baltimore plant (Alexander J. Allen, "Western Electric's Backward Step").

34. The campaign against juvenile delinquency began in late 1944 and was directed at working mothers (Honey, *Creating Rosie the Riveter*, 56, 95, 124). Another good example of how white working mothers were represented by the dominant culture late in the war is an Adel Precision Products Corporation advertisement that appeared in the May 1944 *Saturday Evening Post* that pictured a factory worker on her way to work answering her child's question, "Mother, when will you stay home again?" The ad answers: "Some jubilant day mother *will* stay home again, doing the job she likes best—making a home for you and daddy, when he gets back" (184).

providers, for example, in several of these fictional stories. Although contradicted in part by Paula Giddings' study of black magazines in the 1950s, the work of Jacqueline Jones supports my reading. Her survey of *Ebony Magazine* in the early postwar years shows that working wives and mothers were featured as an integral part of black family life in the postwar years: "[*Ebony*] consistently presented [working married women] in a positive, and frequently heroic, light. . . . [It] offered its wholehearted endorsement of husbands and wives who both followed careers and enjoyed a happy home life together."[35]

It is also important to recognize the central role of the mother as caretaker of the quest for racial equality in this material. While in some ways images of the mother here mirror dominant-culture iconography, they are politicized and therefore quite different portraits. Maternal figures who contemplate the possible death of sons in uniform, for example, vow to carry on the struggle against racism should that happen and thereby become more than adoring props. May Miller's "One Blue Star" showcases just such a mother as she identifies with women of the past who produced fighters for racial advancement. Similarly, the poems "Negro Mother to Her Soldier Son," by Cora Ball Moten, and "Mother's Hope," by Valerie E. Parks, are not so much about maternal reification as they are calls to social action. In contrast, a fictional mother of mixed race ancestry whose soldier son has died is criticized by her daughter for failing to read the legacy left to her by his African American widow and child in Octavia Wynbush's "The Black Streak." This mother cannot overcome her racism, even in the face of her son's love for a black woman, and fails to perceive her maternal mission as one that should encourage the interracial love to which he was committed.

The public role of racial uplift for mothers showcased here differs markedly from white models of motherhood in the dominant culture that counseled stoic patience until the male breadwinner resumed his proper place as paterfamilias. Ruth Feldstein's examination of gender representation in the Emmett Till case of 1955 illustrates this essential difference in attitudes toward the mother. Feldstein describes the ways Till's mother, Mamie Bradley, used her maternal role as a battering ram to attack the racist

---

35. Jones, *Labor of Love,* 269–71. Although she acknowledges the relatively greater tolerance for female wage work in African American communities, Paula Giddings sees parallels between dominant culture representations of traditional gender roles and those in African American magazines later in the postwar period (Giddings, *When and Where,* 249–56).

violence that had killed her boy, while the black press similarly positioned her as a grieving mother in order to challenge the Mississippi judicial system. Feldstein concludes: "[The example of] Mamie Bradley demonstrates that motherhood itself was a battleground on which the meaning of Till's death was fought."[36] This political use of Mamie Bradley's maternal identity in the 1950s civil rights struggle had its roots in wartime rhetoric about the black mother's role in community activities. She was not conceptualized as a homebound figure in African American discourse; rather, she was expected to take up the banner for racial justice in society at large laid down by a martyred child.

For all its racial barriers and limited opportunities for real economic change, then, evidence from these magazines suggests that World War II provided an empowering political base for African American women, one that contrasts markedly with the narrowing of that base for white women. The battle against racism undertaken during the war created a militant discourse for women and men alike that undercut traditional gender construction in the culture at large. The war against racism, in short, furnished African American women with models of pride and resistance, whereas for white women, the battle against sexism suffered a decisive setback with the disappearance of feminist organizations at midcentury. This split aggravated postwar differences between white and black women, ultimately surfacing with great force in the 1960s, when white feminist groups focused on dismantling the suburban, family-oriented ideology that had been interrogated by the black community many years before.[37]

Another fault line separating white from black women that can be traced directly to the war is the contrasting way in which women from both races were portrayed in popular culture of the 1940s. While the war brought about a loss in empowered images of white women on the screen, for

---

36. Ruth Feldstein, " 'I Wanted the Whole World to See': Race, Gender, and Constructions of Motherhood in the Death of Emmett Till." See also Patricia Hill Collins, "The Meaning of Motherhood in Black Culture."

37. The midcentury setback of feminism is the subject of William O'Neill's *Everyone Was Brave: A History of Feminism in America.* Paula Giddings outlines the split between white and black women of the 1960s and 1970s: "Not only were the problems of the White suburban housewife (who may have had Black domestic help) irrelevant to Black women, they were also alien to them. Friedan's observation that 'I never knew a woman, when I was growing up, who used her mind, played her own part in the world, and also loved, and had children' seemed to come from another planet" (*When and Where,* 299). See also Joyce Ladner, *Tomorrow's Tomorrow: The Black Woman.*

example, it represented a breakthrough for African American women, a difference that is highlighted by the extraordinary attention to female singers and dancers in the magazines featured in this anthology. Molly Haskell and others have described the demise of New Woman heroines after the war as Hollywood movies turned away from glamorous images of the female aviator, reporter, aspiring musical star, wartime riveter, or competent professional.[38] Instead, melodramas centering on neurotic or victimized women took center stage along with comedies about fluffy sexpots or stories with domestically oriented heroines. In particular, the ubiquitous wartime pinup ushered in an era of erotic portrayals that lasted well into the fifties. Betty Grable, Rita Hayworth, Marilyn Monroe, Lana Turner, and Jane Russell were all white celebrities with erotic personas who emerged from the war as major stars and created film careers around characters with little else than marriage on their minds.

The situation for black screen stars was quite different. Most notably during this period, Lena Horne and Dorothy Dandridge pioneered film careers that departed dramatically from those of previous African American actresses. Prior to the war, the best-known black female movie stars were Hattie McDaniel and Louise Beavers, who specialized in the part of maids paired with sexy, young, frequently blonde employers relying on them for housework and romantic advice. McDaniel had just won the first Academy Award ever given to an African American when the war broke out in 1939, Best Supporting Actress for her role as Mammy in *Gone with the Wind.* Butterfly McQueen, who played the childlike slave named Prissy in the film, resisted a scene that called for her character to eat watermelon and spit out the seeds (she was successful in having the scene deleted).

Determined to improve these and other servile images of black people, the NAACP undertook a campaign to pressure Hollywood into "normal" treatment of African Americans; thus NAACP representative Walter White began meeting with studio heads and government propaganda specialists in Los Angeles in early 1942. Film historian Thomas Cripps describes the battle White waged to end racist stereotyping and the limited but significant successes that grew out of that effort.[39] One of these was the film

---

38. Molly Haskell, *From Reverence to Rape: The Treatment of Women in the Movies.*

39. For a good description of prewar images of African Americans in the movies, see Thomas Cripps, *Slow Fade to Black: The Negro in American Film, 1900–1942,* 263–308. The anecdote about Butterfly McQueen's resistance is relayed by Martin

career of Lena Horne, who made her debut in *Panama Hattie* (1942). She appeared in eleven movies during the 1940s, singing in sophisticated musical numbers that showcased her physical beauty as well as her voice. Dressed in gorgeous gowns, spotlighted against romantic scenery, and given songs of wit and passion, Horne broke new ground for black women traditionally cast as maternal servants with comic lines. She was joined by the pianist Hazel Scott, dancer Katherine Dunham, and singer-dancer Dorothy Dandridge in projecting a glamorous image of black women heretofore virtually unknown on the Hollywood screen. After the war, Dandridge would become the first African American to be nominated for Best Actress, in the Academy Awards of 1954, for her starring role in *Carmen Jones.*

This is not to say that the breakthrough came without significant problems. It was, after all, an era in which the only African American representative of the home front in a propaganda musical (*Meet the People* [1944]) was a smiling young man with a straw hat picking cotton. Most of the scenes in which Horne, Scott, and others appeared, for instance, were constructed so that they could be cut for southern audiences, and black women were not cast in dramatic roles. The two all-black musicals of the period, *Stormy Weather* (1943) and *Cabin in the Sky* (1943), were criticized by the African American press for perpetuating stereotypes, and stars like Horne and Dandridge found very few roles even at the height of their celebrity. Of all the wartime films seeking to break down stereotyped presentation of African Americans, only one contained a black female character of any substance, *Since You Went Away* (1944), and it was deeply flawed. Hattie McDaniel played a live-in domestic who refuses to be paid for her services by the navy family for which she works because the breadwinner is gone and they cannot afford her. Her loyalty to her white employer is encoded

---

Duberman in his feature article on Paul Robeson, "A Giant Denied His Rightful Stature in Film." For further discussion about *Gone with the Wind* and the role of Hattie McDaniel in the movie, see Cripps, *Slow Fade to Black,* 359–66. Cripps maintains that World War II marks a watershed in images of African Americans in Hollywood cinema and cites the significance of Walter White, in particular, in producing a new era of humanized, positive film roles for blacks: "Although Walter White and the NAACP were not directly responsible for a single beautiful movie, their contractual codification of the social changes of the Great Depression and the second Great War finally destroyed the monopoly of Southern racial attitudes on the screen and made cinematic racism untenable" (Cripps, *Slow Fade to Black,* 383). See also Cripps's study of White's wartime Hollywood activism, *Making Movies Black: The Hollywood Message Movie from World War II to the Civil Rights Era,* 35–63.

in her name, Fidelia, and she has no life other than that of the people for whom she does domestic service.

This portrayal outrageously distorted the massive movement of black women out of domestic service during the war documented by Karen Anderson and others, who point out the immense benefits gained by taking war jobs. Although McDaniel's character was working in a war plant, for example, the film showcased her as a domestic worker. Furthermore, the navy was among the most racist of wartime organizations as it refused to accept black nurses or WAVES until the war was almost over, and it segregated black sailors into mess halls, officer valet service, janitorial work, and assigned them dangerous loading jobs. Although the film integrated black people into crowd scenes and treated Fidelia with respect, early script presentations of African American female defense workers and WACs were dropped, a fate that matched other attempts to include black women war workers in home-front movies.[40]

Nevertheless, an improved image of black women emerged in mainstream popular culture, one that helped move aside the stock loyal maid so entrenched before the war. The erotic pinup that trivialized white women's representation in popular culture was in black magazines connected to this new glamorous image of African American entertainers, who redefined black womanhood to include sexiness, romance, beauty, courage, and passion. Glamorous stars, moreover, represented more than their physical beauty when they spoke out against racism, as they often did. Lena Horne refused to perform for an army audience in which German POWs were seated in front of black soldiers, for example, and Hazel Scott refused to play maids in film roles. Katherine Dunham's choreography relied on Caribbean dance influences and showed off the African American female body as

---

40. Donald Bogle describes the hardships faced by African American actresses in the 1940s in *Brown Sugar: Eighty Years of America's Black Female Superstars*. His recent *Dorothy Dandridge: A Biography* details the racism that derailed this promising star's career. Feminist perspectives on *Since You Went Away* and on African American women characters in the war years appear in Baker, *Images of Women in Film*, 96–110; Doane, *The Desire to Desire*, 78–81; and Hartmann, *The Home Front and Beyond*, 192–93. Thomas Cripps relates that an early script draft of *Since You Went Away* called for one of the white daughters of the main character to fail a dexterity test when she applies for factory work while a young black woman seated by her successfully passes it. This same white character in a later scene is given an African American woman supervisor in this draft. Both scenes were deleted from the final script. Cripps also describes a scene from this film that was actually shot and later cut that contained black WACs at a train station (*Making Movies Black*, 86–87).

an icon of cultural richness. Black female beauty and racial advancement were conjoined by African American periodicals; reflecting the emphasis on black femininity, *The Crisis* and *Opportunity* ran photos predominantly of women on their covers, particularly in 1943 and 1944, the height of female wartime employment. Out of seventy-one total covers for these two publications from 1942–1945, forty-nine had female subjects. This is in line with dominant culture periodicals that represented women on covers, but the captions for these African American "cover girls" emphasized work-related achievements.[41] Differing from white "cheesecake" shots, attractive African American women were contextualized as college students, professional achievers, or trailblazers for their race.

Strengthening the revision occurring in film representation was the African American wartime press's emphasis on female achievement in the arts. As Paula Giddings asserts, the war years witnessed a second African American renaissance in this area, with women at the forefront.[42] Broadway stars like Hilda Simms, Anne Wiggins Brown, and Etta Moten were frequently featured in these periodicals, along with the singer Marian Anderson and promising young talents like Philippa Duke Schuyler, a child prodigy who was composing symphonies by the time she was a teenager. Marian Anderson in particular was framed as a leader in the fight against racism, given her stature on the concert stage and her dignified response to being snubbed by the Daughters of the American Revolution at Constitution Hall in 1939. Barred from performing at the D.A.R. convention, Anderson, with the support of First Lady Eleanor Roosevelt, sang instead at the Lincoln Memorial. Such women were seen as harbingers of a more inclusive future—standard bearers of democracy who would lead black people into the cultural center of American life.

Artists of all kinds, male and female, had been seen as leaders in the fight against racism since the Harlem Renaissance, of course, but the war emphasized performing arts rather than literary achievement, a realm in

---

41. An example is the cover of the summer 1944 issue of *Opportunity*, which features Vivian Currey in a "sweater girl" photo that is at the same time a modest and wholesome image. Although she is described as one of the finalists in a "Pin-Up Girl contest," the magazine highlights her employment as an automatic screw machine operator at a New Jersey manufacturing company.

42. Paula Giddings considers World War II a second renaissance in the arts for African Americans (*When and Where*, 244). Neil Wynn agrees with this assessment, citing, among other things, the fact that the number of African Americans in Broadway plays rose from three in 1940 to twenty-eight in 1946 (*The Afro-American and the Second World War*, 96).

which the female singer, dancer, or stage actress excelled during the 1940s. White celebrities like Eleanor Powell, whose tap dancing was featured in film musicals of the 1930s and war years, or white singers like Kate Smith, Jeanette McDonald, Judy Garland, and the Andrews Sisters were paralleled by African American female performers spotlighted in the pages of these four magazines.

It is important to recognize, however, that the breakthroughs occurring in the arts for African American women, as in film, were piecemeal, incomplete, and largely illusory. There were more failures than successes. The examples of the child prodigy Philippa Duke Schuyler and the soprano Anne Wiggins Brown are instructive. Philippa Duke Schuyler, the daughter of the prominent Harlem Renaissance journalist George Schuyler and his white wife, Josephine Cogdell, was able to read at the age of two and a half; often compared to Mozart, she became a celebrity in the 1930s and 1940s. She played at Carnegie Hall and toured the nation while only a teenager, but by the 1950s, she was forced to tour abroad, since American venues closed rapidly for her once the war was over. Discouraged by the doors closing in her native land, Philippa later acknowledged that color prejudice derailed her concert career:

> I was born and grew up . . . without any consciousness of America's race prejudice . . . [but] I became intellectually aware of it when I . . . entered the world of economic competition as a full-fledged adult. Then I encountered vicious barriers of prejudice in the field of employment because I was the off-spring of what America calls a "mixed marriage." It was a ruthless shock to me that, at first, made the walls of my self-confidence crumble. It horrified, humiliated me. But instead of breaking under the strain, I adjusted to it. I left [America].[43]

Similarly, Anne Wiggins Brown, the first African American vocalist admitted to the Juilliard School of Music and the woman for whom George Gershwin created the stage role of Bess in his opera, *Porgy and Bess,* enjoyed Broadway stardom in the 1930s and 1940s. She found, however, that race prejudice forced her to tour abroad since black classically trained sopranos had virtually no audience in the United States. Brown's problems were foreshadowed by the touring schedule for *Porgy and Bess* in the midthirties. When she learned that the show would be staged at the National Theater, a segregated facility in Washington, D.C., where her family lived,

---

43. Quoted in Kathryn Talalay, *Composition in Black and White: The Life of Philippa Duke Schuyler,* 112. Philippa's father, George Schuyler, was the business manager of *The Crisis* during the war.

she refused to perform until management agreed to admit African American patrons for the one week it would be on.[44] Brown ultimately settled in Norway, where she still lives.

What can we conclude from this material about the legacy of World War II for black women? It is clear that one part of the story is rueful acknowledgment that the much vaunted new roles for women trumpeted by dominant culture propagandists were a joke for most African Americans looking for work. By the time employers were willing to hire black women—and not all of them reached that point—most of the best jobs had been given to whites. As I said earlier, this dismal picture is reflected in the angry words that flow through the prose and poetry of this volume, as well as in the many stories with women in domestic work at the height of the labor shortage and with characters who encounter racism on the job. These characters' inability to take advantage of the many jobs opening up to white women during the war boom mirrors actual workforce patterns that trapped African American women in the most undesirable, low-paying occupations.

Despite black women's lack of progress in the wartime labor force, however, most studies conclude that World War II represents a political watershed for African Americans, one that propelled women as well as men into the civil rights movement of the 1950s and 1960s. Jacqueline Jones asserts, for example, that women's wartime economic failure to cross race barriers did not prevent them from making important political gains: "If black women did not achieve any long-lasting economic gains as a result of the war, they did begin to test the limits of their own collective strength in ways that would reverberate into the future."[45] This study supports that

---

44. Anne Wiggins Brown, "On Hearing Her Sing, Gershwin Made 'Porgy' 'Porgy and Bess,' " interview by Barry Singer, *New York Times,* March 29, 1998, 39.

45. Jones, *Labor of Love,* 235. Similar conclusions are drawn in Anderson, *Changing Woman;* Giddings, *When and Where;* Susan Lynn, *Progressive Women in Conservative Times: Racial Justice, Peace, and Feminism, 1945 to the 1960s;* Manning Marable, *Race, Reform, and Rebellion: The Second Reconstruction in Black America, 1945–1990;* Vicki Crawford, Jacqueline Rouse, and Barbara Woods, eds., *Women in the Civil Rights Movement: Trailblazers and Torchbearers, 1941–1945;* August Meier and Elliott Rudwick, *CORE: A Study in the Civil Rights Movement, 1942–1968;* Dorothy Newman et al., *Protest, Politics, and Prosperity: Black Americans and White Institutions, 1940–1975;* and Leila Rupp and Verta Taylor, *Survival in the Doldrums: The American Women's Rights Movement, 1945 to the 1960s.* See also Darlene Clark Hine and Kathleen Thompson, *A Shining Thread of Hope: The History of Black Women in America;* and Tera W. Hunter, *To 'Joy My Freedom: Southern Black Women's Lives and Labors after the Civil War.*

assessment. Spearheaded by the political accomplishments of Mabel Keaton Staupers, Estelle Massey Riddle, Mary McLeod Bethune, Mary Church Terrell, Ella Baker, and others, black women's voices in these periodicals call for resistance to racism on all levels of American society, but particularly in many of the areas that would become battlegrounds in the postwar period: restricted seating at the back of buses, confinement to urban ghettoes, and exclusion from restaurants. These issues are foregrounded in the war years by black periodicals, and women's roles in particular are framed in terms that are compatible with their political activism.

If they could not break the back of racial discrimination in the wartime labor force or popular culture, then, African American women in this anthology speak up, speak out, and claim their own power to live as equals in American society. Despite the pain running through much of this material, pride and defiance are the most characteristic elements in the black female wartime writing reprinted here. Examples include Grace W. Tompkins, who declares of racist violence, "It stinks to high heaven, this smell of death!" while Ruth Albert Cook lambasts America for imposing a "blackout" on its own dark citizens and hiding its "closeted skeleton" of racism. Elsie Mills Holton says "goodbye to the days of the jig and the shine boy": "We do not amuse so completely as before." Lucia Mae Pitts, a WAC, honors the 99th Pursuit Squadron at Tuskegee for unleashing "a passionate anger against the stalking mob which comes to assault our homes and break our peace" and tells her brother soldiers to stop holding women back from joining the battle: "We have swallowed your disapproval and joined up just the same, because there was a job to be done and we had to do it. . . . We, too, march and soil ourselves with dirty jobs, and rise with the dawn to put in a good day's work at the jobs you did before. . . . Though not in the delicate gowns you knew, . . . we will still seek the stars and the moon." Constance C. Nichols declares: "My beauty cannot be denied. / Look you upon me—fool or sage— / NEGRO WOMAN HAS COME OF AGE!"[46]

Adopting many of the postwar techniques that would prove so effective against segregation, women are shown here defying the sometimes unwritten rules that kept them out of restaurants, department stores, offices, bus seats, desirable neighborhoods, movie roles, and well-paying jobs. Viewed as the opening salvo of the postwar drive against segregation, then, African American women's role in World War II can be seen as a rehearsal for the

---

46. Grace W. Tompkins, "The Smell of Death"; Ruth Albert Cook, "Blackout"; Elsie Mills Holton, "Renunciation"; Lucia Mae Pitts, "A WAC Speaks to a Soldier"; Constance C. Nichols, "Confidence."

coming war to integrate schools, lunch counters, public transport, housing, and popular culture. It is fitting that one of the poems written in 1944 included here, "Time Was, Time Is, Time Shall Be" by Vivien E. Lewis (whose ethnicity is unknown), concludes with the same words Martin Luther King Jr. used to close his "I Have a Dream" speech in the 1963 March on Washington: "Thank Gawd amighty! Free at last." For if they were defeated as individuals—and this material chronicles the bitterness of those defeats—as a collective force African American women found an empowered voice during the war, one that anticipates the fruit of their wartime effort to break silence, to challenge limits, and to change forever the terms of their lives.

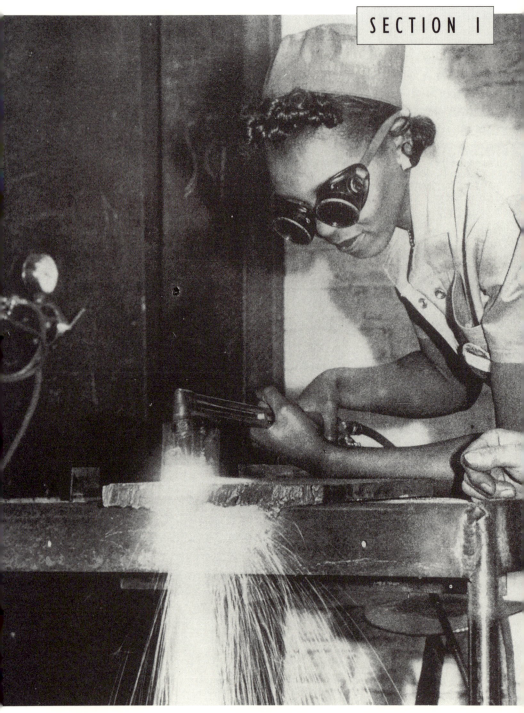

Woman Welder, *The Crisis*, April 1942

War Work

African American magazines were upbeat as they advertised war jobs for women, as is illustrated in war plant supervisor Ida Coker Clark's essay "Negro Woman Worker, What Now?" but the reality was that most black women ran into serious obstacles in their efforts to obtain skilled blue-collar or clerical and other kinds of work. Employers hired them only as a last resort, after white female and black male labor supplies were exhausted, and many war contractors refused to hire them at all. Frequently, they were relegated to night shifts, janitorial positions, or both. This discrimination is illustrated by George E. DeMar, a National Urban League field reporter, in his essay "Negro Women Are American Workers, Too," which describes all the occupational categories in Pittsburgh in which not one African American woman could be found at the height of the labor shortage in 1943. Another essay in this section, "Overly Sensitive," by the African American employment counselor Robert Jones, details the subterfuges employers used to avoid hiring black workers through the U.S. Employment Service.

Two personal essays by factory workers in this section, both entitled "What My Job Means to Me," illustrate the hardships such prejudice created. Hortense Johnson was a munitions worker who describes the considerable physical demands of her job as well as the constant threat of explosion; Leotha Hackshaw, an inspector in a war plant, must take a modeling job to make ends meet. Both complain about the long commutes to their jobs, a problem for most black women who were confined to racial ghettos in the urban areas that drew vast numbers of migrants to manufacturing jobs. The discrimination faced by black women in war work is reflected in Chester Himes's "The Song Says 'Keep on Smiling.'" It concerns a fictional shipfitter's helper whose cramped boardinghouse room over a San Francisco bar diminishes the quality of her life, as does the racism of her coworkers. Basing his story in part on his own experiences as a shipfitter in Los Angeles during the war, Himes fictionalizes the hurtful fractures in home-front unity for black workers, even those who managed to penetrate racial barriers to skilled employment.

Shirley Graham's "Tar" also details the impact of racial bars on African American women when she focuses on a young southern migrant to New York, Mary, who cannot get hired as a sheet-metal worker after taking a government training course. Forced back into domestic work, Graham's protagonist can only get hired by a war plant when her white employer provides her with a reference to a friend of his, and even then she is employed below her skill level pouring tar on the night shift. Graham also alludes to racism in the military in this story. Mary's sweetheart, Tom, has attended engineering school in the hopes of designing bridges and roads, but when he joins the army, he is denied entry into officer ranks, while his white classmates are readily promoted. Instead, Tom is assigned a laboring job. In an incident based on an actual explosion in Port Chicago, California, in 1944 when over 250 black sailors were killed unloading bombs from navy ships, Tom suffers the humiliation of being covered with tar after a tank explodes on his loading dock. Racial discrimination is also at the heart of "The Job," by James Light, when an African American serviceman's wife hired as a waitress in a white establishment is fired after customers complain about her. Devastated by the experience, this protagonist represents the real women who could not find positions in sales, clerical work, and public service occupations, even when the labor shortage was most acute.

Reflecting this lack of access to good jobs are the large numbers of fictional characters in this section who are domestic workers. Although the proportion of working black women employed in domestic service fell dramatically between 1940 and 1944, they continued to fill the majority of such jobs in the wartime labor force as white women eschewed such work for better-paying employment. This was one of the worst paid and most arduous of occupations, particularly in the South, where employers expected maids to be on call up to twelve hours a day and to work six days a week. Zena Dorinson's "Help Wanted" illustrates the automatic equation many whites made between a woman's skin color and her employment status when she fictionalizes a white woman's mistaking a black college graduate for a maid. Zora L. Barnes's "Requiem" concerns another college graduate, who falls down the employment ladder, depicted symbolically as a real ladder, despite her qualifications and ends up doing heavy cleaning as a custodial worker. Having had personal experience as a black domestic worker, Melissa Linn demonstrates in another way the parallel drawn between African American ethnicity and low employment status when, in "All That Hair," a maid's child steals the wig of her mother's employer so she can look like the white children with whom she attends school. Such stories speak to the difficulties African American women had in climbing out of low-wage work even at a time when unprecedented numbers of better jobs were opening up to women.

During the war, black women's ability to gain employment was hindered in part by the entrenched racist attitudes of employers and coworkers alike; employment policies all over the country routinely followed racial lines even though race discrimination in war plants had been forbidden by Franklin Roosevelt. Hate strikes erupted periodically throughout the war when white workers walked off the job over promotion or hiring of African Americans into previously restricted occupational categories. One of the largest of these occurred in a Baltimore Western Electric plant in the summer of 1943, when twenty-two white women walked out over the hiring of black women in an all-white department. Unsuccessful in their effort to change company policy, the white workers returned only to petition for separate toilet facilities, which led to a larger strike in December of that year. This disruptive action resulted in federal troops occupying the plant until the spring of 1944, when management acceded to the racist demands by building segregated rest rooms for white and black workers. Stereotypes of black women as carriers of venereal disease underlay the Baltimore strike. Other racist beliefs are at work in "I Had a Colored Maid," by a *Negro Story* editorial board member and federal clerical worker, Margaret Rodriguez. Here a black clerical worker in a government agency is accused of stealing documents by her white coworker, when they have merely been mislaid. Through such stereotypes, racist discrimination in employment is justified.

On the other hand, African American women did make some meaningful gains as a result of the wartime labor shortage. Executive Order 8802 banned race discrimination in defense industries and civil service jobs in June 1941, and while it was not well enforced, the law set a precedent that would prove useful in the postwar years. Progress was made when federal clerical jobs in Washington, D.C., experienced an unprecedented influx of black workers who had previously only filled janitorial positions. (The number of black women in federal clerical work increased from sixty thousand in 1940 to two hundred thousand in 1944.) Moreover, Mary Church Terrell, Mary McLeod Bethune, Crystal Bird Fauset, and other black leaders were important figures in the White House during the Roosevelt administration, supported in particular by the desire of Eleanor Roosevelt to break down racism in American society. Mabel Keaton Staupers and Estelle Massey Riddle made great strides toward integrating the Army Nurse Corps and saw to it that black women were accepted into the navy as WAVEs by the war's end. The apparel industry underwent a 350 percent increase in black female employment, and increasing numbers of black women left household service for public-sector service jobs that were better paying and had better working conditions. The sense that change was slow but nevertheless real pervades the material in this section, particularly in poetry by the black writers Constance C. Nichols, Hazel L. Washington, Lucia

U.S. Army Major, *Opportunity*, Winter 1945

Mae Pitts, and Marie Brown Frazier. The bittersweet nature of wartime opportunities for black women is palpable, but so is a determination to make the most out of the little being offered.

EBONY RHYTHM, 1948

A Woman at War

HAZEL L. WASHINGTON

I was a woman at war,
Deep in the whirlpools
And intrigues of war;
Dark like the days
That shroud my generation,
Brown like the khaki I wore.

War is hell—
Fire and smoke,
Blood, death, and starvation.
It is greed for conquest,
Lust for power,
Clamor for recognition:
An evil concoction of fiendish minds.

War is sorrow—
Tears and loneliness,
Ancient like the seas,
Wild as jungle beasts.

War is a game—
Played on the earth's checkerboard
By those who move
Out of turn
And change the natural pattern
Into chaos.

I was a woman at war,
Deep in the whirlpools
And intrigues of war;
Dark like the days
That shroud my generation,
Brown like the khaki I wore.

NEGRO STORY, December–January 1944–1945

A WAC Speaks to a Soldier

LUCIA MAE PITTS

Dedicated to Lt. Thomas I. Pitts, to the soldiers at Fort Huachuca,[1] and to all soldiers.

We salute you—
But not with so common a thing as our hands.
Our hands must keep busy working
And we cannot keep them raised
For as long as you need saluting.
It is our hearts that we raise in a gesture of respect—
Quietly and unseen,
But constantly and reverently.

You did not really want us here.
"Women have no place in the Army," you said.
"Women should stay at home and keep the home-fires burning.
We want to think of you as sitting and waiting
For us to come back,
Dressed in the flimsy gowns which were yours alone
And which we remember sentimentally;
Not in uniform like thousands and thousands of others
And so much like our own.
We want to dream of you
As lying down to your rest at night,
Looking up at the stars and the moon above us all
And saying a prayer for us."
Others said, "You were cruel to come in
And push us out to the firing line . . .
Do you know you are sending us to our death?"

We have swallowed your disapproval
And joined up just the same,
Because there was a job to be done

---

1. Fort Huachuca, Arizona, where the army set up a segregated base for African American soldiers.

And we had to do it.
We have tried not to think of things
Like sending you to your death.
We have thought, on the other hand,
Of what would happen to all of us
If you stayed at home . . .
We have come in to share as much as we can
Of your discomfort and your sacrifice.
We, too, march, and soil ourselves with dirty jobs,
And rise with the dawn to put in a good day's work
At the jobs you did before.
When we seek our bunks at night,
Our bodies, too, are weary and sore.
And as we take over and push you from your jobs over here,
We salute you.
With a lump in our throats and determination in our hearts,
We salute you.
We come to do you and our country good.
We believe in you.
We believe it will not be in vain.
You will go forth as men of whom we may be proud,
For whom we shall be glad to have left
The comfort of our homes,
The security of our paying jobs,
The freedom of action we knew—
For whom we shall be glad to have shared
The sacrifice you make.
We will not let you down.
Though not in the delicate gowns you knew,
Though not sitting, but still waiting,
We shall keep the home-fires burning.
And from the austerity of our Army home,
We will still seek the stars and the moon
And say our prayers . . .

We send you forth,
And as you go marching in never-ending files,
With our hearts and the work of our hands
We salute you.

EBONY RHYTHM, 1948

We Launched a Ship

RUBY BERKLEY GOODWIN

On one never-to-be-forgotten day, we launched a ship.[1]
The full-throated voice of Marian Anderson[2] proclaimed,
"I christen thee *Booker T. Washington*."
A bottle broke and champagne sprayed the prow
Of the giant liberty ship as she slid proudly down the ways
And sat serenely on the broad face of the ocean.

We launched a ship and the proud workers
Both black and white stood together and cheered.
They cheered with throats suddenly gone tight
And smiled at each other with eyes blurred
By the happy tears that trembled on lashes,
Or were brushed quickly aside by a calloused hand.

We launched a ship and the captain stood proudly on its deck.
He was a Negro, fearless and soft-spoken,
He breathed deeply and said to his crew,
"This ship—our ship—is more than a ship.
It is a symbol—a symbol of the dream that is America.
We must never let that dream die."

We launched a ship and the crew looked at their captain.
Some have called it a strange crew,
For the men were from many countries,
But all were bound by the love of freedom
And a fervent belief in the equality of man;
So the crew looked at their captain,

---

1. The ship referred to is the *S.S. Booker T. Washington,* brought into service in 1942. Its captain, Hugh Mulzac, was the first African American merchant marine naval officer to command an integrated crew; twenty-two years before, Mulzac had been offered the command of a segregated ship, which he refused. With its crew representing eighteen nationalities, the *Booker T. Washington* made twenty-two round-trip voyages in five years and carried eighteen thousand troops to Europe and the Pacific.

2. African American contralto, 1902–1993.

Black, brown, yellow, and white faces
Looked at the captain.
They answered not in words but each heart said,
"We know—we know—that's why we are here!"

The Captain's voice was silent but his heart asked back,
"And why are you here?"
Their hearts responded,
"Because all men are brothers,
Because black and white workers will
Work together in harmony,
Because there is a place in the world
For black leadership."

The shouting of the crowd on shore
Beat against the hull of the ship.
The black and white workers on the pier said proudly,
"We worked together to build her."
The black and white crew aboard resolved,
"We'll work together and sail her."

We launched a ship—
A ship with a glorious mission,
And it became the symbol of a
Dawning brotherhood throughout the world.

OPPORTUNITY, SUMMER 1944

Army Airport

MAE SMITH WILLIAMS[1]

All the day and thru the night,
I hear recurrent sounds of flight,
The whirr of wings, the drone of plane,
The moan of wind, the creak of crane,—
The lumber piled in the woodyard high,
The ships' masts pointing toward the sky,

---

1. Mae Smith Williams was an African American army airport employee.

Stark skeletons in waiting line
Along the bay—
                    the turbulent whine
Of churning tide and rope-tied scow.
The storm-clouds scowl with angry brow
Til rosy rifts of afterglow
Steal thru the drifts of ether-snow,
Then here and there a silvery beam
A pathway flings across the stream,
The wind-blown, gurgling, flotsam tide,
Where waiting rafts and barges ride.

The silent guards patrol the shore
While busy workmen's voices roar
Their orders forth and pit their strength
To load the cargo, til at length
The ships depart—
                    about the camp
The soldiers move with martial tramp,
Dark soldiers bronzed by blood and sun,
White soldiers garbed in wings and gun.

The army planes in gaunt array
Like giant bats full-poised to play
Their destined part—all silent, still,
O'er stretch of field and rise of hill,
First quivering, then purring slow
Pulsating, throbbing, skimming low,
Like transient meteors they rise
With muffled roar and mount the skies,
Like comets streaking thru the heights,
Now lost, now found by beacon lights
That search the labyrinth of blue,
They signal—disappear from view:
Our planes—with wings of hope they fly,
Our faith their pinions—
                    "Victory!" our cry.

THE CRISIS, SEPTEMBER 1944

To a Lone Negro in a Small Town

CONSTANCE C. NICHOLS

There is peace and calm!
Too much! Too much!
I beat my head with my fist.
How the whirling World
Goes on! Goes on!
Yet never a one to list
To the unechoed moan of my lonesomeness!

Take me out of this lily-white throng!
Let me hear, now, the noise of a city street;
See your smiling brown face pass along!

NEGRO STORY, DECEMBER–JANUARY 1944–1945

The Love We Made

WILLIAM COUCH JR.

Where is the love we made in a parked car
      by the vacant lot
You weeping through the jazz off the dashboard;
      I laughing, strong,
Shaping and sure of everything I shaped for us
      out of the darkness there
Later trying to fit it into a kitchenette
And say it when we both came home from
      factories—Neither remembers:
You, the young mother of an abortion
      will weep at nothing now
I, reasonable, older,
      Dare not fool with dreaming.

NEGRO STORY, OCTOBER–NOVEMBER 1944

Salty River

MARIE BROWN FRAZIER

You shall never see me weep again;
> My tears gall you so;
I shall turn them inward
> Let them flow
Until little salty rivers
> Course through my veins.
Little salty rivers
> Rivers—wide and deep
I shall turn my tears inward
> You shall never know I weep.
Some future day when I weep no more,
> Salty rivers will wash my heart to shore.

THE CRISIS, JUNE 1945

To Friendship

GEORGIA DOUGLAS JOHNSON

How could I live without friendship
Hearts bending low to my call,
Graciously mindful, tenderly dear,
Drying my tears ere they fall.

I could not live without friendship
Life too unequal to bear
Were there no freshets of friendship
Springing for me here and there!

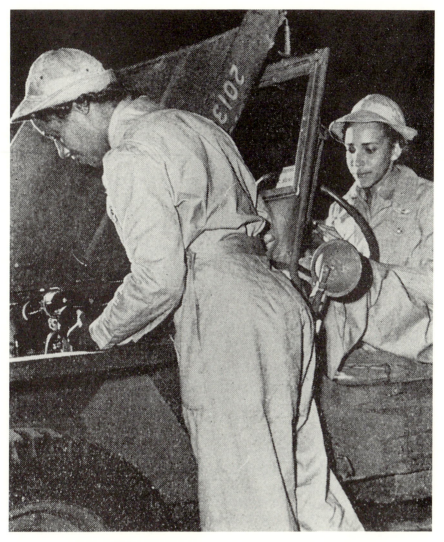

Army Motor Corps Workers, *Opportunity,* **April 1943**

NEGRO STORY, APRIL–MAY 1946

Black Man's Train Ride

RUTH DE CESARE

A black man looks ahead with hope.

Big train wheelin' a rickety track,
Clickety clack, rickety rack,
Old train reelin' the old dead track,
A-carr'in' me home, a-carr'in' me home.
Look out the window, boy, what do you see?
Clickety clee, what do you see?
Great white fences a-starin' at me,
A-starin' at me;
This is a long ride home.
See them poor shacks all in a row,
Whisperin' rows, rickety rows,
What's inside of them, God only knows,
Clickety clack, clackety clack;
I knows:—
Still black faces, all in a row, cryin' their eyes out,
Wantin' to go home.

Look out the other side, everythin' fine:
Sweet mill lumber stacked in a line,
Clickety clack, click, clack;
Beautiful burnt wood, down to the ground,
Down to the Negro shacks, down to the white heart;
I'm comin' home.
Down to the farmland, down to the town,
Down to the milk-white dairy,
With the bottles goin' *clickety clack,*
And the workers in their white coats,
Clackety clack,
And the white machines with no minds at all;
I'll get there yet!
It's a long ride, boy, it's a long hop,
And I'm dead tired out from my journeyin';

Slip, slop,
Slow down, train;
This here's my gettin' off stop.

NEGRO STORY, MARCH—APRIL 1945

Tar

SHIRLEY GRAHAM

It was the moan of the saxophones that did it—deep down, lingering and warm. Mary turned abruptly and began pushing her way towards the door. "Easy there, honey. What's the hurry?" "Lady, can I . . . ?" "Hands off, Alabama, I seen her first!" "Some chick!" "Tall, slim mamma!"

No good. She had to get out. As usual, on Saturday night, the place was crowded, but nobody seemed to mind. Deep red leather, black lacquer, smooth floors, laughter, smoke and good music. No mistake about the music! The U.S.O. down the street offered no competition to the Savoy. Weekends there were always plenty of men in uniform. Plenty of men—not in uniform. Why should there be so many? Why weren't they in the army with—Tom?

Down the street Mary drew a deep breath that hurt. Lenox Avenue was rakish without being tawdry. The air was good, touched lightly with the pungent odor of barbecue, and there were sounds of loud and easy friendliness. But without a glance either way, Mary turned off the avenue into 140th Street, gradually leaving lights and haunting saxophones behind.

This was the way they usually went home—she and Tom—clinging to each other, shadowed by the trees. Then the throb of the saxophones was part of all the breathless night. No—it was pain.

Crazy idea—going to the Savoy without Tom. She had thought to run into some lonely soldier from down home. They were all over Harlem—gawky, slow speaking dark boys from Mississippi, Alabama and Georgia—anxious and defiant, crude and proud. They turned to Mary like cornflowers to sunshine. Mary was one of them. She wasn't long come from Georgia herself.

That's why she could never get over the wonder of Tom. He was so sure of himself. He knew so well what he was going to do—had everything figured out. Nothing was going to stop him. And she had fitted into all his plans. "You're the missing link," Tom had grinned. "Right out of heaven into my arms! Oh, Baby!" Imagine calling Georgia heaven! Tom, who had made heaven for her. Smart Tom, who went downtown to school all day and worked nights. (All except that one night a week when he took her dancing at the Savoy.) Georgia and heaven, Tom and music and the bridges he told her he was learning to build, the shining clean home they were going to have—all mixed up like molasses—sweet!

Then the dirty Japs dropped bombs on Pearl Harbor!

Lord, Tom was mad! "Just like that. Right out of the sky on Sunday morning. Few more months and I'd be finished—set to build all the roads and canals and bridges in the world. But the army needs engineers *right now!*" Just before Christmas he had come in all excited. The entire class was going to be commissioned—wouldn't have to wait till June. All fellows were going into the army right away! He was going to be an officer! And Mary didn't say a mumbling word.

But there seemed to be some delay, and Tom fussed and fumed. Then for several evenings he was very quiet. Mary's heart ached. She recognized *the look*. She'd seen it on the face of a child who had been slapped *hard*. She even remembered it in the eyes of a kitten, which had been kicked. You see, Tom had been so sure! One night he was downright glum until unexpectedly he said, Aw hell, he was going to the army anyway. Wouldn't take long—he'd soon get to officers training camp. They'd see, he had muttered darkly. He'd build bridges yet!

Now he was gone.

The odor of burnt hair assailed Mary's nostrils when she let herself into the walk-up apartment. Cleo was home—had converted the tiny kitchen into a beauty salon. Bits of hair still clung to the sink. With smoking iron she was transforming the thick, spongy mass of her head into a carefully designed and glistening coiffeur.

Cleo was not, however, happy. Her Saturday evening had been a total loss. Washing and pressing her own hair was a chore to which she had been forced only through dire necessity. For Cleo sang in the Abyssinian Baptist Church choir. Attendance at morning service was obligatory. Nor dare she fall below the high standards set by Brother Powell. She sang second alto and intended "to shine for Jesus"—literally. Now, her voice was aggrieved.

"Two hours—two hours I wait at Maybelle's for this shampoo and curl. Then—what you think happens?"

"What?" asked Mary, knowing it must have been terrific.

"In walks that great big balook of a sailor of hers, and she goes wild!

Not nary another head tonight—said I didn't have no appointment—walks right out leavin' two customers. Would you believe it? After two hours!"

"Well . . ." began Mary, doubtfully, "if he was here only one evening, I guess . . ."

"This damn war is ruinin' the country—just ruinin' it," Cleo's voice was bitter.

Mary paused long enough to cluck sympathetically, then sidled into the living room and threw up the window.

"Say," called Cloe, "Mrs. Van Dyke phoned. Wants you to come on Monday."

Mary didn't answer, and Cleo appeared in the doorway, hot iron poised.

"You hear what I said. Mrs. Van Dyke . . ."

"I heard you."

Mary had thrown herself down on the couch and was fumbling with the radio. She added without spirit. "Fat old thing!" Cleo eyed her suspiciously.

"Where you been?" A direct question.

"I stopped by the Savoy."

Mary didn't look up. She didn't need to. Tom might just as well be standing there on the rug. Through the pregnant silence the radio began to sputter.

Cleo hadn't liked Tom. She considered him "uppity." And Cleo felt responsible for Mary. There was some sort of vague relation between the two families. It was Cleo who had suggested that Mary come north. Mary, she said, had a future.

For Mary sewed. Ever since she was a little girl she had been putting pieces together in striking and unusual patterns. And her tiny stitches were perfect. Now, what she could do with a length of cloth was something. She had a feeling for colors, too. The white folks in Maxwell were crazy about her. They all said Aunt Ross's gal was a well-mannered little thing.

"But," Cleo had urged, "why stay in such a dump workin' your fingers to the bone for fifty cents a day when you can come to New York and in a little while have your own shop on Seventh Avenue. Look at Madame Walker!"[1]

Mary couldn't very well look at Madame Walker—but she got the point. So did Aunt Ross, for that matter. There wasn't anybody else to consult. So that's how Mary came to be in Harlem sharing an apartment on West 136th Street with the veteran New Yorker, Cleo. And she was doing very

---

1. Madame C. J. Walker was a Harlem businesswoman, an African American entrepreneur who built a million-dollar beauty products industry during the early twentieth century.

well. Cleo had mentioned Mary's abilities to her boss. All her friends were delighted to find such an "unspoiled" seamstress.

Cleo cooked. She was a good cook, but she had no illusions about *her* future. She refused to live in[2]—got what she could out of her nights as she went along, and accepted fate. But Mary was different. Mary had talent!

And a girl with talent didn't have to get gaw-gaw over the first fast talker who came along. For all his big talk about bridges, the only work that "engineering student" did was odd job man around the Taft Hotel—nights.

Mary had protested. "But Tom's putting in all his time studying. He's going to . . ."

"Bridges!" Cleo had snorted. "Don't make sense for a colored man—no future!"

No, she had not approved. And him going to the army hadn't helped matters. Mary had wanted Tom to marry her before he left. He had explained to a tight-lipped Cleo, "Engineers get in mighty tough spots. Wouldn't be fair to her. When I come back . . . if everything's okay . . . I mean—if I'm all here—you know . . . then we'll . . ." He had turned away from Mary's hungry eyes.

That was six months ago. And look at her now! Limp as a rag—no ambition—not interested in good customers—Mrs. Van Dyke, for instance . . . and her living on Central Park, South!

"This night," Cleo told herself, "I gotta speak my mind!"

But Mary didn't hear a word of it.

For Mary was listening to the radio. Thousands of other people heard that same announcement. They didn't know the man was talking straight to Aunt Ross's Mary—was telling her what she could do—how she could join up with Tom and help get this war over—quickly.

No, she didn't hear a word Cleo said. After she had written down an address she leaned far out the window and watched the blinking lights of a mail carrier high over head. The throbbing of its engines was music. She thought again of the saxophones, but now it was sweet. For she was feeling the beauty of a plane—all silver in the sunlight. How wonderful it would be to make even the tiniest part of a great plane!

It had never occurred to any of Mary's satisfied customers that she knew a war was going on. She said nothing the next afternoon until the job was finished. Then stooping over to pick up a long basting thread from the thick rug she announced in her husky, honey-thick drawl, "I won't be comin' next week."

---

2. To live with her employers as a maid.

The lady was annoyed. These girls, so utterly unreliable.

"I signed up for a defense course."

When the lady remonstrated, Mary was a bit apologetic. (Cleo had told her bluntly she was a fool.)

"I figured I ought do somethin' to help. I . . . I . . . don't think this," she lifted the silken folds, "is awful important. You reckon 'tis?"

Because Mary was skilled in cutting cloth on a bias and fitting uneven edges, she did exceptionally well in the sheet metal class. She took the advanced course. Then showed her certificate proudly.

"Now what?" Cleo asked.

"I'm going into the plane factory."

But Mary didn't get into that factory. Nothing daunted, she tried another and another and another. She stood in long lines day after day—clutching her certificate. At night she had crazy dreams—about flying and dropping through clouds—of her color fading out when she blew a saxophone. One night she dreamed she was green! After a while her face did get sort of ashy. She couldn't just keep on living on Cleo. She put her certificate away.

The customers welcomed her back gladly. "After all," they said. One lady mentioned the circumstances to her husband. "She's so *disappointed.* I thought there was a shortage of help." The husband thought so too and immediately gave Mary a letter to a friend of his. Mary took the letter gratefully. It asserted that she was "honest" and "a personable negress."

Mary got a job—filling vats with tar. She stood and poured tar all night—going on at twelve and returning in the morning spattered with tar.

"For heaven's sake," Cleo asked, "must you push in the tar with your nose?"

"Seems like I'm awful clumsy. It's so thick. I'll move up soon. Everybody has to start with tar."

The folks for whom Cleo cooked went south for the winter. Because Cleo's flesh yearned for the golden warmth of Texas sunshine, she went with them.

It was cold and damp the April morning Cleo returned. She shivered in the dark hallway as she fitted her key. Inside, water was running. From the bathroom door she surveyed Mary vigorously scrubbing tar from her forearms. Mary was thinner.

"Look," Cleo demanded, "you still pourin' tar? Ain't you been promoted?"

Mary shook her head.

"The old so and so . . ." Cleo began, but Mary stopped her.

"Just had a long letter from Tom." Her eyes were shining.

Cleo was trying to stuff her coat into the tiny hall closet. Perhaps the state of that closet rendered her voice acid as she commented, "Naturally Tom's awful busy right now buildin' bridges over the Rhine."

"Tom didn't say nothin' 'bout bridges this time." Then why was Mary's voice singing? "That morning they'd been unloading a ship when . . ."

"Unloading ships—Tom?" Cleo experienced a grim satisfaction. Engineers and their "tough places," indeed!

" . . . planes come. Tom said they was rushin' the stuff to cover when machine fire riddled the wharf."

"Was he . . . ?"

"Not Tom! The tank he was rollin' was shot to pieces and tar gushed all over him—knocking him down—burying him in tar. He said nothing could have hit him. And when they was gone and he managed to get up . . . Lord, he mustta been a sight!" And Mary laughed.

Cleo found herself moistening her lips as she finally managed to close the closet door. Then she turned back to Mary, who asked, "Can't you just see Tom in that tar?"

She shook the soap from her eyes, leaned over and carefully removed a bit of tar from behind her left ear.

Cleo grinned. "You don't do so bad yourself."

"I'll get it all off. I'm stopping by the Savoy tonight. Count Basie's there."

Mary studied a spot just above her right elbow and frowned slightly.

"I reckon it'll take a heap of tar for all the new roads we gotta make. Yeh—a lotta tar!"

THE CRISIS, APRIL 1945

The Song Says "Keep On Smiling"

CHESTER B. HIMES

It had been Jean Delaney who had given them the idea in the first place. She sang with the shipyard orchestra and worked on shipway No. 7 as a shipfitter's helper. And she had a ripe red smile that even the San Francisco fog couldn't dampen.

The white girls used to ask her, "Jean, how on earth do you keep your smile? You're never low—how do you do it?"

One day Jean said, "Look, why don't you chicks organize a club and have some fun. You'll go nuts thinking about your guys and going to bed with memories. Make it just for the girls with boy friends in service."

Assembly Worker, *Opportunity*, April 1943

And that's how it began.

But when they organized the club, they didn't include her, and she only learned about it by accident. She had noticed all that day that the women were avoiding her, but she didn't know the reason until that evening on the bus going home, a girl named Sheila said to her, "Bring some music tonight, Jean; we want you to sing for us."

"Bring some music where?" Jean wanted to know. "What's cooking?"

"To Helen's, of course." And then Sheila looked startled. "You're coming, aren't you?"

"I might if I knew what it was all about," Jean smiled.

Sheila blushed, and then stammered, "Oh, er, I-er, thought you knew. The girls are having a meeting of the *Sweethearts Club*. They, er, asked you to join, didn't they?"

It was the first time Sheila had ever seen Jean lose her smile. "Yes they did, but I, er, I'm not eligible," Jean lied with quick defensiveness. "Er, you see my boy friend's not really in service; he's in the merchant marines."

But it hurt her deeply that they had not asked her to join. All the way up Sutter Street, her hurt slowly intensified, and when she alighted at the corner of Filmore, she felt as close to tears as she had been since leaving New Orleans six months before.

It was a noisy, uncouth corner, always crowded with street loungers who insulted and molested unescorted women. Hurrying into the corner cafeteria, she ate beside a harsh indifferent woman who read the evening paper; and then, running the gauntlet of meddling drunks, went across the street and started up the two flights of stairs to her hall bedroom.

The first floor of the three-storied apartment building was occupied by a black-and-tan jump joint[1] called *Dels Cafe.* Mrs. Dels, who owned both the cafe and the building, lived on the second floor, while the third was given over to rooms for defense workers.

On sudden impulse, Jean stopped and knocked at Mrs. Dels' door. A short, stout, brown-skinned woman with bobbed, wavy hair streaked with gray opened the door and smiled delightedly at the sight of her.

"Why, here's my pretty little daughter," she greeted warmly. "Come in. Where have you been? You must come and see me more often."

Cheered somewhat by the warmth of the greeting, Jean tried to smile again. "I really should, Mrs. Dels," she confessed, taking a seat on the divan. "You're always so wonderfully happy; how do you do it?" And then suddenly,

---

1. A jazz nightclub patronized by African Americans.

she had to laugh—that was exactly what the white girls had always said to her.

But Mrs. Dels was pleased by the remark. "God has been good to me," she replied.

"I suppose He'll get around to the rest of us sooner or later," Jean sighed.

"You young folks and your troubles," Mrs. Dels chided. "Don't know what trouble is. Tell me about yourself, daughter. What have you been doing with yourself?"

"Oh, I've been staying in, reading and sleeping," Jean said, and then all of a sudden she found herself pouring out all of the annoyances that had accumulated on her job. But it was at her mention of the *Sweethearts Club* that Mrs. Dels sensed the difference in her voice.

"So they took your idea and then didn't ask you to join," she surmised.

"I didn't really want to join anyway," Jean denied, trying hard to sound indifferent about the whole business. "But I thought sure they would ask me. Why it's just a hen affair, nobody but just the women; and I've been chummy with them right along."

"Now don't you worry, child," Mrs. Dels comforted. "Those whitefolks will be coming to you yet, begging you to sing for them. Their conscience will get to hurting them and they'll do something extry nice to make up for it. White folks is like that—try to buy their way right straight into heaven.

"You take me, for instance. I worked for a family thirty years and they worked me like a dog; and then I told them I was just tired and I was going to quit and get some rest and enjoyment out of life before I died. And you know, their conscience got to bothering them and they gave me the money to buy this place. All the days I was slaving for them I never thought that some day I'd own a business and a big apartment house. I own a brand new Cadillac automobile, too. I had the money and I just bought it 'cause I always wanted to own a car. Soon as I learn how to drive you got to let me take you for a ride downtown somewhere."

Jean tried to smile again, but the long speech left her depressed. If she had to wait thirty years before she felt she had a place in the world, she would just as soon die now. Soon afterwards she said she was tired, and promising to call again soon, she climbed the stairs to her own room.

Upon entering, she snapped on the light. Although it was only a little after six, inside was pitch dark. Only between the hours of two and three in the afternoon did the one window, opening onto a narrow court, supply enough light by which to read.

Pushed against the inner wall was a faded, moth-eaten davenport of indescribable color; to the right stood a cheap, ivory painted dressing table scarred with numerous cigarette burns. The remainder of the available space was occupied by the bed.

Gathering together her toilet articles—towel, soap, tooth brush and paste, along with cleanser and disinfectant—she peeped out into the hallway to see if it was clear, then tiptoed down the back stairway to the bathroom. She walked daintily, holding the hem of her robe away from the dirty floor.

By the time she had returned, the noise from the cabaret part of the cafe had already begun. Situated directly below her room, every sound came up through the narrow court and issued through her open window as if from an amplifier. But if she closed her window, the dank odor of the room suffocated her.

However, instead of going to bed, she began arranging her hair and making up her face. She was so blue and lonesome she could have screamed just to hear a familiar voice. Satisfied with her makeup, she donned her high-heeled slippers and a print evening gown, and suddenly, a little startlingly, began to sing to the furniture, frowning at the dresser, smiling at the davenport, gesturing to the bed.

"I'll get by as long as I have you . . ."[2] she crooned, throwing wide her arms to the closed door. But after a time she could no longer stand it; she had sung herself into a state of desperation. She had to talk to someone or she would go nuts.

Throwing a coat over her shoulders, she ran downstairs to the cafe. For a moment she stood in the jam which hemmed in the bar, undecided. A hand squeezed her arm and a whiskey-thickened voice whispered, "Wanna drink, babe?"

Before she could reply, the orchestra leader, Bert Saunders, who was just arriving, came up behind them and said, "Easy chum, she's my guest."

Turning quickly, she recognized him. "Oh! It's you."

The cabaret entertainers used the same bath as the upstairs roomers, and once before she had met him in the hallway. He had invited her to come down and have a drink on him; and now he said, presuming she had accepted, "Well, this is a treat. Come on in."

For just an instant she hesitated. Then, smiling, she said, "It's a good deal," and followed him into the cabaret to a table near the orchestra stand.

Although it was only seven-thirty, the place was already filled. All available floor space not occupied by the orchestra was taken up by tables placed so closely together there was scarcely room for the waiters to pass with the

---

2. Words of a popular jazz standard.

drinks. Brown and yellow faces took on strange hues in the orange light, and cigarette smoke formed a bluish haze overhead. Pungent perfumes and whiskey smell clogged in her nostrils; and the incessant din of loud, unrestrained voices filled her ears. But there was something exciting about the place, something primitive, abandoned, wanton, that took her mind from her own troubles.

Sitting opposite her, Bert ignored the clamor of "Let's have some jive, papa," and tried to get acquainted. He was a short, dark man with slicked hair and a worldly smile, clad in an expensive gray suit, light blue shirt, and a dubonnet bow tie. He ordered Scotch and soda for them both, and smiled at her.

"Did you really come down to meet me, sugar, or did I just pop in on the dime?"[3]

"I just got tired of my dingy attic room for which I pay nine good dollars weekly," she said.

His eyes lidded slightly. "A good looking queen like you shouldn't have a hard time finding a place to stay—please believe me."

"That's what you think. I've searched this whole bay area from end to end and there's absolutely nothing to be found."

He leaned a little toward her, his gaze on her face, and suggested, "Well, I have a big apartment—and my wife is in New York. I could rent you a room; why should I be so selfish."

She gave him a level look. "I'm not the girl. I have a sweetheart in the merchant marines; he's at sea now, but when he gets back, I'm going to marry him—"

"And settle down," he supplemented, spreading his hands. "My idea isn't *forever*, sugar," he persisted. "When he comes back, you move out." He lifted his glass, put it down. His eyes narrowed. "Nothing lost. I know where there's a silver fox jacket that's strictly a good deal."

After a moment she asked, "You don't believe in a girl being true to her sweetheart, do you?"

"When I was white," he said in a dead tone voice, "I used to believe in everything." Signaling the waiter to refill their glasses, he added, "But you and I are black, sugar. Now I'm just an opportunist. What I believe in are the days; just the pure and simple days. And this is my day, sugar; I'm making plenty right here in this beatup joint jiving these hicks." He wet his lips and took a breath. "I could be a chump for you, sugar—please believe me."

---

3. Happen in on a conversation with someone else.

A big-boned flashily dressed woman leaned over his shoulder and said, "So you're chippy chasing again—and I caught you!"

Unperturbed, he replied, "So that's your story?"

But Jean quickly arose. "I must be going," she said. "Thank you for the drink."

The waiter served the second round of drinks, but she was halfway to the door. The big-boned woman took the seat which she had just vacated and winked at the people at the next table.

Bert arose to follow Jean. But at the doorway she turned and said breathlessly, "Please, I don't want to cause a scene."

He said, " 'Til the next hand then," and let her go.

Outside, she whistled, "Whew!" And then suddenly laughed.

For an instant she contemplated visiting Hattie, a cook on Nob Hill whom she knew, but decided against it. No need of peeping in the white folks' kitchens when you didn't have to. So she walked down Filmore to Geary and caught the "B" car downtown to Market. She went into the *Western Union* office and asked, "It isn't possible to send a radiogram to a fellow in the merchant marine, is it?"

The girl smiled sympathetically. "Not if he is at sea."

She walked back to Sutter and caught a "2" car home. It was eleven-thirty when she re-entered her room; and the noise from below was tremendous. The male singer was going to town on: "*Yass-yass-yass . . .*" And the patrons were echoing: "*Oh-yass-yass-yass . . .*" The joint was rocking.

She waited for twelve o'clock when it would become quiet and she could go to sleep.

THE CRISIS, DECEMBER 1943

On Saturday the Siren Sounds at Noon
ANN PETRY

At five minutes of twelve on Saturday there was only a handful of people waiting for the 241st Street train. Most of them were at the far end of the wooden platform where they could look down on the street and soak up some of the winter sun at the same time.

A Negro in faded blue overalls leaned against a post at the upper end of the station. He was on his way to work in the Bronx. He had decided to change trains above ground so he could get a breath of fresh air. In one hand he carried a worn metal lunch box.

As he waited for the train, he shifted his weight from one foot to the other. He watched the way the sun shone on the metal tracks—they gleamed as far as he could see in the distance.

The train's worn 'em shiny, he thought idly. Train's run up and down 'em so many times they're shined up like a spitoon. He tried to force his thoughts to the weather. Spitoons. Why'd I have to think about something like that?

He had worked in a hotel bar room once as a porter. It was his job to keep all the brass shining. The door knobs and the rails around the bar and the spitoons. When he left the job he took one of the spitoons home with him. He used to keep it shined up so that it reflected everything in his room. Sometimes he'd put it on the window sill and it would reflect in miniature the church across the street.

He'd think about Spring—it was on the way. He could feel it in the air. There was a softness that hadn't been there before. Wish the train would hurry up and come, he thought. He turned his back on the tracks to avoid looking at the way they shone. He stared at the posters on the walls of the platform. After a few minutes he turned away impatiently. The pictures were filled with the shine of metal, too. A silver punch bowl in a Coca-Cola ad and brass candlesticks that fairly jumped off a table. A family was sitting around the table. They were eating.

He covered his eyes with his hands. That would shut it out until he got hold of himself. And it did. But he thought he felt something soft clinging to his hands and he started trembling.

Then the siren went off. He jumped nearly a foot when it first sounded. That old air raid alarm, he thought contemptuously—always putting it off on Saturdays. Yet it made him uneasy. He'd always been underground in the subway when it sounded. Or in Harlem where the street noises dulled the sound of its wail.

Why, that thing must be right on top of this station, he thought. It started as a low, weird moan. Then it gained in volume. Then it added a higher screaming note, and a little later a low, louder blast. It was everywhere around him, plucking at him, pounding at his ears. It was inside of him. It was his heart and it was beating faster and harder and faster and harder. He bent forwards because it was making a pounding pressure against his chest. It was hitting him in the stomach.

He covered his ears with his hands. The lunch box dangling from one hand nudged against his body. He jumped away from it, his nerves raw, ready to scream. He opened his eyes and saw that it was the lunch box that had prodded him and he let it drop to the wooden floor.

It's almost as though I can smell that sound, he told himself. It's the smell and the sound of death—cops and ambulances and fire trucks—

A shudder ran through him. Fire. It was Monday that he'd gone to work extra early. Lilly Belle was still asleep. He remembered how he'd frowned down at her before he left. Even sleeping she was untidy and bedraggled.

The kids were asleep in the front room. He'd stared at them for a brief moment. He remembered having told Lilly Belle the night before, "Just one more time I come home and find you ain't here and these kids by themselves, and I'll kill you—"

All she'd said was, "I'm goin' to have me some fun—"

Whyn't they shut that thing off, he thought. I'll be deaf. I can't stand it. It's breaking my ear drums. If only there were some folks near here. He looked towards the other end of the platform. He'd walk down that way and stand near those people. That might help a little bit.

The siren pinioned him where he was when he took the first step. He'd straightened up and it hit him all over so that he doubled up again like a jackknife.

The sound throbbed in the air around him. It'll stop pretty soon, he thought. It's got to. But it grew louder. He couldn't see the tracks anymore. When he looked again they were pulsating to the sound and his ear drums were keeping time to the tracks.

"God in Heaven," he moaned, "make it stop." And then in alarm, "I can't even hear my own voice. My voice is gone."

If I could stop thinking about fire—fire—fire. Standing there with the sound of the siren around him, he could see himself coming home on Monday afternoon. It was just about three o'clock. He could see himself come out of the subway and start walking down Lenox Avenue, past the bakery on the corner. He stopped and bought a big bag of oranges from the push cart on the corner. Eloise, the little one, liked oranges. They were kind of heavy in his arms.

He went in the butcher store near 133rd Street. He got some hamburger to cook for dinner. It seemed to him that the butcher looked at him queerly and he could see himself walking along puzzling about it.

Then he turned into 133rd Street. Funny. Standing here with this noise tearing inside him, he could see himself as clearly as though by some miracle he'd been transformed into another person. The bag of oranges, the packages of meat—the meat was soft, and he could feel it cold through the paper wrapping, and the oranges were hard and knobby. And his lunch box was empty and it was swinging light from his hand.

There he was turning the corner, going down his own street. There were little knots of people talking. They nodded at him. Sarah Lee who ran the beauty shop—funny she'd be out in the street gossiping this time of day. And Mrs. Smith who had the hand laundry. Why, they were all there. He turned and looked back at them. They turned their eyes away from him quickly when he looked at them.

He could see himself approaching the stoop at 219. Cora, the janitress, was leaning against the railing, her fat hips spilling over the top. She was talking to the priest from the church across the way. He felt excitement stir inside him. The priest's hands were bandaged and there was blood on the bandages.

The woman next door was standing on the lower step. She saw him first and she nudged Cora.

"Oh—" Cora stopped talking.

The silence alarmed him. "What's the matter?" he asked.

"There was a fire," Cora said.

He could see himself running up the dark narrow stairs. Even the hall was filled with the smell of dead smoke. The door of his apartment sagged on its hinges. He stepped inside and stood perfectly still, gasping for breath. There was nothing left but charred wood and ashes. The walls were gutted and blackened. That had been the radio and there was a piece of what had been a chair. He walked into the bedroom. The bed was a twisted mass of metal. The spitoon had melted down. It was a black rim with a shapeless mass under it. Everywhere was the acrid, choking smell of burned wood.

He turned to find Cora watching him.

"The children—" he said, "and Lilly Belle—"

"Lilly Belle's all right," she said coldly. "The kids are at Harlem Hospital. They're all right. Lilly Belle wasn't home."

He could see himself run blindly down the stairs. He ran to the corner and in excited agony to the Harlem Hospital. All the way to the hospital his feet kept saying, "Wasn't home." "Wasn't home." "Wasn't home."

They let him see the kids at the hospital. They were covered with clean white bandages, lying in narrow white cots.

First time they've ever been really clean, he thought bitterly. A crisp, starched nurse told him that they'd be all right.

"Where's the little one?" he asked. "Where's Eloise?"

The nurse's eyes widened. "Why, she's dead," she stammered.

"Where is she?"

He could see himself leaning over the small body in the morgue. He still had the oranges and the meat and the empty lunch box in his arms. When he went back to the ward, Lilly Belle was there with the kids. She was dressed in black. Black shoes and stockings and a long black veil that billowed around her when she moved. He was thinking about her black clothes so that he only half-heard her as she told him she'd just gone around the corner that morning, and that she'd expected to come right back.

"But I ran into Alice—and when I came back," she licked her lips as though they were suddenly dry.

He could see himself going to work. The next day and all the other days after that. Going to the hospital every day. Living in an apartment across the hall. The neighbors brought in furniture for them. He could hear the neighbors trying to console him.

He could see himself that very morning. He'd slept late because on Saturdays he went to work later than on other days. When he woke up he heard voices. And as he listened they came clear to his ears like a Victrola record or the radio.

Cora was talking. "You ain't never been no damn good. And if you don't quit runnin' to that bar with that dressed up monkey and stayin' away from here all day long, I'm goin' to tell that poor fool you're married to where you were when your kid burned up in here." She said it fast as though she wanted to get it out before Lilly Belle could stop her. "You walkin' around in mournin' and everybody but him knows you locked them kids in here that day. They was locked in—"

Lilly Belle said something he couldn't hear. He heard Cora's heavy footsteps cross the kitchen. And then the door slammed.

He got out of bed very quietly. He could see himself as he walked barefooted across the room. The black veil was hanging over a chair. He ran it through his fingers. The soft stuff clung and caught on the rough places on his hands as though it were alive.

Lilly Belle was in the kitchen reading a newspaper. Her dark hands were silhouetted against its pink outside sheets. Her hair wasn't combed and she had her feet stuck in a pair of runover mules. She barely glanced at him and then went on reading the paper.

He watched himself knot the black veil tightly around her throat. He pulled it harder and harder. Her lean body twitched two or three times and then it was very still. Standing there he could feel again the cold hard knot that formed inside him when he saw that she was dead.

If the siren would only stop. It was vibrating inside him—all the soft tissues in his stomach and in his lungs were moaning and shrieking with agony. The station trembled as the train approached. As it drew nearer and nearer the siren took on a new note—a louder, sharper, sobbing sound. It was talking. "Locked in. They were locked in." "Smoke poisoning. Third degree burns." "Eloise? Why, she's dead." "My son, don't grieve. It will probably change your wife." "You know, they say the priest's hands were all bloody where he tried to break down the door." "My son, my son—"

The train was coasting towards the station. It was coming nearer and nearer. It seemed to be jumping up and down on the track. And as it thundered in, it took up the siren's moan. "They were locked in. They were locked in."

Just as it reached the edge of the platform, he jumped. The wheels ground his body into the gleaming silver of the tracks.

The air was filled with noise—the sound of the train and the wobble of the siren as it died away to a low moan. Even after the train stopped, there was a thin echo of the siren in the air.

NEGRO STORY, JULY–AUGUST 1944

Viney Taylor

LILA MARSHALL

Viney Taylor was a hardworking girl. All her neighbors on Jackson Street in Nashville, Tennessee, liked her and her good for nothing loafer of a husband, Sam.

After years of working for white folks, Viney had a job as a power machine operator, and she loved it. She was buying war bonds each month, and she planned to save as much as she could so that she and Sam could buy a little home of their own. She dreamed about how it would look with the green grass and hedges all around it. She even knew exactly how she would plant the flower garden and what kind of a car they would buy to go in the garage in the back.

They might have children too. Viney had worked too hard to think of them before now, but it gave her a little pleasant feeling to dream of Sam's child. She would want the boy to look just like him, and the girl could look like the both of them. If only Sam could get a good job, and they could put their money together; it wouldn't take them any time to get ahead. And so she worked hard every day and dreamed of their future.

Viney went quietly about her business unless someone molested Sam. For she would fight you about her man, because he was all she had. That he was a lazy tramp was not important. He was tall and big and black and handsome. She loved everything about him, the ripple of his muscles, the way his fresh white shirt clung to his broad wet black chest in the summertime, his deep rich voice, his small black eyes and his wide, quick-flashing grin.

Sam always had to have clean white shirts, and he dressed in the best of clothes—fine gabardine trousers and natty sport coats. On Saturday nights, he borrowed money from Viney so that he could shoot pool with the boys and buy liquor. Often he would come home broke and drunk. Then again, he would swing in jauntily with a pocketful of bills and take Viney to the show. Viney was happy now with her Sam and her defense job. It seemed to her that she was learning something different. She had always wanted to go to night school, but she had been too tired when she came home from the white folks' houses. Now they had lessons and meetings connected with this job and a chance for advancement. Her main recreation had always been her church work, for she was president of the Woman's Home Missionary Society in St. John's A.M.E.[1] Church around the corner, and was an ardent worker. She had tried to get Sam to go to church, but he refused, said he knew more than the preacher and the congregation together.

But as long as Sam called her "honey" and "baby" and treated her sweet and loving, she was satisfied.

"Sam's okeh—jus' smart—needs a break," she would make excuses for him. "Ain't no job good 'nuff for him around here—he's educated more than me."

Sam had finished high school, and Viney had only gone through the ninth grade before she had to quit and get a job. She was a dark brown girl with hair that wasn't "good" like white folks' hair. But it looked nice because she always kept it pressed and curled neatly. She had high cheek bones and pretty, large eyes. Comely, slender and tall, with long lean legs, she was strong from working hard all her life.

When she first began to hear things about Sam and a girl named Lucy Smith, she didn't pay any attention to them. Lucy was fat and ugly and lazy. Sam wouldn't look at no cheap something like her. It was just people jealous and running their mouths, she thought.

Lucy was nineteen, a few years younger than Viney, and her reputation

---

1. African Methodist Episcopal.

was a trifle shady. She lived on Chesnutt Street in an apartment of her own, had lots of gaudy clothes, but did not work.

"You know Viney," Mandesta said—Mandesta lived across the hall with her old mother and was Viney's best friend. "Lucy's got a bedroom just full of all sorts of stuff."

"I know it is full of stuff all right." said Viney. "Jus' like Lucy—she always was messy."

"She's got all kinds of dolls and junk—pink taffeta silk spread, and pretty pictures and one of them radiolas with lots of new records."

"Shucks," Viney spit out the exclamation and made a face.

She looked around at her and Sam's bedroom. The best that could be said for it was that it was light and airy, and she kept it clean. The wallpaper was streaked and hanging off in places, and the furniture was cheap and plain. Their big brass bed bought at the second-hand store was covered with a frayed patchwork quilt. But Viney had scrubbed everything clean, the bare board floor, the three spindly chairs, the table, and her windows were shiny. That was one thing she had learned from the rich folks—how to clean, and she was a good cook.

Mandesta continued, "I wonder where Lucy gets her money—I heard all kinds of men hang around her."

"She looks like a sack of potatoes with a string tied around the middle," answered Viney. "I don't know what they see in her."

"I hear she makes over them—lays the jive thick."

"Sure, she's deceitful—ugly old fat thing."

"Well you know how men is—them whores can really tie a knot in their tails," Mandesta spoke in a shrill baby voice which made everything she said seem funny.

Viney forgot about the rumors, she was so busy. When she got home at night tired, she would have to work at home, and then she would fall asleep and hardly wake up when Sam came and crawled in bed beside her.

After awhile, she began to notice a change in him. He had become sort of indifferent and even cross these days.

"Sam," she had asked plaintively, "whassa matta honey—you sick?"

"Aw get the hell away from here woman—can't a man even be quiet without you bothering him?"

Viney was hurt. Her Sam didn't usually talk that way to her. But the thing that hurt her most was when he took the money she was saving for extra war bonds; said he had to have it to pay for a job he wanted. She let him have it and prayed for him to get the job. But he said no more about it and began to stay out later and later every night.

The neighbors kept on telling her she ought to do something about Lucy. But she didn't know what, and she wasn't quite sure about them. She couldn't really believe her Sam would take up with no other woman. No matter how trifling he was, he had always been crazy about her. Yet the thought of Lucy kept rankling in the back of her mind making her uncomfortable.

This hot Sunday afternoon, Viney was sitting in their small front bedroom fanning and feeling a little sorry for herself. Sam had stayed out late the night before and had slept all morning. Then he had gone out before she came home from church without leaving word. He usually waited for her, ate dinner and took her out. She was watching the couples pass by all dressed in their Sunday finery. Viney had changed her church clothes to a crisp cotton frock. Where was Sam anyhow? Couples were still passing arm in arm, which made her feel lonesome. Every now and then, Viney would call out something to Mandesta, who was sitting in the window with her mother across the hall in the apartment just like hers.

"It sho' is hot," she said in her low quiet voice fanning harder and getting warmer all the time. "I wish Sam would come and take me to the park."

"Jim told me he seen Sam over on Chesnutt Street last night," Mandesta said.

"Chesnutt Street!" Viney felt a little hot and funny in her chest and her underarms were suddenly wet. She kept trying to keep her mind off Lucy. As long as she was working every day, she didn't have time to think. But this was Sunday. What if Sam was fooling around. The thought made her sick at her stomach—especially a cheap ol' something like Lucy. Why she'd be afraid to touch him. She tried to put her mind on God and on the sermon she had heard that morning. What was that the minister had said about jealousy? She kept on rocking, stretching her bare legs out and touching her toes against the bare board as she rocked, but that sick feeling was in the pit of her stomach and creeping all over her body.

"Viney—look," cried Mandesta in her shrill high-pitched voice. "There's Lucy now. Look—look—look!"

Viney started and peered down the street. Yes, there she was—bold thing. What was she doing way over here on Jackson? Where was Sam? Lucy was plump and almost black. Her face was round and good natured and dusted heavily with a brown powder. Gold hoop earrings dangled from her ears. Her lips were painted bright red, and her cheeks were rouged. She twisted from side to side when she walked, mincing along on her high heeled green leather shoes, her large legs in dark silk stockings. She was walking like she owned the world. Dressed in green and yellow, she had a fluffy white pompom in her large green hat.

"Got her nerve," said Mandesta. "Look at her shake—look at her fine clothes."

Viney said nothing—only stared hard. Suppose Sam—Suppose Lucy— Sam was always home on Sunday . . . Sam . . . Lucy . . . Lucy . . . Sam. Thoughts of Sam and Lucy were whirling around in her head until she could not think clearly. Suddenly she bolted from the fast-moving rocking chair and made for the door. She didn't even turn around or stop when she heard Mandesta cry, "Viney—come back here—where you going Viney?"

Mandesta's shrill voice rose to a scream over the bannisters.

"Be careful Viney—Viney!"

But she kept right on, her long legs carrying her quickly down the dirty old stairs of the frame house and out past the green hedges. There was Lucy. She had passed the house, her fat green rump quivering as she strutted. The noise of the passing streetcar roared into Viney's ears.

She broke into a wild trot. She ran up around Lucy and blocked her way, standing akimbo. Lucy jumped and then tossed her head and tried to pass, but Viney wavered in front of her. Lucy stopped.

"Well, Miss Viney?"

"Well, nothing," she stammered.

"What's this I hear about you and Sam?"

"What on earth do you mean, Viney?"

"Keep your airs—I hear you're fooling around with Sam."

Lucy's eyes flashed, and she primped up her mouth.

"Whyn't you keep Sam at home where he belongs if you love him so?"

Viney stared. Then it was true. He had been messing with her. She saw through a haze, a white blur.

"If I couldn't hold a man . . ." Lucy began haughtily but didn't get a chance to complete her sentence.

"You dirty chippie," Viney said, and grabbed for Lucy's short oiled strands of hair, knocking off the pompommed hat. Lucy whirled around, her head gave a crack and down she went on the pavement, screaming. So surprised was she, that for a moment she couldn't try to fight back. Besides, she was pretty fat and squeezed into her tight outfit, which was already beginning to rip. Viney dragged her on the ground, struck her and kicked her like a woman gone mad. With righteous fury, sickeningly heavy blows and kicks rained alternately on Lucy's face and body with regularity. Her screams could be heard for miles. Viney tore her and pulled her until black patches of skin began to be visible through the green of the dress and the white of the lacy underclothes. Bits of green silk and white muslin were everywhere.

On all sides, people had gathered to look. Some were laughing. No one tried to stop them. Men were staring at the curve of Lucy's plump breast and thigh and chuckling. Some of the women and children were covering their eyes with their hands.

Lucy was almost naked. Shreds of clothing were clinging to her. She looked for all the world like a big plucked goose with the feathers lying around. She was striking out wildly, and yelling, but her eyes were half closed, and her nose was bleeding.

"That's right Viney—good for nothing hussy," one woman called. "She needs a beating."

"Taking people's husbands," said another. "Viney's right."

But Viney heard none of this. Sweating and breathing heavily, she was completing her job of beating Lucy. After pounding her unconscious, she picked up a big brick that lay near.

"Viney," Mandesta screamed from the window. "Viney!"

Viney flung the brick at Lucy's back, grabbed Lucy's heavy form and dragged her as fast as she could the few feet to the streetcar line and held her there. Everyone gasped.

"Viney!" someone called. "That's enough!"

The streetcar was coming. Lucy's near-nude body lay still. Viney had jumped back and stood watching with the crowd. Everyone was yelling. The car was lumbering up the track. It roared up clanging and stopped a foot or two from Lucy.

"What the hell's going on here?" cried the motorman, as he jumped out the street car. The crowd gathered around, and Viney ran as swiftly as she could down the cracked pieces of broken pavement skipping over the sandy stretches where there was no pavement, up through the green hedges, up the broken down stairs and ran gasping into her little front bedroom.

Mandesta and her old gray-haired mother were waiting. They had seen it all from the window.

"Hurry," they said and helped her tear off her clothes and slipped a white cotton nightgown over her head. She was perspiring and panting. They covered her up in bed with the white sheet, turning down the patchwork quilt, and wiped her face. She lay there in her huge brass bed, breathing heavily.

No sooner had they covered her than there was a heavy knock at the door, and a deep Southern voice shouted, "Open up here—open up!"

Mandesta opened the door and looked innocently into the red faces of the two big blue-coated policemen.

"Well, where is she?"

"Who?"

"That woman."

"What woman?"

"Fighting—nearly killed another one jus' now—looked like a cyclone struck her."

"Don't know—we been in the kitchen—in the back."

"She ran in here."

"Naw sir—nobody here but Viney—been sick a long time."

"Sick—where?"

"In there, sir." Mandesta's baby voice rose high and she pointed to the bed.

The policemen stood over Viney. She was tossing under the sheet, and her dark face looked twisted and painful.

"Ain't a scratch on her," one of them said, bending over her. They didn't look at her scratched knuckles under the cover.

"Naw, it couldn't be this one."

They turned toward the kitchen, kicked open the door, opened the pantry, and then pulled open every door in the house—closets and all.

"Shucks, these damn niggers ain't gonna tell on each other."

"Naw cause they all jus' alike—one jus' as bad as another."

"Fightin' over some old no-good man, I guess."

"C'mon les' have a drink," said one.

And laughing heartily, the two big officers fell heavily down the dirty stairs and strode down the street, forgetting that there had been two women fighting and that they had come to uphold the law.

OPPORTUNITY, APRIL 1943

What My Job Means to Me

HORTENSE JOHNSON

Employed at Picatinny Arsenal, Dover, New Jersey

Of course I'm vital to victory, just as millions of men and women who are fighting to save America's chances for Democracy, even if they never

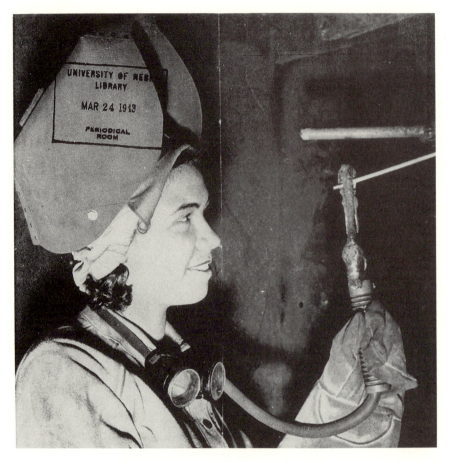

War Worker, *Opportunity*, April 1943

shoulder a gun nor bind a wound. It's true that my job isn't so exciting or complicated. Perhaps there are millions of girls who could do my job as well as I—certainly there are thousands. I am an inspector in a war plant. For eight hours a day, six days a week, I stand in line with five other girls, performing a routine operation that is part of our production schedule. We inspect wooden boxes that are to hold various kinds of munitions, and that range in size from eight inches to six feet. When we approve them they are ready to be packed with shells, bombs, fuses, parachutes—and other headaches for Hitler or Hirohito.

Not much to that, you say. Well, that all depends on the way you look at it. A missing or projecting nail, a loose board or hinge—these are some of the imperfections that we watch for. If we miss them, they may be checked later on, or they may not. If they are not, they may mean injury for a fellow worker on a later operation or an explosion in another part of the plant with dozens of lives lost—or they might even spell disaster for American soldiers in a tight spot in North Africa.

Did I say my job isn't exciting, or complicated? I take that back. It may be a simple matter to inspect one box or a dozen, but it's different when you are handling them by the hundreds. The six of us in my crew sometimes inspect as many as fourteen or fifteen hundred boxes during one shift. That means two hundred and fifty apiece—an average of one every two minutes, regardless of size and not counting any rest periods. Try that sometime and see if it's a simple job! You stand at your bench all day long, with rest periods sometimes seeming years apart. You fight against the eye fatigue that might mean oversight. You probe with your fingers and tap here and there. Your back aches, your legs get weary, your muscles scream at you sometimes—groan at you all the time. But the dozen and one little operations must be carried on smoothly and efficiently if your work output is to keep up. It's exciting all right, and it's plenty complicated—in the same way that jungle warfare must be, hard and painstaking and monotonous—until something goes off with a bang!

And when your shift is finished, you stalk off stiffly to the washroom and hurry to get ready for the bus that brings you forty-five miles back from the plant to your home in the city. You slip on an extra sweater and heavy woolen socks, because the unheated bus is apt to be cold and damp. Even when you get into the bus your day's job isn't over, for you work almost as hard as the driver. You strain with him to see through the heavy winter fog that blankets the highway. You watch with him for the tricky ice that waits at curves to throw you into dangerous skids. When sleet has covered the road and made all travel seem suicidal, you sit ready to get out at the worst spots and walk with the rest of your crowd until the bus pulls across to safety.

So when you get back home, you're glad to jump into bed and die until morning—or until your alarm-clock tells you it's morning, no matter how black it is. Then your two-hour experience of traveling back to the job begins all over again, because in spite of rain, snow, cold or illness, the job is there to be done, and you're expected to do your share. It never occurs to you to figure out how much money you're making, because it isn't much anyhow—after you've had your victory tax deducted, paid for your war bond, set aside money for your bus commutation ticket. By the time you've given grandmother the food and rent money, and paid the doctor for helping you to fight off your frequent colds, and bought the extra-heavy clothes the job calls for, you're just about where the boys in New Guinea are. Don't let Senator Wheeler[1] fool you with his talk about "high wages for war workers!"

So if it's as tough as all that—and it is!—why do you stick on the job? Why did you leave the comfortable job you held with a city business house? Why don't you go back to it and make as much money as you're making now? Why? Because it's not that easy to leave, and it's not that tough to stay! Of course the work is hard and sometimes dangerous, but victory in this war isn't going to come the easy way, without danger. And we brown women of America need victory so much, so desperately. America is a long way from perfect. We resent the racial injustices that we meet every day of our lives. But it's one thing to resent and fight against racial injustices; it's another thing to let them break your spirit, so that you quit this struggle and turn the country over to Hitler and the Talmadges and Dieses[2] who will run this country if Hitler wins. America can't win this war without all of us, and we know it. We must prove it to white Americans as well—that our country can't get along without the labor and sacrifice of her brown daughters, can't win unless we *all* fight and work and save.

So the hardships of war work become willing sacrifices to victory, not to victory for Democracy, but to victory by a country that some day, please God, will win Democracy. In such a spirit, even some of the hardships are forgotten in the daily rewards of the job. After all, we are working today and drawing regular pay checks. And there is fun on the bus trips, even when you're half-frozen. There is a comradeship that comes from working and traveling together, expressed in jokes and singing and laughter on the return trip. Sometimes we have parties on the bus, sharing candy or sandwiches, and even cutting a birthday cake bought from a roadside bakery. Frayed nerves and short tempers show themselves sometimes, and that's understandable, but a real quarrel seldom develops. Ill-tempered remarks are usually understood, and passed over without comeback.

I imagine that our boys at the front develop the same kind of tolerance, the same kind of partnership, for the same reason. Wouldn't it be great

---

1. Senator Burton Kendall Wheeler of Montana (1923–1947) was a noninterventionist.

2. Eugene Talmadge was governor of Georgia from 1933 to 1945 and was a segregationist. Martin Dies was a representative from Texas and headed the Dies Committee from 1938–1945, a precursor to the House Un-American Activities Committee later chaired by Senator Joseph McCarthy.

if the white workers who are fellow fighters with us in war production, would develop more of the same spirit of partnership? What can we do to make them realize that colored people must be given equal opportunity in every walk of life to make that partnership real—to build an impregnable, free, and democratic America?

Well, that's why I stay on the job, and that's what this job means to me. I might shift plants if I get a good chance. I haven't been very well, and the constant strain and exposure have put me into bed too often for my doctor's satisfaction and my own comfort. But one thing is sure; if I leave this job I'll get another one in war work. Victory is vital and I'm vital to victory. It's going to take courageous deeds at the front, and in the Navy and the Merchant Marines to win this war, but it's also going to take top-speed production in the war plants at home—and that's my assignment.

I'm not fooling myself about this war. Victory won't mean victory for Democracy—yet. But that will come later, because most of us who are fighting for victory today will keep on fighting to win the peace—maybe a long time after the war is over, maybe a hundred years after. By doing my share today, I'm keeping a place for some brown woman tomorrow, and for the brown son of that woman the day after tomorrow. Sterling Brown[3] once wrote, "The strong men keep a-comin' on," and millions of those men have dark skins. There will be dark women marching by their side, and I like to think that I'm one of them.

OPPORTUNITY, APRIL 1943

What My Job Means to Me

LEOTHA HACKSHAW

A Minor Inspector in the New York Ordnance District of the War Depart-ment.

Eighteen months ago I told my friends that I was going into the war industry. Mary, a close friend, raised a horrified face and shouted, "Lee, are you crazy? Why, that work is *killing*. You're not accustomed to that kind of thing. I'll bet you that it won't be long before you'll be running out of that place." Another friend, Jean, more logical but just as outraged as Mary,

---

3. African American poet and literary critic.

pointed out that modeling was a "fine profession; the hours are short, the pay is good and it's glamorous besides. And you are leaving it to go into something with hard work, long hours and such a small salary that it doesn't even count."

When my friends were done with me I had the same feeling that Caspar Milquetoast, The Timid Soul, must have when he faces a crowd.

My first crack at war work was with a firm manufacturing finished optical lenses for binoculars. Before the war it consisted of a small group of ten highly skilled workers producing contact lenses. Now it has thousands on its payroll working on three shifts twenty-four hours a day. During the first day at the plant I thought about the four years I had spent at college. One did not need a college degree to do this!

Soon complications set in and the remarks my friends had made came floating back to me.

In order to make eight o'clock time at the plant in Long Island I had to get up at five-thirty in the morning. Before going to work I had to bathe and dress my two-year old son, prepare his breakfast and then get myself ready to leave my home in the Bronx. The girl who cared for the baby during the day was due to arrive at seven but she rarely put in an appearance before seven-thirty. As a result I used to do a sprint from the subway to the plant that must have beaten Jesse Owens' record more than once. That would have been all right if I were Jesse Owens. Since I wasn't, I always arrived at the time clock gasping for breath and would remain a bundle of nerves for the rest of the day. Something had to be done; so I transferred over to the "graveyard shift" from midnight to eight A.M. Then another problem cropped up! Sleeping during the night and sleeping during the day are two different things altogether. I am a habitually good sleeper. But I never realized how many different noises there are until I tried to sleep in the daytime. It seemed as if the Sanitation Department was always collecting garbage, a child was always crying in the street, or somebody's mother was forever yelling for it. I had no idea before how much actually happened right under my window. And of course, Mikie thought it much fun to come in and roll all over Mummy while she slept. After the first two weeks on the "graveyard shift" I got to the point where my eyes stayed open by themselves. When I got home at nine-thirty in the morning, however, I wasn't sleepy any more. I was ready for work then. Partly because I could not sleep during the day and partly because the small salary I was drawing did not stretch far enough, I began accepting modeling engagements for afternoon work. The only sleep I got I snatched in the early evenings before leaving for the plant. During that first month I lost twenty pounds. My blood pressure caught on to the idea and went down too. My doctor cast stern eyes over me and advised me to quit. I needed every pound, she said, and the work was much too hard for me. But I held on and stuck to my guns. Perhaps I would have given up then and there if I did not know what I was working for. But it was not the money I was working for, although I needed it badly, because I could have done much better elsewhere and with less effort.

At the optical firm my duties were first, to cement the lenses; then I changed to polishing them. Finally, I was inspecting them after they had been polished. I could not see the lens as a mere piece of optical glass. I saw it in the finished binocular in the hands of an officer at the front where it would become a tool in winning the war and bringing destruction upon the enemy. How I wished that the company were producing the finished binocs! Soon my wish came true. I went to work for the Army Ordnance inspecting finished binoculars. I was one of eight inspectors in the plant and the only Negro. I remember the morning I reported to the plant. Everyone was too surprised and curious to say much. Many of them had never worked with a Negro before. With them as with me it was a question of adjusting to each other. The company itself, I soon learned, had no Negroes in its employ with the exception of one or two porters. There were plenty of places where they could have fitted in but I saw none around. Shortly after I arrived and very cautiously, a Negro matron was installed in the Women's Lounge. She was followed by other Negro girls in the assembly lines. If anyone had expected a riot between the white girls (mostly Irish-American) and the incoming Negro girls they must have been disappointed. No interest was shown whatever. The company workers were very friendly to me. One Italian boy, a former monk at the age of nineteen, was especially chummy. We would get together at lunch and compare recipes for meat sauces. The government inspectors were friendly too but were too busy to get together. However, once in a while we found time for the things that only girls indulge in. One day one of the Jewish female inspectors took me "basement-bargain-hunting." We made the rounds of several large department stores—always in the basements. Unfortunately, my odd-size measurements, size fifteen,[1] proved to be too odd even for the basement and I came out empty-handed.

The work itself proved interesting. The finished glasses came directly to us as they left the company's inspectors. They were to be checked against specifications supplied us by the Army. Often, as I inspected a glass, I would visualize the use to which it would be put. The scene thus conjured up

---

1. About a size nine today.

in my imagination may vary greatly from the real procedure on the field. Nonetheless, it never fails to stir me with the thrill of knowing that I am doing something worthwhile in the winning of the war. Every binocular becomes a symbol to me; a symbol of the freedom and liberty the world possessed so recently and which it would possess again. It means something else besides. It is the "open sesame" which takes me back to the historical beginning of the Negro in these United States. Before my eyes the first slave-ship landed in Jamestown in 1619. I see them sold on the block. I see the whip fall and hear the lash amid the cries of families torn apart forever. I hear soft voices singing, making haunting music filled with pathos and hope, hope of deliverance some day to come, and joy too. The joy that comes from courage and deep spiritual strength. I see a black man, a slave, go down in death and in history to be known as the first American to fall in the American Revolution. I see a black man, Benjamin Banneker, together with L'Enfant, lay and plan the great capital of this land. And later, I see other men, white men, with sympathy and humanity in their hearts for their fellow men, gather together in an effort to end a monstrous social evil, work out a plan of action. This was to become the first abolitionist society in the U.S. And soon I hear a great man proclaim the black man FREE! And as a result of being free these men feel free and do the things that free men should. And during the Reconstruction Period I see Joseph Rainey and Hiram Revels, first Negro Congressmen, distinguish themselves in our national legislature. On and on they pass before my eyes, achieving and proving their worth. Until today I see over one million black men in the armed forces of the country.

What are they fighting for? They fight to preserve a way of life, the American Democracy. Our forefathers in drawing up our Constitution realized that all men possessed inherent and inalienable rights "that among these are life, liberty, and the pursuit of happiness." They proclaimed it so. It is true that even under this democracy the Negro has been denied these "inalienable" rights; but he must not look elsewhere for a better form of democracy. It is for him to take conditions as they are here, no matter how horrible, and make them suitable. We cannot do this as individuals. We need the dynamic force of the masses exercising agreement in one program, strong methods, and culminating in one concerted action. The Negro masses need not fear being alone in this. There are others who think like him. And he must not allow the stunning impact of prejudice and discrimination to inhibit and restrain him. He must not ignore the hard won gains while facing the present day injustices. In our own time our President has raised the standard of the "Four Freedoms." These Freedoms are not new. They have been fought for over and over again. The Negro has attained one of these and part of another. Freedom from fear and freedom from want he is fighting for now; for under them democracy can reach its fulfillment. He is fighting to guarantee his rights to them.

Lastly, he is fighting for America, the land itself, the geographical boundaries within which he expects his racial group to attain its historical maturity. The little that we at home do day by day seems small in comparison to the sacrifices which the men at the front willingly endure. Our jobs should mean to every one of us much more than a daily routine or an occupation. For work today is more than just livelihood. It is a sharp weapon useful in bringing the day of victory nearer. It is the means of preserving our very lives.

THE CRISIS, APRIL 1945

Civil Service

CONSTANCE C. NICHOLS

My desk sits facing yours across the floor,
Yet your fair head is stiffly held aloof
From my own darker one, though 'neath our roof
With one accord we do a job. For war
Has linked us as no pleading could before.
Yet, seemingly, you wait for further proof
That we are spun the same . . . the warp and woof
Of new, strong fabric, draped at Freedom's door . . .
For you are still reluctant to obey
The impulse that would bring you to my side;
You send your memos on a metal tray,
And coldly kill each overture I've tried.
Why hope to rid charred continents of gloom
'Till *we* have learned to smile across a room?

Clerical Worker, *The Crisis*, May 1942

NEGRO STORY, MAY–JUNE 1944

Growing Up

ROMA JONES

Four.
Muvver, the little boy next door,
He called me "nigger."
Isn't he a funny boy?
Muvver!
What's a nigger?

Fourteen.
Mother, Frances isn't my friend!
I thought she liked me, but today
She called me "nigger"!
Mother, why does she
Hate me so?

Twenty-four.
Mother, the world's a beautiful place,
But the people in it are so queer.
The girls at the office stopped talking
When I came in today.
Mother, I feel sorry for them.
Aren't they funny?

NEGRO STORY, MAY–JUNE 1944

I Had a Colored Maid

MARGARET RODRIGUEZ

Miss Merryweather banged the file drawer shut and whirled around to her desk. Somewhere, somewhere, the report must be somewhere. It was a secret report and was charged specifically to Miss Merryweather. And now the security people wanted it back. They wanted it within an hour. Miss Merryweather was flustered and exasperated. Anger was gathering about her and within her. She sat down in her swivel chair and stared at the papers on her desk. The report was not in the office. She had searched all day and so had Mrs. Martin and Miss Foster. Miss Foster. Miss Merryweather's mind paused in its ransacking and pondered over Miss Foster. Connie Foster was her full name. Although Connie was a colored girl, she seemed honest, and to Miss Merryweather's never-ending abashment Connie was no different in many ways than Miss Merryweather herself. Connie never misspelled words in her typing, nor was she untidy. She never spoke too loudly. Her suits were in as good taste as any Miss Merryweather had seen. But Connie was a colored girl, and this fact was never absent from Miss Merryweather's mind, nor were the implications and possibilities of this fact ever absent.

Miss Merryweather turned her chair to face Mrs. Martin, who was going through a folder in search of the report.

"Mrs. Martin," said Miss Merryweather, "where is Miss Foster?"

Mrs. Martin looked up in her quick, nervous way. "Why, I don't know. Did she go to lunch?"

"Not if she didn't say so," Miss Merryweather answered matter-of-factly. The girl was dependable. She was up to par on all the little routines of a government office. But, all the same, she was a colored girl.

"Tell me, Mrs. Martin," Miss Merryweather asked, "what do you think of Miss Foster?"

"Why, I don't know," Mrs. Martin answered quickly. "I'm sure I don't know. Why do you ask?"

Miss Merryweather became impatient, as she always did with Mrs. Martin. Poor old Mrs. Martin was a little stupid, which could likely be traced to the bad illness she had a few years ago. Washington was full of people with logical reasons for being stupid. The thought struck Miss Merryweather like the tinkle of a new idea, and made her a little more patient with Mrs. Martin as she answered: "My dear, we have lost a secret report. The matter is serious, very serious. We three are the only ones who have handled the report."

Poor old Mrs. Martin took off her glasses and blinked her eyes. Then she turned the faded eyes full upon Miss Merryweather. "You don't think I or Miss Foster took the report, do you?" she asked. And as an afterthought she added: "What on earth would either of us want with it?"

Miss Merryweather was very patient now. "My dear," she said, "I know *you* don't know where the report is."

Mrs. Martin wiped her glasses with a handkerchief and put them on. She straightened papers in the folder in front of her and let her thin-veined hands rest on the folder.

"Do you think Miss Foster took it?" she asked nervously.

Miss Merryweather's face lost its patience and hardened as she thought of Connie Foster.

"You know, Mrs. Martin," she said, "1 don't understand the Government hiring all these colored people to do confidential work. Of course, I didn't say anything when they sent me this colored girl, but—"

Mrs. Martin stood up and moved over to the window. "Connie Foster is a fine person, Miss Merryweather," she said. "Her work is very good, and she's a good girl. Really, she's a good, fine girl."

A gleam came into Miss Merryweather's eyes, and a smart, shrewd smile came to her mouth as she answered Mrs. Martin.

"That's what I thought about Lily," she said triumphantly, and her voice rang as if she made a great announcement.

"Lily?" Miss Martin asked. She had never heard of Lily.

"Yes," answered Miss Merryweather, the triumph rising in her voice. "I had a colored maid named Lily."

Mrs. Martin frowned, trying to see Lily's place in the office.

"I thought she was a fine girl," Miss Merryweather went on. "And do you know what Lily did? She stole two hundred dollars from me and disappeared."

Mrs. Martin said nothing, and Miss Merryweather went on: "Colored people just naturally steal. I guess they can't help it."

They both heard the door open and looked to see Connie Foster coming in. Connie's eyes were brimming with tears. She said nothing to either of the women, but went quickly to her desk and got her purse and gloves from the desk drawer. She cleared her desk, putting away papers and notebooks.

Miss Merryweather looked knowingly at Mrs. Martin and stood up. Briskly she walked over beside Connie.

"Why did you do it, Miss Foster?" she asked in the voice of a judge addressing a criminal.

Connie Foster's hands stopped their clearing of the desk, and Connie's eyes full of tears met Miss Merryweather's accusing eyes.

"What do you mean, Miss Merryweather?" she asked, and there was wonder in her grieving voice.

Miss Merryweather had no patience for this colored girl trying to evade the issue. "Why did you take the report?" Miss Merryweather was sharp and contemptuous.

Connie looked at Miss Merryweather, then looked at Mrs. Martin. Mrs. Martin turned her face to the window and said nothing.

Connie opened her purse, took out a handkerchief and wiped her eyes. Then she rose from her desk chair and faced Miss Merryweather. Connie was tall and slender and superbly neat in her tailored suit. Miss Merryweather thought with abashment that the girl was splendidly poised as if she knew some hidden reason for poise that Miss Merryweather could not fathom in a hired girl.

"Why?" asked Connie without emotion, "Why do you think I took the report? What do you think I would want with it?"

Miss Merryweather considered a second before she answered. The girl had good nerves to appear so calm in asking "Why." Why, indeed. Why do all colored people steal?

"Why are you crying?" Miss Merryweather asked happily.

"It has nothing to do with your report!" Connie hissed the words and the impact of her hiss caught Miss Merryweather in the face like a blow.

"Why, you dirty, lying nigger!" Miss Merryweather screamed, and at that moment the door opened and a man walked in. Mr. Bryan, he was. Chief security officer for the building. He glanced at the three women and cleared his throat. "Miss Merryweather," he said, "I'm sorry to have bothered you about the secret report. The report was returned to us yesterday attached to another report in the wrong envelope. We just discovered it." Mr. Bryan smiled vaguely at Miss Merryweather. "Must have been a mistake, but it's all right," he said. Then he walked out of the room and closed the door behind him.

Miss Merryweather found herself unable to move. Connie stood facing her and Miss Merryweather kept her eyes focused on the closed door. Her mind was not itself. She could not harness her mind, nor could she do anything at all but remain as she was, caught in a pattern too old for Connie and enmeshed in another pattern too new for Miss Merryweather.

Mrs. Martin turned from her place at the window and moved over to Connie. "Miss Foster," she said, "why are you crying? Is something wrong?"

Connie looked at Mrs. Martin and tried to smile, but the smile ended in a gasp as she answered. "Yes, something is terribly wrong. I have just come from the reception desk. My mother came down to tell me—she brought the telegram—" Connie's voice broke, but she went on: "My brother Jimmie was killed in the South Pacific. He was part of a landing crew—"

Mrs. Martin's faded old eyes filled with tears and her mouth quivered. She put her arms around Connie and patted the girl's shoulder with a thin-veined hand. "Don't I know, my child," she said. "Don't I know so well how it is. Two of my boys were taken, too. Twins, they were, and such fine boys." The old woman's grief mingled with the girl's as they clung together, comforting each other.

Miss Merryweather looked at them clinging in common grief, and Miss Merryweather was suddenly assailed by a thousand emotions, too baffling and too tremendous for her austere self to grasp at one time. And so she sat down at her desk, Miss Merryweather did, and stared at Connie. And while she stared, Lily, the war, Connie, Connie's dead brother in the South Pacific, and poor Mrs. Martin's dead twin boys paraded solemnly before her.

OPPORTUNITY, APRIL 1943

Requiem

ZORA L. BARNES

As I lie here in the huge white bed, through the triple mirror on the opposite wall I can see the topmost branches of an old oak tree whose branches are just beginning to waken again. The rusty forsaken look they had worn since fall is smoothing off to a moist sheen. Leaves have not yet begun to peer through, but even from here I can almost see the tiny greenness which will burst forth. The day nurse says any day now. Then, in the other side, the indifferent outlines of the door through which I've been carried—in and out, in and out—so many times and the neat white screen that guards the door reflect only a cold implacability that remains always the same.

I like best the side mirroring the ancient oak. I never am certain whether the marathon I'm in will end with me the victor or whether I shall go out of that door for the last time still not knowing if the tiny greenness breaks through all at once. Or, if twig by twig, limb by limb, the tree will flaunt its leafy banners and proclaim another spring.

That mirror reveals to me six other things. Sometimes in the queer haze that filters through the window-pane just at dusk, I seem to see six people—three of them me and three are those I might have been.

The first time I saw myself, 'twas on a bitter afternoon. The wind had howled and shrieked and rattled madly at the windows the whole afternoon. Then just as evening came, the wind hushed away and a golden red fringe of light escaped from the sunset to paint itself across my mirror.

The light took form and shape. I saw a long-legged round-shouldered girl of fifteen. Her black hair was tied with a bright red bow. And in her dark brown face was reflected all the glory and wonder of the picture she was painting. It was a huge piece of silken cloth—not white, but of the subdued shade of golden that years of waving bravely in a desert sun might softly mellow. At her side was a smoking pot of wax rimmed 'round with many brushes—large, small, fat, lean, of every variety. And on this ivory cloth she painted with smooth dexterity a carnival scene. Beneath her brush in wax the outlines of a sickle moon, a Moorish temple, a balcony fretted with ornament and carving sprang to view. Then cobble by cobble between the rows of quaint dwellings she built a street. And upon it she placed a man of Spain and beside him with head thrown and arm upraised to the turn of the fandango she placed a girl. I could see them dancing there upon the silken cloth. Though it may have been the wind—I seem to hear the click of castanets, the beat of feet, and the laughter of onlookers in the street.

Then—like the pieces of a kaleidoscope which are shaken, then fall into alien patterns, I saw the thin girl look up in blank surprise. Perhaps, it was again the wind—but I heard voices, a voice raised in angry accusation.

"Mary Brown! Where is the leather book you were making?"

"It's there, on the table, Miss Hanson. With my notebook. Why?"

"Lillian Moore can't find hers. It isn't in the drawer where she left it."

Still with no notion of what was yet to come, the girl answered, "I'm sorry, but I haven't seen it."

And back to her smoking wax pot and dripping brushes she turned her attention. Like a moving picture, I could see the faces of all those who were in that room. From the first there had been a strangeness in it. And as I gazed closer and still closer, I discovered the strangeness. The little girl with the brushes had the only brown face.

The tall, straight person with the accusing voice looked vaguely about the classroom then walked to a table on which reposed a single notebook and—a leather book. Picking up the little leather book, she opened its cover and peered closely at an inscription written in it. After a moment, she came with the book to the girl.

"This is not your book."

The girl put down her brush and turned to the person. Quietly, she contradicted, "But it is. See? It has my name in it."

"You could have put that there any time. This book has been marked 'Excellent.' Yours would not have been so well done."

Again the girl contradicted, "You marked that in mine yesterday. And I took it home last night to show to my father."

"You may have taken it home, but it isn't yours. It's Lillian Moore's. *You stole it!*"

The girl winced as if struck and retorted sharply, "That's a lie! I don't steal!"

The person's eyes narrowed to malevolent slits and her pointed tongue flicked once or twice across her lips as she hissed, "Get out of this class! Get out of this school and stay out! We don't want any thieving niggers in this school!"

The branches of the tree waved flirtatiously and their reflection brushed the gay carnival scene from my mirror.

The second time the mirror caught the magic of *now* and turned it aside to reveal the past, I saw another girl. This one too was small, but not fifteen, and her shoulders were straight and her eyes were dauntless. In her hands she held a square of paper. It seemed some kind of report. About her were many other girls. And strangely enough, this girl, too, had the only brown face.

The girls laughed and chatted in friendly banter. And again the wind seemed to speak.

"Mary, you go first! You got the highest marks, so you will get the best job."

"It seems like strutting too much to walk in there with all these 'perfects' on my report. Somebody should have given me 'poor' if only in mending. It would seem more natural, really."

"Go on. You can't help it if you're a genius. Go ahead. Maybe she'll make you assistant librarian."

"And maybe she won't," the girl retorted as she knocked at the door marked PRIVATE.

There was a tiny, gentle-looking woman with snowy hair and candid blue eyes sitting behind a desk. She looked up with a friendly smile and said, "Have a seat, Mary."

"Thank you, Mrs. Wright."

"Have you enjoyed the apprentice class with us this summer? With your college training and teaching experience, you must have been able to contribute a great deal to the class. We're glad to have had you with us."

Without looking at the square of paper the girl had placed before her, she continued, "Now what are your plans?"

"I was hoping to be able to work here in the library. It's my home town and I'd like to work where I'd be near my parents."

This time it was the other person who looked up in shocked surprise, "But you wouldn't be able to do that. That is, I mean . . . you see, there are no positions open here at the library."

"I understand that three of the staff are leaving. Two to go to school and one to be married. Their places will be open, won't they?"

"Not exactly. You see . . . our budget is smaller this year and we'll have to work with a smaller staff. If you really want to do library work, I think you'd be happier working with your own people, say at Hampton or Wilberforce. But if you think you'd rather stay here at home and work . . . my housekeeper has left and we'd love so much, Mr. Wright and I, to have you come take care of us."

The piercing scream of the ambulance as it turned the far corner on the way to an emergency broke the spell of the second picture.

For days I lay here remembering those two scenes. For some reason they wiped out the blank horror I'd been feeling ever since they had carried me back in here that last time. The doctors had been too hearty about telling me that soon I'd be up and able to fall and break something else. The nurses had been too cheerful and too solicitous about how I felt when they knew as well as I that I hadn't felt anything at all for days. They'd shot enough dope in me to make the whole yellow race dream of their ancestors.

Then just a little while ago, this afternoon, I realized that I couldn't feel or move the fingers of my left hand. And I didn't know I was crying until I looked in the center mirror. There I saw great blobs of tears coursing down my face. As I lay here alone with my eyes all drowned with crying, my reflection in the mirror blurred and I saw the last picture.

There was another girl—her shoulders not so straight, her eyes not so glorious, her head not so high. Yet there lingered some faint resemblance to the other girls. She was atop a tall ladder reaching toward a huge lighting fixture overhanging a balcony. In her roughened hands she held a wet rag and with it she was industriously wiping at the large globe. From time to time the ladder swayed precariously over the three flights of stairs. As she worked she sang a song in odd contrast:

> "Oh, Lord! I don't feel no-ways tired,
> Children, Oh, Glory! Hallelujah!"

From below the stairs came a tall fair man with the blue line of his freshly shaven jaw in splendid contrast to the wind-whipped pinkness of his cheekbones. His blue eyes glittered in anticipation and persuasion. He ran his hand through his bright hair and rumpled it becomingly. He paused at the foot of the ladder.

"Mary, you don't want to be a cleaning woman all your life. Do you?"

"Of course not, Mr. Gordon. I applied here for a sales job. The ad said a college graduate with a knowledge of art for the gift department."

"I know, I know. But you see, the customers might not like the idea of a colored girl for a saleslady. Not when there are so many white girls who need jobs."

"I understand, Mr. Gordon. It doesn't really matter much any more."

"Now, now, Mary! I just have to be careful. You see, this is my first big manager job and I have to ease my weight in at first. So to speak. But to show you I'm a good scout, I'll tell you what I'll do. I'll talk to the owners and try to change their policy a bit. . . . But you'll have to be kinda nice to me, Mary. I'll really be sticking my neck out, you know."

He reached up and ran his finger up and down, up and down the seam of her stocking.

He grinned confidently, "You wouldn't mind that. Now would you?"

The girl jerked away from his exploring finger and as she moved, the ladder swayed. She caught futilely at the light, but its glassy strength slipped from her fingers and like a plummet she hurtled to the floor below.

I've known them all—those three. And too, I know the three they might have been—artist, librarian, or even sales clerk.

But life has eyes for choice too keen. Of late, I have thought perhaps this frizzy hair, which might have gone incognito beneath a patterned turban but for the too-thick lips and flattened nose, might be ironically rejected even by death. Then to the legend company of Flying Dutchman and Wandering Jew there might have been added—a Weary Pilgrim. But from the hearty greetings and muted footsteps and evasive eyes I learn the first small bit of hope: Death is blind and knows not of race or creed or color.

This, then, is the first fruit of them that sleep. And as I lie here shrouded in white against that time and rimmed in by the gloom, I only wonder if perhaps tomorrow the tree—

NEGRO STORY, DECEMBER–JANUARY 1944–1945

Help Wanted

ZENA DORINSON

"I hope they won't put a tag on me right away," Alice was saying. "I'm so glad to be going South, I hope they just won't label me 'Northern Negro' and shut me out on account of it."

Alice was a sociologist. She had just taken a job with a southern college, and was going to leave next week, and now she was dreaming her dreams aloud to me.

Alice and I were old friends; we had been to school together. She had just had lunch with me, and we had come in the hot afternoon to sit in the park. On the withered grass of that little patch of parkway between the boulevards, under the shade of a tree, we fanned our hot faces and talked about what we were reading and thinking these days; and, as our eyes took in the scorched bit of park, the children running and screaming under the dusty trees, mammas and nurses languid in the shade, the cars going by beyond, and the water falling colorless against the bronze green of the fountain, we talked, I remember, of the war and the postwar world.

"So much to do . . . ," Alice was saying. Her soft voice had so carried me to the far country of her dreams that I was unaware of one of the women I knew coming across the grass towards us until I looked up into her perspiring face.

She was a woman I knew only slightly from speaking to her in the park. She was a big, well-fed woman who lived in a large apartment across from the parkway. Her daughter and son-in-law and their two children lived in the apartment below hers, and she liked to dictate their lives. Now she leaned her bulk down to us, smiling apologetically, and fanned her face with her hand.

"Hot," she said, smiling.

I agreed. I waited. I could see Alice becoming amused. We didn't know what the woman wanted. She talked to me about the weather, but she was looking at Alice. She was appraising Alice's cool blue dress, her neat small head, her smart white shoes.

"You mind if I sit down?" She sagged her weight carefully to the ground beside me, and wiped the sweat from her neck with a finger. "Such hot weather! Such terrible weather in a big place like we have. My poor daughter! . . . and two children." She leaned towards me confidentially, coyly. "And would you believe me, she can't get help for love or money."

She had explained herself, and now it was her turn to wait. For a moment I didn't get what she wanted, but then almost immediately I did. She saw a white woman and a Negro woman sitting together under a tree. Of course the Negro woman must be working for the white one. So that was it. I began to feel queer across my chest. I turned to Alice.

The woman plunged ahead, determined and apologetic. "I don't want you to misunderstand me," she said. "I just want to ask your girl, possibly she has a friend of hers who would like a job?"

Alice glanced past me at the woman. She didn't seem annoyed or perturbed or anything. She didn't look any different than when we had talked about more schools and more scholarships in a bright world after the war.

"It would be a good job," said this woman into the silence. "My daughter is very kind to her help, and she'll pay as much as anybody."

Alice gave herself a little shake. "None of my friends needs the job."

"Well," said this woman, straightening up with her hand in the small of her back, and grinning at me again: "I don't want you to misunderstand me, I don't mean to take your girl away from you . . . I just thought . . ."

"She doesn't work for me," I said. "She is my friend."

The strangest look came over the woman's hot face. She looked down at me leaning against the bark of the tree and at Alice leaning back against the same tree trunk, and at our hands, black and white, resting a few inches apart on the trodden brown grass.

"Well!"

I remember how she walked away, fast and disturbed. She even turned to look at us. Then she merged with a group of women around the pool of the fountain. Their heads all came together as over a calamity. They threw looks over their shoulders at Alice and me, and I saw the women shaking their heads and gesturing excitedly. I was sure I made out on the lips of the woman who had approached us, one damning word: "Crazy."

I was so ashamed. But Alice placed her hand over mine, as if to absolve me of blame.

NEGRO STORY, JULY–AUGUST 1944

The Job

JAMES LIGHT

There was this girl and this thing happened to her, nothing big, nothing to shake the world, but it came so sudden, so unexpected, that it's kind of knocked her flat, put her down for awhile. The name of this girl is Regina Smith, and, right now, she is sitting in the ladies' room of the Palace theatre. The theatre is showing a double feature, but she is staring straight ahead, trying to figure out exactly what to do, not caring that they are showing a double feature and she is wasting her thirty-five cents' admission.

Take a good look at her. See her soft brown eyes, swimming and liquid, like they're close against your face, a little wet now, maybe, but that won't last long. Look at her tall, slim figure, and her cool, firm breasts, and the straight, haughty line of her nose; look at the statuesque proudness of her, and remember it, because it's not often that you see her like.

Looking at her, you wouldn't think she's married and has two children, and her husband's home on furlough. You'd think she'd be hurrying home to that family of hers, rushing to get there, maybe shopping around to get them something good to eat because she loves them all so much and her husband is leaving again tonight. Sure, that's what you'd think, but there she sits, staring ahead, thinking of this thing that has happened to her and wondering what to do.

You see she's a waitress. She's been through college, and she's got a good brain, but now she waits on tables. This place where she's been working is called Wolfe's and it is pure tone a yard deep. It is one of those places where they have a violinist who plays *Melody in F* and *Minuet in G*, things like that, and where there is a hostess who takes you to [your] table and brushes off the spotless linen tablecloth and treats you like a king.

It was just luck she got the job in the first place, what you call an experiment. This day she was walking along, feeling low down, and then suddenly, no reason at all, she wanted a cup of coffee, and there was this big red neon sign, *Wolfe's,* staring her in the face. It looked like a pretty expensive place and, at first, she walked past, but, what the hell, a cup of coffee can't cost much, and so she came back.

The restaurant was just starting to fill up and she got her coffee quick. Fondling it, waiting for it to cool, she heard a shrill voice. It said, "You can take your job and play with it." She looked up and this tiny, blondined girl was yelling at a small, chinless man dressed all black and white, like a stiffly starched penguin. She had a plate in her hand and, while Regina was watching, she threw it underhand at the man. He caught the plate and stood watching while the girl walked fast, getting away.

Regina got up, took a few steps, slow and steady, got there, and then, like it was nothing extraordinary or anything, said, clear and loud, "I need a job."

The small, penguin-looking man looked at her, queerly at first, not understanding, and then after it finally sunk in, said, "Well, I dunno, it might be okeh, and then again it might not."

She knew exactly what he meant of course, but she pretended not to, and, quick, she began to pour out reasons. "Look," she said, "why not? It's rush hour; you gotta have someone. I'm light on my feet, and there isn't too much of me, so I can squeeze through the aisles without any trouble at all."

The place was beginning to fill up more and more. One whole section was being ignored, and they were getting impatient. The man noticed that, and he looked at Regina, real close, stripping her with his eyes. She's got a light coffee and cream skin, so that she can almost pass for white, and that helped. There was a little noise and a lot of dignified frowns from the section that wasn't getting any service, and that helped, too.

"Well, I dunno," the man mumbled, "we ain't never 'ployed no Negroes before." He put one hand to the lobe of his ear, and jerked his head skyward, "It might be all right, though, you ain't bad lookin' and, thank God, you ain't coal black." He hesitated, thinking it through, letting it soak in, and then he flicked a thumb towards the kitchen. "Come on."

Regina followed him as he rocked along through a swinging door with "In" lettered on it. There was a long special counter along one wall of the kitchen, and a shorter salad counter along the side. A fat, perspiring woman was behind the special counter cutting a slab of ham. Her hands were tense, and long deep veins stood out on them like blue ink canals.

A few blue-uniformed girls were lounging around the kitchen smoking cigarettes and talking, and the small, penguin man waddled his way through them until he reached the special counter. When he got there he raised himself to his full height, thrust out the whiteness of his chest, put one hand on the massive back of the woman cutting ham, and whispered into her ear. The woman raised her head and gazed at Regina from behind bushy, black eyebrows. Then she boomed, "Take her; it don't matter." She beckoned impatiently, the blue ink canals rippling along her forearm. "Give her a uniform; we gotta get rid of this food."

The small man rocked his way back to Regina. "Well," he said, tugging at his ear again, "Mrs. Wolfe—that's my wife—says it's all right. You've had 'sperience of course."

"No," Regina said, "but I can learn; I learn quick."

Mr. Wolfe frowned, and she thought she was cooked, but the booming voice ordered, "Hurry it up, ain't got all day," and he hurried her around to a short staircase. "Dress down there," he said, "and hurry."

She had her hat and coat off before she got to the bottom of the staircase, and in another three minutes flat, she was hurrying back up it, all dressed and everything. When she came into the kitchen Mrs. Wolfe gave her a few directions. "Be polite," she said, "Don't get in nobody's way, and be sure and get the right prices. Those are the main things. Remember 'em."

"I will," Regina said, "I'll remember all of them." She went into the dining room then, looking around, wondering where to start. The other girls had been working her section while she was being hired, and everyone had soup and salad starters, but she had to pick up from there.

A little bald man was sitting at one of the tables, eating his soup, looking down at his plate. Mild and benevolent he seemed, and she went up to him, "May I take your order, sir?" she asked.

The bald head turned upwards to let the face get a chance. It looked startled when it saw Regina, and then, "Why . . . yes," it said, expanding itself into a slight smile, "but I thought . . . I mean . . . I had another waitress."

"No," Regina said, "that was temporary; I was just hired and this is my section."

"Oh, then," the man said, "that's different." He hesitated. "Then *Wolfe's* is employing Negroes?"

"Yes, sir," she said, remembering the politeness, holding the anger in, "and what was your order, sir?"

The smile flickered off his face. "Well," he said, "I want the number two special; I ain't got my salad yet, and I'd like it without mayonnaise. I'll choose dessert later."

"Yes, sir," she said. Quickly she walked back to the kitchen. Just inside, she bumped one of the other girls, not hard, barely enough to notice it. "I'm sorry," she said.

The other girl stared at her, hard and cold. "Stay that way," she spit out. "Don't get in my way."

Regina took a few steps; everything blurred up a little. She heard the swish of the out swinging door, as the other girl left.

"Don't mind her," someone said. "She's got a complex." Through the blur Regina could see most of the girls smiling at her.

"Number two special," she yelled, and then, like she'd heard the other waitresses, "one plain salad, hold the mayonnaise."

"Like a pro," a girl smiled, and she was in, one of them.

Look at her now, sitting where she is and staring straight ahead. Her brain is whirling, thinking through this thing that happened to her, but you can't tell it to look at her sitting there so cool and calm. She's taking a cigarette now, lighting it, concentrating on the smoke swirling around her, and this peculiar idea is coming into her head.

Looking at her, you can tell she'd make a good waitress. She's got that lithe, greyhound figure, and that book-on-the-head balance that points out the really good ones. But that doesn't matter much. There's other things.

You see she came in to work today, went down to the dressing room, and put on her blue, wrap-around uniform. She was light and singy inside because her husband had come in town on a forty-eight hour pass. If she'd have had the nerve she'd have called up and got a day off, but this job is a pretty good one and she didn't want to take any chances. When you've got to earn money for two kids and an old mother, you think of those things.

So she padded upstairs, loitering over it, thinking over the night before, and all the good things her husband, Bill, had said. She had cooked supper; it was something solid, something she could put her teeth into, and she did it slow and easy because she didn't want to cry at all the happiness that was bubbling around inside her. And then when supper was finished, they had put the children to bed, tucking them tight like before the war, and had gone into the living room and talked for a while.

Regina told Bill about the dainty old men and the fussy old women who never tipped, and the young girls who combed their hair over the soup. "But it's a good job," she finished. "The people are pretty nice and I kind of like the work. It's sure a lot better than doing other people's cleaning."

Regina's mother was sitting in her own chair near the window, looking out into the darkness, making herself inconspicuous like some old folks have a way of doing. Now she said, "It's different from my day. Then no Negro woman was good enough for that."

"Yes, we know," Bill said, low and tender, "but things are changin'. They ain't now like they were then, and in a little while they won't be like they are now. They're gettin' better all along. Things are changin'."

"That's right," Regina had said, "Things are changing."

As she climbed the stairs toward the kitchen, Regina thought of these things. The last phrase dwelt pleasantly on her tongue, and she said it softly aloud.

When she got upstairs she remembered she needed a lunch pad, and she strode over to Mrs. Wolfe at the special counter. Mrs. Wolfe was stirring the soup, and when she saw Regina, she said, "Didn't see you come in." Her fat bosom was heaving, pendulum like, doing it in double, and while she talked, she looked steadily at the soup. "I think Mr. Wolfe would like to talk to you."

"Oh," Regina said. She went through the out swinging door looking for Mr. Wolfe. The restaurant hadn't yet begun to fill up, and he was over near the cashier's cage, his head cocked towards the sky, talking to the girl there. He looked down then and saw Regina. "Uh," he said. He came over, took her by the hand, and waddled along with her to one of the empty tables. "Look," he said, "I don't like to say this—I like you, you're a good waitress, and I wish the 'speriment had worked, but it ain't." The chinlessness of him, as he talked, made him more like a penguin than ever now, a quite futile, quite helpless penguin.

"You're firing me," Regina whispered. Her eyes misted up a little, and her insides began to feel all trembly weak.

"No," Mr. Wolfe said, "I don't want you to get that idea. I ain't firin' you; like I said, you suit me fine. But there's been complaints . . . and . . . well, I'm only sayin' what I've gotta. I speak the words, sure, but others make the music. You can see that."

"Yes," Regina murmured. "I can see that." She took her hands from her lap and placed them palm downwards on the table. "They're brown," she said.

Mr. Wolfe was fumbling around in his pockets. "I got your check somewhere around here," he mumbled. He found it finally, rose, and pushed it towards her as he rocked away.

She sat at the table for a while and then, when the restaurant began to fill up for the lunch hour rush, she got up. Mrs. Wolfe saw her as she passed through the kitchen and rushed up to her. The fatness of her was quivering all over, and she was clenching and unclenching her hands so that the ink blue veins rose and fell. "Gosh honey, I'm sorry," she said. "Me 'n Mr. Wolfe didn't want to do it, but we just had to." She took one of Regina's hands into her own, large, globular ones and patted it. "Take this," she panted and left, hurrying away as quickly as her bulk allowed.

Regina looked at the paper that had been put into her hand. It was a twenty dollar bill,[1] and Regina tore it quickly into little bits, keeping out of her mind what the money would buy. She went downstairs to the dressing room, slipped out of the blue, wrap-around uniform, and hurried out.

She kept walking, the breeze pushing against her dress, pressing in on her like some live and hostile thing, until finally her legs gave out, and then she paid her thirty-five cents' admission and went into the Palace theatre.

She's sitting there now sweating it out. The smoke is swirling around her head, and this peculiar idea has come into her head. Look at her. She is getting up now, and is putting out her cigarette. She is standing there, taut and tense, like a thoroughbred just after he's quit running. She is putting on her hat and coat and is leaving. Bravely, haughtily, she walks out to go home and face her soldier husband Bill with a smile.

You see she loves her husband very deeply. She loves the uniform he is wearing, and she is proud to see him in it, he looks so neat and trim. Tonight he is leaving her, going to a P.O.E.[2] where he will be shipped out to fight for democracy.

---

1. Equivalent to about $100 in the late 1990s.
2. Port of exit.

And so she has this peculiar idea that she should not say anything to him about this thing that has happened to her. Things are changing; she knows it, and she wants him to go on knowing it, too.

NEGRO STORY, APRIL–MAY 1946

All That Hair

MELISSA LINN

Seven year old Minnie Mae looked longingly at the sidewalk as she walked from school to her mother's place of work. It was noon. Several little girls passed her without so much as a hello. Minnie Mae knew why they ignored her. She wasn't like them. She didn't have the right kind of hair.

More than anything else in this world Minnie Mae wanted pretty curly hair crowned by a stiff pink butterfly bow. All the little girls in her room at school had soft, silken, flexible locks, and from her seat in the rear of the room she could look over the room and see all the smooth heads: brown, yellow, black, and red. All of them topped by pink, blue, plaid, or yellow butterfly bows. They were just simply beautiful. Oh, if only she could run a comb through her hair as nonchalantly as Sally Lou, and have it leave little rows where the teeth had been! Or to have it fall down into her eyes when she stooped over, or to run in the wind and have it blow before her eyes. But no, she must have these kinky stiff naps that made her cry every time her mother washed them. If only a fairy would come and change her like she did Cinderella! Maybe a fairy would. So Minnie Mae dreamed on as she walked slowly toward the white folks' house where her mother worked and where she ate her lunch every day.

Ever since she could remember she had been going to Mrs. Whitham's to see mama. Once, mama dressed her up, and she was presented to Mrs. Whitham to speak her Easter piece; then Mrs. Whitham gave her cookies and fifty cents for her new pocketbook. Mrs. Whitham was awfully nice— she was little, almost as little as Minnie Mae. She looked just like a china doll. Her hair was light and curled all over her head in tiny, silken curls. But mama told Aunt Joe that Mrs. Whitham's hair was false, just like the wigs you wore on Halloween.

Minnie Mae turned up a broad white driveway and followed it around to the back door. She opened a screen door softly, and stepped into a clean white kitchen. It was empty. She went on through to the stairs and started softly up. Mamma was probably making up the beds, and perhaps she would let her help.

On reaching the top of the stairs, Minnie Mae peered into the first bedroom. It was empty. She tiptoed to the second room and stopped, for there lay Mrs. Whitham, sound asleep. Minnie Mae knew she was asleep, because her eyes were shut and her mouth, hanging loosely open, allowed a thin trickle of saliva to escape and roll down to the pillow. Minnie Mae stared with wide eyes at the white lady because her head was as smooth and shiny as her little baby brother's. It looked just like a new potato that mother had scraped very carefully in order to cream whole.

Close by, on the dresser, where its owner had placed it in order to relieve an aching head, was the wig of beautiful hair, the silken curls shining in the sun. When Minnie Mae saw it, her eyes grew big and she began to breathe harder. If she could just try it on. Oh, if she just dared. She looked again at the sleeping lady, then stepped softly across the room, picked up the wig and placed it gently on her head.

She looked into the mirror and saw a transformed creature. The inch-long, stubborn, greasy kinks were gone, and silk curls tumbled profusely in their place. Oh, if only she could wear it to school! The kids would like her then. She gave one look at the sleeping lady, then turned, ran quickly out of the room and down the stairs. She stopped. Mama! Where was she? Then she heard a slow boop-a-boop-aboop-aboop—and she knew her mother was washing in the basement. She picked up a piece of cake from the table and ran out of the door. She ran all the way to school, holding the wig on with one hand, and thinking all the time. Now maybe Mary Lou, that pretty little fat girl, would play with her at recess. Maybe all the girls, Sally Jane, Lillian and Ruth, would come and ask her to play jack-stones. Maybe they'd even ask her to come over to their houses after school and play "grown-up." Carried away by her realistic dream, her heart bounded in delightful anticipation, and she reached the school, ran up the steps, and into her room.

At first the teacher didn't see her. Then, as a surreptitious tittering arose and gradually grew to open snickering and suppressed laughter, she looked frowningly up. As her eyes focused on Minnie Mae, they widened with incredulity, her large mouth fell open, and red splotches began to spread slowly on her coarse neck. And then, the little brown girl, whom class and teacher alike had ignored all year, was suddenly the amused and contemptuous center of attraction.

The child stopped, dismayed. Her eyes, grown enormous, stared in horror and fright from under the white wig. The sound of laughter roared in her ears, and as her heart began to pound with misgivings, the teacher's strident voice cried, "You! Come here!"

At the sound of the angry voice, the laughter ceased, and it was very quiet in the room. Minnie Mae felt the whole sea of white faces staring, mocking, burning her. Laughing at her. Suddenly everything became blurred, and a greater panic seized upon her, for she felt a wet scalding run down her legs, and to her horror and shame saw a puddle grow as big as a river at her feet, and start rolling down the aisle, under the seats, a long, wide condemning river. They would never like her now!

Shame mingled with the fright and tears came. Despairing sobs rose in her throat, and she burst into uncontrollable crying. Loud, racking sobs shook her body, and she stood rooted to the spot, her stockings clinging cold and wet to her legs. She bowed her head in the crook of her arm, and the sobs made the absurd white curls of Mrs. Whitham's wig jiggle precariously on the little brown head.

Annoyed and contemptuous, the teacher strode down the aisle, pushed the child into the cloak room and demanded, "Where did you get that hair?" Minnie Mae was sobbing so much she couldn't answer, whereupon the teacher half pushed, half shoved her down to the principal's office. That buxom lady gave a glance at the mournful brown girl, her eyes took in the wet soaked stockings, and she told her to go home.

Minnie Mae, crying as though her heart would burst, ran into her mother's place of work, and when that good woman saw her child come in wearing her employer's hair, her heart jumped violently.

"God *a'mighty,* Minnie Mae . . . here . . ."

Without another word she snatched the wig from the child's head, hastened quick and soft as a cat upstairs where her mistress was still sleeping, and put the wig back in its proper place, then descended rapidly and shaking the child violently, she whispered fiercely, "*Hush!* Do you want to wake Mrs. Whitham and have her find out you've had her wig, so I'll lose my job? Where would we be then?" She released the child and said, "You go on home, and I'll tend to you tonight after work." She gave the child a shove out the door, and turned back to her work, cooking food. She muttered, "Children sure are more bother than they are worth, always doing something to upset folks."

Minnie Mae went slowly out the door, toward her home, and as she walked along in the warm afternoon sun, long shuddering sighs escaped from her heart. By the time she had finished the long walk home the sighs had stopped, but a new wisdom and sadness was buried deep in a brown child's heart.

OPPORTUNITY, SUMMER 1945

Overly Sensitive

ROBERT G. JONES

Suppose your boss had ordered you to carry out an assignment which was against your conscience and the best interests of your country. Would you follow the discipline of "Theirs not to reason why?"

Stretch your imagination a bit more. If you knew your refusal would be labeled "insubordination," that you would be called "overly sensitive" and possibly face dismissal during a mass unemployment period, would that affect your decision?

That was precisely my situation from 1938 through 1941, as a worker in a public employment agency. During those years I was forced by procedure to work on employers' orders which limited my recruiting to about ten percent of the available manpower in the community we were supposed to serve.

To state the problem simply, I, as an employment interviewer, working in an office covering a territory largely inhabited by Jews, Negroes, Puerto Ricans, Italians and Irish Catholics, was daily given job orders to fill which called for "white Christian Protestants of North European stock" only. Frequently these discriminatory orders required "three generations of American background." Of course, the agency was not in Germany, nor in the comparatively backward sections of the United States. New York City was our operating location.

How many times I boiled over, all inside, I can't recall. The number of nights that I tossed, unable to sleep because of a troubled conscience, I don't remember. What I do know is that often I would dream about some poorly clad, unemployed father of kids, standing at my desk. Like all other applicants he sought a job so that he could feed his children and pay the rent for their shelter. Then I would jump up in bed, frightened by the lie that I had to tell him when I knew the job was still open.

Most of us in that office were members of some minority groups, and as employment interviewers and counselors we had to maintain a certain "professional" attitude towards our work. If we complained about being forced to behave in keeping with the racist theories of our now despised enemies, the fascists, we were criticized as "not adjustable" or "overly sensitive." I was probably considered in both categories.

In looking back across the years, perhaps I was "overly sensitive." I don't know. Perhaps I had been conditioned to believe in democracy without reservations. Again, it might have been that my inability to become callous about denying the right to earn a living to "certain people" was the result of my previous job experience. I had worked with these applicants and their children for five years. Many of the young people had now grown up and were fathers and mothers themselves. As a social worker I knew their problems. In my former job as head worker in a social agency, discrimination was considered un-American and something which had no place in our community. We not only believed that, but we taught and practiced it in our every action. In that organization, both staff and those whom we served knew that the community meant all of the people within its confines. Our membership and staff extended to the entire community.

The president, one of the best boys in this agency, was a member of a minority group. Eddie ————, the leader of the self-governing body, had been elected by the membership under democratic procedure. I remember how we had frequently discussed the necessity for his completing high school. His arguments come back as if we had talked only yesterday. "What's the use of getting an education if they won't hire you. . . . No sense in going to high school to be a flunky . . . ," and the one that almost got me, "Look at you, with college, law school and then some, and you can't even get a decent job." His arguments at that time were all too true.

Three years later he graduated from high school to join the long list of unemployed. Often he would look at me and say, "So I got a diploma, but what good is it?" With faith in the future of America, I urged him to go to college at night. For a time I did not see him. When he turned up again he was married and about to become a father. He appeared at the employment office seeking a job "with a future."

I guess Eddie, Izzie, Tony, and all the rest were influences in making me "overly sensitive" of responsibility to get them jobs. These kids, their fathers and mothers, had been indelibly stamped on my mind. I could not forget them; nor could I escape, for I was assigned to an office right in the same community where I had literally preached the all-inclusive definition of the word "community."

When I first started to work I was very happy. I thought that at last I could alleviate some of the sufferings of those whose problems I knew. I remember the familiar faces of those looking for work. They were bright with hope. It would not be necessary for them to impress me of their needs.

When I became an interviewer the year was 1938 and the number of jobs was small. I could, with a clear conscience, tell my young friends, as well as their parents, the truth. And they would always leave with a feeling of confidence in the validity of my statement. But when the jobs began to come in, the trouble started. My conscience became a factor in my work. All of the theories that I had learned about democracy seemed to be a hindrance to doing my job effectively. It hurt me to lie to those in need of work.

Yes, there were jobs, but it was extremely difficult to meet the "specifications." In our files were hundreds of qualified workers who just could not measure up to the little refinements so essential to getting employment in those days. These ethnic qualifications were raised not only by private industry, but Government as well.

I was happy when I was given an assignment to work with the needle trades industry, which had not entirely succumbed to practicing exclusion because of race, creed, and all the other unimportant factors in running a machine. But even here there was trouble. Certain sections of this industry were equally as bad as some of the entirely discriminatory trades. Discrimination was evident in the manufacture of the more expensive garments as the custom trade. In this line I could not even send Eddie for a job as a delivery boy.

I remember Eddie saying to me, shortly after his wife had given birth to their first child, "Gee, it's funny; we all go to the same schools and all the other things, but when we go to work, it's another world." He knew the score as well as those of us in the office. That was in 1940. At that time he had found his own job, but would come to the office each Saturday looking for something better. He would come with a smile and announce himself as "a first class high school graduate porter with a wife and kid living on fifteen bucks a week."

Came 1941, with the hundreds of job orders, and we breathed a sigh of relief. Our office had the people. Qualified workers? Our files contained some thirteen thousand of them. But when I began to search for those who could meet the racial, religious and nationality qualifications, our files were practically worthless.

There were jobs at military bases, defense factories and other activities necessary in the preparation for our country's defense. Still our files remained filled. We then began to get trainee orders for hundreds of young people. At last, I thought, here is the chance for Eddie and all of the other unemployed youth in our bulging files. Our entire staff was elated. Now we would do something worthwhile. We talked among ourselves. The initial conversations were within the ethnic groups. Then Negro and Jewish staff members talked with one another about the new situation. And finally the entire office talked openly for the first time. We learned that some of the staff in the group not discriminated against had been concerned about the racist practice. However, when the formal orders were handed to us for the trainees, we found that "discrimination as usual" continued. This time the entire staff wondered how employers still insisted on discriminating when there was such a great need for workers. Each day we would get new orders—orders with the undemocratic features.

Eddie had learned of this tremendous demand for workers. How could anybody not hear the call? The cry was everywhere. In the press, on the radio and in many other places one heard, "Go to your nearest public employment agency!"

He, like others in that community, would come in and inquire, be lied to, and say, "Gosh, I heard it on the radio at eight this morning and rushed here to be first on line, and you say they don't need anybody. I don't get it." Others became belligerent and many were demoralized. Just what the fascists wanted!

Even as Eddie didn't "get it," neither did the staff members, who recognized that one cannot prepare for a global war by limiting participation to a select few.

Two months before the late President Roosevelt issued his famous Executive Order 8802,[1] which became an effective weapon against the "divide and rule" Nazi theory, I stood at my desk fingering discriminatory trainee orders for an airplane manufacturer. I had just completed a file search and had discovered but four people who could meet the superficial specifications. The hundreds of otherwise qualified workers were immobilized. Quite disgusted, I turned in time to see a young girl, a former member of my old agency, approaching my desk. Putting on my best professional smile, I greeted her, "Hello. I have a job for you—trimmer of women's housedresses. Understand they pay . . ."

"Mr. Jones," she interrupted, "Did you hear about Eddie?"

"No, but I saw him last Saturday. He was in looking for a better paying job. Told me that his wife is going to have another baby in a couple of months. Usually comes up here every week."

For a moment there was silence. I remembered that last Saturday I had jobs for trainees that would have fitted Eddie to a "T," but his ethnic background made all of his education of no value. I didn't tell him, but he left, saying, "This can't last forever."

---

1. Executive Order 8802 forbade race discrimination in war plants with federal contracts.

To break the awkward pause, I said, "It's about time for him to pop up, for he usually comes in about this time."

"I see," she remarked quietly. "Mr. Jones, did you know . . . did you know they found Eddie's clothes on the bank of the East River three days ago?"

I still see myself standing there, dazed, while digging my nails into my palms to repress the mixed feeling of shame, anger and remorse. Somehow I felt as guilty as if I had pushed him into those icy, black waters. . . .

Now I am convinced by the people of the State of New York that my early attitudes regarding discrimination were quite right. It is a wonderful feeling to know that being "overly sensitive" in 1938 was merely acting in accord with the spirit of 1945. . . .

OPPORTUNITY, APRIL 1943

Negro Women Are American Workers, Too
GEORGE E. DEMAR

Manpower problems, concomitant with the maintenance of huge armies, and the production of subsistence consumer goods for the civilian population, have forced women in increasing numbers onto industrial thresholds. For the masses of Negro women, the war economy offers the initial opportunity to enter American industry. The newness of their position, the rebuffs experienced by the Negro male, the necessity for the full citizenship of the Negro, the need for work-democracy in America seems only to give the Negro woman added incentive to work on production lines. Today, conscientiously, with studied seriousness, led by such outstanding characters as the "training conscious Bethune" and the inimitable "Marian,"[1] they are pounding on the door of American Democracy . . . asking to be let in.

Paradoxically, the Negro woman is a newcomer to the American industrial scene; her history in American life is that of a worker and wage earner. The desire for careers was very evident during the "20s." Frustration snapped at the heels of many during the "30s." Today, at the beginning of the "40s," for many Negro women the idea of a "career" outside the "cook

---

1. Mary McLeod Bethune, head of the Division of Negro Affairs of the National Youth Administration; Marian Anderson, the famous concert singer.

kitchen" looms for the first time as a reality. Negro women know they can do a job properly. Negro high school graduates have known for a long time that, given the opportunity, they could be clerks, stenographers, secretaries, and saleswomen, or do any job in a particular classification which did not demand college training. Negro college graduates, who have finished accredited schools, have known they were equal in ability to many whites who in numerous instances were trained with them. Always, however, the maze of prejudice has encircled the Negro woman, to baffle and balk her entry into industry. Few have been able to rise above the situation so as to affect customs and the traditional jobs in America. Negro women who completed high school or college courses, qualifying them as teachers or for business, have been forced to rely upon Negro schools, colleges, and agencies, or limited Negro business opportunities for employment. Unable to gain entry-employment in a white industrial economy, Negro women have been employed chiefly in domestic and personal service (the closest possible work-contact with whites), and today their employers are reluctant to let them go . . . to work in war industry. If high school, vocational school, or college education tends to make good cooks, it also tends to create better office and factory workers.

. . . However, the Negro woman has not been as wholeheartedly accepted in training and in industry in Pittsburgh as the white woman. . . .

In spite of proper training and wise counseling, and clinging to faith in America, the aspirations of the Negro woman worker are frequently "dimmed out" at the factory employment offices when company representatives say: "There must be some mistake"; "No applications have heretofore been made by colored women"; "You are smart for taking the courses, but we do not employ colored"; "We have not yet installed separate toilet facilities"; "A sufficient number of colored women have not been trained to start a separate shift"; "The training center from which you come does not satisfy plant requirements"; "Your qualifications are too high for the kind of job offered"; "We cannot put a Negro in our front office"; "We will write you . . . but my wife needs a maid"; "We have our percentage of Negroes."

The "percentage of population" fixation having its origin in one-tenth of the nation's population being Negro has operated not only to give employment to Negroes, but also has placed limitations upon the employment of Negro women. The reason advanced for the practice is "to keep a proper balance." Percentages as a fixed guide may well indicate that a firm is employing Negroes, but to turn away a qualified worker purely on the basis that a percentage has been hired is to court disaster in this war emergency. And those who talk most of percentages do not have a percentage of clerks, a percentage of accountants, a percentage of secretaries, or a percentage of executives. Generally, and without reference to skill and training, the percentage for the entire population is confined in the work picture to unskilled workers. . . .

The Public Utilities of Pittsburgh, like many war industries, have their own employment service and have not hired Negro women in many of the categories open to white persons. Though the total Negro population of the Pittsburgh Metropolitan District is 115,000, and 20,000 Negro women are potential industrial workers, in Pittsburgh there is not a single Negro clerk, stenographer, telephone operator, receptionist, meter reader or even elevator operator to say nothing of bookkeepers, accountants, secretaries, or motor vehicle operators employed by the Public Utilities. Few, other than menial jobs, are available to Negro women.

A small number of firms, of Allegheny County's 400 concerns employing more than 100 persons, in the spirit-of-democracy and all-out war production, have begun the placement of the unskilled and semi-skilled Negro woman. Many do not admit Negroes to the classifications where white women are employed. One firm, the only one employing Negro women in unlimited numbers, is glad that it is getting the "cream of the crop, excellent girls with two and four years' high school training." And yet, this firm's wage scale hovers on the minimum of the Fair Labor Standards Act and is noticeably lower than wages paid by other war industries in the area. The girls have been confined to the night shift. Westinghouse Electric Manufacturing Company, East Pittsburgh, employing approximately 3,500 women, has hired a few more than 100 Negro women on the night shift only. They work as punch press, drill press, milling machine operators, engravers, painters, and grinders. The H. J. Heinz Company has hired 400 new employees, of which thirty-four are Negro women woodcraft workers. Machinist trainees have also been employed by the S & R Grinding Company and the Western Electric Company. Sheet metal trainees have been employed by the Berger Company, Linoback and the Iron City Companies. Draftswomen have been employed by Carnegie-Illinois Steel Corporation, the Blaw Knox Company and the War Department. The Penn Trouser Company has increased the number of its Negro power machine operators. The Union Switch and Signal Company has accepted several Negro women for training; and the Oliver Iron and Steel Corporation proposes far-reaching plans.

The problems of the Negro woman and victory are complex, but management has found the Negro capable and equal to job requirements. America at war cannot afford the luxury of racial discrimination; experience has shown that management which is efficient, and firm, can harness Negro womanpower energy for essential production needs. It is imperative that petty personal prejudices reflected in attitudes toward use of plant facilities, working on the same assembly line, and opportunities for upgrading must be subordinated to the larger need of producing sufficient munitions, food and clothing for this "arsenal of democracy" and its allies, the United Nations. Necessity has forced every large city to achieve a measure of this in its peacetime transportation, health and educational activities. It is a thousandfold more urgent that industry achieve the full integration and utilization of Negroes today whether it be from deep convictions of the soul or simply as a means of saving its hide!

Serious, though faltering, steps are being taken. Training has been initiated in schools, colleges and the NYA [National Youth Administration]; the U.S. Employment Service has facilities for the screening of womanpower; industry in some few instances has introduced Negroes into its personnel offices; and the creation of a new full-time board to take the place of the ill-fated FEPC [Fair Employment Practice Commission] gives rise to the hope that No. 8802 will be implemented in fact. Negro women welcome each and all of these steps. They stand ready to accept the cloak of democracy, offered so hesitantly.

Time is of the essence, as the Negro woman crosses the thresholds into industry to save manpower, money and time. The Negro woman must grasp zealously and courageously the invitation to succeed, extended by genuine Americans, through obtaining full knowledge and necessary job skills and by earning for herself the reputation of being "a responsible efficient worker." She must realize that powerful forces, black and white, stand ready to help her. American industry, that bulwark of the United Nations, if it would discredit Hitler and our native brand of Fascists, must proclaim with Franz Boas[2] that it does not hate color—it dislikes ignorance. With such a united approach to womanpower problems, women—women of all races—working together can become the determining factor in the winning of the war; they will be an important factor in deciding the peace.

---

2. Franz Boas was a well-known anthropologist with progressive views on race; Zora Neale Hurston studied under him in the 1920s.

OPPORTUNITY, SPRING 1944

Negro Woman Worker, What Now?

IDA COKER CLARK

In every section of America Negro women are closing up manpower gaps—in far Western plants, on mid-Western farms, in labor-starved New England cities, in conservative Eastern factories, and as far South as Jacksonville, Florida, and Huntsville, Alabama. During the past year we have also seen Negro women and girls hired in many non-defense jobs left vacant by other Negro women, Negro men, white women and white men who joined the armed services or who were hired on other jobs. When questioned as to their occupational status before their present employment, many of these workers tell of domestic jobs, odd jobs, or days' work. Others tell of having migrated from areas where they worked as rural teachers, hairdressers or clerical workers. Others boast of the fact that they are now making "real money"—their last regular jobs having been on work relief projects.

It is difficult at this stage in World War II to think of other than general unemployment during the era that will follow the present one. With the release of millions of men and women from the armed forces, with the expected return of many white women and girls to jobs that they held before certain transfers and promotions were made, and because of lack of training for peacetime industries, the Negro woman worker may be faced with problems similar to those encountered after World War I, but of a graver nature.

A brief review of two Women's Bureau bulletins released during the depression—"Negro Woman Worker" and the "Occupational Progress of Women from 1910 to 1930"—gives a fairly comprehensive picture of the occupational status of Negro women after World War I. These reports indicate that the majority of these women had to leave jobs made available to them during the wartime period of labor scarcity and return to low-bracket jobs, to unemployment, and to suffering. As we look forward to another year with an increasing need for women in the war-work program, and as we think of the Negro woman worker in the post-war world, what facts do we have to help in shaping the occupational pattern that may come out of the present?

The Negro woman worker is daily making adjustments on a par with other workers, although she continues to find it necessary to make double and triple adjustments. There is the ever-present adjustment that she usually has to make because of race. Then there is the adjustment that she makes, as do other women workers, because of sex. Now in 1944 as a war industry worker she finds many problems confronting her because she is new and inexperienced. . . .

Firsthand information from the workers themselves gives broader implications and definitely answers the question as to whether Negro women workers are making adjustments. Eight months ago two young Negro women who entered a factory as the first Negro women to be employed started as workers in the maintenance section. They were told by those who had worked in the factory for years that they would not be transferred to any other section. It was interesting to note that these two women daily took advantage of each opportunity to get ahead by learning the names and positions of those in authority, making friends with workers in the preferred section, becoming familiar with the work routine, keeping up with plant bulletins, and staying on the job. When the promotions came, they were assigned to new jobs. They promoted themselves because of their ability, persistence, resourcefulness, and tact.

In present attempts to solve certain work problems, Negro women workers are in the same class with other women workers. In this all-out effort women must prove that in spite of physical limitations they can reduce absenteeism to an absolute minimum. As weeks go by they are proving that they can stand the rotating shift as well as men. Studies have been made in various plants to prove this.

A survey made in Kansas by the U.S. Employment Service showed that contrary to first beliefs mixed crews proved more satisfactory than all-men or all-women crews in many occupations. It was pointed out that employee morale was raised; absenteeism was only six percent greater among women than among men; after rest periods women reported to production lines quicker; women were more careful of material and tools; and there was a noticeable decrease in employee accidents since the hiring of women.

Among other problems of women workers is the problem of working mothers who find it difficult to maintain normal family life at home. Despite efforts of mothers to find relatives, friends, and hired persons to help in caring for their children, and despite employers' efforts to adjust assignments to shifts of women with young children, this continues to constitute a major problem in every war production area in America. As more public and private funds are appropriated, more aid will be available from nurseries, day care centers, agencies, churches, and other institutions.

For the past three or four months the Negro woman worker, as well as other workers, has been affected by cutbacks in many industries. This means that many women are out of work for a period until they are transferred, or until they find employment in another industry where increased production is essential as the war scene changes. As more cutbacks will be experienced in 1944, this will constitute another major problem for the Negro woman worker.

To have a "sense of belonging" is as important to the Negro woman worker as getting and holding a job, whether the job be in a defense plant or in non-essential industry. It has been pointed out by personnel directors and others who have close contacts with women workers, that the worker's ability to find her place in the everyday life of the plant is in direct proportion to her life as an active citizen in the community in which she finds herself. Many Negro women new to their jobs and to their communities need counseling on and off the job to help them feel a "sense of belonging." As little or no counseling is given to Negro women on the job, either through the offices equipped for such services or through union activities, agencies and groups outside have the broader job of helping these women plan their community activities and carry through the education in their behalf that is needed at the present time.

Negro women and Negro men as well are gradually getting into the "thick of things" and are beginning to understand their place in the total effort. On the nights that both Negro and white men and women attended the U.S.O.-Y.W.C.A. midnight skating parties at the Negro Branch of the Germantown (Philadelphia) Young Women's Christian Association, contacts were made with various small groups to listen in on the trend of conversation. These men and women were employed at the Signal Corps Depot, Frankford Arsenal, Bendix Corporation, Navy Yard, Midvale Steel Corporation, Quartermaster Depot, Pennsylvania Railroad, and Sun Shipbuilding Company. Whether white or Negro, the "shop talk" was different according to whether the worker was an old worker or a new defense one. This was to be expected, but over a period of three months many of the Negro women who were still attending the "Y" activities were beginning to talk of their part in bond rallies and in beneficial suggestion campaigns, their appearance with the glee club on lunch hour programs, their contributions to plant bulletins, and other programs of a cultural, recreational, or informational nature. Such "on the job" participation by Negro women may seem trivial, but there are implications for the future in the way that our women become represented in plant activities.

Other check-ups on women in the group mentioned above showed that the workers who brought to their new jobs experience in club groups, youth movements, church work, or extra-curricular activities in school were the women more able to gain recognition from plant officials and fellow employees as well.

One of the leaders in the National Industrial Program of the Y.W.C.A. took five months away from her office to study the rapid industrial changes and the importance of women workers, especially on the Pacific Coast. She reported that the "matter of groups is receiving serious consideration for various kinds are springing up among war workers." While some of these groups are feared because of certain tensions, community agencies working with women and girls may play a dynamic role in helping such groups get a sense of direction. She also reported that "women are generally overlooked on labor-management committees, but there is an eagerness now among trade unions to use women on these committees." In this connection, Negro women have not penetrated the field of plant and industrial committees, but here and there Negro men are being elected and added to these committees that are concerned with self-government.

It is quite significant at this time that a few workers in each group are seeking help in solving the problem of keeping present jobs from being "duration" jobs. During the early months of last year, a counseling period was planned in conjunction with the U.S.O.-Y.W.C.A. program mentioned above. Among the queries and comments from women workers the following are significant:

> "How can I get more training for the type of work that I am now doing?"
> "I need help with typewriting and shorthand."
> "Is it possible for me to go to night school when my shift changes so often?"
> "We want more in-training classes."
> "Now that we can afford it, should I take a business course or should I get another defense job?"
> "What can be done to make domestic jobs more attractive for those of us who may have to return to them?"

These questions and comments coming from the few workers who were attracted to the counseling hour are vital to the life of women everywhere, and especially to Negro women, whether they work in a shop or an office. Community agencies and interested groups should plan programs that will help the bulk of Negro women become more concerned about their economic security. . . .

When questioned as to their affiliation and interest in unions, the majority of Negro women workers had little or no comments to make, mainly because they have not been exposed to unionism. There is need for a definite plan of workers' education and training in trade union principles for Negro women. A survey of local unions is now being made by the Women's Bureau of the U.S. Department of Labor. This survey will give information on both union policies for women members, and women's activities in unions.

The Negro woman worker should make the job of planning for her future a part of her daily routine. The same spirit which is increasing her contribution to winning the war can help her as she plans now for the immediate future.

OPPORTUNITY, FEBRUARY 1942

The Editor Says
An Enemy of Democracy

ELMER CARTER

It was the South that created the "mammy" tradition—the tradition of the gentle, uncomplaining, patient Negro woman who brought the children of the southern aristocracy into the world, who watched over them during the years of their infancy, who nursed them in illness and who beguiled them with weird stories during childhood and cared for them and guided them from adolescence into maturity.

After Reconstruction, the mammy tradition became one of the indicia of status. "Dear old mammy"—"my old black mammy"—was the passport which the white southerner often employed when in the North to indicate that he or she was descended from the master class and that he was not "po white." No southern lady or gentleman would depreciate the virtues of the Negro mammy. She has been extolled in song and story. She was the soul of devotion and loyalty.

This being true, the latest order from the War Department of the government, relative to the participation of Negro citizens in the war, borders on the fantastic, for Surgeon General James C. Magee of the United States Army, after a fervid plea for 50,000 young women to enter nursing schools in order to fill a pressing need which exists in the Army and Navy, has

An Army Nurse, *The Crisis,* **February 1943**

refused to accept Negro nurses for service except in "hospitals or wards devoted exclusively to the treatment of Negro soldiers."

The inference is, of course, that wounded white soldiers would refuse to accept the ministrations of colored nurses. Evidently Major General Magee does not know that colored women nursed soldiers of the Confederacy and Union Armies during the Civil War. Harriet Tubman, heroic figure of that era, herself was a nurse who brought many a wounded Union soldier out from the shadow of death.

We don't know who Major General Magee is, or where he came from, but his order warrants an immediate investigation by the Congress of the United States. The citizens of this country have a right to know just what motivates a high official of the government who seems bent on creating resentment, if not inciting disloyalty, on the part of a significant section of the population.

There are hundreds of young colored women who are graduate nurses. They are eager to serve in the Army, the Navy, the Marine Corps. They have the same patience, the same devotion, the same gentleness as their grandmothers, and in addition they possess scientific knowledge of modern medical and surgical practice, and skills acquired through long apprenticeship in recognized hospitals. Given equal opportunity for training, the Negro nurse has no superior in any national or racial group in the world.

THE CRISIS, APRIL 1945

You Will Say (Tu Diras)
ANDRE SPIRE (TRANSLATED BY JOHN F. MATHEUS)

And you will say:

My nurse was black, the one I had,
Yes, mesdemoiselles,
When I was born in the U.S.A.
In Europe, then,
A tiger raged,
The woeful tracks of jackals followed him.

You will say to them:

My nurse was black, the one I had,
No half-breed she,
Perhaps a shade of yellow
With a profile quite projection
And straightened hair, shining,
Tiara shaped, with glistening oil,
So when she walked in the sunlight

Amidst her braids
All colors flashed of rainbow hues.
Somersaults we turned on the lawn.
Yes! Like me she bent into a ball,
And put her head down in the grass
So, then flipflop!

And when I climbed upon her front,
What chuckling laughs,
Like firecrackers, like water falling
And how I felt each spasm on my skin!

She used to talk to the dishes in the sink,
To the grater, to the pots, to the bottles.
In her pink palms how they bustled about,
Then stood in rows in the cupboard shelves
Like magic of the enchanter's wand.

My glass and my bowl
To my pouting lips are raised
And sleep comes down
Upon mine eyes resistless now,
Comes down with wooing and with smiling
Like the lips of all the angels in Paradise.

And why should she not have an angel's smile
On her dark face, my ebon nurse?
There is in truth an ebon Virgin in Chartres church
And upon many a Byzantine mosaic.
And Balthazar, who followed the Star to the manger bed,
Was he not black of face and swart
As the rock of Mount Moriah in Jerusalem?

And why should not the face of God be dark,
With long black locks
And ebon beard, with eyes afire
Like King Cophetua's, of Burne-Jones'[1] art in London,
Sitting at the feet of the little white servant maid
With periwinkle eyes, whom he adores?

---

1. Sir Edward Burne-Jones, the nineteenth-century English painter.

U.S. Cadet Nursing Corps Ad, *The Crisis*, July 1944

THE CRISIS, NOVEMBER 1945

Like a Winding Sheet

ANN PETRY

He had planned to get up before Mae did and surprise her by fixing breakfast. Instead he went back to sleep and she got out of bed so quietly he didn't know she wasn't there beside him until he woke up and heard the queer soft gurgle of water running out of the sink in the bathroom.

He knew he ought to get up but instead he put his arms across his forehead to shut the afternoon sunlight out of his eyes, pulled his legs up close to his body, testing them to see if the ache was still in them.

Mae had finished in the bathroom. He could tell because she never closed the door when she was in there and now the sweet smell of talcum powder was drifting down the hall and into the bedroom. Then he heard her coming down the hall.

"Hi, babe," she said affectionately.

"Hum," he grunted, and moved his arms away from his head, opened one eye.

"It's a nice morning."

"Yeah," he rolled over and the sheet twisted around him, outlining his thighs, his chest. "You mean afternoon, don't ya?"

Mae looked at the twisted sheet and giggled. "Looks like a winding sheet," she said. "A shroud—." Laughter tangled with her words and she had to pause for a moment before she could continue. "You look like a huckleberry—in a winding sheet—"

"That's no way to talk. Early in the day like this," he protested.

He looked at his arms silhouetted against the white of the sheets. They were inky black by contrast and he had to smile in spite of himself and he lay there smiling and savouring the sweet sound of Mae's giggling.

"Early?" She pointed a finger at the alarm clock on the table near the bed, and giggled again. "It's almost four o'clock. And if you don't spring up out of there you're going to be late again."

"What do you mean 'again'?"

"Twice last week. Three times the week before. And once the week before and—"

"I can't get used to sleeping in the day time," he said fretfully. He pushed his legs out from under the covers experimentally. Some of the ache had gone out of them but they weren't really rested yet. "It's too light for good sleeping. And all that standing beats the hell out of my legs."

"After two years you oughtta be used to it," Mae said.

He watched her as she fixed her hair, powdered her face, slipping into a pair of blue denim overalls. She moved quickly and yet she didn't seem to hurry.

"You look like you'd had plenty of sleep," he said lazily. He had to get up but he kept putting the moment off, not wanting to move, yet he didn't dare let his legs go completely limp because if he did he'd go back to sleep. It was getting later and later but the thought of putting his weight on his legs kept him lying there.

When he finally got up he had to hurry and he gulped his breakfast so fast that he wondered if his stomach could possibly use food thrown at it at such a rate of speed. He was still wondering about it as he and Mae were putting their coats on in the hall.

Mae paused to look at the calendar. "It's the thirteenth," she said. Then a faint excitement in her voice, "Why it's Friday the thirteenth." She had one arm in her coat sleeve and she held it there while she stared at the calendar. "I oughtta stay home," she said. "I shouldn't go outta the house."

"Aw, don't be a fool," he said. "To-day's payday. And payday is a good luck day everywhere, any way you look at it." And as she stood hesitating he said, "Aw, come on."

And he was late for work again because they spent fifteen minutes arguing before he could convince her she ought to go to work just the same. He had to talk persuasively, urging her gently, and it took time. But he couldn't bring himself to talk to her roughly or threaten to strike her like a lot of men might have done. He wasn't made that way.

So when he reached the plant he was late and he had to wait to punch the time clock because the day shift workers were streaming out in long lines, in groups and bunches that impeded his progress.

Even now just starting his work-day his legs ached. He had to force himself to struggle past the out-going workers, punch the time clock, and get the little cart he pushed around all night because he kept toying with the idea of going home and getting back in bed.

He pushed the cart out on the concrete floor, thinking that if this was his plant he'd make a lot of changes in it. There were too many standing up jobs for one thing. He'd figure out some way most of 'em could be done sitting down and he'd put a lot more benches around. And this job he had—this job that forced him to walk ten hours a night, pushing this little cart, well, he'd turn it into a sitting-down job. One of those little trucks they used around railroad stations would be good for a job like this. Guys sat on a seat and the thing moved easily, taking up little room and turning in hardly any space at all, like on a dime.

He pushed the cart near the foreman. He never could remember to refer to her as the forelady even in his mind. It was funny to have a woman for a boss in a plant like this one.

She was sore about something. He could tell by the way her face was red and her eyes were half shut until they were slits. Probably been out late and didn't get enough sleep. He avoided looking at her and hurried a little, head down, as he passed her though he couldn't resist stealing a glance at her out of the corner of his eyes. He saw the edge of the light colored slacks she wore and the tip end of a big tan shoe.

"Hey, Johnson!" the woman said.

The machines had started full blast. The whirr and the grinding made the building shake, made it impossible to hear conversations. The men and women at the machines talked to each other but looking at them from just a little distance away they appeared to be simply moving their lips because you couldn't hear what they were saying. Yet the woman's voice cut across the machine sounds—harsh, angry.

He turned his head slowly. "Good evenin', Mrs. Scott," he said and waited.

"You're late again."

"That's right. My legs were bothering me."

The woman's face grew redder, angrier looking. "Half this shift comes in late," she said. "And you're the worst one of all. You're always late. Whatsa matter with ya?"

"It's my legs," he said. "Somehow they don't ever get rested. I don't seem to get used to sleeping days. And I just can't get started."

"Excuses. You guys always got excuses," her anger grew and spread. "Every guy comes in here late always has an excuse. His wife's sick or his grandmother died or somebody in the family had to go to the hospital," she paused, drew a deep breath. "And the niggers are the worse. I don't care what's wrong with your legs. You get in here on time. I'm sick of you niggers—"

"You got the right to get mad," he interrupted softly. "You got the right to cuss me four ways to Sunday but I ain't letting nobody call me a nigger."

He stepped closer to her. His fists were doubled. His lips were drawn back in a thin narrow line. A vein in his forehead stood out swollen, thick.

And the woman backed away from him, not hurriedly but slowly—two, three steps back.

"Aw, forget it," she said. "I didn't mean nothing by it. It slipped out. It was a accident." The red of her face deepened until the small blood vessels in her cheeks were purple. "Go on and get to work," she urged. And she took three more slow backward steps.

He stood motionless for a moment and then turned away from the red lipstick on her mouth which made him remember that the foreman was a woman. And he couldn't bring himself to hit a woman. He felt a curious tingling in his fingers and he looked down at his hands. They were clenched tight, hard, ready to smash some of those small purple veins in her face.

He pushed the cart ahead of him, walking slowly. When he turned his head, she was staring in his direction, mopping her forehead with a dark blue handkerchief. Their eyes met and then they both looked away.

He didn't glance in her direction again but moved past the long work benches, carefully collecting the finished parts, going slowly and steadily up and down, back and forth the length of the building and as he walked he forced himself to swallow his anger, get rid of it.

And he succeeded so that he was able to think about what had happened without getting upset about it. An hour went by but the tension stayed in his hands. They were clenched and knotted on the handles of the cart as though ready to aim a blow.

And he thought he should have hit her anyway, smacked her hard in the face, felt the soft flesh of her face give under the hardness of his hands. He tried to make his hands relax by offering them a description of what it would have been like to strike her because he had the queer feeling that his hands were not exactly a part of him any more—they had developed a separate life of their own over which he had no control. So he dwelt on the pleasure his hands would have felt—both of them cracking at her, first one and then the other. If he had done that his hands would have felt good now—relaxed, rested.

And he decided that even if he'd lost his job for it he should have let her have it and it would have been a long time, maybe the rest of her life before she called anybody else a nigger. The only trouble was he couldn't hit a woman. A woman couldn't hit back the same way a man did. But it would have been a deeply satisfying thing to have cracked her narrow lips wide open with just one blow, beautifully timed and with all his weight in back of it. That way he would have gotten rid of all the energy and tension his anger had created in him. He kept remembering how his heart had started pumping blood so fast he had felt it tingle even in the tips of his fingers.

With the approach of night fatigue nibbled at him. The corners of his mouth dropped, the frown between his eyes deepened, his shoulders sagged, but his hands stayed tight and tense. As the hours dragged by he noticed that the women workers had started to snap and snarl at each other. He couldn't hear what they said because of the sound of the machines but he could see the quick lip movements that sent words tumbling from the sides of their mouths. They gestured irritably with their hands and scowled as their mouths moved.

Their violent jerky motions told him that it was getting close on to quitting time but somehow he felt that the night still stretched ahead of him, composed of endless hours of steady walking on his aching legs. When the whistle finally blew he went on pushing the cart, unable to believe that it had sounded. The whirring of the machines died away to a murmur and he knew then that he'd really heard the whistle. He stood still for a moment filled with a relief that made him sigh.

Then he moved briskly, putting the cart in the store room, hurrying to take his place in the line forming before the paymaster. That was another thing he'd change, he thought. He'd have the pay envelopes handed to the people right at their benches so there wouldn't be ten or fifteen minutes lost waiting for the pay. He always got home about fifteen minutes late on payday. They did it better in the plant where Mae worked, brought the money right to them at their benches.

He stuck his pay envelope in his pants' pocket and followed the line of workers heading for the subway in a slow moving stream. He glanced up at the sky. It was a nice night, the sky looked packed full to running over with stars. And he thought if he and Mae would go right to bed when they got home from work they'd catch a few hours of darkness for sleeping. But they never did. They fooled around—cooking and eating and listening to the radio and he always stayed in a big chair in the living room and went almost but not quite to sleep and when they finally got to bed it was five or six in the morning and daylight was already seeping around the edges of the sky.

He walked slowly, putting off the moment when he would have to plunge into the crowd hurrying toward the subway. It was a long ride to Harlem and tonight the thought of it appalled him. He paused outside an all-night restaurant to kill time, so that some of the first rush of workers would be gone when he reached the subway.

The lights in the restaurant were brilliant, enticing. There was life and motion inside. And as he looked through the window he thought that everything within range of his eyes gleamed—the long imitation marble counter, the tall stools, the white porcelain topped tables and especially the big metal coffee urn right near the window. Steam issued from its top and a gas flame flickered under it—a lively, dancing, blue flame.

A lot of the workers from his shift—men and women—were lining up near the coffee urn. He watched them walk to the porcelain topped tables carrying steaming cups of coffee and he saw that just the smell of the coffee lessened the fatigue lines in their faces. After the first sip their faces softened, they smiled, they began to talk and laugh.

On a sudden impulse he shoved the door open and joined the line in front of the coffee urn. The line moved slowly. And as he stood there the smell of the coffee, the sound of the laughter and of the voices helped dull the sharp ache in his legs.

He didn't pay any attention to the girl who was serving the coffee at the urn. He kept looking at the cups in the hands of the men who had been ahead of him. Each time a man stopped out of the line with one of the thick white cups the fragrant steam got in his nostrils. He saw that they walked carefully so as not to spill a single drop. There was a froth of bubbles at the top of each cup and he thought about how he would let the bubbles break against his lips before he actually took a big deep swallow.

Then it was his turn. "A cup of coffee," he said, just as he had heard the others say.

The girl looked past him, put her hands up to her head and gently lifted her hair away from the back of her neck, tossing her head back a little. "No more coffee for awhile," she said.

He wasn't certain he'd heard her correctly and he said, "What?" blankly.

"No more coffee for awhile," she repeated.

There was silence behind him and then uneasy movement. He thought someone would say something, ask why or protest, but there was only silence and then a faint shuffling sound as though the men standing behind him had simultaneously shifted their weight from one foot to the other.

He looked at her without saying anything. He felt his hands begin to tingle and the tingling went all the way down to his finger tips so that he glanced down at them. They were clenched tight, hard, into fists. Then he looked at the girl again. What he wanted to do was hit her so hard that the scarlet lipstick on her mouth would smear and spread over her nose, her chin, out toward her cheeks, so hard that she would never toss her head again and refuse a man a cup of coffee because he was black.

He estimated the distance across the counter and reached forward, balancing his weight on the balls of his feet, ready to let the blow go. And then his hands fell back down to his sides because he forced himself to lower them, to unclench them and make them dangle loose. The effort took his breath away because his hands fought against him. But he couldn't hit her. He couldn't even now bring himself to hit a woman, not even this one, who had refused him a cup of coffee with a toss of her head. He kept seeing the gesture with which she had lifted the length of her blond hair from the back of her neck as expressive of her contempt for him.

When he went out the door he didn't look back. If he had he would have seen the flickering blue flame under the shiny coffee urn being extinguished. The line of men who had stood behind him lingered a moment to watch the people drinking coffee at the tables and then they left just as he had without having had the coffee they wanted so badly. The girl behind the counter poured water in the urn and swabbed it out and as she waited for the water to run out she lifted her hair gently from the back of her neck and tossed her head before she began making a fresh pot of coffee.

But he walked away without a backward look, his head down, his hands in his pockets, raging at himself and whatever it was inside of him that had forced him to stand quiet and still when he wanted to strike out.

The subway was crowded and he had to stand. He tried grasping an overhead strap and his hands were too tense to grip it. So he moved near the train door and stood there swaying back and forth with the rocking of the train. The roar of the train beat inside his head, making it ache and throb, and the pain in his legs clawed up into his groin so that he seemed to be bursting with pain and he told himself that it was due to all that anger-born energy that had piled up in him and not been used and so it had spread through him like a poison—from his feet and legs all the way up to his head.

Mae was in the house before he was. He knew she was home before he put the key in the door of the apartment. The radio was going. She had it turned up loud and she was singing along with it.

"Hello, Babe," she called out as soon as he opened the door.

He tried to say "hello" and it came out half a grunt and half sigh.

"You sure sound cheerful," she said.

She was in the bedroom and he went and leaned against the door jamb. The denim overalls she wore to work were carefully draped over the back of a chair by the bed. She was standing in front of the dresser, tying the sash of a yellow housecoat around her waist and chewing gum vigorously as she admired her reflection in the mirror over the dresser.

"Whatsa matter?" she said. "You get bawled out by the boss or somep'n?"

"Just tired," he said slowly. "For God's sake do you have to crack that gum like that?"

"You don't have to lissen to me," she said complacently. She patted a curl in place near the side of her head and then lifted her hair away from the back of her neck, ducking her head forward and then back. He winced away from the gesture. "What you got to be always fooling with your hair for?" he protested.

"Say, what's the matter with you, anyway?" She turned away from the mirror to face him, put her hands on her hips. "You ain't been in the house two minutes and you're picking on me."

He didn't answer her because her eyes were angry and he didn't want to quarrel with her. They'd been married too long and got along too well and so he walked all the way into the room and sat down in the chair by the bed and stretched his legs out in front of him, putting his weight on the heels of his shoes, leaning way back in the chair, not saying anything.

"Lissen," she said sharply. "I've got to wear those overalls again tomorrow. You're going to get them all wrinkled up leaning against them like that."

He didn't move. He was too tired and his legs were throbbing now that he had sat down. Besides the overalls were already wrinkled and dirty, he thought. They couldn't help but be for she'd worn them all week. He leaned further back in the chair.

"Come on, get up," she ordered.

"Oh, what the hell," he said wearily and got up from the chair. "I'd just as soon live in a subway. There'd be just as much place to sit down."

He saw that her sense of humor was struggling with her anger. But her sense of humor won because she giggled.

"Aw, come on and eat," she said. There was a coaxing note in her voice. "You're nothing but a old hungry nigger trying to act tough and—" she paused to giggle and then continued, "You—"

He had always found her giggling pleasant and deliberately said things that might amuse her and then waited, listening for the delicate sound to emerge from her throat. This time he didn't even hear the giggle. He didn't let her finish what she was saying. She was standing close to him and that funny tingling started in his finger tips, went fast up his arms and sent his fist shooting straight for her face. There was the smacking sound of soft flesh being struck by a hard object and it wasn't until she screamed that he realized he had hit her in the mouth—so hard that the dark red lipstick had blurred and spread over her full lips, reaching up toward the tip of her nose, down toward her chin, out toward her cheeks.

The knowledge that he had struck her seeped through him slowly and he was appalled but he couldn't drag his hands away from her face. He kept striking her and he thought with horror that something inside him was holding him, binding him to this act, wrapping and twisting about him so that he had to continue it. He had lost all control over his hands. And he groped for a phrase, a word, something to describe what this thing was like that was happening to him and he thought it was like being enmeshed in a winding sheet—that was it—like a winding sheet. And even as the thought formed in his mind his hands reached for her face again and yet again.

A WAC, *The Crisis,* **September 1942**

Racism on the Home Front

Although women in the military were unquestionably hurt by racism, male soldiers became the symbol of besieged black America in the African American press as segregated army bases provided the flash point for protest and civil disturbances; these issues are reflected in this section. In November of 1941, representatives of the black press, including Roy Wilkins, the editor of *The Crisis,* met with heads of the War Department and were told, under protest, that the military would segregate African Americans from other troops. Although it would reverse itself in 1948 when Harry Truman desegregated the armed forces, the War Department's position was that it was not a "sociological laboratory" and that racial integration would interfere with prosecuting the war. Jim Crow facilities at training camps included separate buses, PX counters, and sections in movie theaters, hospital wards, and dormitories; domestic travel via train meant segregated cars in the South; and buses between army camps and southern towns were initially segregated as well. Furthermore, black battalions were often put under the command of white officers, frequently southern, and at times forced to perform menial tasks. In at least one instance, a state (Arizona) demanded that black troops be released to pick cotton. These conditions are alluded to in the material of this section as are other incidents. Adding to the humiliation and dangers of these undesirable tasks were the barring of black troops from combat until late in the war (they were used mainly in labor battalions) and the imposition of quotas on numbers of African Americans allowed to be pilots, officers, nurses, doctors, and skilled technicians in the military.

Aggravating these discriminatory practices were the numerous instances of violence against black soldiers at training camps, such as the shooting of a soldier by white police when he sat in the white section of a bus in Beaumont, Texas, or the killing of another soldier in Durham, North Carolina, by a white bus driver. In 1942, three soldiers based in Alexandria, Louisiana, were convicted of rape and sentenced to death, a cause taken up by Thurgood Marshall and the NAACP. Not one World War II black soldier was awarded the Congressional Medal of Honor (the first was given in 1998). These cases and others were mentioned by African American magazines, and they fueled a dramatic rise of support for the NAACP and the National Urban League.

Women were by no means immune from such attacks, as is illustrated in Sergeant Aubrey E. Robinson Jr.'s letter to *The Crisis,* in which he describes the assault by a white bus driver on a black female passenger who dared to challenge his authority. These situations form the backdrop for material in this section, including African American journalist Thelma Thurston Gorham's angry depiction of women's quarters at Fort Huachuca, Arizona, where most black troops were stationed; a letter from a soldier's wife who objects to a racist shrimp-can label on the shelves of a Safeway store near her husband's base in Temple, Texas; and another letter, from the sister of a black serviceman, Mrs. Charles H. Puryear, describing an incident in which a white lieutenant ordered five soldiers and two WACs to give up their train seats to Italian prisoners.

Such accounts flowed from a home front fractured by legal segregation in the South and de facto segregation in the North. African Americans were heavily policed in southern communities, where their numbers were the greatest, but they were restricted by unspoken rules from white neighborhoods in the North as well. White protest over the Sojourner Truth housing project set up in Detroit to accommodate in-migrating black defense workers was symbolic of resistance to integrated housing, as were racial covenants excluding black people from postwar subdivisions like the planned community of Stuyvestant Town in New York City.

Gwendolyn Williams's "Heart against the Wind"; Esta Diamond's "Something for the War"; Chester Himes's "All God's Chillun Got Pride"; and Ruby Rohrlich's "Citizen in the South" are all fictional representations of these home-front conditions but also of African American defiance of them. Himes's story grew out of his WPA jobs in Cleveland, where he worked during the Depression. He describes this period in his memoirs as humiliating, and we get glimpses here of what he went through, but the fictionalized court-martial incident is drawn from army-camp reports, well publicized in the African American press, of black soldiers rebelling against demeaning treatment. Ruby Rohrlich, who worked for the Office of War Information and wrote "Citizen of the South" as part of its antiracism campaign, describes another such challenge to Jim Crow patterns. Here an African American physician on a train trip to visit her army-doctor husband refuses to change cars when she hits Washington, D.C., and the color bar. Williams's "Heart against the Wind" and Diamond's "Something for the War" describe rebellion of another sort as black women resist a racist status quo while supporting the war effort through, respectively, writing to a soldier and giving blood. Diamond's story is especially noteworthy for its critique of the Red Cross policy of segregating blood, and for its display of autonomy by a domestic worker who refuses to subordinate her own community activities to her employer's importunate demands.

Anger over discrimination against black soldiers, coupled with crowded living conditions, segregated public space, and encounters with white southern migrants erupted in 242 violent clashes in forty-seven cities throughout 1943, a topic that informs much of the material in this section. Such military incidents created such anger in Harlem that an altercation between a black soldier and a white policeman sparked a three-day riot in which four people were killed, four hundred injured, and five hundred arrested in August of that year. James Baldwin, in "Notes of a Native Son," commented on the incident: "It would have demanded an unquestioning patriotism, happily as uncommon in this country as it is undesirable, for these people not to have been disturbed by the bitter letters they received [from soldiers], by the newspaper stories they read. . . . It was only the 'race' men, to be sure, who spoke ceaselessly of being revenged . . . for the indignities and dangers suffered by Negro boys in uniform; but everybody felt a directionless, hopeless bitterness, as well as that panic which can scarcely be suppressed when one knows that a human being one loves is beyond one's reach, and in danger."[1] The future Supreme Court justice Thurgood Marshall, in "The Gestapo in Detroit," critiques police action in Detroit when over twenty-four black people were killed and a thousand injured in a June 1943 race riot and suggests the operation of tensions larger than the one that triggered the melee.

Significantly, the catalyst for both the Harlem and Detroit riots was gender-related. The Harlem fracas developed out of an incident at the Braddock Hotel when a black woman named Margie Polite had an altercation with a white policeman in the hotel lobby. A black soldier intervened on her behalf and was shot by the policeman, prompting her to shout on the street that he had been killed, a cry that incensed the population. The genesis of the Detroit riot was twofold: in the black community there was a rumor that white sailors had thrown a black woman and her baby off a bridge at Belle Isle (a recreation park), while whites believed a black man had raped a white woman there. Preceding both outbreaks was the Los Angeles "zoot-suit" riot in early June, when white sailors went on a rampage beating Chicano and African American young men for allegedly flirting with white women. That tension over women should be at the heart of these major disturbances illustrates the way gender merged with race issues during the war to produce volatile home-front conditions. Reflecting this aspect

---

1. James Baldwin, "Notes of a Native Son," 84.

of racial clashes in 1943, short stories by Pearl Fisher ("Riot Gold"), Lila Marshall ("Sticks and Stones"), and Ann Petry ("In Darkness and Confusion") place women centrally in their plot constructions around the race riots of that year.

Gender conflict is also a central issue in this section's poetry and fiction, which concern other racist violence on the home front, such as the lynchings in October 1942 of three young black men in Mississippi who were accused of raping white women. In January of that year, Cleo Wright, charged with assaulting a white woman, was shot three times while being arrested, taken from jail by a mob, dragged through the streets by a car, and burned alive in Sikeston, Missouri. These and other events prompted writers to indict wartime America for waging a Nazi-like domestic war on its own citizens of color while purportedly fighting for democracy abroad. Women are anguished bystanders to such violence in the poetry of James Baldwin, Gloria Clyne, and others, who depict them as helpless mothers bearing the cross of their sons' martyrdom. They emerge as victims of brutal racist aggression, echoing images of white women in dominant culture propaganda as vulnerable targets of Axis rapaciousness. In African American treatment, however, black women are the innocent targets of white supremacist evil: the enemy is at their door on the home front, not in a foreign land.

OPPORTUNITY, MARCH 1942

Blackout

RUTH ALBERT COOK

The census says fifteen million of us—
I say thirty million—live
In this great democracy.

Add it for yourself.

Last night, a man with a Groton-Harvard accent[1]
Talked into the bedrooms, and parlors,

---

1. President Franklin Roosevelt, who gave radio addresses to the American public during the war.

And kitchens,
And automobiles,
Of fifteen million Americans who listened,
Proud, and frightened,
With the pride and fear
Of sanity
Among the insane.

Last night, fifteen million Americans
Were paled
Into identity
With one hundred fifteen million
Other Americans.

But today,
The same fifteen million Americans,
Became America's "tenth Americans,"
Became America's largest minority,
Became Negroes again.

Black troops marched with empty guns
Through Southern towns
Bristling with loaded guns.

The South killed another Negro.

In Wilmington, Delaware,
A very blond woman showed
Her very blond child
A brown child.
"See? That is a darky."

In Chicago, Illinois,
A woman went to a doctor—said—
"Oh! You're colored!"
And scurried away.

And the voice of Kate Smith[2]
Blared out of loudspeakers
On street corners—

---

2. Popular white singer of the time, famous for her rendition of Irving Berlin's
"God Bless America."

In drug stores—
In barber shops—
"God bless America—"

And the same fifteen million
Watched with accustomed eyes
Their pleasant pigmentation
Grow black as hell
And as evil.

The same fifteen million
Listened to Kate.
Became fifteen million
Nauseated
Niggers.

And as always, W. C. Handy,
And Duke Ellington,
And Ethel Waters,
And Count Basie,
And Maxine Sullivan,
And Jimmie Lunceford,
And Ella Fitzgerald,
Helped entertain
In juke boxes
During the blackout,
In gaudy, chromium-streaked,
Smoke-fogged,
Dugouts.

Sultry rhythm,
And heat,
And laughing water,
Made part of the fifteen million
Almost forget
For as long as fifteen minutes at a time,
That there was a blackout.

Add it yourself.
Fifteen million last night,
And fifteen million today,
Makes thirty million different people.

Or fifteen million
Split personalities.

It's all in how you look at it.

And America salutes
The stars and the stripes.

And shakes a defiant,
Half mailed fist
At un-American
Systematized cruelty
Everywhere—

Except its own
Rattling,
Closeted,
Skeleton.

Any bonds today?

THE CRISIS, FEBRUARY 1945

Only in America

RHOZA A. WALKER

ONLY, IN AMERICA—
    Can a child
        Sit and Dream:
    Golden Dreams,
    Fantastic
        Dreams,
    Dreams
        that are aggrandized;
    And then awake one morning,
    To find them
        Realized!

ONLY, IN AMERICA—
    Can a person

start from Scratch;
Scummy Scratch,
Scrawny Scratch,
Barrenly imbued—
And shed Scratch like a motley'd shell;
Rebirthed . . . Rebreathed . . . Renewed!

ONLY, IN AMERICA—
Can a mother
tell her Son
Someday,
You'll be the President!
Leader of the Mass!
And before Age tints with silver tones,
This thing
has come to pass.

ONLY, IN AMERICA—
Can a Man
boldly say;
He doesn't like the government
Or the men who run the state:
Here the laws are FOR THE PEOPLE:
This does not alternate.

ONLY, IN AMERICA—
Is a whole Nation Free;
Free to vote,
To enterprize,
With impartiality;
And Opportunity lends to ALL
A Free and Equal hand . . .
Did I say ALL?
Well, that is ALL except the Negro Man.

NEGRO STORY, APRIL–MAY 1946

Despair

HELEN S. FRIERSON

Out of the night
    There comes a song
Full of heartbreak
    And sounds forlorn.
The Negro's plaintive cry
    To be Nationally free,
But his hope will die
    And his faith will flee.
Sighs and hot tears
    Breast full of hate,
Doubts and fears
    Decrees of fate.
Labor and sweat,
    Live and learn
No time to fret
    A living to earn.
Sunshine and rain
    Comes from above,
Showers of blessings
    Gifts of love.
Nightmares at night,
    Dreams by day.
Cruel to fight,
    Crime to slay.
Waiting for light,
    Groping in dark,
Nerves all tight,
    Hear brutes bark.
Men and dogs,
    Birds and fish,
Jive and lies,
    Truth and myth.

EBONY RHYTHM, 1948

Black Recruit

GEORGIA DOUGLAS JOHNSON

At home, I must be humble, meek,
Surrendering the other cheek;
Must be a coward over here,
And yet, a brave man—over there.

This sophistry is passing strange,
Moves quite beyond my mental range—
Since I must be a hero there,
Shall I prepare by crawling here?

Am I a faucet that you turn
To right—I'm cold—to left—I burn!
Or but a golem[1] wound to spring
This way or that—a soulless thing!

He surely is a master-man
Who formulated such a plan.

EBONY RHYTHM, 1948

Guilty

RUBY BERKLEY GOODWIN

(A Negro soldier was killed by a bus driver in a southern state because he did not know the jim crow section of the car)

I did not know my place—
That is the crime for which I died.
I did not know where to sit,
Or how to bow low,
Or when to say "Yes, sir," to Mr. George.

---

1. A golem is a figure from Jewish mythology; a kind of Frankenstein, it looks human but has no soul.

I grew up with stardust in my eyes,
Stardust gathered from a million
Hopes and dreams of great men
Who died to make this a strong free nation.

True, all was not stardust.
I remembered Jamestown, Virginia,
And Harper's Ferry.
But a war was fought to end the shame
Of human slavery, or so I was told
By my teachers in New York.

I became a man and I heard
Of the Four Freedoms,
How good they sounded to me:

Freedom from want,
No more breadlines,
No more Salvation Army clothes,
No more relief doles,
No more hard-boiled case workers.

Freedom to worship,
I could sing "Steal Away" and "Ave Maria"
On Beale Street or in Carnegie Hall.
I could serve an invisible God
Or worship an image of gold or brass.

Freedom of speech,
I could laugh with Rochester[1] on the radio,
Disagree with the Dies committee,[2]
Yell for the Brooklyn Dodgers,
Or criticize the President.

And freedom from fear.
That was the greatest freedom
Of them all;

---

1. Eddie Rochester was the African American sidekick of comedian Jack Benny.
2. The Dies Committee, headed by Congressman Martin Dies, investigated "anti-American" activities in the postwar period. It was the precursor to the House Un-American Activities Committee headed by Joseph McCarthy.

For the man who has no fear
Is the only free man in the world.

I wrapped the Four Freedoms around me
When I put on my uniform
And started south to become a soldier
To save the world from tyranny.

But I did not know my place—
That is the crime for which I died.
I did not know where to sit,
Or how to bow low,
Or when to say "Yes, sir," to Mr. George.

OPPORTUNITY, SUMMER 1944

Paradox

FRENISE A. LOGAN

I'm a fighter for democracy:
I fight for justice and equality;
I fight for the four freedoms;
I fight to keep free men free;
That's what they tell me.

I hear their say,
And I look away,
'Cause they wouldn't understand
The question in my eyes;
Nor the conflict in my mind.

THE CRISIS, JANUARY 1944

Letter to the Editor
Safeway Stores Insult Negroes

A SOLDIER'S WIFE

While visiting my husband in one of our Texas army camps, I found the shelves of the Safe Way chain stores located in Temple, Texas, lined with these insulting products. Thinking this may be of interest to you and other "American Citizens," I am sending this label.[1]

Also at the request of many soldiers stationed there, with whom I had the privilege of talking, I would like to mention a few more things.

Within this "Gov't. Reservation" of Camp Hood, Texas, posted over public water fountains, toilets, theaters, etc., are signs "For Colored" and "For White." Our boys and civilian employees of the camp, including myself, have stood at bus stops for five and six hours while dozens of drivers refused to stop in colored areas until the whites had been accommodated. Frequently we have been asked out of our seats so that the whites could sit down. Many other things, too numerous to go into detail, are forcing the morale of our colored soldiers to a new low.

Why must our second lieutenants remain second lieutenants indefinitely, regardless of efficiency or capabilities?

Why must our husbands and brothers go abroad to fight for principles they only "hear" about at home?

Does our War Department believe in the Constitution of our country? Are the "Four Freedoms" excluding our Southern States? Does the "Commander in Chief" realize what's going on in the hearts and minds of his colored soldiers? How long does he expect them to tolerate these deplorable conditions? Is he training them to be brave, courageous soldiers on foreign soil and mere mice here at home? Does it matter to him whether or not these men leave the shores of their homeland with the deep feeling of peace in knowing they must go to protect, and insure, Liberty and Justice to ALL here at home?

Is the appeasement of the South worth the sacrifice of America's most loyal citizens? How long will this farce of Democracy continue before

---

1. *The Crisis* reprinted the "Nigger Head Brand Shrimp" can label, which has a derogatory cartoon of a young black man eating shrimp. The label indicates that this was a product of the Aughinbaugh Canning Company, Biloxi, Mississippi.

our President and War Department begin practicing what they preach? I wonder.

A Soldier's Wife

THE CRISIS, MARCH 1945

Letter to the Editor

MRS. CHARLES H. PURYEAR

Enclosed you will find an excerpt from a letter which my 19-year-old brother wrote me this week. He has been in the Army a year and is a member of the Air Corps. This incident occurred while he was en route from New York to Texas, where he is now stationed. The excerpt follows:

"The trip was excellent until we reached St. Louis, Missouri. When the train was ready to pull out a First Lt. MP (white) came into our jim crow car and ordered five soldiers, two WACs and me to get up and give our seats to fifteen Italian prisoners. We wouldn't move, so after a while he took the prisoners off. It seems that the Italians were sitting in the best seats in a white car and the lieutenant thought that they weren't good enough to sit there, but could sit with us. I could not help but give the incident a great deal of thought. I may be wrong in calling the Italians prisoners; perhaps I should have said 'Co-belligerents,' but I can't help thinking that some time or other those fellows fought against us and shot at, if they did not kill, Americans. I wondered if I were in the same situation on a Nazi train whether or not one of their officers would come through and order their soldiers to give up their seats for even a short distance. It is just such incidents as that that make me wonder what I am fighting for."

That, Mr. Editor, is what many a Negro soldier is puzzling his brain over today. It seems incredible in such critical times as these that an officer of the American Army would have the audacity to order American WACs, who are volunteers, let alone American soldiers, to give up their seats for any distance because of such prejudice. Just such incidents as these are the stepping stones in such cases as the recently publicized clash between Negro soldiers and Italians on the West Coast.[1]

---

1. Black soldiers at Fort Lawton in Walla Walla, Washington, rioted and killed an Italian P.O.W. because the Italians were in white-only facilities. The incident occurred in 1944.

I hope that you will find space in your paper for this, or part of this, letter.

Mrs. Charles H. Puryear
Long Branch, New Jersey
January 10, 1945

Editor's Note:

Nothing so lowers Negro morale as the frequent preferential treatment of Axis prisoners of war in contrast with deprecatory Army policy toward American troops who happen to be Negro. Just a few weeks ago in Camp Joseph T. Robinson, Arkansas, Lena Horne found herself the featured entertainer of Nazi prisoners of war to the exclusion of our own Negro soldiers. And some months ago in Texas Negro troops found that they as loyal Americans could not eat in the same station dining room which fed German prisoners of war. The Germans were white—and welcome; the Negroes, black and American, and therefore persona non grata.

OPPORTUNITY, WINTER 1945

Letter to the Editor
SERGEANT AUBREY E. ROBINSON JR.

This letter from a soldier to the Interracial Committee of his home town is a true story of a shocking experience.

November 6, 1944

This afternoon my Company Commander brought to my attention the letter he received from you concerning your request for an investigation of the incident in which I was involved in Aiken, S.C., prior to my transfer to this station. Unfortunately there seems to be little that he can do and I believe that he will write to you to that effect. It is his suggestion that such a request be directed to the proper authorities in Washington, preferably the Department of the Inspector General. Whether such authorities have been notified I cannot say.

Your letter came as a distinct surprise but I am most grateful for your expressions of confidence in my personal integrity. Your interest deserves an account of the events of that incident.

One Saturday evening I left Camp Gordon, Ga., on pass to visit some friends in nearby Aiken, S.C. I boarded a Valley Coach Line bus in Augusta,

Ga., to make the eighteen mile trip to my destination. Complying with the Jim Crow laws of the state I moved to the rear of the bus. The bus, although crowded, was quiet and the passengers, mostly civilians, were orderly. About eight miles from Augusta, one of the seats near the middle of the bus was emptied when one of the passengers got off. This seat was an aisle seat next to a white soldier. Standing in the aisle was a colored soldier who continued to stand by the empty seat until the white soldier touched his arm and told him to go ahead and sit down, he didn't mind. This the colored soldier did and the two men engaged in conversation until the bus reached Warrenville, S.C. There the bus driver saw the two soldiers sitting together and ordered the colored soldier to move. This he did without hesitation and without protest. The white soldier was indignant and protested against the driver's action but he was told that the laws of the state did not permit such seating and besides he would run the bus the way he wanted it run.

At this same stop several colored passengers got on the bus. There was standing room only except for one seat three quarters of the way to the rear of the bus. This was occupied by an elderly white civilian who was asleep. A middle aged colored woman got on the bus, noticed the empty seat and turned and asked the driver if he would ask the man to move to a seat in the front which had just been emptied. The bus driver very gruffly told her no, that he would not ask the man to move, and if she didn't like it she could get her money back and get off the bus. She went to the front to get her refund and as she started down the steps of the bus the bus driver took his fist and struck her across the back of the head. The blow almost felled her and she half-fell, half-staggered from the bus.

Several white soldiers grabbed the driver and prevented him from inflicting further blows. From our seats in the rear we demanded that he cease before we ourselves used force. Not one of us did more than raise a verbal protest. The bus driver grabbed up his money box and left the bus. We remained seated until it was evident that he would not move the bus. In about fifteen minutes another bus pulled in. The driver of our bus went to the driver of this bus and told him not to let the eleven colored soldiers on the bus because they had created a disturbance on his bus. So we were left five miles from our destination on an empty bus.

We then asked to have the Military Police notified and believing that they had been, we sat on the empty bus. There we made our mistake for instead of Military Police, two car-loads of county police and armed civilians pull up and order us to the rear of the bus. We were then driven directly to the county jail and locked up without being questioned, arraigned or without any of the usual procedures. We asked to be allowed to notify our units. We were told that they would be notified. Later we learned that they had not been notified.

The eleven of us remained locked up from 9 P.M. Saturday until 6 P.M. Monday. I cannot describe here the condition of that jail; it was absolutely miserable. Monday evening we were taken before a court, the bus driver was there, but there were no other witnesses. He testified and perjured himself in every sentence. He said that we had beaten him, that we had in general raised a rumpus. All of this was absolutely untrue. We were then called on to give our story. It so happened that I was called on first. I told the court everything that I saw and heard and told it just as it happened. The other men all agreed, only one or two having details to add. We pleaded not guilty, but it was evident from the start that the "trial" was a farce.

The judge gave us a tongue-lashing and fined us for "disorderly conduct." I was fined $25 or 30 days on the South Carolina chain gang as were two other fellows. The remainder were fined $15 or 30 days on the chain gang. We were fined $25 because we had taken seats in the front of the bus while it was empty of all other passengers and after the bus driver had left it. We were sitting waiting for the Military Police, or so we thought. No one of us had money enough to pay his fine, so we pooled our money and paid the fine of one of my buddies. The rest of us were loaded into cars and taken to the county farm.

En route to the farm, I was able to contact Mrs. Cummins, the hostess at the colored U.S.O. I told her that I needed $25 immediately. Asking no questions she said that she would get it for me immediately. She got the money and brought it out to the farm and thus secured my release but not before I had been forced to take off my military uniform and put on the filthy, black and white striped clothes of a convict and have an iron chain riveted to my right ankle.

This happened to each one of us. Mrs. Cummins came just after we had been penned up. She took me back to town and gave me a meal, my first in three days. I called my battalion at 9:45 Monday evening and that was the first time that they knew what had become of us. I returned to camp as soon as possible and notified the commanding officers of the units to which the other men belonged. Not one of them knew the whereabouts of their missing soldiers.

The men were furious when they heard what had happened to us. They collected money for the fines of the other men and early Tuesday morning went to get them. They did this of their own initiative. Our officers did nothing in behalf of the men. The men on the chain gang were found 25 and

Canteen Hostess, *The Crisis*, June 1943

30 miles out in the country working under armed guards. By mid-afternoon the five men in my unit had been released. The others were released later as their commanders saw fit to go after them.

The entire series of events was like one long nightmare. It was an experience that I shall never forget and one that I did not think could happen in "This Great Democracy." It shook to the very core my faith in a nation where such things could receive the sanction of so many people as it does here in the South. I had to call upon every ounce of training and pre-military experience to keep from becoming bitter, and to realize that I must continue to sacrifice to be a soldier so that I may fight and if necessary give my life for my country. If I did not believe that there are some Americans of all colors, nationalities, creeds who are truly seeking to make the necessary adjustments—that all Americans might participate fully and freely in American life—I would be unwilling and unable to be a good soldier. We who now fight and are about to fight will contest wrong wherever we find it, abroad or as a cancer in our own nation.

Organizations such as yours point the way for a better life for all and not just a few American citizens. Meeting in organized groups is a start; it isn't enough. To work, to play, to talk, to argue with a man is to know him. To know a man and understand him is the key to your tolerance of him in your society. To tolerate the differences, assimilate the likenesses, is to weave an indestructible social order.

Again let me express my deepest appreciation for your interest in me, I shall always seek to merit it.

Very truly yours,
Sgt. Aubrey E. Robinson, Jr.

OPPORTUNITY, DECEMBER 1942

Citizen in the South

RUBY ROHRLICH

The train pulled out of Pennsylvania Station. Melanie Thornton smiled as her small son pressed his nose against the window. Eleven hours, she thought, that's less than half a day, practically nothing in time. When you're in the hospital working, it passes quickly; but on a train, when you haven't seen your husband for six months—eleven hours is a lot! Still, she thought, as she mused lazily on the relativity of time, still it's only hours . . . and her breath quickened.

Billy climbed on her lap. "The wheels are singing, mum—gonna see da-dee, gonna see da-dee." Billy heard a song, rhythm in everything. Melanie pictured Randall's amazed delight when he saw the boy. "How he's grown!" he would say, and measure him. At five they grew so fast they needed new shoes before the old were half worn. Billy straightened his visor cap, pulled down his soldier's coat, and raised two fingers to his forehead. "Is this it, mum, is this how pop does it?" The white baby teeth gleamed through the slightly pendulous lips, the dark eyes dilated in excitement.

In her loneliness for Randall the sight of Billy never failed to comfort her—to comfort, and yet to wrench her heart, too, for the boy looked so like his father. It was hard this separation, their first separation in seven years of a marriage that had made her complete, sane. They were both physicians, they loved their work and shared it closely; they had their boy, and their delight in him. Randall, who had taught her to love life and people—how she missed him. She had wept when his Christmas furlough had been canceled, for she had not seen him since his enlistment in June. But he had phoned the next day, urging her to come to him instead, and her laughter became frequent and easy. It had been hard for her to arrange her own leave—so many doctors had already left for the Army that the hospital was seriously under-staffed. But they knew Randall's regiment might be sent overseas any day, and by pleading she had wrested a week from them. One week, 168 hours, and twenty-two of them had to be spent in travelling. And then—when again would she see him?

The sound of the wheels came to her muted, and sad, and monotonous. Melanie shook herself impatiently—they, the three of them, would have a long week together, and it would begin in about ten hours. Dreamily she made her son comfortable with a cookie and a picture book.

"Tickets, lady."

Melanie started, and showed the conductor her tickets. The wheels were screeching to a stop; they had reached Philadelphia.

"You'll have to change cars at Washington, lady."

Melanie was puzzled. "I thought this was a through train."

The conductor did not meet her inquiring look. "It's a through train all right, but from Washington on, colored folks have to sit in a separate car."

Melanie sat up straight, her bronze face resuming the impassive mask of the time before Randall. "My boy and I are going to Fort Bragg. My husband's in the Medical Corps there."

"That's the rule, ma'am. They haven't changed the rule." The conductor kept toying with his ticket-punch.

Her voice deep with firmness, Melanie said, "These are reserved seats. I paid for them, and I'm not changing."

The conductor shrugged his shoulders as he walked away, but his eyes were sympathetic.

Billy tugged at her hand; her stern face frightened him a little. "What'd the man want, mum?"

"It's all right, Billy."

The joy had run out of her, but she managed a reassuring smile and motioned to a double seat where three children were playing. "Why don't you play with the children, dear? Show them your book."

For the next two hours, until they reached Washington, she would have something to think about.

The children were laughing at something Billy was saying. He was probably telling them one of his made-up stories. Now he and a little girl began to bounce a ball against the plush back of the seat. Melanie's face softened as she looked at him. Then she frowned, and her hand flew out toward him in a small, unconscious protecting gesture. How had she dared bring Billy to the South? He would be burned deep, would never forget. She *had* remembered the South, but she had thought, now? . . . surely not now.

Suddenly she felt confined, cramped, in this train. It was so narrow, so close. She wanted to stretch her legs, walk somewhere, fast. The even spacing of the seats, their faded bilious green irritated her. Melanie passed her hand wearily over her forehead and through her thick, short, curly hair. She stood up, straight and slim, and walked to the water faucet, lurching with the movement of the train. She thought, shall I move? Randall, what shall I do?

When she returned, she found the children playing on her seat. Billy was whirling his spinning top for them. As she watched how naturally these children accepted him, she realized again that the rejection of her people was not instinctive, was not transmitted in the genes and chromosomes. Poor little Billy. And yet she and Randall couldn't have protected him much longer. He would have to learn in the usual, the bitter way.

Melanie swallowed an aspirin for her aching head. She gave the children some of the sandwiches she had prepared that morning, and milk from a thermos bottle. Billy's eyelids were drooping, he needed a nap. Melanie asked his playmates to go. She held her son on her lap, and he soon fell asleep. The afternoon sun was strong and hot in the train. She drowsed a little, then fell into a troubled sleep.

The train stopped. Melanie awoke.

"All 'board . . . Washington."

She waited.

"You gotta change cars here," the new conductor said, as he waited for Melanie to get up and leave.

"These are my seats," said Melanie quietly. "I reserved them and paid for them."

"That don't make no difference. Colored people sit in their own car down here." His light-blue middle-aged eyes looked hard at her, unashamed.

"My husband is in the Army. We're going to visit him at Fort Bragg," Melanie explained, very patiently. Billy stirred in her arms, and opened his eyes.

"That don't make no difference. You gotta change cars here. Come on now."

Billy clung to her. He looked with blinking eyes from his mother to the conductor. Melanie tried to conceal her growing anger. "I'm an American citizen, I've got the same rights as anyone else. I'm not giving up seats that I reserved and paid for."

"You'll leave this car if I have to put you out." His face an apoplectic red, eyes furious, he left the car, almost running. He returned in a moment, with two men of the train crew.

"Here she is, the nigger woman. Now let's get her out of here."

He put his hand heavily on Melanie's shoulder. She threw it off. "Don't you touch me." Her voice shook with the outrage she was damming up. Billy burst into tears. She thought, I mustn't cry . . . please, I mustn't cry.

The other passengers were craning to see what was happening. Melanie said to the men, who looked uneasy and helpless, "I'm not moving, do you hear?" Her eyes were wide with determined hatred.

One of the crew tugged at the conductor's arm. "Look, you can't fight a woman and a kid." They left the car, the conductor reluctant, trailing threats: "Sassy Northern nigger . . . they'll show her what's what in Virginia . . . she won't get away with it there."

Billy was hiccuping with sobs, the tears oozing through his tightly-shut eyes. His fists clenched. Melanie held him tightly. "Don't, baby . . . Mama's here . . . nothing will hurt you . . . don't baby." It was quiet in the train. The clicking of the wheels sounded subdued, futile. Melanie gritted her teeth, and ached from the thumping violence in her heart. I hate . . . I hate . . . I hate. Billy in the South, and little girl Melanie in the South. From her scarred memory came the ghastly resurgence of the scene—her father bleeding on the floor of the hut and with his last breath urging his wife to take Melanie and get out of the South; the anguished words pouring out of her mother, "That's enough—you'll kill him. For Jesus' sake, that's enough." And the white man, stated, "You niggers gotta learn your place. I tell him what's comin' to him—he don't tell me." But he *had* killed him. A little girl of seven, with the first crust of hardness.

Then the Harlem room, her mother coming back bone-tired from the cleaning of white folks' homes. But now the glad renewal was before her, and even on the way to church her step grew lighter. Night after night Melanie watched her mother and the others in the room of intricately-blended smells, thick sweet and rotten: the sweat, the stale sour cooking from below, the exaggerated flower perfumes. Proudly they wore the white, loose angels' gowns, clapping hands and stamping feet to the hot rhythm of the hymns. . . . I been saved all the day, and I'm glad. The voice of the preacher, ear-hurting, sense-beating . . . the moans, the swaying, the testimonials . . . "I been wicked, Lord, but I'm gonna keep my mind steadfast on Jesus."

Billy, exhausted by his sobs, was clutching her in his sleep. Melanie looked at the dull, flat greenness of the passing Virginia fields.

She remembered the awe she had felt in the beginning, and the wild, forgetful soaring from the hymns. But with slow understanding had come pity, then boredom and shame. After that her mother went to church alone.

A few seats ahead a man turned on his portable radio, and Melanie heard the beat of boogie-woogie. This was Harlem singing, singing in the night, Harlem black and red, stepping fast to the crashing of juke-hymns-radio from Swingland and church and whorehouse. Whores they make of us, whores or servants, with music in the night to make us forget.

It was good this hatred; it strengthened and hardened you. The first clear consciousness of it had come in high school, when it had driven her to win prizes and honors. Grimly triumphant, she had silently challenged the white girls: Can you do better? Her turbulence swept fiercely over the people in the moving train, all the white people she had ever known: Can you? Can you?

But then the warning of defeat through loneliness when her mother had first coughed up blood. The pity and love she had buried welled up and spilled over. With her mother she waited at the clinics, watching incredulously, afraid, as day by day the skeletal form emerged. It was then, brooding the long hours in the crowded, antiseptic waiting rooms, that she had first determined to be a doctor. Terror of loneliness had forced a feeling of identity with her people, and then had come the will to fight for them, to succor their poor flesh in the name of her father and her mother.

The train was speeding through the country, hills in the distance vague with the first grayness of night. She wrapped a coat around Billy against the chill, and remembered the winter bleakness at the employment agencies, the hard oblivious eyes . . . we can't do anything for you, don't bother to register . . . no office jobs for colored. So college student Melanie scrubbed the floors of white homes, and medical student Melanie washed the diapers of white babies. Did I discriminate? Was Mrs. Brown's white baby less to me than Bessie's black?

No, Randall, you're wrong. I believed you; to become soft and whole I wanted to believe you. But you're wrong, Randall, wrong. Unto the third and fourth and fifth generations do they destroy us. Why are you fighting, Randall? You've given up everything. Your practice, slowly and patiently built up, it's gone now. And why did we have Billy? My little boy, crying his heart out. You may die, Randall . . . you may die for democracy, die with the white men. My life may be emptied like a white wife's, my boy fatherless like a white boy. But why? For what, Randall?

Billy woke up, restless, fretful. "I'm hungry, mum." Melanie glanced at her watch—7:40. She gave her son the last of the sandwiches and milk. "We'll see Daddy soon, darling."

The train stopped—Richmond, Virginia. Melanie thought tiredly, again it will happen.

The conductor paused at her seat, immensely surprised. "What you doin' here? Didn't you change cars at Washington?" His lips remained stupidly open.

Melanie felt Billy become tense. She stared straight ahead of her, and said evenly, "I saw no reason to change cars. These are the seats I reserved and paid for."

"You saw no reason to change! Why, woman, get out of this car." Incredulity had raised his voice to a high falsetto. His eyes blinked rapidly, and his mouth stayed open.

Melanie wondered dimly if she had the physical strength to oppose this one, too. She clenched the arms of her seat to brace herself.

"You just let her be, buddy. She's had enough." The voice was deep, angry. Melanie looked up. Why, it was a white man, a white man in uniform, thrusting his face challengingly close to the conductor's. She memorized unconsciously the wheat-colored hair and large, firm mouth.

"That's right, leave her alone."

"It's disgraceful, hounding a woman and child like that."

"This is a free country; she's got her rights like anyone else."

But these protests were coming from all over the car! Unbelievingly, Melanie searched the faces nearest her; yes, she had heard the words. The conductor backed away toward the exit, as if afraid to turn his face from this anger. His mouth still open, he left the car.

The soldier watched him until he had gone. Then he raised a finger to his cap in a half salute. "Sorry you've been bothered, ma'am. I should have spoken up before, but. . . ." He stopped, embarrassed by her brimming eyes. "You see, the uniform . . . I wondered if I should . . . then I decided, yes, *because* of the uniform. . . ."

She whispered, "Thank you."

The soldier sat down opposite Billy. "Hello," he said. "I've got a brother about your age. His name is Billy."

"That's *my* name!" said Billy, astonished. He smiled shyly. "We're going to see my pop; he's a soldier, too." And he settled down to talk.

Now Melanie let the tears fall, tasting the salt, her heart slowly easing itself of the heavy burden. You fool, she thought, letting yourself go blind with the old hate. . . . Randall warned you against it . . . save it, he said, save it for the real enemy.

Her mind was washing itself clear now. Never again must she let herself go blind and deaf from the red haze, the wild drumming in the ears. In her paean of hate she had pushed far back in her consciousness the certainty of their friendships, the sure warmth of the many who did not think in terms of black and white. She had ignored, too, her knowledge of the others, her patients—the wives of workers, white and black. She had heard them talk together, borrow and lend of each other, solace each other in pregnancies and childbearing. She had seen their children play together, naturally, as children play.

She turned to the soldier, her voice strong. "It was knowing that I wasn't alone any more that made me cry. And that I could stop hating."

His mouth widened in a smile of admiration, tribute. "You really didn't need help. You'd make a good soldier."

"I come from a tough family." Her pride was in her eyes. "My great-grandfather was a runaway slave, and his son fought against the South in the Civil War. My father was killed fighting for his crop. You see we do need help, we can't get anywhere alone."

"Yes. I often wonder why so many of your men enlist, the way things are."

Melanie spoke with quick eagerness. "That's wrong. Though a while back, I was feeling that way myself. But things are better now than they were. I'm still sitting here, isn't that so? It's the slowness you're thinking of. But now at least we can fight to make it come faster. If we lose this war, we won't be able to fight at all."

The soldier's voice was doubtful. "It's a hard thing for many Negroes to see, and I can't say I blame them. You certainly need a long-range point of view."

"We're fighting for two things." Her words came more slowly now, as if she was clarifying it for herself, too. "We're fighting for a country which does give us a chance to solve our special problems. I know it's slow, but we are not powerless to make things better. While if Hitler wins, we'd be slaves again, and even our friends would find it hard to help us. The other thing is that in fighting Hitler and defeating him, we'd beat those elements that are keeping us down."

The soldier said, "Putting it that way, we're really all in the same boat, I suppose." He got up and held out his hand. "We'll be in camp in a few minutes. I hope I see you there, ma'am."

Melanie clasped his hand. "We'll all meet again soon." And he left.

She hugged Billy tightly, with sudden exuberance. I'm going to the other extreme, she thought, but it's such a relief.

As the train slowed to a stop, Melanie felt herself sharing the general excitement and bustle, and she smiled at her vision of a train crowded with people of many colors, talking together and laughing.

THE CRISIS, JANUARY 1944

Heart against the Wind

GWENDOLYN WILLIAMS

No part of the day is more beautiful than the twilight with its faint tinge of gold left by the sun as it disappeared beyond the horizon. It brings a quietness that rests the very soul; it distills a gentleness upon the world that is the magic of dancing stars and another new moon.

Lys sat at her desk by the window and gazed raptly at the evening sky. It would be dark in another hour; then that lovely pale sky would become inky so that the stars would be as specks of glistening metal and the moon would be all silvery in her flight across the heavens. It would be dark, and she'd be alone again. Alone for how many more nights? Lys's expression changed, and her eyes fell on the letter she had just written Stephen. Stephen! How glad she would be when he came home again. How different she hoped the word "home" would be then. . . .

Dearest Stephen:

How's everything with you? Where are you? Don't tell me; I know. You're far off in a strange land where you will see many wonderful things probably both beautiful and horrid, and I won't be there to share them all with you. You're sorry, aren't you? I wish I were there beside you wading through the mud or whatever it is you wade through at any time.

I didn't write to say that though. I am writing to make an announcement: We are going to have a baby. I waited this long to tell you, because I had to be absolutely certain. And, Stephen, forgive me for being so cruel, but I don't want it. Doesn't that sound bad! You are shocked; I can see the sad shame for me creep into your eyes; then I see you catch your head with your hands as you number the reasons why I should be one of the happiest women in the world. Of course, I picture the whole thing.

So much has happened to change me! You long to know why I don't want our child. First of all he has no heritage. Stephen, a heritage is more than an innate quality—it's a birthright. He has no birthright; he's a little black boy. He can be anything. A doctor, lawyer, businessman, or even an actor or a preacher. He might be a teacher or pull people's teeth without giving them gas. But there are other things: those possibilities must run parallel with hate, prejudice, and any outrage that might occur. If all the unkindness in existence could be erased—

Secondly, he has no country. No, don't take that literally. I suppose what I mean is does his country want him. His ancestors died with the scars of chains and whips upon them, but that was yesterday, and yesterday is dead. Today is important, Stephen. Through the years black men have proved themselves to the country, but the country . . . to be honest, the people of the country have never thanked them for their faithfulness.

The oration at Gettysburg has lived through the ages as a masterpiece; yet those words delivered so hopefully have not had much meaning for the step-citizens of our country. Shall we listen to our son recite them some day? Of course, and he shall weep over their futility. He shall grow up observing the Fourth of July. Truly, we will never tell him that independence is a reality for some and a lie for others. No. We shall hang out the proud flag and pledge allegiance to it. Independence is freedom, so maybe by the time he is eighteen he will be free. A black boy's freedom is measured out by teaspoonsful.

He shall swear by his constitutional rights. He can lick any man who dares him to board a trolley or demands that he sit in the back of a train. He shall spit in the face of fear and want; he shall worship as he chooses whom he chooses, and he shall say what he pleases to say and to the right people. I'm laughing, Stephen.

Gettysburg, July the Fourth, and constitutional rights are ashes. The people who read them have made them so. They have degraded the words associated with them so that they are destroyed surely as if lighted by a match. There was no speech, no declaration; the bill of rights is a hoax. Because it does not work both ways.

Stephen, why are you fighting? It boils down to the fact that you are on a foreign soil to free the enslaved peoples of a foreign land while at home they step on the faces of your brothers. A man can be murdered for no other reason than he is black. We are slaves of a modern age. Who will free us this time that there is no Lincoln and no states seceding from the Union? And we won't stoop to violence because we are a few. And we acknowledge the good privileges we have been permitted.

What difference does it make about the color of a man's skin? A man's a man in spite of that—with ambition, passion, and blood flowing in his veins. All men have a head with hair upon it until neglect or age eats away the roots; and eyes, a nose, a mouth; also every normal body is a trunk with the correct appendages attached. All men have that whether they are white, black, brown, red or foreign. Strip one at random and prove it for yourself.

And women. A woman is subject to the same dangers when she conceives a child and again when she is in labor in spite of her color. The babe in her womb is recipient of the same opportunities to be perfect or afflicted.

All men spring from the same source. Sure, and all men die. There is evidence that no man is superior to another; if he were, his progeny would inherit the earth, and he would be as God, with life everlasting.

Oh, Stephen! I would rather destroy this child and go to hell than to deliver it into a world like this where those who cry democracy and are so prolix in their love of freedom are reeking with hypocrisy. He will have friends, our son, but he will also have foes. And, Stephen, could he fight them!

I'd rather he never know the anguish of being black nor the pride—nor the injustice of being an unsung hero.

Tears stole down Lys's cheeks. She crushed the paper; it dropped short of the wastebasket and made a slight thud on the floor. There it lay until the wind, blowing in the open window, chased it into a corner.

Lys sighed. She lifted another mail form from the box, dipped her pen in the ink. She studied the blank paper for a while. She must write against the thoughts in her heart. Stephen had enough to go through without her writing a lot of foolishness over there to him.

But things were in such a muddle that they didn't even make horse sense. One way you looked at it, it was downright funny: here we are trying to help fight a war and promote a victory for freedom. How do you spell it! What does it mean! There are those who know; and still there are those who believe it is the state of being the boss of everything and everybody this side of tan. It's a lust for power, any kind of power, over the step-citizens of this country. It's the talking against nazis, fascists, and all the other ists, isms, et cetera.

It will be, as it has been, a shame if a country whose people have sworn by Liberty fails to sponsor a fair play program after this great world struggle. How will they curb the laughter if they help to win a struggle for the freedoms of other peoples and changes its spots in the very places where they should not have been for bigger spots.

We all ought to begin now to count the differences that color established in some circles. If we did, Lys wondered, would we be honest enough to apologize for the instances where prejudices were silly?

She began to laugh. It was absurd to realize that a country of such distinguished folks should sponsor a promulgation so like the one it was striving to liquidate. Democracy is an example of a serpent which gorged itself on a supposed prey and didn't find out till too late that it was eating its own tail.

Lives have been forfeited, liberty has been raped, and happiness has been pursued into the gutter.

Lys twisted a button and the room flooded with light. With the light came a fresh point of view, Stephen's point of view: We men will fight for what we have now, that's more than we have had before; it's worth something, but maybe we won't be wrong in expecting some more of that which we honestly deserve.

And there was Stephen, and all black people, in the room.

Her pen touched the paper.

Dearest Stephen,

We are going to be the proud parents, within this year, of a very special citizen. Don't worry about me, everything is going swell.

I've waited so long to tell you because I had to get me straightened out on a few points which you can well guess.

All the folks say howdy and send best wishes for your continued safety. . . .

Love, love, love,
Lys

THE CRISIS, NOVEMBER 1943

All He Needs Is Feet

CHESTER B. HIMES

Ward was walking down the sidewalk in Rome, Georgia, when he came to a white woman and two white men; so he stepped off the sidewalk to let them pass.

But the white man bumped into him anyway, and then turned and said, "What's the matter with you nigger, you want all the street?"

"Now, look, white folks—" Ward began, but the white man pushed him: "Go on, beat it, nigger, 'fore you get in trouble."

"All right, Mr. Hitler," Ward mumbled and started off, but the white man wheeled and grabbed him and spun him about: "What was that last crack, nigger?"

"I din say nothing," Ward replied. "Just cussin' old Hitler."

"You're a damn lie!" the white man snarled. "You called me Hitler and I'll not take that from anybody!"

So he hit Ward on the side of the head. Ward hit the white man back. The other white man ran up, and Ward drew his knife. The woman screamed, and Ward cut the white man on the arm. The other white man grabbed him from behind and Ward doubled forward and wheeled, swinging him off. The first white man kicked Ward in the stomach and Ward stabbed him in the neck. The woman kept screaming until some other white people came running and overpowered Ward.

A policeman came up finally, but by then the mob was too big to handle, so he did the best he could. He said, "Don't lynch him here, take him out in the country."

But the people didn't want to lynch him. He hadn't cut the man so bad, so all they wanted to do was teach him a lesson. A man with a C card[1] furnished some gasoline and they soaked his feet, tied his arms behind him, set his feet on fire, and turned him loose. He ran through the streets with his feet flaming until his shoes had burned off and his feet had swelled twice their normal size with black blisters; then he found an ice wagon and crawled in it and stuck his feet on the ice and fainted.

All up and down the street, the people laughed.

---

1. Ration card.

Two weeks later a doctor came out to the city jail where Ward was serving ninety days for assault with a deadly weapon—a very lenient sentence, the judge had declared—and cut off both his feet.

Ward had a brother in the navy and one in the army and a brother-in-law working in a defense plant in Chicago. They got together and sent him enough money to go to Chicago when he got out of jail.

When his ninety days were up, some church people gave him some crutches, and when he had learned how to use them a little, he caught the train and left. In Chicago, his sister gave him enough money to buy some leather knee pads and he got a job shining shoes and was doing all right.

He bought three $25 war bonds and was saving up money to buy a fourth.

The picture, *Bataan,* was showing in a downtown theatre that week, so one night he took off early and went down to see it. He had heard them talking about this colored man, Mr. Spencer, playing the part of a soldier, and he wanted to see it for himself.[2]

He sat next to the aisle so as not to disturb anybody passing over them, and shoved his crutches underneath his seat. It was a good picture, and he enjoyed it. Just shows what a colored man can do if he tries hard enough, he thought. Now there's that Mr. Spencer, actin' like a sho-nuff soldier, just like the white men in the picture.

But when the picture came to an end, a big, beautiful American flag appeared on the screen, and the stirring strains of the National Anthem were heard. The audience rose rapidly to their feet and applauded.

Ward did not arise.

A big, burly white man, standing behind him, reached down and thumped him on the head. "Stand up, fellow," he growled. "What's the matter with you? Don't you know the National Anthem when you hear it?"

"I can't stand up," Ward replied.

"Why can't you?" the white man snarled.

"I ain't got no feet," Ward told him.

For an instant the white man stood there in a sort of frustrated fury; and then he drew back and hit Ward on the side of the head. Ward fell forward

---

2. *Bataan* was a 1943 film directed by Tay Garnett and starring Robert Taylor, George Murphy, and Desi Arnaz, among others. Kenneth Spencer played the sole African American soldier in the film. This drama was based on an actual Pacific island World War II incident, the Bataan Death March, in which American soldiers were forced on a grueling foot journey by their Japanese captors.

down between the rows of seats, and the white man turned and ran up the aisle toward the exit.

A policeman, who had been standing in the foyer, and had witnessed the incident, grabbed the white man as he came out of the aisle.

"You're under arrest," he said. "What's the trouble, anyway?"

"I just couldn't help it," the white man blubbered, tears running down his cheeks. "I doan understand you people in Chicago; I'm from Arkansas, myself. I just couldn't stand seein' that nigger sitting there while they played the National Anthem—even if he din have no feet!"

THE CRISIS, JUNE 1944

All God's Chillun Got Pride

CHESTER B. HIMES

He is twenty-nine now and he is in the guard-house.

He was guilty.

Simple.

He was twenty-five in 1940 and she was twenty-three, and they had been married since the summer of 1937 and in all that time he had only kept one secret from her. That was a thing he could not tell her; if he had ever told her that they would have both been lost. Because the way had been rocky; dark and rocky. And the only thing that had kept them going was his posed belligerence, his air of bravado, disdain, even arrogance.

As the white girl, Helen, said in 1939, when he had been promoted from labor to research and assigned to work in the public library, "When I first saw you, I said to myself, 'What's this guy doing on his muscle? What have we done to him?' "

But don't condemn him from the start. Because he needed it; he needed being on his muscle, he needed his tight-faced scowl, his high-shouldered air of disdain, his hot challenging stare, his manner of pushing into a pleasant room and upsetting everyone's disposition with the problem that he rolled in front of him, as big and as vicious and as alive as if it was a monster on a chain; he needed all of his crazy, un-called-for and out-of-place defiance, his lack of civility and rudeness; he needed every line of the role he assumed in the morning upon arising and played throughout the day, not even letting down when alone with his wife, the role of swaggering, undaunted, and unafraid, and even ruthlessly through the ever-coming days, through the hard-hurried crush of white supremacy, through the realization of odd identity, through the ever-present knowledge that if he lost the ball no one would pick it up and give it to him; if he ever fell down he'd be trampled, unmercifully, indifferently, without even being thought of, that he was alone and would always be alone without defense or appeal; he needed every ungracious thing he ever did.

Because every morning that he lived, he awakened scared. Scared that this day, maybe, toleration of him would cease; scared that this day, maybe, he would just give up and quit the struggle—what was the use, anyway? What could he hope for? He was tired, so terribly tired; he doubted if he could get through the day; scared not only of his giving up but of his crushing out, scared of saying to himself, "I'm gonna break out of here, I'm gonna crush out this existence of being a black beast in white America; I'm gonna take a running head start and butt a hole through this wall, no matter how thick it is, or I'm gonna splatter my brains from end to end of Euclid." Scared of just being black—that was it. One of the ancient librarians who avoided him as if he were diseased, who refused to hear when he addressed them directly, who were vitriolic when finally replying, who let him stand unattended before their desks while they carried on thirty-minute conversations over the telephone concerning everything under God's sun and would then arise and walk away, who made it as tough as they possibly could, would some day say to him, "Why in heaven's name can't you colored people be patient?" and he would snarl at her right off the very top of his muscle, "Why you-you, why go to hell, you beatup biddy!" And he would be out of a job. All of the Negroes who ever hoped to work in the library project of the WPA[1] in Cleveland, Ohio, would be out of jobs; the whole race would feel it and he would be a traitor not only to himself but to twelve million other people who didn't have a thing to do with it. He'd have to go home and tell Clara that he blew up and lost his job; and God knows they couldn't go hungry anymore. He hated to think of what might happen, because they couldn't take another period of that hungry hopelessness. Or he would go into a store and raise cain because the white clerks would not wait on him and the police would come and he would tell them he was a citizen and they would laugh and take him down to central station and beat his head into a bloody pulp; and the only thing he could do would be just to fight back physically as long as he could. Scared of walking down

---

1. Works Progress Administration. This Roosevelt administration agency put people to work during the Depression with taxpayers' money.

the street and being challenged because some one might think he walked too proudly. Scared of asking for a white man's job; just scared to do it, that's all. Not scared because he might not be able to do it, because he might turn out to be the very best. Nor scared so much of being refused, because being refused was something that he always expected; being black and being refused were synonymous. Being refused had its own particular sensation; not so much scare, not even anger so much—just a dead heavy weight that he must carry, just an eternal pressure, almost too much, but not quite, to bear, impossible to ignore, but too tightly smothering to rebel, too opaque, too constant, too much a part of the identification of color; it was impossible to realize what it would mean not being refused, impossible to visualize the mind outside of this restriction, impossible to rationalize acceptance. Why, good Lord! To cut him loose from the anchoring chains of refusal, he'd go running, jumping mad. As mad as Thomas Jefferson when he wrote, "All men are created equal . . ." As mad as all those crazy, freezing men that crossed the Delaware, fighting for the right to starve—and be independent. As mad as all the other running, jumping, insane people who shoulder through the world as if they owned it, as the women who flounce down Broadway with silver foxes dragging, knowing they are accepted. Mad! He'd go stark, raving mad! Mad as all free people. . . . Just scared to walk in and ask; scared of the act. Why? Why are little children scared to cross the street? Surely they are not scared of what's on the street. Because they have been taught not to; because they know they will get a whipping if they do. And although he tried to get outside this teaching of America, it was inside of him, making him scared. Scared to talk to a white girl, to laugh with her and tell her she was beautiful. Not of being rebuffed; he was a handsome chap and the chances were against his being rebuffed by any woman. Not of being lynched; this was Cleveland, Ohio. They don't hang Negroes in the north; they have other and more subtle ways of killing them. Just scared of talking to her, of the act.

He could not tell this to anyone; especially not to Clara. She was scared, herself; and she couldn't tell him. No Negro can tell another, not even wife, mother, or child, how scared he is. They might discover that they are all scared, and it might get out. And if it ever got out then they wouldn't have but two choices; one would be to quit, and the other would be to die. Whereas now they have three; they have self-delusion. If he told Clara, they wouldn't have had a chance; because what kept her going was thinking he wasn't scared.

So each day, of a necessity, in order to live and breathe, he did as many of these things of which he was scared to do as he could do short of self-destruction. He did them to prove he wasn't scared so the next day he would be able to get up and live and breathe and go down to the library and work as a research assistant with a group of white people.

The necessity of his continuing to live and breathe troubled him to some extent because he could not really understand it. Having been educated in America, he had learned of course that living and breathing, unaccompanied by certain other inalienable rights, such as liberty, and the pursuit of happiness, were of small consequence; but he had learned, also, that this ideology did not apply to him. He never really sat down and thought about it for any length of time; because he knew that if he ever did, living in America would become impossible. That if he ever made an honest crusade into abstract truth and viewed Negroes and whites in physical, spiritual, mental comparison, detached from false ideologies and vicious, man-made traditions, dwelling only on those attributes which made of what he saw a man, and not of what his forebears might have been nor what he claimed to be by race, he would see, aside from pigmentation of skin and quality of hair, little difference in anatomy, mentality, and less difference in soul. He would see the same flesh, the same bones, the same blood, the same ability to walk upright, differentiating them all from other, and supposedly lower species of animals, the same organs of reproduction; he would see the same false convictions, taught by the same teachers and learned in the same way; the same capacity for good and evil, for viciousness and generosity, for lust and philanthropy; he would see the passions in both compelling them to rape, steal, maim, murder; he would see the impelling urge for wealth, the destructive desires for power, the seeds of untold lies and the skeletons of deceits; he would see the same knowledge gleaned from the same founts; and when he looked into their souls and saw all the rotted falseness of ideologies imposed upon them all so that the few of any race could live and fatten from the blood, sweat, and tears of the many of all races, all the corruption of religions and philosophies and laws by which they all chained themselves to spiritual and physical slavery, and dedicated their offsprings for untold generations to ever-recurring horrors, for the life of him, God be his solemn judge, he could not have told the black from the white.

And after that, after he had seen the truth sheared of all the falseness of tradition and ideology, there would have been nothing to have done with that "nigger" but to have taken him out and shot him.

But he did not ever seek the conviction of his truth—or its strength; he let it remain vague and unexplored in the fastness of his mind like some hidden, vicious monster that would destroy him once it was released. He never once opened *that* door, although he opened many others. Simply because he was scared; that was all—just scared.

His name was Keith Richards, but people called him "Dick." He was about five-nine, weighed between one-fifty-five and one-sixty, and walked with a stiff-backed swagger. He had never had more than two good suits of clothes and one good pair of shoes since he had been grown, but he always managed to look well-groomed, perhaps because he was handsome. His complexion was black and he had features like an African prince, and when he forgot his scowl and accidentally laughed, he came on like bright lights.

Women could have loved him if he had given them a chance, but illness and poverty had thrown him mostly into contact with white women and he had always been on his muscle. He seldom relaxed enough for them to get to know him.

He had often wondered why Clara Street had married him; she was a really beautiful girl. She could have married any one of a number of handsome and very well-to-do men of all races; and why she chose to string along with him, a rebel more or less who had been kicked out of college in his sophomore year and who didn't know how to do anything at all but starve, he never knew. He could sketch a little and he dabbled in water colors and occasionally he wrote a feature article for one of the weekly newspapers; but this did not make him extraordinary—there are a million Negro youths with that much talent on the ball.

So he was a little scared of this, also. Some day some crazy impulse would prompt him to touch it, to prod into it to see if it was real, to search for its dimensions and perspective, to see if it was another practical joke the white folks were playing on him, and he would discover that Clara was not there at all, and that Negroes were even denied the emotion of love and the holy state of matrimony.

At first their marriage had been a series of shabby rooms, somehow anchoring their sordid struggle for existence—for bare existence; room rent when it was due and enough food for each meal coming up. Not once during all that time did they buy any salt, nor sugar either until each landlady learned to keep hers put away. Just a dark-brown-toned plane of nothingness no deeper than sex relationship on which they lay as darker silhouettes while time pushed them on, not as individuals, separate identities, but as an infinitesimal part of universal change.

At times they got drunk together and imagined things. This was the best, the highest they could reach in the dark-brown-toned pattern—this imagining. It was something burnished—almost silver, almost gold; really it was brass. When they both caught it at the same time, it was beautiful in a way. All the pageantry and excitement and luxuriousness of rich white life in white capitalism was there—the Rainbow Room and the Metropolitan Opera, Miami and Monte Carlo, deluxe liners and flights by night. And doing things, noble, heroic, beautiful things for her—"Because I love you." . . . Things he had been taught to desire from birth—denied him before he was born.

Because I love you. . . . If I really loved you, baby, I would blow out your brains. Right now! Because all you can ever look forward to, baby, is never having nothing you ever dreamed about. Low lights and soft music, luxury and ease, travel and pleasure—*acceptance!* Not for you, baby, not for us. We got dipped in the wrong river, baby, we got dipped in the mud. Your soul might be white as snow; but the color of your soul doesn't count in America, baby.

However, all that was before he got on WPA. He wasn't born on WPA as in after years white industrialists seemed to think when he applied for work. During the first year of their married life he had several jobs—busboy in a hotel dining room, porter in a drug store; he even tried writing policy,[2] but the players didn't like him. He couldn't show the proper degree of sympathy when some one played 341 and 342 came out. It was a dirty clip racket as far as he could see and he felt sorry for them. And that just didn't do. The pickup man took his book one day, and he told Clara, "We should have been on the other end."

The best job he had was one at the Country Club in the spring of 1939. He was serving drinks in the tap room. But it was hard to take. When the members got in their cups, all their white supremacy came out. They were very, very white when they got drunk.

He could have borne their disgustingness, for after all that didn't prove their racial superiority. They were no more disgusting when drunk than the Negroes down on Scovil avenue in the prostitution area. He could even have put up with their "mammies"; their dear old "black mammies" who raised them, and in later years gave cause to, and proof of, the fact that all white people love Negroes. He came to feel that a white person without a "black mammy" just didn't count. And the exhibitions of odd and unusual sex presented by some of the members in their stages of drunkenness did not shock him, nor even disturb him—he could see this coming up and dodge.

But what finally got him and drove him away from a really good job; a job where all he had to do to earn his ten and fifteen dollars in tips every night

---

2. Playing the numbers; gambling.

was just to be a nigger; what finally gnawed him down to a jittery wreck was the fear that he might take a drink of Scotch some day and it would go to his head and make "that nigger crazy" and he could pull Mr. John Sutter Smythe out from under the table and ask him, "Look, Mr. Smythe, just what makes you think you are so superior to me?"

He quit the night Mr. Hanson told the joke about an old "black mammy," her daughter, and the white traveling salesman. If Mr. Hanson's wife and daughter had not been present, and a number of other members and their wives, he would never have repeated it a year later to white women on WPA who insisted that white men treat Negro women with the greatest respect and chivalry—because it was really a dirty story.

"You understand, Miss Wilson," he apologized at the end, "I would not have dared tell you such a story if I had not heard a respectable white gentleman tell it in the presence of a number of respectable white gentlewomen."

Miss Wilson got up and walked away.

But he had not told her the most important part. The most important part was simply that after having listened to the joke, after having remained until it was too late to leave, having allowed himself to be maneuvered into a position where he had either to be a fool or a coward, he turned and went inside the office and quit.

He could have stepped over to the table, picked up some "blunt instrument" as the prosecution says, and knocked Mr. Hanson unconscious. But that would have given him three beatings and a sentence of one to twenty years for assault with intent to kill; and he would have not been released under the twenty years unless Mr. Hanson had relented, and that was to say the least, unlikely.

On the other hand it was also a matter of the value of his pride. It was problematical from the first whether his pride was worth all of those beatings and twenty years to boot. Or if it was worth it, whether he was prepared to spend that much to keep it.

Now the value of pride is something that either goes up or down with the passing of years. Keith's went up. Some time during his wearing of the proud uniform of a soldier in the Army of the United States it went priceless.

Keith is in the guard-house now.

U.S. Army Nurses in Australia, *The Crisis,* **April 1944**

NEGRO STORY, DECEMBER–JANUARY 1944–1945

Something for the War

ESTA DIAMOND

It was a good day. June, but it had the snap and tanginess of early October. Lily liked it better this way than when it got so hot and muggy everything stuck to you, and you couldn't whisk through your work in record time, and the heat robbed you of all your energy.

Lily worked quickly in the clean white kitchen, slicing bread for dinner in one heap, and bread for sandwiches for Mrs. Lloyd's committee in another heap. Then she concentrated on the second heap, trimming the crusts deftly, and cutting the slices into narrow little strips, some of which she spread with cheeses, and some with anchovy paste. She arranged them prettily on a platter and took them into the living room. Mrs. Lloyd smiled approvingly at Lily, indicating that she wanted the platter on the coffee table. Then she went on talking to the members of her Red Cross committee, Mrs. Doodall, Mrs. Flynn, and Mrs. Keen.

"But we must do something about the group," Mrs. Lloyd said. "Hardly anyone shows up at bandage rolling any more. They just don't seem interested."

"Yes," said Mrs. Keen. "I'm afraid they've gotten used to the war, and it just doesn't excite them any more, they don't feel a call to arms, so to speak."

Mrs. Doodall didn't say anything, just nodded her head up and down in violent approval, the little green and blue parrot on the brim of her hat bobbing and dipping agitatedly.

Mrs. Flynn watched Lily with obvious envy as she walked across the deep-piled golden rug back to the kitchen.

"Wanda," Lily heard her say to Mrs. Lloyd as the kitchen door swung slowly back and forth. "You don't know how lucky you are with that maid. So polite, so efficient, and *so* attractive."

Lily smiled and hummed a little bit to herself. She liked it here. Mrs. Lloyd was pleasant and always let Lily know when a dinner was well executed, a new cake particularly good, or a flower arrangement attractively done. The pay was good, too, and Mrs. Lloyd herself furnished the uniforms, gray for the morning and early afternoon, and black with a starched white apron for late afternoon and evening. The white set off the rich coffee color of her skin and the lustrous blackness of her eyes and hair.

Lily got the ice cubes out of the refrigerator and put two cubes in each of four glasses. Mrs. Lloyd would appreciate her common sense in using only two cubes apiece in such cool weather. She filled the glasses with fruit punch and floated half a strawberry in the top of each glass.

"Yes," Mrs. Keen was saying as Lily came out with the punch, "that's an excellent idea. We can set aside two bridge tables for bandage rolling, and then rotate the bridge players. Then everyone will spend about half of the afternoon playing bridge, and half rolling bandages."

"That's settled, then," said Mrs. Lloyd. "Now what about a date? It should be week after next."

"How about Monday?"

"No. You couldn't get enough people on Monday. They're usually too done in after the weekend."

"That looks fine, Lily," said Mrs. Lloyd and Lily murmured "Thank you, ma'am" and glided back to the kitchen.

She was washing the dishes when she heard Mrs. Lloyd call her.

"Yes?" she said, standing just inside the room.

"Lily, come here," said Mrs. Lloyd. "I want to ask a special favor."

Lily walked into the room and stood politely in front of Mrs. Lloyd. She felt that Mrs. Lloyd was showing her off, showing off her own good fortune in having this maid when the other women were forever having maid trouble.

"Lily, you know the kind of work our little group does, Red Cross war work?"

"Yes, ma'am."

"Well, Lily, we're trying to arrange a very important meeting of the group, and we can't get them together on any day but Thursday, that is a week from this Thursday."

They both waited, then Mrs. Lloyd went on.

"I hate to ask you to give up your day off, but this is very important, and you can take Wednesday instead."

Lily lowered her eyes in embarrassment. She hated to refuse, in front of all these people. She wished Mrs. Lloyd had waited to ask her when they were alone.

"I'm sorry, ma'am, but I'm busy on Thursday."

Mrs. Lloyd smiled tolerantly. "But surely you can make some arrangement? This is really very important, Lily. It's for the war, you know."

"I know, ma'am," said Lily, "but—well, this is, too."

Mrs. Lloyd's eyebrows flew up in inquiry.

Lily hated to explain before the whole committee.

"You see, ma'am, we have a little group in the building I live in, and we do whatever we can—most of us has husbands or boy friends in the service. Sometimes we wrap packages for them, or write letters, and week from Thursday we're going to give blood."

"But, Lily," said Mrs. Flynn, forgetting that this was Mrs. Lloyd's affair in her excitement at finding a flaw in the perfect maid. "Lily, you can go there on Wednesday."

"No," said Lily, "we going in a group, together. That way we gets the most people to go."

"Suppose we discuss it later, Lily," Mrs. Lloyd said kindly. "I'm sure we can find a way of managing it, and," she turned to the other three, "I'll call you tonight and let you know what Lily and I have arranged."

She dismissed Lily with a sweet smile, but Lily stood there, her eyes wide with nervousness.

"Really, ma'am, I can't do it."

"That will be all now, Lily" said Mrs. Lloyd, flushing slightly.

Lily went.

"Well," she heard Mrs. Flynn say, as the kitchen door swung softly to and fro, to and fro. "Well!!"

"Still," said Mrs. Doodall, "you have to admire her for donating blood." There was a pause and then Mrs. Doodall continued. "There was so much talk about it, but I just can't remember. They wouldn't give Negro blood to our boys, would they?"

Then the kitchen door stopped swinging and remained shut, and it was very, very quiet in the clean white kitchen.

THE CRISIS, OCTOBER 1945

The Black Streak

OCTAVIA B. WYNBUSH

"And you won't go, mother?"

Lucia Manton leaned eagerly forward from the cushions on the long, rust-colored divan and stared hard and expectantly at the slight, brown-haired woman standing across the room, framed in the exquisite lace curtains through which the late afternoon sun, streaming in, illuminated the woman's lovely profile.

The beautifully-cared-for hand grasping one edge of the curtain tightened; the face turned more resolutely toward the window, as Marianna Manton shook her sleekly-groomed head a determined no.

"Mother, you're wrong, so very wrong!"

Springing from the divan, Lucia moved in graceful slenderness across the thickly padded Oriental rug, and stood beside her mother. Gently the girl covered the hand on the curtain with her own.

"Don't try to persuade me!"

Marianna's hand slid down from the curtain, found its mate, and twined with it tightly. She turned her face fully to the window. Through a blur of quick tears, her eyes fixed on what hung before her.

Drawing back the curtain, Lucia stepped closer to her mother, then let the curtain fall into place, so that they were both framed within its folds. Her eyes, too, rested on the emblem hanging in the window.

For two years it had hung there, a blue star, bravely saying, "He will come back some day." A month ago yesterday, it had changed to gold.[1]

"Grant would want you to go, mother."

The last, slanting rays of the sun, gold sparkling her brown hair, caught the frown that wrinkled Marianna's high, fair forehead, scintillated the icy fire that flared quickly in her gray eyes, and splashed more deeply the sudden red which encarmined her cheeks

"Don't say that!" she rasped.

Lucia sighed. A more tactful daughter would have known how to handle this difficult mother. But Lucia had never been known for tact.

"You know he would, mother."

There was no gentle, tactful persuasion in the girl's tone. Her words rang with a passionateness which, although controlled, was plainly evident.

Marianna's brow straightened; the icy fire flickered out before astonishment, and the crimson faded from her cheeks. Really, this could not be her daughter, Lucia, speaking in such a tone to her. Tactless, Lucia always had been, but quiet and deferentially worshipful, at all times; always seeing eye to eye with her parents—after a little persuasion.

Disengaging her hands from her daughter's, Marianna pushed aside the curtains and, with all the stateliness her five feet four inches could command, she stalked across the dim room to the long, wide mahogany desk that occupied much of the center floor space. Flicking on the fluorescent desk lamp, she slipped into the desk chair, and began nervously thumbing through a neat pile of typed manuscript.

---

1. A gold star signified death of a soldier.

Slowly Lucia followed her mother. Perching herself on the opposite side of the desk, she rested one foot on the floor, and began swinging the other deliberately back and forth. What she had to say did not come readily, and her mother was giving her no cooperation whatever.

"You see, mother, it's getting awfully awkward for me."

"And why should it be getting awkward for you?" petulantly snapped Marianna, as she snatched a disarranged sheet of the manuscript back into place. She did not, however, look up at Lucia.

"Well, the kids at school are saying things."

"What things?"

"Oh—things. Innuendoes, I guess you'd call them, if older, more refined people said them, but the kids at High aren't very old, and they're not very refined. They just crash things down on your head—like—like—"

"Yes?"

This time Marianna looked up, as Lucia's sentence faded into the stillness of the room.

"I didn't mean to go at it like this, mother, but today one of the girls at the table where I sat in the cafeteria spoke up and said that she thought it a shame when the whole world is fighting for democracy that some people right here in Homeville were so darn color-crazy they couldn't forgive a black girl for marrying into their family, even—even—after her husband had been killed."

"She said that to you?" Marianna's voice seemed thin and far away.

"Not *to* me, mother, but *at* me. When I got up and left, she pretended that she didn't know I was at the table, but everybody there knew better. Everybody knew she meant us, because—because Sylphania's the only— dark girl, and Grant's the only—"

Lucia's voice choked, and her sentence remained suspended.

With one delicate hand Marianna waved the incident away—completely away. As her hand moved in the graceful arc of the gesture, it passed through the light cast by the desk lamp. How beautiful my hand is, thought Marianna gazing for an enraptured second at that member, and how fair. How very transparent it is, in this light.

"Don't let those ignorant children at High worry you, Lucia. I'm sorry that you have to be thrown with them, but it's your father's idea, not mine, that you go to public school. If I had my way, you'd be in a good boarding school."

Leaning forward, Marianna lifted her pen from its bronze stand, and held it tentatively over the first page of the manuscript.

"Now, run along like a good, dear child, I must finish proofing my speech.

You know, I have to deliver it before the Interracial Committee tomorrow night."

Lucia smiled—a sour, comprehending smile. Such an old dodge! Didn't her mother know that she couldn't work it forever on a sixteen-year-old miss? And, too, the speech had been proofed three days ago, and she, Lucia, had helped with the proofing.

"I'm not going, mother, until we talk this thing through."

Marianna stretched out her hand to put the pen back into place. Her eyes fixed on Lucia, she missed the stand twice before the pen was safely lodged. If ten years could miraculously disappear, she would put this fractious youngster across her knee, and settle the argument with a well-placed slipper.

"Just what is there to talk about? I've said my say."

"After all, mother, Sylphania is Grant's wife, and Grant's your son, and my brother. I say *is*, because, to me, his being dead doesn't change the relationship. And Sylphania's still his wife."

A bitter smile wreathed the corners of Marianna's mouth. She would never forget the resentment which had run through her deepest grief like a discordant note; resentment over the fact that it was through a telephone message from the father of her son's wife that she had learned of the boy's death. The circumstance had served to impress the one fact that she was trying so hard to erase. That Grant had married this black girl. Marianna propped her elbows on the desk, twined her fingers together, and pressed them against her forehead.

Slowly Lucia moved a hand over the highly-waxed surface of the desk. As her hand came within the glow of the light, she involuntarily compared it with her mother's hands, twined so tightly together. Lucia's hands were alabaster; Marianna's, a warm ivory with the soft patina of age.

"You shouldn't hate Silly and her people, mother, just because they're black."

"I don't hate them. It's—it's just—"

Marianna's voice trailed off. Her hands gestured vaguely.

Lucia swung herself down from the desk and faced her mother. The sudden movement forced Marianna to look up.

How like her father the girl looks now, thought the mother. The way her hair grows in a widow's peak from her slightly rounding forehead, with its vertical wrinkle; the black eyes aflame with inward lightning; the slightly flaring nostrils quivering with emotional stress; the firm, slightly square chin thrust out just now in unfamiliar defiance makes her look more like her father than ever.

"Look, mother!" Lucia's little fist beat the desk. "All that was good in your day—I guess—when you were growing up, I mean. Color must have been about all there was to make a distinction, wasn't there? I'm just guessing, you know. I mean—it must have been that the people who had the best chance got it because of color—Oh, I can't know what made it that way here, in Homeville."

Lucia paused, hoping that her mother would help her, but Marianna merely regarded the girl with hard, unfriendly eyes.

Lucia stumbled on, "I recall hearing Aunt Carlotta boast, when I was little, that all the 'elite' could trace their ancestry back to some of the best—white folks—in the state. That must be why we considered ourselves so much better than the dark colored people—being able to wear the bar sinister."

"Lucia, I never thought I would live to hear my own daughter talk in such a vulgar manner!"

"I'm not being vulgar. I'm just talking the way everything is done nowadays. Straight and plain. I think it's downright shameful the way this family has behaved to Silly and her folks. When the whole world's talking about democracy."

"Democracy! If democracy means I have to wallow with all sorts of people because I am unfortunate enough to have, somewhere, a black ancestor—"

"Being nice to Silly's folks is not wallowing, mother! They're respectable and well-thought-of."

"Silly! Such a common, made-up name. Her real name is bad enough, but a nick-name like Silly!"

"Grant liked it. In fact, he gave it to her."

Lucia's voice lowered to its usual cultivated pitch; her lips trembled, as she added, "and he would have adored Grant, junior, I'm sure."

Marianna looked sharply at Lucia. "Have you seen—the baby?" she demanded.

"Only at a distance. I've never been to the house, because you told me not to go."

Marianna nodded, a smugly complacent nod. Lucia was still her obedient, unquestioning child.

"The day I saw Sylphania," Lucia went on, "she was coming down Main street, with the baby in her arms. When she got sight of me she turned into Roswell's store. I feel sure she did so just to avoid meeting me. And now, the baby is sick."

Marianna stirred uncomfortably. Lucia was back where she had started.

It was the news of the baby's illness, conveyed to her by one of her high school friends, which had begun this argument.

"It's nothing serious, I'm sure," Marianna said. "All babies get sick some time."

"Helen said he's pretty sick, mother. Even if he weren't sick, we ought to go call on his mother, especially since he's all we've got to remind us of Grant. It's the only decent thing to do, don't you think?"

The jangling of the telephone bell in the hall cut off any reply that Marianna might have made.

"Answer it, please, Lucia. Katie doesn't like to be interrupted when dinner is so nearly ready, and I'm quite fatigued, myself."

Marianna's face took on that peaked, exhausted look which usually brought her family to her feet. Lucia slipped swiftly into the hall. Marianna sighed and sat back in her chair. Closing her eyes, she gave herself over to her thoughts.

Words of her quadroon mother[2] came floating back over the still years. "Keep 'em on their own side of the fence, girls. If you once let the bars down, you can't put 'em back up again. You can't rub a black streak out, and we don't want any more great-grandmother Janes in this family."

Great-grandmother Jane, the bete noir of the family; great-grandfather Hugh's black African wife. Marianna had never seen her, but she had often shuddered at the vivid description given by her own mother. Every generation, since great-grandmother Jane's day, had feared the black streak that might, at any time, show up in some child.

Sister Carlotta had borne no children, because of her mortal fear of the streak. Toni, brother John's third child, possessing the most beautiful features and the loveliest hair that had ever been known in the family, was a constant problem to the others. She could never accompany her parents, or her brothers and sisters on any of their excursions to theatres, restaurants or other places where a dark skin would not be countenanced. Lucia, herself, had barely escaped. There had been no more children for Marianna after Lucia. The risk was too great. And Sylphania, Grant's widow, had brothers. Lucia must be protected. The bars must be kept up.

"Mother, you haven't heard a word that I've said!"

With a quick jerk of her shoulder muscles, Marianna returned to consciousness of her surroundings.

"What is it?" she queried, looking up.

---

2. *Quadroon* is a term, rarely used today, that indicates a person had one-quarter African heritage.

"The telephone, mother."

"Oh, yes." Marianna started to rise. "Who wants me? Nobody? Then why interrupt me?"

"Helen just telephoned to say that the baby died a few minutes ago."

Frozen into a half-sitting, half-standing position, Marianna stared at Lucia, down whose cheeks a rivulet of tears was coursing.

"Surely you'll go now, mother?"

Keep the bars up—once they are down—the black streak—Sylphania's brothers—Grant gone—Lucia alone left.

"No!"

"Mother!"

With an angry twirl of her short skirt, Lucia swung around and started for the hall door.

Marianna sprang up.

"Lucia!" she cried, amazement, anger and authority struggling for mastery in her voice. "Lucia, come back here!"

The answer came in a furious stamp of running feet on the hall stairway, and the faint sound of an upstairs door being slammed.

Marianna walked swiftly to the hall door, looked up the stairway, and opened her mouth to call out. However, her habitual restraint, her distaste for scenes and the thought that Katie, in the kitchen, would know that something was unusually wrong with this well-conducted household overmastered her impulse. A step or two more took her to the foot of the stairs. Tentatively she placed her hand on the newel post, stood undecided a moment longer, then, turning slowly, walked back into the living room and sank down in the chair before her desk.

"She'll throw herself on her bed, have a good cry, and be herself again by the time Katie serves dinner." Marianna spoke aloud, in the manner of one who is trying to convince herself by the sound of her own voice. She rested her elbows on her desk once more, twined her fingers, and pressed her forehead against them.

In her heart there was a strange mix-up of emotions. She was sorry and she was glad. Sorry because her son, Grant, had married a black woman. Sorry because Grant was dead. Sorry for the grief of the black woman for her dead baby. Of course, she was sorry for that; but glad, darkly glad, that the baby who, she had heard, was very brown, would no longer hold a claim upon the Manton family. Lucia—

Running footsteps descending the stairs broke in upon Marianna's thoughts. Lucia had recovered quickly, too quickly. Marianna raised her head. The hall light was on. Lucia, hatted and coated, drawing on her gloves, flashed past.

Quickly Marianna got to her feet.

"Lucia!" she called, knocking against the side of the desk in her haste to reach the hall.

"Lucia!"

Marianna stood panting in the hall, staring at her daughter, who was turning the door knob.

"Where are you going, Lucia?"

"Out, mother! Definitely, out!"

Lucia wrenched the door open as she spoke, letting in the sharp, tangy autumn air.

"Where? Tell me!"

Marianna was at the door, grasping Lucia's hand, as it held the knob.

The girl turned her face to her mother. Dark lightings quivered and flashed in Lucia's black eyes.

"It seems to me, mother, that a woman of your intelligence could answer that question with very little trouble."

It was but for a moment, the clashing of wills in the looks that were exchanged. In that moment a battle was fought and won. Marianna knew that never again would Lucia give unthinking obedience to her mother.

Slowly her hand dropped; slowly she turned and walked back into the living room. As she crossed the threshold, the outer door slammed decisively shut. Marianna crossed to the window. By the light of the street lamp directly in front of the gate, she watched Lucia's quickly retreating figure until it vanished from her sight.

Sighing, Marianna walked back to her desk and sat down. For a long while she slumped there, eyes closed, brows drawn in a black frown. Her fingers, thrashing about on the desk, finally touched the manuscript. Opening her eyes, Marianna drew the first sheet toward her. The speech. It wouldn't hurt to go through it again. A reading would help quiet her nerves.

Page by page she re-read the manuscript. Little by little the frown erased itself from her brows, and her lips relaxed their grim tautness. When she reached the last page, her face was clear and complacent.

"This," she murmured, "is a perfect ending. The best I've ever written."

In a half-whisper, she read the concluding paragraph aloud: "And finally, there can be no real peace, no successful realization of democracy until all people, everywhere, learn to look beneath the accidents of birth, creed and color, and find the man in God's own likeness hidden there."

NEGRO STORY, JULY–AUGUST 1944

Justice Wears Dark Glasses

GRACE W. TOMPKINS

The gray-haired man had a kind face, thought Mamie. He would believe her. He removed his glasses and slowly polished them as she nervously shifted from one foot to the other. The big man's hold on her arm tightened as she cleared her throat in an attempt to speak. Carefully replacing his glasses, the man behind the desk spoke, "Yes, Spraggins?"

"Another one, sir. Stole two dresses."

"I—I—," Mamie's voice died away.

"What are you trying to say?" The man's voice was gentle.

"Mistuh . . . I never stole anything. Just wanted to try on the dresses . . ."

"Salesgirl saw her duck, sir, caught her with them. Here they are." Spraggins laid the dresses on the desk.

"Yes, sir. I mean, no . . ." Mamie's voice mounted to a wail.

"She wouldn't let me try them on. I asked her and she . . ."

The gray-haired man held up his hand for silence. He pushed one button in the long row that edged the glass-topped desk. Then he began to write rapidly on a pad of paper. A young woman came in. He detached the sheet and handed it to her, and she left.

An agonizing twitch had set up in Mamie's stomach. She scratched her head nervously and shifted her weight again. The silence only increased her terror. Spraggins cleared his throat, and the sound echoed like a shot in the room.

The man at the desk had not once looked in her direction. She stared hard, trying to catch his eye. You know I didn't steal them, she thought. You're just trying to scare me. She didn't want to wait on me. I didn't steal . . . you know I didn't steal . . . she didn't want to wait on me. . . . The sentences chased each other around and around in Mamie's mind, but her throat was dry and not a word came out.

The office door opened, and the young woman returned with two more. Mamie recognized the salesgirl, but she had never seen the other one.

"Miss Donovan, did you see this theft?"

"Yes, Mr. Feldman."

Mamie was bewildered, for the reply had come from the strange woman.

"And you, too?" He turned to the salesgirl.

"Yes, sir." Her reply was hardly audible, and she reddened.

Mamie found her voice: "No, no. . . . You said I had to ask the floorwalker, and when I tried to talk to him, this man brought me up here!"

"A likely story!" The man behind the desk no longer looked kind and gentle. "You're not only a thief but a liar too. Here are three witnesses who saw you take them. We're going to teach you . . . you folks to stay out of Manson's and there's just one way to do it!"

He nodded to Spraggins, who immediately caught Mamie by the arm and started for the door. She struggled.

"What are you going to do? What—!" Her voice ended in a cry as a vicious upward jerk of her bent arm put an abrupt end to the struggle.

They went down in the freight elevator and out the side door to the rotunda. The blue of the patrol wagon made her wonder who was being arrested. And then she was hustled unceremoniously between two big rough policemen, and the grilled door was slammed shut.

The flies buzzing around a spittoon held Mamie's eyes as she plucked and twisted a corner of her jacket. The mumbled words of the bondsman were lost in the roar of the blood pounding in her ears. A colored policeman stopped to talk to the bondsman. A hopeful gleam lighted Mamie's pain-dulled eyes, but died quickly as the man laughed and sauntered away. After a long wait, she was free to go home until Monday morning. The bondsman had her lone ten dollar bill in his pocket.

On reaching the street, she found that she did not have carfare. It was a long way to 33rd Street, but she did not have the courage to ask anyone for eight cents. After the first ten blocks she walked in a pain-ridden daze. Passers-by thought she was drunk. A man flung a coarse remark at her.

Lena saw her coming and ran down the rickety steps to meet her.

"Mamie! You're sick!"

"I've been arrested."

"Arrested? Jesus!"

Lena helped her into the stuffy bedroom and began taking her street things off. She finally got her to sleep.

Mamie awoke refreshed. Then she remembered, I have to go to court Monday. They arrested me for stealing. I had better get a lawyer, but I haven't any money. She had a strange empty kind of feeling. Lena came in.

"Get dressed," she said. "We're going to see Mr. Clark."

"I ain't got no money to get no lawyer."

"He'll take it in payments. You can't let 'em get away with this."

"They can't do nothin'. I didn't steal them dresses."

"They had you arrested, didn't they? It's a lousy frame! They framed you 'cause they don't want colored people in their damn store. It shoulda been me! You just ain't no fighter!"

"What could I do? The big man grabbed me before you could say 'scat,' and the boss man thought I was lying. Both them women lied. I never even seen the big one with the yellow hair."

"It's a lousy frame. A damn lousy frame!" said Lena.

Mr. Clark was both ponderous and suave. Much of what he said was so veiled in legal terminology that it went over Mamie's head.

"Of course Illinois has a Civil Rights Law under which you may sue when exonerated. Now if you sue for punitive damages the court may award you a dollar. What the hell? It won't pay back what you lose. AND . . . you could go right back in the store again tomorrow and the same thing might happen again. Now if you sue to obtain revocation of license you won't get to first base. And of course that's all based on your being exonerated."

Mamie looked perplexed.

"Now if they find you guilty . . ."

"But I ain't," she interrupted him.

"I know, I know," his voice was soothing, "but the law's a funny thing. If those women and the store detective testify under oath that they saw you, then it's your word against three. Of course we can produce character witnesses. Now if you'll . . ."

Court was crowded. Mamie's case was near the end of the docket. Her lawyer sat importantly inside the railing with half a dozen others. She listened carefully to each case, to the testimony of witnesses, to the pleas of the attorneys. Lena patted her hand reassuringly. After six cases in a row had been dismissed for lack of sufficient evidence, she took heart and relaxed a little.

"Manson versus Mamie Jones, shoplifting. Mamie Jones!"

Mamie got to her feet trembling and walked through the enclosure.

As she looked in the face of the judge, her fear left her. To her right stood Spraggins, the two women, and another elderly man, counsel for the store. Her pastor and her doctor had joined her lawyer on the left. Lena stood directly behind her with a protective hand resting on her shoulder. The judge was white-haired, and his seamed face was calm. There was an amused twinkle in his eyes as he looked at her, and she almost smiled at him.

Her fear gone, she told her story in a clear steady voice. The judge nodded sympathetically several times as she talked. Then the strange blond woman was talking. She said that she had watched Mamie paw through the dresses on the counter, walk around a bit and return to the counter. Mamie had taken two dresses and started away.

"Did you say anything to her?" asked the judge.

"No. I thought she was going to approach a salesgirl and try the dresses on."

"Then what happened?"

"She looked around in a furtive sort of way and then started in the direction of the ladies' washroom."

"No . . . I don't even know where the washroom . . ." began Mamie.

"Please," said the judge.

"A salesgirl accosted her," continued the woman. "And she broke into a run. Mr. Spraggins caught her."

Mamie stared fascinated at the woman as she talked clearly with every evidence of telling the truth. The salesgirl corroborated every word. Spraggins said he had seen the commotion and had arrived in time to see Mamie drop the dresses to the floor.

As Mr. Clark began to talk, Mamie felt a surge of relief.

"Your Honor, this woman had no need to steal. She entered the store in good faith with a ten dollar bill to buy two of the dresses advertised at $3.99 in the basement sale. She was treated with discourtesy, denied the privilege of trying on her selection, roughly handled by the store detective and the floor walker, and called a liar and a thief by the manager. This woman is respectable. Her reputation is unimpeachable as these three witnesses will affirm. It is quite obvious that Manson's is trying to intimidate the Negroes who insist upon trading in the store when their publicized policy is not to wait upon colored people."

The last statement brought a quick reprimand and a warning from the judge. He waived the testimony of the character witnesses, and Mamie felt satisfied that she had won.

The lawyer for Manson's was speaking: "For the past six months, there has been a wave of petty thieving in the store. Women's apparel sections are the hardest hit. We have got to stop it. This woman was caught red-handed. Probably inexperience made her unsuccessful in making away with the merchandise without detection. But the fact remains that three people say the attempt was made. Manson's must make an example of her and deter the others with whom she may be associated."

The judge was nodding sympathetically. He turned inquiringly toward Mr. Clark, but the lawyer had nothing to add. The court was very quiet. Mamie was sure everyone could hear the pounding of her heart against her ribs. Then the judge began to speak and his voice was low and friendly: "I do not believe you are an habitual thief. You work. That is to your credit. Your friends are here in defense of your character as they know it. That is also in your favor. The morale of their working staff must be preserved. I cannot believe that three witnesses have lied under oath. In view of the facts as presented, I have no alternative but to find you guilty and sentence you to thirty days in jail."

In the ante-room, Abe Clark was saying, "My fee is thirty-five dollars. I have a note here for the amount. Will you sign it, please?"

Mamie signed.

THE CRISIS, MAY 1944

"Whatsoever Things Are Lovely"
FLORENCE MCDOWELL

Saturday afternoon was on Seventh avenue. Lavinia Randall recognized the signs. Down on Eighth avenue she had done her marketing just as a shower was ending. Then, with her yams and corn-meal and pork-chops and coffee and okra, she had hurried through the narrow cross-street that was cluttered with children and crap-games. On Seventh avenue it was easier to move and breathe. And perhaps there she could find a clue or catch an idea for what she must soon be doing.

Surely there was more beauty on Seventh avenue than on any other street in Harlem. Where else could one feel the space that let her spread out inside? Where else could one see trees marching up the center? Her biology teacher had told her that they were Chinese plane trees. Lavinia liked the balls that hung like toy fruit or grace-notes after the leaves had given up, and she liked the rich brown and gray bark with its undergarment of cream and yellow. If she were walking on Morningside avenue, she could get close to such trees and sniff the bitter, teasing odor of the bark while it was still wet from the rain. Now the leaves were new with May. Those Seventh avenue plane trees did bring something to Harlem—more than could have been foreseen when they were planted.

On this day there were always more people sauntering or loitering in clusters. The usual swarm was in front of the movie theatre. Barber shops and beauty parlors had plenty of customers. Lavinia had once written a theme on "Kinks." It seemed queer that while hair was being uncurled down here, kinks should be crimped and set and baked just above Morningside Park—all at the same time, on Saturday afternoon.

She shied away from the pale, unwholesome man, like a potato-sprout, who was trying to sell "reefers" and from a pack of women and girls whose blatant slacks and suspenders matched their insolence and their insinuations.

It was a relief to look at some men in uniform. They knew how to carry themselves, these young Negroes, and there was dignity in their faces. Some day she'd like to marry a man like that and have four children. One would sing like Marian Anderson, one would be a doctor, one would build houses entirely unlike Harlem houses, and one would be a policeman who couldn't even think of letting graft come near him.

Here was a man dealing out handbills. She knew what they would contain—bait for the kind of Negroes who are so sick of all that is that they are ready to risk anything that isn't. There, one block east, was the church that always made her look up. The steeple insisted that there was something above it. And, sure enough, although most of the sky was still clouded, over that steeple was a scrap of blue in which a gull was a white airplane.

Too soon she must turn off into her own dirty block. On the corner was the gang of slouching hoodlums who could snatch a handbag when they were not shooting craps or making trouble in some other way. Only night before last they had beaten up a soldier who was walking through the block. He was still in the hospital with a fractured skull. One of the ruffians had said, "We ain' agoin' teh have any eh them uniform squares a comin' aroun' here, 'cause ef they do, then the girls they won' pay us no mind."

Stoops, steps, and pavement were covered with children of all sizes. Boys were playing "stick ball," and she had to dodge as she passed. Here were garbage cans still unemptied and piles of refuse that must wait until the unsoiled portions of the city could be regroomed.

Before going into her house she would do what had been proved helpful. Tucking her bags under her arm, she took from her pocket a handkerchief and held it over her face. Never could she get used to the smell of that hallway and those stairs—a smell that was made up of so many bad smells that one tried not to inhale or think. She always went very fast up the steep steps and down the dark little corridor that led to her home.

Inside that door she would find cleanliness that had been won and kept, but at what a price! When they had first tried to reconcile themselves to that flat, they had agreed that they would stay only until they could get out of debt. That was just after her father had broken his leg, when her mother's wages in the millinery shop were all they had, for the slim insurance could not last long. Now that her father was back in his job on night shift, her mother was in the hospital mending after an operation. Lavinia had thought that she should seek work and gain her diploma in evening school, but both parents had said that since she was a senior, she must go on. They would wiggle through somehow, and some day they would be out of debt and away from smells. They had seen the model flats (*Paradise Found* they should be called). Some day—!

She would slip in quietly, for her father was still sleeping. About four she would give him his dinner. Early that morning she had cleaned the bedroom so that it would be ready for him, and later she had cleaned the kitchen and the room that was living-room and dining-room for the family and bedroom for her. Tomorrow her mother would be coming home, and she would find things as she had left them, as decent as soap and water and disinfectants could make them.

But there was something to be done at once, and she must turn to her task. She must sit by the window and try to discover what she was almost sure was not there to be discovered.

She had been glad to remain in school for several reasons, but one of the weightiest was Miss Palmer, her English teacher. Miss Palmer was young and invigorating, with black hair that she didn't try to kink. Her blue eyes had lashes that were like black petals, and her skin was like the inside of the seashell that Lavinia had picked up on her one excursion to the sea. Miss Palmer rode horseback and played tennis when she could get away from English papers. Air from out-of-doors seemed to come in with her, to be a part of her. Being in her class meant more than learning punctuation and grammar or any facts. One felt that this person really lived, that she had roots through which she could draw what was needed for herself and others. And she gave it. She made Lavinia feel that life could be interesting and rewarding, even for a Negro girl in Harlem.

Miss Palmer had commended Lavinia's work and had told her that she had ability in writing. Several of her poems would be in the school magazine, and one of her stories was to be entered in a national contest for high school pupils. Some day she might write what many would read.

The night after that revelation Lavinia had forgotten that her bed-spring sagged and squeaked and that neighbors were swearing and fighting. She had sat up in the bed and had written down in her notebook lines and thoughts that gurgled up. Seeing the light through the cracks about the door, her mother had come in with, "What's the matter, Honey? Can't you sleep?"

Lavinia had hesitated. Then she had repeated Miss Palmer's words. The wonderful thing about having a real mother is that she can be told what one couldn't tell other people without sounding conceited. This mother had hugged her girl and had said, "Lavinia, if you can truly write someday, I'll be the proudest woman that ever tried to put a hat on anybody's head." They had laughed together, and then her mother had said, "Let's sing a little bit—just low—so we won't bother anyone. Then we can get to sleep. Don't forget that morning's just around the corner." And they had sung very softly "Goin' Home."

Now at her window she was trying to see what Miss Palmer had asked the class to see—something beautiful. " 'Whatsoever things are lovely'— write about them." That was the assignment. But the lovely things were to be observed from one's own window. "No, this is not an exercise in truth- telling," Miss Palmer had explained, "but you will do better work if you stick to what you really see." And Lavinia would play the game if she could.

From their rear apartment she was gazing into the long, cramped area. If it were winter, there might be some hope, for when snow fell like popcorn, even that sordid spot had its brief moment of transfiguration.

She was looking out upon windows and fire-escapes that were jammed with everything that ought not to be in a window or on a fire escape: mops, milk bottles, wads of clothing, beer-bottles, pails, tin cans, empty flower- crocks, dish-pans, cartons, old newspapers, brooms, shoes, pillows, police dogs, soiled bedding, jars of food, an old mattress that told too much—the catalogue might equal one of Walt Whitman's. Strutting back and forth were clothes-lines drooping under dejected garments that could furnish another weary review. All were limp, for they had been in two showers. The second was just ceasing. How could anyone wish clothing or bedding to be out in the rain?

Below, on what should have been grass or cement, were mounds of rubbish and filth in which rats grew hardy and nourished fleas. Three live cats and one dead one were visible. Once a dead man had lain there for a whole morning. A list of what was down there would rival the recipe for the witches' brew in "Macbeth." Yes, and more was coming, for another installment of garbage was being thrown down. If only an ailanthus tree, the patron saint of city courtyards, had braved this wretched hole! But there was none. Where was loveliness? Could Miss Palmer or St. Paul, with his shining words, find it here?

And the sounds! Although the neighbors were not in evidence, their voices were. Voices that might have been like velvet, the heritage of the race, had lost their native quality and were shrill and raucous. Nagging, screaming and cursing, they banged against her ears, while dogs barked and babies cried. Enough of that!

Her father had told her that pitying oneself was like eating poison, but she did feel sorry for herself. Why did she have to live in such a place? Why did such squalor have to be? Why couldn't that area be cleaned up and kept clean? Why couldn't people who liked cleanliness and beauty live with flowers and sunshine and quiet? She was honestly trying to find one thing that was not unattractive or repellent, and she was losing.

She was about to give up. This would mean failure on Monday, but she couldn't help it. Then something happened.

The disgusting mattress was on the fire-escape across from Lavinia. In front of it protruded a piece of sheet iron that she had not noticed. Kerosene had been used liberally, and the iron had caught and retained some of it.

The kerosene was there because of a diseased mattress, but now it was associating with water brought by the showers and with the mystery of light rays. The result was a miracle—colors! There they were: clear violet and indigo; strange greens; gingerbread yellow and coppery orange; and, instead of triumphant red, purple and a darkened rose-violet. No, these were not the rainbow colors of the sky as Lavinia had once seen them, free, keen, and joyous. Here were deeper, mingled tones, for water and light had come down to earth.

NEGRO DIGEST, JUNE 1944

My Most Humiliating Jim Crow Experience
ZORA NEALE HURSTON

My most humiliating Jim Crow experience came in New York instead of the South as one would have expected. It was in 1931 when Mrs. R. Osgood Mason was financing my researches in anthropology. I returned to New York from the Bahama Islands ill with some disturbances of the digestive tract.

Godmother (Mrs. Mason liked for me to call her Godmother) became concerned about my condition and suggested a certain white specialist at her expense. His office was in Brooklyn.

Mr. Paul Chapin called up and made the appointment for me. The doctor told the wealthy and prominent Paul Chapin that I would get the best of care. So two days later I journeyed to Brooklyn to submit myself to the care of the great specialist.

His reception room was more than swanky, with a magnificent hammered copper door and other decor on the same plane as the door.

But his receptionist was obviously embarrassed when I showed up. I mentioned the appointment and got inside the door. She went into the private office and stayed a few minutes, then the doctor appeared in the door all in white, looking very important, and also very unhappy from behind his rotund stomach.

He did not approach me at all, but told one of his nurses to take me into a private examination room.

The room was private all right, but I would not rate it highly as an examination room. Under any other circumstances, I would have sworn it was a closet where the soiled towels and uniforms were tossed until called for by the laundry. But I will say this for it, there was a chair in there wedged in between the wall and the pile of soiled linen. The nurse took me in there, closed the door quickly and disappeared. The doctor came in immediately and began in a desultory manner to ask me about symptoms. It was evident he meant to get me off the premises as quickly as possible. Being the sort of objective person I am, I did not get up and sweep out angrily as I was first disposed to do. I stayed to see just what would happen, and further to torture him more. He went through some motions, stuck a tube down my throat to extract some bile from my gall bladder, wrote a prescription and asked for twenty dollars as a fee.

I got up, set my hat at a reckless angle and walked out, telling him that I would send him a check, which I never did. I went away feeling the pathos of Anglo-Saxon civilization.

And I still mean pathos, for I know that anything with such a false foundation cannot last. Whom the gods would destroy, they first make mad.

THE CRISIS, JANUARY 1943

Negro Army Wives

THELMA THURSTON GORHAM

The WAACS and the WAVES will not produce all the heroines of World War II. Quite a number of them (unsung and unheralded) are being produced by the WIVES—particularly the wives who are trying to help maintain the morale of their soldier-husbands by accompanying them wherever they are sent this side of "over there."

They cannot follow their husbands "across," but they can follow, or precede, them to isolated posts like Ft. Huachuca, Arizona,[1] and to posts in the deep and "chivalrous" Southland where they must adjust themselves to the other side of the American way of life.

It takes fortitude and plenty of it to be an Army wife. Especially at a place like Ft. Huachuca. You see, when it was decided to isolate Negro troops from the rest of civilization by walling them up, high and dry, out there above the Arizona desert, WIVES and such things were not taken into consideration. Especially wives of enlisted men.

An Army wife whose husband was recently retired recalls laughingly that when she joined her soldier out there 25 years ago she lived in a tent and had to buy water for drinking and bathing at a dollar per barrel. Twenty-five years ago, Ft. Huachuca was not the modernized, thriving and populous wartime community that it now is. Nevertheless, today, living conditions out there leave much to be desired by women who are self-sacrificing enough to want to share the fortunes of their soldier husbands. Many of them would welcome even tents to what they're getting.

A typical example of what was provided by way of housing for enlisted men and their wives during the past summer at Ft. Huachuca is the structure known variously as "the Castle on the Hill," "Bonnie Blink Plaza," and "Bonnie Blink Palace."

It is an unpainted plywood shack that rivals the best that some slum dwellings have to offer: Eleven rooms about seven feet square, each furnished with two G.I. (government issue) cots and bedding.

---

1. Fort Huachuca housed the largest contingent of African American soldiers in the U.S. Army.

The twenty-two persons (eleven soldiers and their wives) who occupied the place all used the same sanitary facilities: one shower (with hot and cold water), one stool and two enameled iron sinks that served as face basins, laundry tubs, and in lieu of bathtubs. There were no facilities for cooking. The "Castle" was provided at a rental fee of $12 a month after a delegation of non-coms called on the post utilities officer and asked for something better for their wives than the "Girls' Dormitory."

The "Dormitory" is an unconverted barrack of the old Twenty-fifth Infantry in which unmarried girls and married women (all of whom have jobs on the post) have been given quarters. Lockers have been added for storage of personal belongings of those who live there. Otherwise, with G.I. cots lining the walls and no partitions in between, the "Dormitory" inmates have about the same degree of privacy and comfort as their soldier-husbands and sweethearts in the other barracks.

However, for large numbers of white women who work on the post (and whose husbands are not enlisted men in the U.S. Army) excellent quarters are provided. Rooms are spacious, but afford privacy. Sanitary and laundering facilities are adequate, and bathtubs supplement showers. There are cozily-furnished rooms in which to entertain visitors, and there is a kitchen where they can prepare their own meals or have them prepared.

As one old-timer on the post observed. "Nowadays, it's the civilians—and the white ones at that—who get consideration out here!"

White army wives have few complaints to make at Ft. Huachuca—unless it's about the isolation of the post. Nor do wives of white civilian workers (who get choice quarters) have anything to gripe about. It's the Negro army wife and her civilian sister who haven't been counted into the scheme of things out there. And if she cares enough about her soldier to want to "rough it" with him at Ft. Huachuca she must have fortitude and plenty of it.

A desert fortress, walled-in by mountains, Ft. Huachuca is a man's town. Yet in spite of the talk that one hears about the importance of soldier morale, there is still much that could be done for the morale (and morals) of the enlisted lads in khaki out there. . . .

For the happiness of Ft. Huachuca's approximately 14,000 enlistees there is everything except feminine companionship. The women out there number about 300, excluding the WAACS. They include nurses, hospital technicians, civilian employees and wives of officers, enlisted men and civilian workers—Negro, white, Mexican, Indian and Filipino.

When troops of tramping doughboys see anything in skirts out there, they have difficulty keeping step to the platoon leader's "Hup, hup, hup, hup!" Instead of "eyes front," it's eyes right, left and backwards. But two-thirds of the women on the post are married and most of the single ones are engaged. Therefore, as one private remarked, "It's tough!"

However, for the adventurous and amorous soldier, there is always the notorious "Hook," and the equally as infamous unincorporated town of Fry, Arizona. The "Hook" and Fry are located just outside the eastern entrance to Ft. Huachuca. The only places that justify the area outside "the Gate" are a theater and an attractive and capably-staffed type "A" USO building.[2]

The "Hook" is what its name implies — a place where suckers are "hooked" in more ways than one. There are whiskey and gambling, of course—and women.

Neither Fry nor the "Hook" have hot and cold running water in their adobe huts, corrugated metal shanties, tents, and packing-box shacks. The women who live there have limited sanitary facilities, notwithstanding the fact that on paydays men flock to the area by hundreds. Scores of soldiers "await their turns" for hours and many "double back" to stand in line again.

Always after these first-of-the-month forays on the "Hook," the G.U. wards on the post (where venereal cases are treated) are filled to capacity. Some far-sighted fellows go to Nogales and Aqua Prieta, Mexican border towns, where some of the "ranchitos" have their own prophylactic stations and dangers of landing in the G.U. wards are not so acute. Trips to Douglas, Bisbee and Tucson also help to break the monotony of the Ft. Huachuca soldier's state of womanlessness.

Nevertheless, the woman problem out here is acute from no matter what angle you view it. You see, Ft. Huachuca was built for soldiers. It's a man's town and, until nurses for the 93rd Division Station Hospital and the WAACS started arriving, not too much thought was given to the comforts of women on the post.

The WIVES out there have always had to "soldier"—almost as hard as their husbands.

Last summer, the summer after Pearl Harbor, found them at Ft. Huachuca in large numbers—wives of Negro enlisted men who were being trained daily to sacrifice themselves for the cause of the four freedoms and "the American way of life."

They were high school girls, college graduates, school teachers, ca-reerists, housewives, and young girls who should still have been under

---

2. United Service Organization, a federally financed entertainment group.

their parents' supervision. Youngsters and oldsters alike, all were learning and living life "the hard way" in order to be near their soldier-husbands.

They had gone out to Ft. Huachuca to spend a week or two weeks, and were staying "indefinitely," which meant that they'd be there until their lads in khaki were sent to another camp on a cadre or "over there."

They were more concerned about the morale of their menfolk than about their own personal comforts or the luxuries of civilian life. They realized that they could not have all the conveniences in an army camp that they had had at home. They weren't crying about the lives they had left behind them. They knew they weren't the only women in the world whose well-balanced lives had been upset, nor the only women who would give their chance of heaven for a normal home-life again. They were self-sacrificing enough to take almost anything in their stride—and try to learn to like it! . . .

They worked: In order to qualify for quarters as civilian employees on the post. They closed their eyes and ears to the fact that white civilian workers were furnished far more liveable lodgings.

They worked: In the Station Hospital offices as typists and clerks. In the Station Hospital nurses' quarters as maids. In the stucco and stone house on the "officers' line" as maids-of-all-work. In the post exchanges where some soldiers are respectful and some are not. In the laundry, where they have "graveyard" shifts, and in the warehouses. In the Service Club as cooks' helpers, fountain attendants, and what-have-you.

They did not receive transportation to and from work like the white clerical workers who live in the cozy dormitories.

They earned: As typists and clerks, $120 a month. As maids in the hospital, $90 a month. As maids in white officers' homes, whatever their employers felt like paying in addition to room and board. As post exchange employees, $50 a month. As laundry and warehouse workers, $50 to $60 a month. As Service Club employees, $35 a month plus board and lodging.

They had to rely on typical "country store" shopping facilities of the post exchanges where ceiling prices try to reach the peaks of the mountains that surround the post. Or they paid equally as exorbitant prices for merchandise at the wide space in the highway nearby, known as Fry, Arizona. Otherwise, they went 45 miles to Bisbee, 65 miles to Douglas, 60 miles to Nogales or 105 miles to Tucson to shop.

They paid $2.00[3] for a "shampoo, press and curl" at the beauty shop

---

3. This would have been expensive at the time, about twenty dollars today.

provided for them on the post (with a Negro operator under white supervision).

They did their weekly wash in 14-inch galvanized pails, purchased from the post exchange grocery store. They did their ironing on sheets spread across army cots. They became adept at inventing makeshifts.

Yet, they managed always to be attractive, fresh and uncomplaining when they greeted their soldiers after retreat. They had learned that training for a combat unit is a hard life at its best and that a man can't "soldier" well if he has to carry an extra burden of worry.

The WAACS who have been assigned to Ft. Huachuca will find the going made immeasurably easier for them because of these women—the WIVES who have preceded them.

The WAACS have their work pretty well cut out for them and provisions have been made for their comfort. But the WIVES, and this goes for many posts besides Ft. Huachuca, have had to clear away the underbrush alone, blaze their own trails and learn to "soldier" the hard way, along with their menfolk.

THE CRISIS, JULY 1943

Lily White "Walled City"

CONSTANCE H. CURTIS

On June 3, the Board of Estimate of the City of New York, which is the highest legislative section of the New York City Council, ratified a contract with the Metropolitan Life Insurance company for the construction of a $50,000,000 post-war housing project, to be called "Stuyvestant Town," on the lower east side of New York City. In this city within a city, where approximately 24,000 people will reside, the Metropolitan Life Insurance company has stated that no Negro tenants will be accepted. Frederick H. Ecker, chairman of the board of Metropolitan, expressed the company's position in these words, "Negroes and whites don't mix. Perhaps they will in a hundred years but they don't now. If we brought them into this development, it would be to the detriment of the city, too, because it would depress all the surrounding property."

With the clearly outlined policy of the company before them, the New York Board of Estimate voted 11 to 5 in favor of the project. With their approval went a grant of tax exemption of more than $1,000,000 annually for 25 years, or a total exceeding $25,000,000; a contribution of 504,449 square feet of city owned land, representing 19% of the site area; and an empowerment of the company with the right of eminent domain to aid it in assembling the land.

Newbold Morris, president of the City Council, and Edgar J. Nathan, Jr., Manhattan borough president, cast their votes against the housing plan. In his statement of disapproval of the undemocratic undertaking Mr. Morris said: "Now in casting my vote in the negative, I know full well the responsibility I am taking. I know full well that if my point of view prevails, it may mean the end of Stuyvesant houses. As Commissioner Moses says, it may mean the end of all such privately initiated projects. Huge as this project is it dwindles down into insignificance as compared to the principle.

"The principle of equality is as old as our nation. Men of all races have thought it good enough to make supreme sacrifices for it in every generation. It is enunciated in the Declaration of Independence; it is written in the Constitution. It is the law of the land. It is the keystone of the arch of our free society.

"Once we are committed to that principle we can not be content to invoke it on some occasions and discard it for compelling reasons on other occasions. As we sit here, men are dying for that principle, the least we can do is to live for it.

"Therefore, because I care more about the principle than I do about the project, because I cannot vote for public aid and public sponsorship of a private project whose officers state with candor that racial consideration will enter into the selection of tenants, I cast the three votes of my office in the negative."

Prior to the vote of approval by the Board, organizations and individuals throughout the entire city protested the project. From the offices of the National Association for the Advancement of Colored People went a plea to 2,000 selected local members to send telegrams and letters stating their opposition to the measure to Mayor LaGuardia and other members of the Board.

A telegraphed plea asking for a delay in the vote on the project was sent in by 15 civic organizations and was signed by the American Civil Liberties Union, the CIO, the International Ladies Garment Workers Union, the AF of L, the City Affairs Committee, the City-Wide Citizens' Committee on Harlem and other organizations.

An amendment to the Administrative Code was introduced in the May 21 meeting of the City Council by Councilmen Stanley M. Isaacs and A. Clayton

Powell, Jr., the latter the only Negro member of the group. This amendment, if passed, will prevent the Metropolitan Life Insurance company and all other such future contracting parties from following a policy of racial discrimination.

In addition to the Isaacs-Powell anti-discrimination amendment, which has not yet been voted upon, the City Council has adopted, by a vote of 23 to 1, a resolution upholding equal opportunity for all citizens to become tenants in all housing projects.

Court action has been instituted by Julius L. Goldstein, counsel of the Non-Sectarian Anti-Nazi League, to restrain the city from carrying out the contract with Metropolitan. The action was based on the contention that approval of the contract by the Board was invalid. Mr. Goldstein contends that a three-fourths vote was necessary, which was not reached when only 11 of the 16 votes were cast in favor of the plan.

Counsel of the staff of the NAACP are studying means by which legal action may be taken which will either insure the admission of all races into the project or will bar such a plan entirely.

A temporary stay has been granted restraining any action on the project, pending argument before the courts in yet another suit brought by the property owners of the area affected.

The Metropolitan Life Insurance company, which owns Parkchester, an all-white development in the Bronx, has not only flatly stated that no Negroes are wanted as tenants in the proposed "Stuyvestant Town," but has made no provisions for a school within the entire area of their "city." A Metropolitan official has been quoted as giving as the reasons for the company's failure to provide adequate educational facilities that "there is no room for it" and that it does not wish to have outside children enter the project, particularly Negro children.

Plans for the building of "Stuyvestant Town" were first known to the public April 19, when Mayor LaGuardia revealed that a "delightful residential community with an atmosphere of trees and parks" was under consideration. On May 5, the City Planning Commission held its first hearing on the proposal, and on May 20, voted its approval. June 3, the Board of Estimate completed the city's approval of the plan by voting in favor of it also. In less than three months Metropolitan had laid its plans for a $50,000,000 "walled city" before the government of the State and the City of New York, and had rushed them through to final approval!

The Metropolitan project was made possible by the Hampton bill, which was passed by the legislature and signed by New York's Governor Thomas E. Dewey on April 3 of this year. When Governor Dewey signed the bill he admitted some doubts about the law but added: "The purpose of the bill, however, is of such great importance that I have resolved the doubt in favor of the bill.

"The immediate practical problem is housing or no housing. The answer is in favor of housing."

Prior to the passage of the Hampton bill, insurance companies were not allowed to take part in real estate operations of this type.

Liberal, labor, Negro and post-war planning organizations are greatly concerned over this action of the City of New York. It is felt that it will furnish a pattern for the nation, when, in the post-war world, planned housing will be carried on in giant scale. Negroes especially are disquieted for fear of the freezing of the idea of racial segregation in public housing. They are dismayed because many have felt that one of the dividends of the war for the Four Freedoms would be not to strengthen but to lessen the patterns of segregation which have been set up in America.

The fight, however, is by no means ended. In spite of the fact that the Metropolitan Life Insurance company is a five billion dollar corporation which therefore wields untold strength, fair-minded citizens, both Negro and white, have pledged themselves to try in every way to defeat the erection of a lily white town within the City of New York.

THE CRISIS, AUGUST 1943

The Gestapo in Detroit

THURGOOD MARSHALL

Riots are usually the result of many underlying causes, yet no single factor is more important than the attitude and efficiency of the police. When disorder starts, it is either stopped quickly or permitted to spread into serious proportions, depending upon the actions of the local police.

Much of the blood spilled in the Detroit riot is on the hands of the Detroit police department. In the past the Detroit police have been guilty of both inefficiency and an attitude of prejudice against Negroes. Of course, there are several individual exceptions.

The citizens of Detroit, white and Negro, are familiar with the attitude of the police as demonstrated during the trouble in 1942 surrounding the

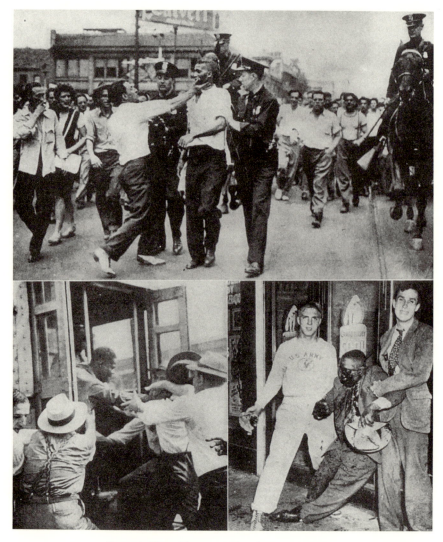

Detroit Riot Pictures, *The Crisis*, July 1943

Sojourner Truth housing project.[1] At that time a mob of white persons armed with rocks, sticks and other weapons attacked Negro tenants who

---

1. A federally funded housing project intended for African American war workers who had migrated to Detroit. A white mob prevented them from moving in when it was built in 1942.

were attempting to move into the project. Police were called to the scene. Instead of dispersing the mob, which was unlawfully on property belonging to the federal government and leased to Negroes, they directed their efforts toward dispersing the Negroes who were attempting to get into their own homes. All Negroes approaching the project were searched and their automobiles likewise searched. White people were neither searched nor disarmed by the police. This incident is typical of the one-sided law enforcement practiced by Detroit police. White hoodlums were justified in their belief that the police would act the same way in any further disturbances.

In the June riot of this year, the police ran true to form. The trouble reached riot proportions because the police once again enforced the law with an unequal hand. They used "persuasion" rather than firm action with white rioters, while against Negroes they used the ultimate in force: night sticks, revolvers, riot guns, submachine guns, and deer guns. As a result, 25 of the 34 persons killed were Negroes. Of the latter, 17 were killed by police.

The excuse of the police department for the disproportionate number of Negroes killed is that the majority of them were shot while committing felonies: namely, the looting of stores on Hastings street. On the other hand, the crimes of arson and felonious assaults are also felonies. It is true that some Negroes were looting stores and were shot while committing these crimes. It is equally true that white persons were turning over and burning automobiles on Woodward avenue. This is arson. Others were beating Negroes with iron pipes, clubs, and rocks. This is felonious assault. Several Negroes were stabbed. This is assault with intent to murder.

All these crimes are matters of record. Many were committed in the presence of police officers, several on the pavement around the City Hall. Yet the record remains: Negroes killed by police—17; white persons killed by police—none. The entire record, both of the riot killings and of previous disturbances, reads like the story of the Nazi Gestapo.

Evidence of tension in Detroit has been apparent for months. The *Detroit Free Press* sent a reporter to the police department. When Commissioner Witherspoon was asked how he was handling the situation he told the reporter: "We have given orders to handle it with kid gloves. The policemen have taken insults to keep trouble from breaking out. I doubt if you or I could have put up with it." This weak-kneed policy of the police commissioner coupled with the anti-Negro attitude of many members of the force helped to make a riot inevitable.

Belle Isle is a municipal recreation park where thousands of white and Negro war workers and their families go on Sundays for their outings. There had been isolated instances of racial friction in the past. On Sunday night, June 20, there was trouble between a group of white and Negro people. The disturbance was under control by midnight. During the time of the disturbance and after it was under control, the police searched the automobiles of all Negroes and searched the Negroes as well. They did not search the white people. One Negro who was to be inducted into the army the following week was arrested because another person in the car had a small pen knife. This youth was later sentenced to 90 days in jail before his family could locate him. Many Negroes were arrested during this period and rushed to local police stations. At the very beginning the police demonstrated that they would continue to handle racial disorders by searching, beating and arresting Negroes while using mere persuasion on white people.

A short time after midnight disorder broke out in a white neighborhood near the Roxy theatre on Woodward avenue. The Roxy is an all night theatre attended by white and Negro patrons. Several Negroes were beaten and others were forced to remain in the theatre for lack of police protection. The rumor spread among the white people that a Negro had raped a white woman on Belle Isle and that the Negroes were rioting.

At about the same time a rumor spread around Hastings and Adams streets in the Negro area that white sailors had thrown a Negro woman and her baby into the lake at Belle Isle and that the police were beating Negroes. This rumor was also repeated by an unidentified Negro at one of the night spots. Some Negroes began to attack white persons in the area. The police immediately began to use their sticks and revolvers against them. The Negroes began to break out the windows of stores of white merchants on Hastings street.

The interesting thing is that when the windows in the stores on Hastings street were first broken, there was no looting. An officer of the Merchants' Association walked the length of Hastings street, starting 7 o'clock Monday morning, and noticed that none of the stores with broken windows had been looted. It is thus clear that the original breaking of windows was not for the purpose of looting.

Throughout Monday the police, instead of placing men in front of the stores to protect them from looting, contented themselves with driving up and down Hastings street from time to time, stopping in front of the stores. The usual procedure was to jump out of the squad cars with drawn revolvers and riot guns to shoot whoever might be in the store. The policemen would then tell the Negro bystanders to "run and not look back." On several occasions, persons running were shot in the back. In other instances, bystanders were clubbed by police. To the police, all Negroes on Hastings street were "looters." This included war workers returning from work. There is no question that many Negroes were guilty of looting, just as there is always looting during earthquakes or as there was when English towns were bombed by the Germans.

Woodward avenue is one of the main thoroughfares of the city of Detroit. Small groups of white people began to rove up and down Woodward beating Negroes, stoning cars containing Negroes, stopping street cars and yanking Negroes from them and stabbing and shooting Negroes. In no case did the police do more than try to "reason" with these mobs, many of which were, at this stage, quite small. The police did not draw their revolvers or riot guns and never used any force to disperse these mobs. As a result of this, the mobs got larger and bolder and even attacked Negroes on the pavement of the City Hall in demonstration not only of their contempt for Negroes, but of their contempt for law and order as represented by the municipal government.

During this time, Mayor Jeffries was in his office in the City Hall with the door locked and the window shade drawn. The use of night sticks or the drawing of revolvers would have dispersed these white groups and saved the lives of many Negroes. It would not have been necessary to shoot, but it would have been sufficient to threaten to shoot into the white mobs. The use of a fire hose would have dispersed many of the groups. None of these things was done and the disorder took on the proportions of a major riot. The responsibility rests with the Detroit police.

At the height of the disorder on Woodward avenue, Negroes driving north on Brush street (a Negro street) were stopped at Vernor Highway by a policeman who forced them to detour to Woodward avenue. Many of these cars are automobiles which appeared in the pictures released by several newspapers showing them overturned and burned on Woodward avenue.

While investigating the riot, we obtained many affidavits from Negroes concerning police brutality during the riot. It is impossible to include the facts or all of these affidavits. However, typical instances may be cited. A Negro soldier in uniform who had recently been released from the army with a medical discharge, was on his way down Brush street Monday morning, toward a theatre on Woodward avenue. This soldier was not aware of the fact that the riot was still going on. While in the Negro neighborhood on Brush street, he reached a corner where a squad car drove up and discharged several policemen with drawn revolvers, who announced to a small group on the corner to run and not look back. Several of the Negroes who did not move quite fast enough for the police were struck with night sticks and revolvers. The soldier was yanked from behind by one policeman and struck in the head with a blunt instrument and knocked to the ground where he remained in a stupor. The police then returned to their squad car and drove off. A Negro woman in the block noticed the entire incident from her window and she rushed out with a cold, damp towel to bind the soldier's head. She then hailed two Negro postal employees who carried the soldier to a hospital where his life was saved.

There are many additional affidavits of similar occurrences involving obviously innocent civilians throughout many Negro sections in Detroit where there had been no rioting at all. It was characteristic of these cases that the policemen would drive up to a corner, jump out with drawn revolvers striking at Negroes indiscriminately, ofttimes shooting at them, and in all cases forcing them to run. At the same time on Woodward avenue, white civilians were seizing Negroes and telling them to "run, nigger, run." At least two Negroes, "shot while looting," were innocent persons who happened to be in the area at that time.

One Negro who had been an employee of a bank in Detroit for the past eighteen years was on his way to work on a Woodward avenue street car when he was seized by one of the white mobs. In the presence of at least four policemen, he was beaten and stabbed in the side. He also heard several shots fired from the back of the mob. He managed to run to two of the policemen who proceeded to "protect" him from the mob. The two policemen, followed by two mounted policemen, proceeded down Woodward avenue. While he was being escorted by these policemen, the man was struck in the face by at least eight of the mob, and at no time was any effort made to prevent him from being struck. After a short distance this man noticed a squad car parked on the other side of the street. In sheer desperation he broke away from the two policemen who claimed to be protecting him and ran to the squad car, begging for protection. The officer in the squad car put him in the back seat and drove off, thereby saving his life.

During all this time, the fact that the man was either shot or stabbed was evident because of the fact that blood was spurting from his side. Despite this obvious felony, committed in the presence of at least four policemen, no effort was made at that time either to protect the victim or to arrest the persons guilty of the felony.

In addition to the many cases of one-sided enforcement of the law by the police, there are two glaring examples of criminal aggression against innocent Negro citizens and workers by members of the Michigan state police and Detroit police.

On the night of June 22 at about 10 o'clock, some of the residents of the St. Antoine Branch of the Y.M.C.A. were returning to the dormitory. Several were on their way home from the Y.M.C.A. across the street. State police were searching some other Negroes on the pavement of the Y.M.C.A. when two of the Y.M.C.A. residents were stopped and searched for weapons. After none was found they were allowed to proceed to the building. Just as the last of the Y.M.C.A men were about to enter the building, he heard someone behind him yell what sounded to him like, "Hi, Ridley." (Ridley is also a resident of the Y.) Another resident said he heard someone yell what sounded to him like "Heil, Hitler."

A state policeman, Ted Anders, jumped from his car with his revolver drawn, ran to the steps of the Y.M.C.A., put one foot on the bottom step and fired through the outside door. Immediately after firing the shot he entered the building. Other officers followed. Julian Witherspoon, who had just entered the building, was lying on the floor, shot in the side by the bullet that was fired through the outside door. There had been no show of violence or weapons of any kind by anyone in or around the Y.M.C.A.

The officers with drawn revolvers ordered all those residents of the Y.M.C.A. who were in the lobby of their building to raise their hands in the air and line up against the wall like criminals. During all this time these men were called "black b——— and monkeys," and other vile names by the officers. At least one man was struck; another was forced to throw his lunch on the floor. All the men in the lobby were searched.

The desk clerk was also forced to line up. The officers then went behind the desk and into the private offices and searched everything. The officers also made the clerk open all locked drawers, threatening to shoot him if he did not do so.

Witherspoon was later removed to the hospital and has subsequently been released.

On the night of June 21 at about eight o'clock, a Detroit policeman was shot in the two hundred block of Vernor Highway, and his assailant, who was in a vacant lot, was, in turn, killed by another policeman. State and city policemen then began to attack the apartment building at 290 E. Vernor Highway, which was fully occupied by tenants. Searchlights were thrown on the building and machine guns, revolvers, rifles, and deer guns were fired indiscriminately into all of the occupied apartments facing the outside. Tenants of the building were forced to fall to the floor and remain there in order to save their lives. Later slugs from machine guns, revolvers, rifles, and deer guns were dug from the inside walls of many of the apartments. Tear gas was shot into the building and all the tenants were forced out into the streets with their hands up in the air at the point of drawn guns.

State and city policemen went into the building and forced out all the tenants who were not driven out by tear gas. The tenants were all lined up against the walls, men and women alike, and forced to remain in this position for some time. The men were searched for weapons. During this time these people were called every type of vile name and men and women were cursed and threatened. Many men were struck by policemen.

While the tenants were lined up in the street, the apartments were forcibly entered. Locks and doors were broken. All the apartments were ransacked. Clothing and other articles were thrown around on the floor. All of these acts were committed by policemen. Most of the tenants reported that money, jewelry, whiskey, and other items of personal property were missing when they were permitted to return to their apartments after midnight. State and city police had been in possession of the building in the meantime.

Many of these apartments were visited shortly after these events. They resembled part of a battlefield. Affidavits from most of the tenants and lists of property destroyed and missing are available.

Although a white man was seen on the roof of an apartment house up the street from the Vernor apartments with a rifle in his hand, no effort was made to either search that building or its occupants. After the raid on the Vernor apartments, the police used as their excuse the statement that policeman Lawrence A. Adams had been shot by a sniper from the Vernor apartments, and that for that reason, they attacked the building and its occupants. However, in a story released by the police department on July 2 after the death of Patrolman Lawrence A. Adams, it was reported that "The shot that felled Adams was fired by Homer Edison, 28 years old, of 502 Montcalm, from the shadows of a parking lot. Edison, armed with a shot gun, was shot to death by Adams' partner." This is merely another example of the clumsy and obvious subterfuges used by the police department in an effort to cover up their total disregard for the rights of Negroes.

Justification for our belief that the Detroit police could have prevented the trouble from reaching riot proportions is evidenced in at least two recent instances. During the last month in the town of Atlanta, Georgia, several white youths organized a gang to beat up Negroes. They first encountered a young Negro boy on a bicycle and threw him to the ground. However, before they could beat this lone Negro, a squad car drove up. The police promptly arrested several of the white boys, and dispersed the group immediately, thus effectively forestalling and preventing what might have resulted in a riot. On the Sunday preceding the Detroit riots, Sheriff Baird, of Wayne County, Michigan, with jurisdiction over the area just outside Detroit, suppressed a potential riot in a nearby town. A large group of Negroes and a large group of white people were opposing each other and mob violence was threatened. The sheriff and his deputies got between the two groups and told them that in case of any violence, the guilty parties would be handled and that the law enforcement officers would do everything possible to prevent the riot. Because of this firm stand, the members of both groups dispersed.

If similar affirmative action had been taken by the Detroit police when the small groups were running up and down Woodward avenue beating, cutting and shooting Negroes, the trouble never would have reached the bloody and destructive magnitude which has shocked the nation.

This record by the Detroit police demonstrates once more what all Negroes know only too well: that nearly all police departments limit their conception of checking racial disorders to surrounding, arresting, maltreating, and shooting Negroes. Little attempt is made to check the activities of whites.

The certainty of Negroes that they will not be protected by police, but instead attacked by them is a contributing factor to racial tensions leading to overt acts. The first item on the agenda of any group seeking to prevent rioting would seem to be a critical study of the police department of the community, its record in handling Negroes, something of the background of its personnel, and the plans of its chief officers for meeting possible racial disorders.

THE CRISIS, AUGUST 1943

Mr. Roosevelt Regrets

PAULI MURRAY

What'd you get, black boy,
When they knocked you down in the gutter,
And they kicked your teeth out,
And they broke your skull with clubs
And they bashed your stomach in?
What'd you get when the police shot you in the back,
And they chained you to the beds
While they wiped the blood off?
What'd you get when you cried out to the Top Man?
When you called on the man next to God, so you thought,
And you asked him to speak out to save you?
What'd the Top Man say, black boy?
"Mr. Roosevelt regrets . . . ."

Upon reading *PM* newspaper's account of Mr. Roosevelt's statement on the recent race clashes: *"I share your feeling that the recent outbreaks of violence in widely spread parts of the country endanger our national unity and comfort our enemies. I am sure that every true American regrets this."*

THE CRISIS, FEBRUARY 1943

Hate

SIMEON BOOKER JR.

Every time the skull rocked—
        back
                forth
        back
                forth
The mighty jaws mocked—

Nig
    ger
Nig
    ger
Hating must be in the bone from Dixie to Maine.
Some white skulls have no brain.

NEGRO STORY, AUGUST–SEPTEMBER 1945

The Smell of Death

GRACE W. TOMPKINS

The smell of death? I know it well.
At Buchenwald, you say?
I wasn't there . . .
But here at home . . . in Georgia
I smelled it once
Even before the hounds gave voice at his scent
The hate-filled eyes . . . and curse upon the lip
The coiled rope, the lash, the loaded gun
And the stench of death clogged my nostrils.
Just one man died
Not thousands as at Buchenwald
But each man dies but one death
It is an individual matter
And all the others
Touch him not at all
When his turn comes for dying
Mass murder is appalling, yes
But each death of the whole is one
The total makes the mass.
I smelled death on a bus
In Carolina.
One vacant seat . . . and a uniformed black brother
An irate driver
Armed MPs

And the odor of death borne in the acrid smoke
Of a revolver.

I smelled it first in Natchez
A brief encounter . . . the cry of "Rape"
The milling mob . . . and shuttered windows
Yet the odor crept beneath the bolted door
To tease the nostrils of the cowed folk within
And whether uniformed officials
And Congressional Representatives
Stand appalled at huge grave's edge . . .
Or terror stricken blacks
Steal forth soft-footed in the night
To cut down or gather up these pitiful remains . . .
It stinks to high heaven
This smell of death!

THE CRISIS, OCTOBER 1942

Black Girl, Shouting

JAMES BALDWIN

Stomp my feet
An' clap my han's.
Angels comin'
To dese fair lan's.

Cut my lover
From dat tree!
Angels comin'
To set me free.

Glory, glory
To de Lamb.
Blessed Jesus,
Where's my man?

Black girl whirl
Your torn red dress.

Black girl hide
Your bitterness.

Black girl stretch
Your mouth so wide.
None will guess
The way he died

Turned your heart
To quivering mud
While your lover's
Soft red blood

Stained the scowling
Outraged tree.
Angels come
To cut him free!

THE CRISIS, MAY 1943

Stabat Mater

GLORIA CLYNE

The mother stood
And watched the tortured, half-burnt thing
That once had been her son,
This broken, bleeding thing,
Swing from a crueler tree
On an American Calvary.

COMMON GROUND, WINTER 1944

Black Mother Praying in the Summer of 1943

OWEN DODSON

Dedicated to Negro mothers everywhere
and especially to Lillian C. Dodson

My great God, You been a tenderness ta me,
Through the thick and through the thin;
You been a pilla ta my soul;
You been like the shinin light a mornin in the black dark,
A elevator ta my spirit.

Now there's a fire in this land like a last judgment,
And I done sat down by the rivers a Babylon
And wept deep when I remembered Zion,
Seein the water that can't quench fire
And the fire that burn up rivers.
Lord, I'm gonna say my say real quick and simple:

You know bout this war that's bitin the skies
And gougin out the earth.
Last month, Lord, I bid my last boy away ta fight.
I got all my boys fightin now for they country.
Didn't think bout it cept it were for freedom;
Didn't think cause they was black they wasn't American;
Didn't think a thing cept that they was my only sons.
And there was mothers all over the world
Sacrificin they sons like You let Yours be nailed
To the wood for men ta behold the right.

Now, I'm a black mother, Lord, I knows that now,
Black and burnin in these burnin times.
I can't hold my peace cause peace ain't fit ta mention
When they's fightin right here in our streets
Like dogs—mongrel dogs and hill cats.
White is fightin black right here
Where hate abides like a cancer wound

And Freedom is writ big and crossed out:
Where, bless God, they's draggin us outta cars
In Texas and California, in Newark, Detroit,
Blood on the darkness, Lord, blood on the pavement,
Leavin us moanin and afraid.
What has we done?
Where and when has we done?
They's plantin the seeds a hate down in our bone marrow
When we don't want ta hate.

We don't speak much in the street where I live, my God,
Nobody speak much, but we thinkin deep
Of the black sons in lands far as the wind can go,
Black boys fightin this war with them.
We thinkin deep bout they sisters stitchin airplane canvas
And they old fathers plowin for wheat
And they mothers bendin in wash tubs,
They brothers at the factory wheels.
They all is bein body beat and spirit beat
And heart sore and wonderin.

Listen, Lord, they ain't nowhere for black mothers ta turn.
Won't You plant Your Son's goodness in this land
Before it too late?
Help these men ta see they losin while they winnin
Long as they allow theyselves ta lynch
In the city streets and on country roads?

When can I pray again,
View peace in my own parlor again?
When my sons come home,
How can I show em my broken hands?
How can I show em they sister's twisted back?
How can I present they land ta them?
How, when they been battlin in far places for freedom?
Better let em die in the desert drinkin sand
Or holdin onta water and shippin inta death
Than they come back an see they sufferin for vain.

I done seen a man runnin for his life,
Runnin like the wind, from a mob, ta no shelter.
Where were a hidin place for him?

Saw a dark girl nine years old
Cryin cause her father done had
The light scratched from his eyes in the month of June.
Where the seein place for him?
A black boy lyin with his arms huggin the pavement in pain.
What he starin at?
Good people, hands up, searched for guns and razors and pipes.
When they gonna pray again?

How, precious God, can I watch my son's eyes
When they hear this terrible?
How can I pray again when my tongue
Is near cleavin to the roof of my mouth?
Tell me, Lord, how?

Every time they strike us they strikin Your Son;
Every time they shove us in, they cornerin they own children.
I'm gonna scream before I hope again.
I ain't never gonna hush my mouth
Or lay down this heavy, black, weary, terrible load
Until I fights ta stamp my feet with my black sons
On a freedom solid rock and stand there peaceful
And look out into the star wilderness of the sky
And the land lyin about clean, and secure land,
And people not afraid again.

Lord, let us all see the golden wheat together,
Harvest the harvest together,
Touch the fullness and the hallelujah together.

                                        Amen

NEGRO STORY, DECEMBER–JANUARY 1944–1945

World of Sin

VALERIE E. PARKS

"It's a world of sin we're living in,"
Cried the preacher, blue eyes shining bright,
"It's a world of sin we're living in . . .

"God's children must follow God's light!"
Then he quenched his thirst and with violent outburst
Cried the preacher, blue eyes blazing bright,
"It's a world of sin we're living in;
"God's children must spread God's light."

Then he walked down the aisle . . .
With his most reverent smile,
(God's child spreading God's holy light)
And he walked up the aisle . . .
With his best heav'nly smile,
And with blue eyes shining bright
Said he to an usher:

"In God's name, don't rush her,
"But there's a BLACK WOMAN in here . . .
"Perhaps a newcomer just here for the summer
"Who's mixed up her churches, I fear."
"What a world of sin we're living in,"
Said the preacher who shared not God's light;
"Go forth, good man, be polite as you can,
"And tell her THIS CHURCH is for WHITE."

THE CRISIS, FEBRUARY 1944

Of Myself

EDNA L. ANDERSON

I see not myself for what I am,
But for what I long and wish to be.
I see my dreams that are untold
Like leaves that from a book unfold.
I see my soul as an ember untouched,
Unkindled by flame not lit.
I cherish my thoughts in solace be;
I spend my days in reverie.
I see my hopes fall down and lay
Like souls bewitched in torment lie,

Each wishful thought in passion's rise
Beckons me to the height of the skies.
And from mine heart there springs a fear
That none but I can see it there.

THE CRISIS, OCTOBER 1945

Troubled Night

LANGSTON HUGHES

Harlem
Knows a song
Without a tune.
The rhythm's there:
But the melody
Is bare.

Harlem
Knows a night
Without a moon:
Darkness,
Stars
Nowhere.

OPPORTUNITY, JANUARY 1942

Dixie Hospitality

FRENISE LOGAN

One of these days I'm gonna get tired
Of ridin' the back end of street cars.
I'm gonna get tired of goin' down side alleys
To a picture show.
Yes, and I'm gonna get damn tired
Of sitting "up front" on a passenger train;

One of these days I'm gonna get mad;
And all the hurts heaped up inside of me—
Hurts I've taken and swallowed from years back,
They gonna burst like a big stick of dynamite,
And everybody's gonna hear that blast,
'Cause it's gonna go off with a loud boom.

NEGRO STORY, APRIL–MAY 1946

Riot Gold

PEARL FISHER

Clem Davis had been sent up to Harlem to cover the riot for his paper. He had often come to me for leads or angles on the color question. This time, however, I was as much in the dark as he was. We decided to go the rounds together.

Of course everyone knew the story in brief: a colored soldier—a prostitute—a white cop—a fight—a shot—then rumor spreading like fumes from a gas bomb, choking thought and reason, releasing the reflexes of the primitive—and finally disaster.

But we were looking for the stories behind the news. We talked to shopkeepers, policemen, social workers, preachers, idlers. We saw the injured in hospital emergency wards; the loot of every description in police stations; the hundreds of men and women and boys and girls in the courts arraigned on various charges—some arrogant, others sheepish, defiant, sullen, loutish, swaggering, leering, dead-pan, waiting to be called to account for the wild orgy of the night before.

We had enough copy for dozens of articles and feature stories. We were tired, stifled, surfeited with the visible aspects of the sordid, futile outburst. All of it was disturbing, much of it unintelligible. The violence born of impotence, the sudden release of bottled-up emotions, the long-endured injustices and discriminations, housing, delinquency, crime waves—all this we knew. We knew the leads that the press would carry—ad infinitum—ad nauseam. But some of the things we had seen didn't add up to sense. You looked at some of the faces and you wanted to cry out—

"Why? Why? Why? You over there, and you, why did *you* do it? What was your own individual drive for taking part in this—this extravaganza?" One felt baffled.

Davis had to meet a deadline and, anyway, we had seen enough. We were pushing our way through the crowds to get out of the station-house, and had reached the door, when a patrol wagon drove up. Instead of the hodge-podge of humanity we expected to see, there emerged from the rear, two officers half-dragging half-supporting an elderly woman. She didn't look at all like a Carrie Nation. She was of medium height, rather stout and was probably about sixty years old. She had mixed gray hair, and a grayish pallor showed through her haggard brown face. She didn't seem to be aware of what was going on about her. As she passed us, a heavy sigh escaped her and a low, agony-filled prayer, "Have Mercy, Lord, Mercy," repeated over and over again.

We stood a moment, undecided, then Davis looked at his watch.

"You follow through on the woman," he said. "Let me know if there's a story in it." I promised, and he left while I re-entered the building to see if I could find out on what charges the woman was to be booked.

Well, after considerable wangling I was able to get to her and draw from her, her story. Here it is much as I gave it to Davis after piecing the parts together.

There was nothing unusual about Mrs. Cicely Jones. She was just an ordinary citizen of the big city living in that overpopulated region known as Harlem. She was honest, law-abiding, Godfearing. She went occasionally to the movies and to church on Sundays. She had "raised" her daughter's two boys from little "shavers." Sonny was sixteen "going on seventeen," and Tim—God have Mercy—Tim would have been twenty "come next January." The boys' father had deserted their mother and then the mother had died, leaving the grandmother to struggle along on her slim earnings as a domestic, with the old problem of making ends meet, which they never did. Things were a little better when Tim got big enough to get odd jobs. The only difference between Cicely Jones and others whom circumstances had forced to shoulder a like burden, was that Miss Cicely's crimpy hair and brown skin made the going harder for her.

Miss Cicely's story did not flow easily from her lips. She was too stunned by all that had happened. I had to ask questions, and piece the answers together to get a connected story. Miss Cicely (She told me to call her that. She said everybody did) was glad to talk to someone. She was all alone now; there was nobody since Tim—.

I had to wait for Miss Cicely to regain a degree of composure before she told me about Tim.

Tim had always been a source of great pride to Miss Cicely.

"My boy Tim was a good boy. He didn't bother nobody. He was sort of proud like, maybe, but he always done what was right. Sonny, now—Sonny was always getting into some sort of 'scrape,' and Tim would somehow always get him out. I didn't have so much to worry about as long as Tim was around. Then Tim was drafted. Sonny's been sort of lost without Tim. Started going around with some boys Tim hadn't liked. Tim said they were bad eggs. Called themselves some kind of club and wore the name of the club, on the backs of their coats—."

Miss Cicely's story trailed off into recollections of incidents in the lives of her boys. Between her sobs she moaned again and again, "Lord have Mercy. I fell by the way-side. Oh, Lord, have Mercy."

"Tell me about Tim," I prodded.

Miss Cicely continued, "I should have warned Tim. It was all my fault. He was so proud of his uniform. He was getting along right nice—sending me an allotment every pay day—and then they made him a corporal and sent him down south."

Miss Cicely had difficulty going on. It seems that Tim, brought up in New York, did not know what serious consequences could follow a breach of Jim Crow etiquette in the South. He had boarded a bus, taking a seat in the rear to avoid trouble. A Negro sitting behind him left the bus. The driver told Tim to move back. Tim sat still. The driver went over to him and slapped his face.

"Move back, Nigger, I told you," he snarled.

For answer Tim smashed him in the jaw, knocking him down. From the floor the driver pulled his gun and fired. Tim crumpled. They threw him off and the bus drove on. In the town the bus driver reported that he had been attacked by a "nigger soldier."

They found his body on the side of the road.

"My boy Tim was a good boy," moaned Miss Cicely. "Never did bother nobody—"

In the three months since, the tragedy was aggravated by her deep concern for Sonny. She tried in the best ways she knew to teach him "right from wrong" and to be a good boy like Tim. On one occasion Sonny had answered, "Yeah! What'd it get him?"

"What happened last night, Miss Cicely?" I said gently. She went on.

Miss Cicely had attended evening church service and returned to the little flat she and Sonny called home. Sonny was not there. She looked at the clock. It was long past ten. Sonny should have been home. Now if Tim were there, he would go out and get Sonny. To pass the time Miss Cicely turned on the small radio. Then she went to the window, her eyes searching the street below for the familiar figure of Sonny. She picked up her Bible. She dozed, for how long she did not know. Suddenly she was aware of something wrong. The program had been interrupted. The music had stopped. Someone was talking—.

"Stay at home—people of Harlem—only a rumor—stay at home—don't lose your heads—nothing to fear—."

Miss Cicely looked down into the street. It seemed strangely quiet, but from the direction of the avenue came a sudden roar—people's voices surging upward then fading away,—a crash—the sound of splintering glass.

Sonny was her first thought. Where was Sonny? In a frenzy of fear Miss Cicely snatched up her shabby handbag, locked the door and hurried down the four flights of stairs and into the street. She didn't know what was wrong. She knew only that she must find Sonny to keep him out of trouble. Tim wasn't there. She had to do it herself.

Reaching the avenue, she found herself among groups of excited people —all Negroes. There wasn't a white face to be seen. Moving from one group to another, straining her eyes up and down the street for a sight of Sonny, she heard jumbled comment.

A colored soldier—a white cop—a shot—

Sonny! Sonny!

A colored soldier—a white bus driver—a shot.

Tim! Oh, Tim!

A soldier—a cop—a shot—a fight—a crowd—plunder—murder—riot.

A police siren screamed. Not Sonny, too. Dear Lord. Miss Cicely stumbled on.

It was later that same evening that I found Sonny in the emergency ward to which he had been taken, and got his part of the story. His long slim body even under the covers seemed to be taut with resentment. I studied his features and found in them some resemblance to his grandmother, minus her resignation. His tight lips refused to succumb to any expression of pain. His eyes blazed hatred of the world in general and at that moment of myself in particular. It took quite a while to break down the barriers and get him to talk. He was wounded but not fatally.

It seemed that Sonny instead of going to church with his grandmother had elected to attend a "picture show" with some of his buddies. When they left the theater, the boys gathered at one of their corner store hangouts. They stood around drinking cokes, dropping nickels into a juke box, jitter-bugging to the music, jiving, and in general, having what they considered a good time. Sonny thought of Miss Cicely and knew that she expected him to stay out late because there was no Tim to come after him. He knew his grandmother's grief for Tim was still raw. He thought he would give her a break and a surprise by going home early just to prove he could be as good as Tim if he wanted to. The trouble with Tim was he'd been a killjoy. He never let himself go—never had any fun. Anyway, there wasn't anything going on. The session wasn't so hot. The joint wasn't jumping.

Just as he was about to leave, some other fellows rushed in with electrifying news—news about a colored soldier being shot and killed by a cop. All the rumors with added details were repeated.

At that moment, they heard the roar of the mob. They rushed out. A few blocks away they could see the milling throng. Somebody called out, "What we waiting for! Let's go," and up the avenue they ran.

They joined the crowd at first just to see what was going on. In the middle of the next block they pulled up beside a group milling around a tall Negro who harangued them.

"Ladies and gentlemen—this sonervabitch has robbed us out of enough money to buy this store twice over. Suppos'n we help ourselves to a little refreshment in his honor—everything on the house."

He flung a rock through the plate glass window of the liquor store before which he was standing. The crowd screamed with glee.

"Step right up, folks, and help yourself—all free for nothin'—"

The crowd surged forward, yelling, laughing. A woman uttered a piercing scream and put her hands to her bleeding face. The human mass had pushed her against a jagged piece of glass in the broken window.

Further up the street a group had collected in front of a small tailor shop. A Negro had planted himself before the door trying to stand off the crowd.

"But I tell you, this ain't no Jew's place. Jew here works for *me*. What you want to ruin me for?"

The crowd hesitated. A smash across the street split the air. Everybody turned and raced across the street leaving the little tailor mopping the sweat from his face.

Sonny's bunch kept up with the crowd that grew larger every minute. Finally, one of the boys heaved a missile into the air.

"Why?" I asked.

"Oh, just for the hell of it," said Sonny.

Then another of the boys spoke up.

"Let's get into this. How 'bout gettin' that pawn shop guy that wouldn't give us but two dollars on that sax—"

At that moment another attraction caught the attention to the crowd. Down the middle of the street marching to the rhythm of the leaders— "H'rup two! three! four!" came a squad of soldiers. The first impulse of the gang was to get away—take cover. As the soldiers came nearer, however, somebody laughed and several bystanders began to fall in behind the army. Sonny looked on, but somehow the uniforms didn't seem to fit the wearers, and he soon realized that the "soldiers" were just a part of the tatterdemalion mob decked out in uniforms most likely raided from some store.

All of a sudden, a picture of Tim came into his mind—Tim in his khaki uniform with the double corporal's stripes on his arm—Tim standing straight and tall before him as he had last seen him—shaking his hand man to man like. "Take care of grandma, Sonny, while I'm away." Sonny could stand no more. He turned away and started for home on the run.

Well, Miss Cicely wasn't very coherent about what she did or how long she stayed in the streets, hoping against hope that Sonny would be in the next group or on the next corner. Tired from her wanderings, she took refuge in a doorway as she saw another throng of people surging towards her. The pattern repeated itself—crashes, yells, shrieks, cries of glee, curses,—more crashes,—people passing with loaded arms, loud talk—.

"Ain't that a goddam shame! I got two *left* shoes."

"Come on folks! Ain't you tired of relief and fat back? Want some ham what is. Know where to get it, too."

Too late, Miss Cicely saw that the mob was headed straight towards her, and realized that the grocery store behind her was the goal. The mob crowded in upon her. She was knocked down—stunned. Then she remembered someone picking her up roughly. "Auntie, what you doin' out here—you better get out of this—. Here, this will do you. Better not go back in there with them cats."

A heavy bag was thrust into her hands—somebody led her out of the mob—she could breathe. And now all she wanted to do was to go home.

Wearily she climbed the four flights to her little flat. As she unlocked and opened the door, she was aware that the radio was going. She knew she had turned it off before going out. Then she saw him.

"Sonny!" she cried. "Oh, Sonny, I been so worried 'bout you—."

Sonny jumped up and stared at his grandmother in amazement. He looked at the heavy bundle she had dropped to the floor in her joy over seeing Sonny safe at home.

"Sonny, where've you been? I looked everywhere—."

"Where've *I* been! For crying out loud! Where've *you* been?" He pushed the bag contemptuously with his foot and brushed past Miss Cicely.

"Sonny! Where you goin'?"

"Jesus! You! Out gettin' that junk while I was hurryin' home thinkin' you'd be worried 'bout me. I could have pinched real stuff—diamonds—

gold—." He laughed derisively, as with another kick at the bundle on the floor, he pulled on his cap and rushed out, banging the door.

"Sonny! Sonny!" screamed Miss Cicely over the bannisters but her only answer was the sound of Sonny's footsteps as he sped down the stairs.

Morning came at last. Miss Cicely had spent the rest of the night after Sonny's departure on her knees.

"Forgive me, dear Jesus—Lord have mercy—You took Tim—Dear Lord— Spare my Sonny—Lord have mercy—."

The sun was high in the sky when there came a heavy knocking on the door, an ominous sound to Miss Cicely's tired mind.

"Open up in the name of the Law!"

The two red-faced blue-coated officers completely filled the doorway. Miss Cicely quaked.

"Are you Cicely Jones?"

"Know a boy named Samuel Jones or Sammy Jones?"

"Any relation to you?"

And on and on—. Miss Cicely couldn't answer. She could only shake her head.

"Where is he?" she moaned. "What have you done with him?"

The officer stumbled over the bundle still lying where Miss Cicely had dropped it.

"What's this? Stolen stuff. Search the place, Jim," he called to his companion.

"Nothing here."

"Guess you'd better come along with us, sister. Bring that stuff along, Jim. Accepting stolen goods, huh?"

"Where's my Sonny?" pleaded Miss Cicely, who hadn't moved. "Please, Mr. Officer, tell me where he is."

"Harlem Hospital, lady, if you want to know. Guess he wasn't satisfied with this—tried for bigger pickin's—caught him coming out of a jewelry store. That's when he got his. Tried to run. A bullet stopped him. Come on, sister, we ain't got all day," but Miss Cicely had dropped limply, mercifully unconscious, at his feet.

The following day I sought Clem and gave him the story.

"Can't we do something?" said Clem. "How is the boy?"

"He'll come around all right. Stands to do a stretch for burglary."

"Are they still holding the old woman?" asked Clem. "Maybe we could get somebody interested in her."

He picked up the telephone and called the police station.

"About that Jones case—Cicely Jones—" He gave the needed details.

After a long wait there came an answer. Clem slammed down the receiver and turned to me, his face strained.

"Come on, I feel the need of a drink," he called as he got up and started out.

I looked my question. Clem answered.

"Cicely Jones died in her cell last night," he said. "Heart attack."

NEGRO STORY, OCTOBER–NOVEMBER 1944

Sticks and Stones

LILA MARSHALL

Mary was a whitish little colored girl with long shiny black braids and dark eyes. She had lived in this new all-white neighborhood for a couple of weeks, and she was lonely. Every day she watched the white children play—long lanky white ones, short fat ones, the ugly girl with the glasses and the one with the pretty red hair. She didn't know them, and you couldn't just walk up to strange children and ask them to play with you, especially if they were white.

There was that one little girl with the big fat red curls that shone brightly in the sun. Mary looked at this little girl all of the time because she had never before seen such beautiful hair. She pretended that this little girl was her special friend, and at night she dreamed that they had lots of fun together. She even imagined a name for her friend. In her mind she called her Rella because she liked that name.

Finally, one day when she was coming home from the store, she saw this little girl's house, which was the only shabby one in the block. It was near the corner. Mary wondered why the prettiest girl in the neighborhood lived in the poorest house. It was frame, and the side-wall shingles were shedding their paint. Great whelps of paint remained showing the bare wood underneath and they made Mary's flesh crawl. They reminded her of her skin when she was peeling from scarlet fever. Boards were missing, leaving ugly gaps in the steps, and at the dirt-streaked windows hung frayed curtains and crazy shades. The back yard was full of old cars and wagons. Mary had often thought what a grand place it would be in which to play and pretend that you were Indians or people in covered wagons being killed by the Indians as she used to play in the old neighborhood.

The other houses rose high in arrogance and splendor, as if they were sneering down on the poor little corner house. Mary's was the most imposing; it was three stories high. Mother had said something about daddy getting their house "for a song" because all the white folks were scared and moved out. She had also said that the house on the corner was a disgrace to the neighborhood, and that the three old ladies next door were trying to get it torn down.

This day when she passed from the store, the little girl was sitting on her rickety porch. Mary was close enough to see that she had tiny freckles; but she was pretty, just the same. When she smiled at Mary and said "Hello," Mary trembled with pleasure. Then she smiled back shyly and quickly ran home with her groceries. In a moment, she was out again with a big, red ball. She bounced it hard on the sidewalk in front of her house, throwing her foot over it at each bounce. She kept shooting furtive glances from under her long lashes in the direction of the house on the corner. In a few minutes the little white girl began to edge slowly toward Mary's house with her first finger stuck in her little moist, red mouth; she began to sway a little. Then she gathered courage and came closer.

"What's your name?" she asked, thrusting her face forward a trifle.

"Mary Taylor—what's yours?"

"Mine's Jane Forbes."

"Oh!"

"Do you like to jump rope?"

"Yes."

"Wanta jump?"

Mary ran up the steps, skipping one each time, her long, thin legs carrying her quickly into the house and out again, trailing a red-handled rope behind her. The screen door banged loudly.

"Your turn," she said.

Jane jumped to one hundred and two, without stopping; then she gave the rope to Mary.

"Now, your turn."

Mary counted 250-251-252. She jumped to 301 and wasn't even tired.

"Don't you believe I can Double Dutch?" she asked.

"Can you, really?"

"Uh-huh!"

Jane's eyes betrayed her admiration.

After that Jane and Mary were inseparable. They usually played all day in Mary's backyard. Sometimes they pretended they were Indians or Pilgrims and the wagons in Mary's back yard became forts or covered wagons.

Sometimes they played Hide and Seek. But best of all, Mary liked to make mud pies. In her back yard she and Jane would press the firm but yielding substances into fascinating shapes. It would spread under their continual manipulations into round, crinkled lumps or smooth elongated ones. Not a dent or furrow could be found to mar the smoothness of these forms. Often Mary had to restrain herself, to keep from tasting them; especially when she pulled and patted them into a flat pie. They never tired of making these mud pies. The long summer days were passing fast. Each day that passed cemented the feeling of the two girls into a stronger friendship.

Each day the girls became closer friends until you could hardly see one without the other. They were always talking and playing and laughing. Mary played with all of the white girls, but Jane was her best friend. Her life had become full now, very happy and gay.

Mary did not see very much of Jane's family, only occasionally caught a glimpse of the tall thin white-haired woman who was her mother, and of the thin blond boy who was her brother and of her red-haired father. Sometimes they smiled at her and Jane told her they thought she was pretty and nice.

Jane often ran into her house, and Mary's mother always gave them cookies and lemonade. Mary's mother seemed to know just what children needed.

"Is your mother white, Mary?" Jane asked.

"No, she's colored—like me."

"I don't see how you can be colored, and your mother is so white."

Mary had no answer for this. In fact, she was not sure she understood it herself. So she went right on playing and swinging in the big porch swing. They played all day every day, only stopping to eat and sleep.

One evening, when the sun was moving down behind the tall buildings in the West, Mary stood on the porch, watching it with great interest. Where the sun had been, the sky looked like a huge cauldron of fire with black seething smoke rising from it; but above this riotous coloring, stretched the usual calm sky—white and placid blue—untouched by the angry sun which had scarred it below.

Later, only a few flame-colored streaks were left in a drab sky. The air was flower-scented and heavy with a damp freshness. Mary took long breaths and jumped from step to step. She would pause to watch the leafy scallops of the trees and would stare up at the clouds which looked like fluffy dabs of moving cotton and which formed sheep and dogs and an entire floating menagerie. She never tired of finding shapes in these ever-changing white masses.

Seven-thirty came and when her mother called her, she dragged herself into the house. Her look was sullen. Daddy had gone out, leaving them there alone.

That night Mary dreamed she and Jane were running fast, with all of the neighborhood kids chasing them. Just as they ran around the corner, they sailed gracefully up into the air as if they had wings. There they were, floating away, while the others shouted and beckoned to them. The children on the ground were like tiny specks.

Then suddenly, they began to fall from a great height. Mary could feel the dizzy fear of falling, and then they hit the earth; simultaneously her body jerked her into consciousness.

Mary could hardly tell whether she was asleep or awake. She could feel herself being held tightly. She heard a terrific noise. The noises seemed to be coming from everywhere. The whole world was confused. Shouts and shrieks came from afar. The sound of shots could be heard in the distance. There was one prolonged din. She realized that she was awake—in her mother's arms.

"Mother, what's that? "

But mother was running to the front window. Mary followed, her bare feet padding against the cool boards of the floor. She crouched beside her mother near the big, bay window. The noises were coming closer. She stood up, but her mother snatched her down behind the window.

The shouts were louder.

She jumped up, just in time to see three men running hard. The street light flooded into their wild dark faces.

Other men pursued them. She saw their pale grim faces. There seemed no end to them.

"Stop them!"

"Stop those niggers!"

She saw a black man drop down, his long body jerking grotesquely backward. He lay with his arms out-stretched and his right leg doubled under him. Blood gushed out, until he lay in a pool of it, a huge black stain on the pavement.

She screamed, and her mother held her tightly.

"Oh, Lord," she heard her mother moan, "God have mercy on us." She covered her face. She was weak. Her knees sagged. When she looked again, the other two were running ahead of the crowd, zigzagging wildly. They looked like dolls in the distance—little puppets that she had seen in the circus. Her heart sank within her as she saw one of the men fall forward on his face, and then the other stopped, suddenly reeled on his toes, clutched his shirt front, and fell heavily to the ground.

All was quiet now except for her mother's moaning.

"God have mercy—on my poor John—God have mercy."

Mary began to cry. She looked out at the dead man under the street light. He had a queer surprised look. She hid her face in her mother's dress, and they both cried . . .

Mother was sobbing and she was praying to God to send daddy safely home. Mary prayed too.

She waited. She clung to her mother. She asked her mother why the white men killed the black ones. Her mother could not answer. She could only pray for her husband, and moan. Her throat was raw and queer. She had never seen death before.

As they waited, she heard the dull thud of feet running up their steps. She caught her breath. She felt her mother's hold tighten. She could scarcely breathe. Then she felt herself being half carried to the head of the stairs. She shrank against the wall with her mother, trembling and peering down the dark stairs. Her ears were strained for the least sound. Would they be shot like those men out there? She held in her breath. She listened.

The front door lock turned with a click, and footsteps were heard on the floor below. Breathing a heavy sigh, her mother ran quickly downstairs with Mary close behind her. It was daddy.

They threw themselves on him, almost knocking him over with their caresses.

"Thank God," breathed her mother, clinging to her husband. "Thank God!"

Then she fell, senseless, to the floor.

When she had recovered and lay on the couch in the parlor, Mary and daddy were standing over her. She heard her mother say:

"Oh, John! A man—a man was killed."

"Yes, darling—I know—calm yourself."

"John, what is it—what's happened?"

"A riot."

"Riot? What riot?"

"Colored and whites fighting all over the city."

Now that her husband was safe, Mrs. Taylor seemed to regain her strength.

She sat up.

"What happened?"

"A colored boy was drowned at the lake."

"How?"

"A bunch of white ruffians!"

"Are we in danger?"

"I don't know."

"I was so worried about you—what'll we do? "

"I don't know."

"Lord have mercy, John—Lord have mercy on us."

Her mother covered her face with her hands.

When she was stronger, she took Mary upstairs, while daddy went down in the basement to see if all of the doors were locked.

Far off in the distance could be heard guns barking away in the night. They listened to the staccato of the guns, their ears peeled to hear closer reports.

Then, "Look, mother—look!"

She pointed across the street.

Three or four half-grown boys had gathered around the street light. She recognized their white faces. One was Jane's brother. They were talking. Several others joined them.

Grabbing her cold hand, Mother ran down to the basement. As they tiptoed across the cement floor, her ears fairly ached with the silence. She clung to her mother—speechless with fear. She could feel the pressure of her mother's hand as they crept over near daddy. Standing near the window, she saw that he had pushed something long and shiny through the iron bars and pointed toward the street.

"Hush," he whispered. The black, musty silence enveloped them. The odor of dust and dampness made her feel faint and weak. She thought of Jane. Would Jane's father kill her father or would her father kill Jane's?

"Look," her father whispered.

They could see the dark forms of the boys moving around in the moonlight. The street light was bright. One boy stood up on the stone steps above the others. He was waving his hands furiously. Soon the others began to shout shaking their clenched fists. She heard the angry shouts in the darkness of the basement.

"We ought to kill all the damn niggers!"

"Killing white men!"

"Black sons of bitches, taking white men's jobs!"

"God damn niggers!"

The bright moonlight shone on their angry faces. Some were red and furious. Others where pale. But they were all waving and shouting, their shadows making fantastic figures on the wall behind them.

Now one of the figures was pointing toward Mary's house. All turned toward them. Fear clutched at her heart. It seemed that she would drop down on the cement floor. She wrapped her arms tightly around her mother's waist.

"Niggers," they shouted, "niggers over there!"

"Niggers is killing white folks!"

"Get those damn niggers!"

The young ruffians began to stir. They moved restlessly.

"Come on, kill the niggers!"

"Come on, kill all the damn niggers!" At once, there was a rush toward her house and a loud yell.

Mary was too frightened to move or cry. Now they would die, die like that man in the street. Terror gripped her dry throat. She clung to her mother. Then she saw her father move. There was a flash. A shot rang out! And another!

The leader stopped short—hesitating.

"A gun!" someone yelled.

"Nigger's gotta gun!"

"The nigger's got a gun!"

"God damn!"

As if by magic, the streets were cleared. She saw them running in all directions. There was not one left.

"Dirty cowards!"

"That got 'em!"

"We'll die fighting."

"The dirty white trash!"

She couldn't believe it was her daddy's voice. She had never heard him say such a thing before.

She shivered. What were niggers? What was white trash? Her father stood motionless—waiting. Mary cowered. She didn't want to be a nigger. She didn't want to die. She began to cry.

"Mother!" she cried in great fright. "Mother, are they comin'? Will they kill us too? Mother? Mother? What's a nigger?"

Mother hushed her furiously, shaking and threatening her, frantically. She stopped crying. She listened. All night long they waited there in the blackness. At intervals, Mary dozed against her mother's warm body. But she always awoke with a start, hearing the shots in the distance. The boys did not return.

Dawn came. During the days that followed, they did not so much as stick their heads out the door. They ate the canned food that was in the house.

They played cards and had fun. Her father stayed home from work. That was fun. The shades in the house were all pulled low. Her father slept in the day sometimes. At night, while they slept, he kept up his tireless vigil, shotgun close by.

Several days later, a phone call from a friend in a distant neighborhood announced the close of the riot. She was glad. The horror of the past week was over. It was like a dream. Everyone went back to work as if nothing had happened.

She danced and sang. Her heart was light. Now she could make mud pies again and play games with Jane. She forgot all about the riot. She skipped to the store. How good it was to be out in the fresh air again. She looked up into the smooth blue and white of the sky. On her way home, as she neared the poor little house on the corner, she saw Jane on the porch, her red curls shining in the sun. She had on a blue dress. Her heart leaped.

"Yoo hoo, Jane," she called, waving her hand, in her joy at seeing her friend.

But as she approached, she saw no answering wave. Jane was frowning at her.

She stood still—a few feet from her friend. Then Jane took a step forward. Her small red tongue darted out.

"Dirty nigger," she spat, "my mother says I don't play with you no more— cuz you ain't nothin, but an ol' dirty nigger—you ol' nigger girl."

Mary wanted to fight—hit someone. She wanted to cry. But, somehow she drew herself up as tall as she could, her black braids flying, her face pale, and with a toss of her head and all of the dignity she could muster, said in a voice that trembled.

"Sticks and stones will break my bones, but names will never hurt me."

She wanted to run home quickly, but she turned and walked slowly away. Her knees wobbled. Her feet were heavy. Tears were swelling into her eyes ready to overflow. The world seemed ended. What could she do? How could she live? She put her head higher into the air, but she was all hurting inside, and when she got into her home, she threw herself down and sobbed: her throat was choked with horror and despair.

SUBMITTED TO *THE CRISIS*, AUGUST 1943

In Darkness and Confusion

ANN PETRY

William Jones took a sip of coffee and then put his cup down on the kitchen table. It didn't taste right and he was annoyed because he always looked forward to eating breakfast. He usually got out of bed as soon as he woke up and hurried into the kitchen. Then he would take a long time heating the corn bread left over from dinner the night before, letting the coffee brew until it was strong and clear, frying bacon, and scrambling. He would eat very slowly—savoring the early-morning quiet and the just-rightness of the food he fixed.

There was no question about early morning being the best part of the day, he thought. But this Saturday morning in July it was too hot in the apartment. There were too many nagging worries that kept drifting through his mind. In the heat he couldn't think clearly—so that all of them pressed in against him, weighed him down.

He pushed his plate away from him. The eggs had cooked too long; much as he liked corn bread, it tasted like sand this morning—grainy and coarse inside his throat. He couldn't help wondering if it scratched the inside of his stomach in the same way.

Pink was moving around in the bedroom. He cocked his head on one side, listening to her. He could tell exactly what she was doing, as though he were in there with her. The soft heavy sound of her stockinged feet as she walked over to the dresser. The dresser drawer being pulled out. That meant she was getting a clean slip. Then the thud of her two hundred pounds landing in the rocker by the window. She was sitting down to comb her hair. Untwisting the small braids she'd made the night before. She would unwind them one by one, putting the hairpins in her mouth as she went along. Now she was brushing it, for he could hear the creak of the rocker; she was rocking back and forth, humming under her breath as she brushed.

He decided that as soon as she came into the kitchen he would go back to the bedroom, get dressed, and go to work. For his mind was already on the mailbox. He didn't feel like talking to Pink. There simply had to be a letter from Sam today. There had to be.

He was thinking about it so hard that he didn't hear Pink walk toward the kitchen.

When he looked up she was standing in the doorway. She was a short, enormously fat woman. The only garment she had on was a bright pink slip that magnified the size of her body. The skin on her arms and shoulders and chest was startlingly black against the pink material. In spite of the brisk brushing she had given her hair, it stood up stiffly all over her head in short wiry lengths, as though she wore a turban of some rough dark gray material.

He got up from the table quickly when he saw her. "Hot, ain't it?" he said, and patted her arm as he went past her toward the bedroom.

She looked at the food on his plate. "You didn't want no breakfast?" she asked.

"Too hot," he said over his shoulder.

He closed the bedroom door behind him gently. If she saw the door was shut, she'd know that he was kind of low in his mind this morning and that he didn't feel like talking. At first he moved about with energy—getting a clean work shirt, giving his shoes a hasty brushing, hunting for a pair of clean socks. Then he stood still in the middle of the room, holding his dark work pants in his hand while he listened to the rush and roar of water running in the bathtub.

Annie May was up and taking a bath. And he wondered if that meant she was going to work. Days when she went to work she used a hot comb on her hair before she ate her breakfast, so that before he left the house in the morning it was filled with the smell of hot irons sizzling against hair grease.

He frowned. Something had to be done about Annie May. Here she was only eighteen years old and staying out practically all night long. He hadn't said anything to Pink about it, but Annie May crept into the house at three and four and five in the morning. He would hear her key go in the latch and then the telltale click as the lock drew back. She would shut the door very softly and turn the bolt. She'd stand there awhile, waiting to see if they woke up. Then she'd take her shoes off and pad down the hall in her stockinged feet.

When she turned the light on in the bathroom, he could see the clock on the dresser. This morning it had been four-thirty when she came in. Pink, lying beside him, went on peacefully snoring. He was glad that she didn't wake up easy. It would only worry her to know that Annie May was carrying on like that.

Annie May put her hands on her hips and threw her head back and laughed whenever he tried to tell her she had to come home earlier. The smoky smell of the hot irons started seeping into the bedroom and he finished dressing quickly.

He stopped in the kitchen on his way out. "Got to get to the store early today," he explained. He was sure Pink knew he was hurrying downstairs to look in the mailbox. But she nodded and held her face up for his kiss. When he brushed his lips against her forehead he saw that her face was wet with perspiration. He thought, With all that weight she must feel the heat something awful.

Annie May nodded at him without speaking. She was hastily swallowing a cup of coffee. Her dark thin hands made a pattern against the thick white cup she was holding. She had pulled her hair out so straight with the hot combs that, he thought, it was like a shiny skullcap fitted tight to her head. He was surprised to see that her lips were heavily coated with lipstick. When she was going to work she didn't use any, and he wondered why she was up so early if she wasn't working. He could see the red outline of her mouth on the cup.

He hadn't intended to say anything. It was the sight of the lipstick on the cup that forced the words out. "You ain't workin' today?"

"No," she said lazily. "Think I'll go shopping." She winked at Pink and it infuriated him.

"How do you expect to keep a job when you don't show up half the time?" he asked.

"I can always get another one." She lifted the coffee cup to her mouth with both hands and her eyes laughed at him over the rim of the cup.

"What time did you come home last night?" he asked abruptly.

She stared out of the window at the blank brick wall that faced the kitchen. "I dunno," she said finally. "It wasn't late."

He didn't know what to say. Probably she was out dancing somewhere. Or maybe she wasn't. He was fairly certain that she wasn't. Yet he couldn't let Pink know what he was thinking. He shifted his feet uneasily and watched Annie May swallow the coffee. She was drinking it fast.

"You know you ain't too big to get your butt whipped," he said finally.

She looked at him out of the corner of her eyes. And he saw a deep smoldering sullenness in her face that startled him. He was conscious that Pink was watching both of them with a growing apprehension.

Then Annie May giggled. "You and who else?" she said lightly. Pink roared with laughter. And Annie May laughed with her.

He banged the kitchen door hard as he went out. Striding down the outside hall, he could still hear them laughing. And even though he knew Pink's laughter was due to relief because nothing unpleasant had happened, he was angry. Lately every time Annie May looked at him there was open, jeering laughter in her eyes, as though she dared him to say anything to her. Almost as though she thought he was a fool for working so hard.

She had been a nice little girl when she first came to live with them six years ago. He groped in his mind for words to describe what he thought Annie May had become. A Jezebel, he decided grimly. That was it.

And he didn't want Pink to know what Annie May was really like. Because Annie May's mother, Lottie, had been Pink's sister. And when Lottie died, Pink took Annie May. Right away she started finding excuses for anything she did that was wrong. If he scolded Annie May he had to listen to a sharp lecture from Pink. It always started off the same way: "Don't care what she done, William. You ain't goin' to lay a finger on her. She ain't got no father and mother except us . . ."

The quick spurt of anger and irritation at Annie May had sent him hurrying down the first flight of stairs. But he slowed his pace on the next flight because the hallways were so dark that he knew if he wasn't careful he'd walk over a step. As he trudged down the long flights of stairs he began to think about Pink. And the hot irritation in him disappeared as it usually did when he thought about her. She was so fat she couldn't keep on climbing all these steep stairs. They would have to find another place to live—on a first floor where it would be easier for her. They'd lived on this top floor for years, and all the time Pink kept getting heavier and heavier. Every time she went to the clinic the doctor said the stairs were bad for her. So they'd start looking for another apartment and then because the top floors cost less, why, they stayed where they were. And—

Then he stopped thinking about Pink because he had reached the first floor. He walked over to the mailboxes and took a deep breath. Today there'd be a letter. He knew it. There had to be. It had been too long a time since they had had a letter from Sam. The last ones that came he'd said the same thing. Over and over. Like a refrain. "Ma, I can't stand this much longer." And then the letters just stopped.

As he stood there, looking at the mailbox, half-afraid to open it for fear there would be no letter, he thought back to the night Sam graduated from high school. It was a warm June night. He and Pink got all dressed up in their best clothes. And he kept thinking, Me and Pink have got as far as we can go. But Sam—he made up his mind Sam wasn't going to earn his living with a mop and a broom. He was going to earn it wearing a starched white collar and a shine on his shoes and a crease in his pants.

After he finished high school Sam got a job redcapping[1] at Grand Central.

---

1. Being a porter at a train station.

He started saving his money because he was going to go to Lincoln—a college in Pennsylvania. It seemed like it was no time at all before he was twenty-one. And in the army. Pink cried when he left. Her huge body shook with her sobbing. He remembered that he had only felt queer and lost. There was this war and all the young men were being drafted. But why Sam—why did he have to go?

It was always in the back of his mind. Next thing Sam was in a camp in Georgia. He and Pink never talked about his being in Georgia. The closest they ever came to it was one night when she said, "I hope he gets used to it quick down there. Bein' born right here in New York there's lots he won't understand."

Then Sam's letters stopped coming. He'd come home from work and say to Pink casually, "Sam write today?" She'd shake her head without saying anything.

The days crawled past. And finally she burst out. "What you keep askin' for? You think I wouldn't tell you?" And she started crying.

He put his arm around her and patted her shoulder. She leaned hard against him. "Oh, Lord," she said. "He's my baby. What they done to him?"

Her crying like that tore him in little pieces. His mind kept going around in circles. Around and around. He couldn't think what to do. Finally one night after work he sat down at the kitchen table and wrote Sam a letter. He had written very few letters in his life because Pink had always done it for him. And now standing in front of the mailbox he could even remember the feel of the pencil in his hand; how the paper looked—blank and challenging—lying there in front of him; that the kitchen clock was ticking and it kept getting louder and louder. It was hot that night, too, and he held the pencil so tight that the inside of his hand was covered with sweat.

He had sat and thought a long time. Then he wrote: "Is you all right? Your Pa." It was the best he could do. He licked the envelope and addressed it with the feeling that Sam would understand.

He fumbled for his key ring, found the mailbox key and opened the box quickly. It was empty. Even though he could see it was empty he felt around inside it. Then he closed the box and walked toward the street door.

The brilliant sunlight outside made him blink after the darkness of the hall. Even now, so early in the morning, it was hot in the street. And he thought it was going to be a hard day to get through, what with the heat and its being Saturday and all. Lately he couldn't seem to think about anything but Sam. Even at the drugstore where he worked as a porter, he would catch himself leaning on the broom or pausing in his mopping to wonder what had happened to him.

The man who owned the store would say to him sharply, "Boy, what the hell's the matter with you? Can't you keep your mind on what you're doing?" And he would go on washing windows, or mopping the floor or sweeping the sidewalk. But his thoughts, somehow, no matter what he was doing, drifted back to Sam.

As he walked toward the drugstore he looked at the houses on both sides of the street. He knew this street as he knew the creases in the old felt hat he wore the year round. No matter how you looked at it, it wasn't a good street to live on. It was a long cross-town street. Almost half of it on one side consisted of the backs of the three theaters on 125th Street—a long blank wall of gray brick. There were few trees on the street. Even these were a source of danger, for at night shadowy, vague shapes emerged from the street's darkness, lurking near the trees, dodging behind them. He had never been accosted by any of those disembodied figures, but the very stealth of their movements revealed a dishonest intent that frightened him. So when he came home at night he walked an extra block or more in order to go through 125th Street and enter the street from Eighth Avenue.

Early in the morning like this, the street slept. Window shades were drawn down tight against the morning sun. The few people he passed were walking briskly on their way to work. But in those houses where the people still slept, the window shades would go up about noon, and radios would blast music all up and down the street. The bold-eyed women who lived in these houses would lounge in the open windows and call to each other back and forth across the street.

Sometimes when he was on his way home to lunch they would call out to him as he went past, "Come on in, Poppa!" And he would stare straight ahead and start walking faster.

When Sam turned sixteen it seemed to him the street was unbearable. After lunch he and Sam went through this block together—Sam to school and he on his way back to the drugstore. He'd seen Sam stare at the lounging women in the windows. His face was expressionless, but his eyes were curious.

"I catch you goin' near one of them women and I'll beat you up and down the block," he'd said grimly.

Sam didn't answer him. Instead he looked down at him with a strangely adult look, for even at sixteen Sam had been a good five inches taller than he. After that when they passed through the block, Sam looked straight ahead. And William got the uncomfortable feeling that he had already explored the possibilities that the block offered. Yet he couldn't be sure. And he couldn't bring himself to ask him. Instead he walked along beside him, thinking desperately, We gotta move. I'll talk to Pink. We gotta move this time for sure.

That Sunday after Pink came home from church they looked for a new place. They went in and out of apartment houses along Seventh Avenue and Eighth Avenue, 135th Street, 145th Street. Most of the apartments they didn't even look at. They just asked the super how much the rents were.

It was late when they headed for home. He had irritably agreed with Pink that they'd better stay where they were. Thirty-two dollars a month was all they could afford.

"It ain't a fit place to live, though," he said. They were walking down Seventh Avenue. The street looked wide to him, and he thought with distaste of their apartment. The rooms weren't big enough for a man to move around in without bumping into something. Sometimes he thought that was why Annie May spent so much time away from home. Even at thirteen she couldn't stand being cooped up like that in such a small amount of space.

And Pink said, "You want to live on Park Avenue? With a doorman bowin' you in and out? 'Good mornin' Mr. William Jones. Does the weather suit you this mornin'?" Her voice was sharp, like the crack of a whip.

That was five years ago. And now again they ought to move on account of Pink not being able to stand the stairs anymore. He decided that Monday night after work he'd start looking for a place.

It was even hotter in the drugstore than it was in the street. He forced himself to go inside and put on a limp work coat. Then broom in hand he went to stand in the doorway. He waved to the superintendent of the building on the corner. And watched him as he lugged garbage cans out of the areaway and rolled them to the curb. Now, that's the kind of work he didn't want Sam to have to do. He tried to decide why that was. It wasn't just because Sam was his boy and it was hard work. He searched his mind for the reason. It didn't pay enough for a man to live on decently. That was it. He wanted Sam to have a job where he could make enough to have good clothes and a nice home.

Sam's being in the army wasn't so bad, he thought. It was his being in Georgia that was bad. They didn't treat black people right down there. Everybody knew that. If he could figure out some way to get him farther north, Pink wouldn't have to worry about him so much.

The very sound of the word Georgia did something to him inside. His mother had been born there. She had talked about it a lot and painted such vivid pictures of it that he felt he knew the place—the heat, the smell of the earth, how cotton looked. And something more. The way her mouth had folded together whenever she had said, "They hate niggers down there. Don't you never none of you children go down there."

That was years ago; yet even now, standing here on Fifth Avenue, remembering the way she said it turned his skin clammy cold in spite of the heat. And of all the places in the world, Sam had to go to Georgia. Sam, who was born right here in New York, who had finished high school here—they had to put him in the army and send him to Georgia.

He tightened his grip on the broom and started sweeping the sidewalk in long, even strokes. Gradually the rhythm of the motion stilled the agitation in him. The regular back-and-forth motion was so pleasant that he kept on sweeping long after the sidewalk was clean. When Mr. Yudkin, who owned the store, arrived at eight-thirty he was still outside with the broom. Even now he didn't feel much like talking, so he only nodded in response to the druggist's brisk "Good morning! Hot today!"

William followed him into the store and began polishing the big mirror in back of the soda fountain. He watched the man out of the corner of his eye as he washed his hands in the back room and exchanged his suit coat for a crisp white laboratory coat. And he thought maybe when the war was over Sam ought to study to be a druggist instead of a doctor or a lawyer.

As the morning wore along, customers came in in a steady stream. They got Bromo-Seltzers, cigarettes, aspirin, cough medicine, baby bottles. He delivered two prescriptions that cost five dollars. And the cash register rang so often it almost played a tune. Listening to it he said to himself, Yes, Sam ought to be a druggist. It's clean work and it pays good.

A little after eleven o'clock three young girls came in. "Cokes," they said, and climbed up on the stools in front of the fountain. William was placing new stock on the shelves and he studied them from the top of the stepladder. As far as he could see, they looked exactly alike. All three of them. And like Annie May. Too thin. Too much lipstick. Their dresses were too short and too tight. Their hair was piled on top of their heads in slicked set curls.

"Aw, I quit that job," one of them said. "I wouldn't get up that early in the morning for nothing in the world."

That was like Annie May, too. She was always changing jobs. Because she could never get to work on time. If she was due at a place at nine, she got there at ten. If at ten, then she arrived about eleven. He knew, too, that she didn't earn enough money to pay for all the cheap, bright-colored dresses she was forever buying.

Her girl friends looked just like her and just like these girls. He'd seen her coming out of the movie houses on 125th Street with two or three of them. They were all chewing gum and they nudged each other and talked too loud and laughed too loud. They stared hard at every man who went past them.

Mr. Yudkin looked up at him sharply, and he shifted his glance away from the girls and began putting big bottles of Father John's medicine neatly on the shelf in front of him. As he stacked the bottles up he wondered if Annie May would have been different if she'd stayed in high school. She had stopped going when she was sixteen. He had spoken to Pink about it. "She oughtn't to stop school. She's too young," he'd said.

But because Annie May was Pink's sister's child, all Pink had done had been to shake her head comfortably. "She's tired of going to school. Poor little thing. Leave her alone."

So he hadn't said anything more. Pink always took up for her. And he and Pink didn't fuss at each other like some folks do. He didn't say anything to Pink about it, but he took the afternoon off from work to go to see the principal of the school. He had to wait two hours to see her. And he studied the pictures on the walls in the outer office, and looked down at his shoes while he tried to put into words what he'd say—and how he wanted to say it.

The principal was a large-bosomed white woman. She listened to him long enough to learn that he was Annie May's uncle. "Ah, yes, Mr. Jones," she said. "Now in my opinion—"

And he was buried under a flow of words, a mountain of words, that went on and on. Her voice was high-pitched and loud, and she kept talking until he lost all sense of what she was saying. There was one phrase she kept using that sort of jumped at him out of the mass of words—"a slow learner."

He left her office feeling confused and embarrassed. If he could only have found the words he could have explained that Annie May was bright as a dollar. She wasn't any "slow learner." Before he knew it he was out in the street, conscious only that he'd lost a whole afternoon's pay and he never had got to say what he'd come for. And he was boiling mad with himself. All he'd wanted was to ask the principal to help him persuade Annie May to finish school. But he'd never got the words together.

When he hung up his soiled work coat in the broom closet at eight o'clock that night he felt as though he'd been sweeping floors, dusting fixtures, cleaning fountains and running errands since the beginning of time itself. He looked at himself in the cracked mirror that hung on the door of the closet. There was no question about it; he'd grown older-looking since Sam had gone into the army. His hair was turning a frizzled gray at the temples. His jawbones showed up sharper. There was a stoop in his shoulders.

"Guess I'll get a haircut," he said softly. He didn't really need one. But on a Saturday night the barbershop would be crowded. He'd have to wait a long time before Al got around to him. It would be good to listen to the talk that went on—the arguments that would get started and never really end. For a little while all the nagging worry about Sam would be pushed so far back in his mind, he wouldn't be aware of it.

The instant he entered the barbershop he could feel himself begin to relax inside. All the chairs were full. There were a lot of customers waiting. He waved a greeting to the barbers. "Hot, ain't it?" he said, and mopped his forehead.

He stood there a minute, listening to the hum of conversation, before he picked out a place to sit. Some of the talk, he knew, would be violent, and he always avoided those discussions because he didn't like violence—even when it was only talk. Scraps of talk drifted past him.

"White folks got us by the balls—"

"Well, I dunno. It ain't just white folks. There's poor white folks gettin' their guts squeezed out, too—"

"Sure. But they're white. They can stand it better."

"Sadie had two dollars on 546 yesterday and it came out and—"

"You're wrong, man. Ain't no two ways about it. This country's set up so that—"

"Only thing to do, if you ask me, is shoot all them crackers and start out new—"

He finally settled himself in one of the chairs in the corner—not too far from the window and right in the middle of a group of regular customers who were arguing hotly about the war. It was a good seat. By looking in the long mirror in front of the barbers he could see the length of the shop.

Almost immediately he joined in the conversation. "Them Japs ain't got a chance—" he started. And he was feeling good. He'd come in at just the right time. He took a deep breath before he went on. Most every time he started talking about the Japs the others listened with deep respect. Because he knew more about them than the other customers. Pink worked for some navy people and she told him what they said.

He looked along the line of waiting customers, watching their reaction to his words. Pretty soon they'd all be listening to him. And then he stopped talking abruptly. A soldier was sitting in the far corner of the shop, staring down at his shoes. Why, that's Scummy, he thought. He's at the same camp where Sam is. He forgot what he was about to say. He got up and walked over to Scummy. He swallowed all the questions about Sam that trembled on his lips.

"Hiya, son," he said. "Sure is good to see you."

As he shook hands with the boy he looked him over carefully. He's changed, he thought. He was older. There was something about his eyes that was different than before. He didn't seem to want to talk. After that first quick look at William he kept his eyes down, staring at his shoes.

Finally William couldn't hold the question back any longer. It came out fast. "How's Sam?"

Scummy picked up a newspaper from the chair beside him. "He's all right," he mumbled. There was a long silence. Then he raised his head and looked directly at William. "Was the las' time I seen him." He put a curious emphasis on the word "las'."

William was conscious of a trembling that started in his stomach. It went all through his body. He was aware that conversation in the barbershop had stopped. It was like being inside a cone of silence in which he could hear the scraping noise of the razors—a harsh sound, loud in the silence. Al was putting thick oil on a customer's hair and he turned and looked with the hair-oil bottle still in his hand, tilted up over the customer's head. The men sitting in the tilted-back barber's chairs twisted their necks around— awkwardly, slowly—so they could look at Scummy.

"What you mean—the las' time?" William asked sharply. The words beat against his ears. He wished the men in the barbershop would start talking again, for he kept hearing his own words. "What you mean—the las' time?" Just as though he were saying them over and over again. Something had gone wrong with his breathing too. He couldn't seem to get enough air in through his nose.

Scummy got up. There was something about him that William couldn't give a name to. It made the trembling in his stomach worse.

"The las' time I seen him he was O.K." Scummy's voice made a snarling noise in the barbershop.

One part of William's mind said, Yes, that's it. It's hate that makes him look different. It's hate in his eyes. You can see it. It's in his voice, and you can hear it. He's filled with it.

"Since I seen him las'," he went on slowly, "he got shot by a white MP. Because he wouldn't go to the nigger end of a bus. He had a bullet put through his guts. He took the MP's gun away from him and shot the bastard in the shoulder." He put the newspaper down and started toward the door; when he reached it he turned around. "They court-martialed him," he said softly. "He got twenty years at hard labor. The notice was posted in the camp the day I left." Then he walked out of the shop. He didn't look back.

There was no sound in the barbershop as William watched him go down the street. Even the razors had stopped. Al was still holding the hair-oil bottle over the head of his customer. The heavy oil was falling on the face of the man sitting in the chair. It was coming down slowly—one drop at a time.

The men in the shop looked at William and then looked away. He thought, I mustn't tell Pink. She mustn't ever get to know. I can go down to the mailbox early in the morning and I can get somebody else to look in it in the afternoon, so if a notice comes I can tear it up.

The barbers started cutting hair again. There was the murmur of conversation in the shop. Customers got up out of the tilted-back chairs. Someone said to him, "You can take my place."

He nodded and walked over to the empty chair. His legs were weak and shaky. He couldn't seem to think at all. His mind kept dodging away from the thought of Sam in prison. Instead the familiar detail of Sam's growing up kept creeping into his thoughts. All the time the boy was in grammar school he made good marks. Time went so fast it seemed like it was just overnight and he was in long pants. And then in high school.

He made the basketball team in high school. The whole school was proud of him, for his picture had been in one of the white papers. They got two papers that day. Pink cut the pictures out and stuck one in the mirror of the dresser in their bedroom. She gave him one to carry in his wallet.

While Al cut his hair he stared at himself in the mirror until he felt as though his eyes were crossed. First he thought, Maybe it isn't true. Maybe Scummy was joking. But a man who was joking didn't look like Scummy looked. He wondered if Scummy was AWOL.[2] That would be bad. He told himself sternly that he mustn't think about Sam here in the barbershop—wait until he got home.

He was suddenly angry with Annie May. She was just plain no good. Why couldn't something have happened to her? Why did it have to be Sam? Then he was ashamed. He tried to find an excuse for having wanted harm to come to her. It looked like all his life he'd wanted a little something for himself and Pink and then when Sam came along he forgot about those things. He wanted Sam to have all the things that he and Pink couldn't get. It got to be too late for them to have them. But Sam—again he told himself not to think about him. To wait until he got home and in bed.

_____

2. Absent Without Leave.

Al took the cloth from around his neck and he got up out of the chair. Then he was out on the street heading toward home. The heat that came from the pavement seeped through the soles of his shoes. He had forgotten how hot it was. He forced himself to wonder what it would be like to live in the country. Sometimes on hot nights like this, after he got home from work, he went to sit in the park. It was always cooler there. It would probably be cool in the country. But then it might be cold in winter—even colder than the city.

The instant he got in the house he took off his shoes and his shirt. The heat in the apartment was like a blanket—it made his skin itch and crawl in a thousand places. He went into the living room, where he leaned out of the window, trying to cool off. Not yet, he told himself. He mustn't think about it yet.

He leaned farther out of the window, to get away from the innumerable odors that came from the boxlike rooms in back of him. They cut off his breath, and he focused his mind on them. There was the greasy smell of cabbage and collard greens, smell of old wood and soapsuds and disinfectant, a lingering smell of gas from the kitchen stove, and over it all Annie May's perfume.

Then he turned his attention to the street. Up and down as far as he could see, folks were sitting on the stoops. Not talking. Just sitting. Somewhere up the street a baby wailed. A woman's voice rose sharply as she told it to shut up.

Pink wouldn't be home until late. The white folks she worked for were having a dinner party tonight. And no matter how late she got home on Saturday night, she always stopped on Eighth Avenue to shop for her Sunday dinner. She never trusted him to do it. It's a good thing, he thought. If she ever took a look at me tonight she'd know there was something wrong.

A key clicked in the lock and he drew back from the window. He was sitting on the couch when Annie May came in the room.

"You're home early, ain't you?" he asked.

"Oh, I'm going out again," she said.

"You shouldn't stay out so late like you did last night," he said mildly. He hadn't really meant to say it. But what with Sam—

"What you think I'm going to do? Sit here every night and make small talk with you?" Her voice was defiant. Loud.

"No," he said, and then added, "but nice girls ain't runnin' around the streets at four o'clock in the mornin'." Now that he'd started he couldn't seem to stop. "Oh, I know what time you come home. And it ain't right. If you don't stop it, you can get some other place to stay."

"It's O.K. with me," she said lightly. She chewed the gum in her mouth so it made a cracking noise. "I don't know what Auntie Pink married a little runt like you for, anyhow. It wouldn't bother me a bit if I never saw you again." She walked toward the hall. "I'm going away for the weekend," she added over her shoulder, "and I'll move out on Monday."

"What you mean for the weekend?" he asked sharply. "Where you goin'?"

"None of your damn business," she said, and slammed the bathroom door hard.

The sharp sound of the door closing hurt his ears so that he winced, wondering why he had grown so sensitive to sounds in the last few hours. What'd she have to say that for, anyway, he asked himself. Five feet five wasn't so short for a man. He was taller than Pink, anyhow. Yet compared to Sam, he supposed he was a runt, for Sam had just kept on growing until he was six feet tall. At the thought he got up from the chair quickly, undressed, and got in bed. He lay there trying to still the trembling in his stomach; trying even now not to think about Sam, because it would be best to wait until Pink was in bed and sound asleep so that no expression on his face, no least little motion, would betray his agitation.

When he heard Pink come up the stairs just before midnight he closed his eyes. All of him was listening to her. He could hear her panting outside on the landing. There was a long pause before she put her key in the door. It took her all that time to get her breath back. She's getting old, he thought. I mustn't ever let her know about Sam.

She came into the bedroom and he pretended to be asleep. He made himself breathe slowly. Evenly. Thinking I can get through tomorrow all right. I won't get up much before she goes to church. She'll be so busy getting dressed she won't notice me.

She went out of the room and he heard the soft murmur of her voice talking to Annie May. "Don't you pay no attention, honey. He don't mean a word of it. I know menfolks. They's always tired and out of sorts by the time Saturdays come around."

"But I'm not going to stay here anymore."

"Yes, you is. You think I'm goin' to let my sister's child be turned out? You goin' to be right here."

They lowered their voices. There was laughter. Pink's deep and rich and slow. Annie May's high-pitched and nervous. Pink said, "You looks lovely, honey. Now, have a good time."

The front door closed. This time Annie May didn't slam it. He turned over on his back, making the springs creak. Instantly Pink came into the bedroom to look at him. He lay still, with his eyes closed, holding his breath for fear she would want to talk to him about what he'd said to Annie May and would wake him up. After she moved away from the door he opened his eyes.

There must be some meaning in back of what had happened to Sam. Maybe it was some kind of judgment from the Lord, he thought. Perhaps he shouldn't have stopped going to church. His only concession to Sunday was to put on his best suit. He wore it just that one day and Pink pressed the pants late on Saturday night. But in the last few years it got so that every time he went to church he wanted to stand up and yell, "You goddamn fools! How much more you goin' to take?"

He'd get to thinking about the street they lived on, and the sight of the minister with his clean white collar turned hind side to and sound of his buttery voice were too much. One Sunday he'd actually gotten on his feet, for the minister was talking about the streets of gold up in heaven; the words were right on the tip of his tongue when Pink reached out and pinched his behind sharply. He yelped and sat down. Someone in back of him giggled. In spite of himself a slow smile had spread over his face. He stayed quiet through the rest of the service but after that, he didn't go to church at all.

This street where he and Pink lived was like the one where his mother had lived. It looked like he and Pink ought to have gotten further than his mother had. She had scrubbed floors, washed and ironed in the white folks' kitchens. They were doing practically the same thing. That was another reason he stopped going to church. He couldn't figure out why these things had to stay the same, and if the Lord didn't intend it like that, why didn't He change it?

He began thinking about Sam again, so he shifted his attention to the sounds Pink was making in the kitchen. She was getting the rolls ready for tomorrow. Scrubbing the sweet potatoes. Washing the greens. Cutting up the chicken. Then the thump of the iron. Hot as it was, she was pressing his pants. He resisted the impulse to get up and tell her not to do it.

A little later, when she turned the light on in the bathroom, he knew she was getting ready for bed. And he held his eyes tightly shut, made his body rigidly still. As long as he could make her think he was sound asleep she wouldn't take a real good look at him. One real good look and she'd know there was something wrong. The bed sagged under her weight as she knelt down to say her prayers. Then she was lying down beside him. She sighed under her breath as her head hit the pillow.

He must have slept part of the time, but in the morning it seemed to him that he had looked up at the ceiling most of the night. He couldn't remember actually going to sleep.

When he finally got up, Pink was dressed and ready for church. He sat down in a chair in the living room away from the window, so the light wouldn't shine on his face. As he looked at her he wished that he could find relief from the confusion of his thoughts by taking part in the singing and shouting that would go on in church. But he couldn't. And Pink never said anything about his not going to church. Only sometimes like today, when she was ready to go, she looked at him a little wistfully.

She had on her Sunday dress. It was made of a printed material—big red and black poppies splashed on a cream-colored background. He wouldn't let himself look right into her eyes, and in order that she wouldn't notice the evasiveness of his glance, he stared at the dress. It fit snugly over her best corset, and the corset in turn constricted her thighs and tightly encased the rolls of flesh around her waist. She didn't move away, and he couldn't keep on inspecting the dress, so he shifted his gaze up to the wide cream-colored straw hat she was wearing far back on her head. Next he noticed that she was easing her feet by standing on the outer edges of the high-heeled patent leather pumps she wore.

He reached out and patted her arm. "You look nice," he said, picking up the comic section of the paper.

She stood there looking at him while she pulled a pair of white cotton gloves over her roughened hands. "Is you all right, honey?" she asked.

"Course," he said, holding the paper up in front of his face.

"You shouldn't talk so mean to Annie May," she said gently.

"Yeah, I know," he said, and hoped she understood that he was apologizing. He didn't dare lower the paper while she was standing there looking at him so intently. Why doesn't she go, he thought.

"There's grits and eggs for breakfast."

"O.K." He tried to make his voice sound as though he were so absorbed in what he was reading that he couldn't give her all of his attention. She walked toward the door, and he lowered the paper to watch her, thinking that her legs looked too small for her body under the vastness of the printed dress, that women were sure funny—she's got that great big pocketbook swinging on her arm and hardly anything in it. Sam used to love to tease her about the size of the handbags she carried.

When she closed the outside door and started down the stairs, the heat in the little room struck him in the face. He almost called her back so that he wouldn't be there by himself—left alone to brood over Sam. He decided that when she came home from church he would make love to her. Even in the heat the softness of her body, the smoothness of her skin, would comfort him.

He pulled his chair up close to the open window. Now he could let himself go. He could begin to figure out something to do about Sam. There's gotta be something, he thought. But his mind wouldn't stay put. It kept going back to the time Sam graduated from high school. Nineteen seventy-five his dark blue suit had cost. He and Pink had figured and figured and finally they'd managed it. Sam had looked good in the suit; he was so tall and his shoulders were so broad it looked like a tailor-made suit on him. When he got his diploma everybody went wild—he'd played center on the basketball team, and a lot of folks recognized him.

The trembling in his stomach got worse as he thought about Sam. He was aware that it had never stopped since Scummy had said those words "the las' time." It had gone on all last night until now there was a tautness and a tension in him that left him feeling as though his eardrums were strained wide open, listening for sounds. They must be a foot wide open, he thought. Open and pulsing with the strain of being open. Even his nostrils were stretched open like that. He could feel them. And a weight behind his eyes.

He went to sleep sitting there in the chair. When he woke up his whole body was wet with sweat. It musta got hotter while I slept, he thought. He was conscious of an ache in his jawbones. It's from holding 'em shut so tight. Even his tongue—he'd been holding it so still in his mouth it felt like it was glued there.

Attracted by the sound of voices, he looked out of the window. Across the way a man and a woman were arguing. Their voices rose and fell on the hot, still air. He could look directly into the room where they were standing, and he saw that they were half-undressed.

The woman slapped the man across the face. The sound was like a pistol shot, and for an instant William felt his jaw relax. It seemed to him that the whole block grew quiet and waited. He waited with it. The man grabbed his belt and lashed out at the woman. He watched the belt rise and fall against her brown skin. The woman screamed with the regularity of clockwork. The street came alive again. There was the sound of voices, the rattle of dishes. A baby whined. The woman's voice became a murmur of pain in the background.

"I gotta get me some beer," he said aloud. It would cool him off. It would help him to think. He dressed quickly, telling himself that Pink wouldn't be home for hours yet and by that time the beer smell would be gone from his breath.

The street outside was full of kids playing tag. They were all dressed up in their Sunday clothes. Red socks, blue socks, danced in front of him all the way to the corner. The sight of them piled up the quivering in his stomach. Sam used to play in this block on Sunday afternoons. As he walked along, women thrust their heads out of the opened windows, calling to the children. It seemed to him that all the voices were Pink's voice saying, "You, Sammie, stop that runnin' in your good clo'es!"

He was so glad to get away from the sight of the children that he ignored the heat inside the barroom of the hotel on the corner and determinedly edged his way past girls in sheer summer dresses and men in loud plaid jackets and tight-legged cream-colored pants until he finally reached the long bar.

There was such a sense of hot excitement in the place that he turned to look around him. Men with slicked, straightened hair were staring through half-closed eyes at the girls lined up at the bar. One man sitting at a table close by kept running his hand up and down the bare arm of the girl leaning against him. Up and down. Down and up. William winced and looked away. The jukebox was going full blast, filling the room with high, raw music that beat about his ears in a queer mixture of violence and love and hate and terror. He stared at the brilliantly colored moving lights on the front of the jukebox as he listened to it, wishing that he had stayed at home, for the music made the room hotter.

"Make it a beer," he said to the bartender.

The beer glass was cold. He held it in his hand, savoring the chill of it, before he raised it to his lips. He drank it down fast. Immediately he felt the air grow cooler. The smell of beer and whiskey that hung in the room lifted.

"Fill it up again," he said. He still had that awful trembling in his stomach, but he felt as though he were really beginning to think. Really think. He found he was arguing with himself.

"Sam mighta been like this. Spendin' Sunday afternoons whorin'."

"But he was part of me and part of Pink. He had a chance—"

"Yeah. A chance to live in one of them hell-hole flats. A chance to get himself a woman to beat."

"He woulda finished college and got a good job. Mebbe been a druggist or a doctor or a lawyer—"

"Yeah. Or mebbe got himself a stable of women to rent out on the block—"

He licked the suds from his lips. The man at the table nearby had stopped stroking the girl's arm. He was kissing her—forcing her closer and closer to him.

"Yeah," William jeered at himself. "That coulda been Sam on a hot Sunday afternoon—"

As he stood there arguing with himself he thought it was getting warmer in the bar. The lights were dimmer. I better go home, he thought. I gotta live with this thing some time. Drinking beer in this place ain't going to help any. He looked out toward the lobby of the hotel, attracted by the sound of voices. A white cop was arguing with a frowzy-looking girl who had obviously had too much to drink.

"I got a right in here. I'm mindin' my own business," she said with one eye on the bar.

"Aw, go chase yourself." The cop gave her a push toward the door. She stumbled against a chair.

William watched her in amusement. "Better than a movie," he told himself.

She straightened up and tugged at her girdle. "You white son of a bitch," she said.

The cop's face turned a furious red. He walked toward the woman, waving his nightstick. It was then that William saw the soldier. Tall. Straight. Creases in his khaki pants. An overseas cap cocked over one eye. Looks like Sam looked that one time he was home on furlough, he thought.

The soldier grabbed the cop's arm and twisted the nightstick out of his hand. He threw it half the length of the small lobby. It rattled along the floor and came to a dead stop under a chair.

"Now what'd he want to do that for?" William said softly.

He knew that night after night the cop had to come back to this hotel. He's the law, he thought, and he can't let—Then he stopped thinking about him, for the cop raised his arm. The soldier aimed a blow at the cop's chin. The cop ducked and reached for his gun. The soldier turned to run.

It's happening too fast, William thought. It's like one of those horse race reels they run over fast at the movies. Then he froze inside. The quivering in his stomach got worse. The soldier was heading toward the door. Running. His foot was on the threshold when the cop fired. The soldier dropped. He folded up as neatly as the brown-paper bags Pink brought home from the store, emptied, and then carefully put in the kitchen cupboard.

The noise of the shot stayed in his eardrums. He couldn't get it out. "Jesus Christ!" he said. Then again, "Jesus Christ!" The beer glass was warm. He put it down on the bar with such violence some of the beer slopped over on his shirt. He stared at the wet place, thinking Pink would be mad as hell. Him out drinking in a bar on Sunday. There was a stillness in which he was conscious of the stink of the beer, the heat in the room, and he could still hear the sound of the shot. Somebody dropped a glass, and the tinkle of it hurt his ears.

Then everybody was moving toward the lobby. The doors between the bar and the lobby slammed shut. High, excited talk broke out.

The tall thin black man standing next to him said, "That ties it. It ain't even safe here where we live. Not no more. I'm goin' to get me a white bastard of a cop and nail his hide to a street sign."

"Is the soldier dead?" someone asked.

"He wasn't movin' none," came the answer.

They pushed hard against the doors leading to the lobby. The doors stayed shut.

He stood still, watching them. The anger that went through him was so great that he had to hold on to the bar to keep from falling. He felt as though he were going to burst wide open. It was like having seen Sam killed before his eyes. Then he heard the whine of an ambulance siren. His eardrums seemed to have been waiting to pick it up.

"Come on, what you waitin' for?" He snarled the words at the people milling around the lobby doors. "Come on!" he repeated, running toward the street.

The crowd followed him to the 126th Street entrance of the hotel. He got there in time to see a stretcher bearing a limp khaki-clad figure disappear inside the ambulance in front of the door. The ambulance pulled away fast, and he stared after it stupidly.

He hadn't known what he was going to do, but he felt cheated. Let down. He noticed that it was beginning to get dark. More and more people were coming into the street. He wondered where they'd come from and how they'd heard about the shooting so quickly. Every time he looked around there were more of them. Curious, eager voices kept asking, "What happened? What happened?" The answer was always the same. Hard, angry. "A white cop shot a soldier."

Someone said, "Come on to the hospital. Find out what happened to him."

In front of the hotel he had been in the front of the crowd. Now there were so many people in back of him and in front of him that when they started toward the hospital, he moved along with them. He hadn't decided to go, the forward movement picked him up and moved him along without any intention on his part. He got the feeling that he had lost his identity as a person with a free will of his own. It frightened him at first. Then he began to feel powerful. He was surrounded by hundreds of people like himself. They were all together. They could do anything.

As the crowd moved slowly down Eighth Avenue, he saw that there were cops lined up on both sides of the street. Mounted cops kept coming out of the side streets, shouting, "Break it up! Keep moving. Keep moving."

The cops were scared of them. He could tell. Their faces were dead white in the semidarkness. He started saying the words over separately to himself. Dead. White. He laughed again. Dead. White. The words were funny said separately like that. He stopped laughing suddenly because a part of his mind repeated, Twenty years, twenty years.

He licked his lips. It was hot as all hell tonight. He imagined what it would be like to be drinking swallow after swallow of ice-cold beer. His throat worked and he swallowed audibly.

The big black man walking beside him turned and looked down at him. "You all right, brother?" he asked curiously.

"Yeah," he nodded. "It's them sons of bitches of cops. They're scared of us." He shuddered. The heat was terrible. The tide of hate quivering in his stomach made him hotter. "Wish I had some beer," he said.

The man seemed to understand not only what he had said but all the things he had left unsaid. For he nodded and smiled. And William thought this was an extraordinary night. It was as though, standing so close together, so many of them like this—as though they knew each other's thoughts. It was a wonderful thing.

The crowd carried him along. Smoothly. Easily. He wasn't really walking. Just gliding. He was aware that the shuffling feet of the crowd made a muffled rhythm on the concrete sidewalk. It was slow, inevitable. An ominous sound, like a funeral march. With the regularity of a drumbeat. No. It's more like a pulse beat, he thought. It isn't a loud noise. It just keeps repeating over and over. But not that regular, because it builds up to something. It keeps building up.

The mounted cops rode their horses into the crowd. Trying to break it up into smaller groups. Then the rhythm was broken. Seconds later it started again. Each time the tempo was a little faster. He found he was breathing the same way. Faster and faster. As though he were running. There were more and more cops. All of them white. They had moved the colored cops out.

"They done that before," he muttered.

"What?" said the man next to him.

"They moved the black cops out," he said.

He heard the man repeat it to someone standing beside him. It became part of the slow shuffling rhythm on the sidewalk. "They moved the black cops." He heard it go back and back through the crowd until it was only a whisper of hate on the still hot air. "They moved the black cops."

As the crowd shuffled back and forth in front of the hospital, he caught snatches of conversation. "The soldier was dead when they put him in the ambulance." "Always tryin' to fool us." "Christ! Just let me get my hands on one of them cops."

He was thinking about the hospital and he didn't take part in any of the conversations. Even now across the long span of years he could remember the helpless, awful rage that had sent him hurrying home from this same hospital. Not saying anything. Getting home by some kind of instinct.

Pink had come to this hospital when she had had her last child. He could hear again the cold contempt in the voice of the nurse as she listened to Pink's loud grieving. "You people have too many children anyway," she said.

It left him speechless. He had his hat in his hand and he remembered how he wished afterward that he'd put it on in front of her to show her what he thought of her. As it was, all the bitter answers that finally surged into his throat seemed to choke him. No words would come out. So he stared at her lean, spare body. He let his eyes stay a long time on her flat breasts. White uniform. White shoes. White stockings. White skin.

Then he mumbled, "It's too bad your eyes ain't white, too." And turned on his heel and walked out.

It wasn't any kind of answer. She probably didn't even know what he was talking about. The baby dead, and all he could think of was to tell her her eyes ought to be white. White shoes, white stockings, white uniform, white skin, and blue eyes.

Staring at the hospital, he saw with satisfaction that frightened faces were appearing at the windows. Some of the lights went out. He began to feel that this night was the first time he'd ever really been alive. Tonight everything was going to be changed. There was a growing, swelling sense of power in him. He felt the same thing in the people around him.

The cops were aware of it, too, he thought. They were out in full force. Mounties, patrolmen, emergency squads. Radio cars that looked like oversize bugs crawled through the side streets. Waited near the curbs. Their white tops stood out in the darkness. "White folks riding in white cars." He wasn't aware that he had said it aloud until he heard the words go through the crowd. "White folks in white cars." The laughter that followed the words had a rough, raw rhythm. It repeated the pattern of the shuffling feet.

Someone said, "They got him at the station house. He ain't here." And the crowd started moving toward 123rd Street.

Great God in the morning, William thought, everybody's out here. There were girls in thin summer dresses, boys in long coats and tight-legged pants, old women dragging kids along by the hand. A man on crutches jerked himself past to the rhythm of the shuffling feet. A blind man tapped his way through the center of the crowd, and it divided into two separate streams as it swept by him. At every street corner William noticed someone stopped to help the blind man up over the curb.

The street in front of the police station was so packed with people that he couldn't get near it. As far as he could see they weren't doing anything. They were simply standing there. Waiting for something to happen. He recognized a few of them: the woman with the loose, rolling eyes who sold shopping bags on 125th Street; the lucky-number peddler—the man with the white parrot on his shoulder; three sisters of the Heavenly Rest for All movement—barefooted women in loose white robes.

Then, for no reason that he could discover, everybody moved toward 125th Street. The motion of the crowd was slower now because it kept increasing in size as people coming from late church services were drawn into it. It was easy to identify them, he thought. The women wore white gloves. The kids were all slicked up. Despite the more gradual movement he was still being carried along effortlessly, easily. When someone in front of him barred his way, he pushed against the person irritably, frowning in annoyance because the smooth forward low of his progress had been stopped.

It was Pink who stood in front of him. He stopped frowning when he recognized her. She had a brown-paper bag tucked under her arm and he knew she had stopped at the corner store to get the big bottle of cream soda she always brought home on Sundays. The sight of it made him envious, for it meant that this Sunday had been going along in an orderly, normal fashion for her while he— She was staring at him so hard he was suddenly horribly conscious of the smell of the beer that had spilled on his shirt. He knew she had smelled it, too, by the tighter grip she took on her pocketbook.

"What you doing out here in this mob? A Sunday evening and you drinking beer," she said grimly.

For a moment he couldn't answer her. All he could think of was Sam. He almost said, "I saw Sam shot this afternoon," and he swallowed hard.

"This afternoon I saw a white cop kill a black soldier," he said. "In the bar where I was drinking beer. I saw it. That's why I'm here. The glass of beer I was drinking went on my clothes. The cop shot him in the back. That's why I'm here."

He paused for a moment, took a deep breath. This was how it ought to be, he decided. She had to know sometime and this was the right place to tell her. In this semidarkness, in this confusion of noises, with the low, harsh rhythm of the footsteps sounding against the noise of the horses' hoofs.

His voice thickened. "I saw Scummy yesterday," he went on. "He told me Sam's doing time at hard labor. That's why we ain't heard from him. A white MP shot him when he wouldn't go to the nigger end of a bus. Sam shot the MP. They gave him twenty years at hard labor."

He knew he hadn't made it clear how to him the soldier in the bar was Sam; that it was like seeing his own son shot before his very eyes. I don't even know whether the soldier was dead, he thought. What made me tell her about Sam out here in the street like this, anyway? He realized with a sense of shock that he really didn't care that he had told her. He felt strong, powerful, aloof. All the time he'd been talking he wouldn't look right at her. Now, suddenly, he was looking at her as though she were a total stranger. He was coldly wondering what she'd do. He was prepared for anything.

But he wasn't prepared for the wail that came from her throat. The sound hung in the hot air. It made the awful quivering in his stomach worse. It echoed and reechoed the length of the street. Somewhere in the distance a horse whinnied. A woman standing way back in the crowd groaned as though the sorrow and the anguish in that cry were more than she could bear.

Pink stood there for a moment. Silent. Brooding. Then she lifted the big bottle of soda high in the air. She threw it with all her might. It made a wide arc and landed in the exact center of the plate-glass window of a furniture store. The glass crashed in with a sound like a gunshot.

A sigh went up from the crowd. They surged toward the broken window. Pink followed close behind. When she reached the window, all the glass had been broken in. Reaching far inside, she grabbed a small footstool and then turned to hurl it through the window of the dress shop next door. He kept close behind her, watching her as she seized a new missile from each store window that she broke.

Plate-glass windows were being smashed all up and down 125th Street— on both sides of the street. The violent, explosive sound fed the sense of power in him. Pink had started this. He was proud of her, for she had shown herself to be a fit mate for a man of his type. He stayed as close to her as he could. So in spite of the crashing, splintering sounds and the swarming, violent activity around him, he knew the exact moment when she lost her big straw hat; when she took off the high-heeled patent leather shoes and flung them away, striding swiftly along in her stockinged feet. That her dress was hanging crooked on her.

He was right in back of her when she stopped in front of a hat store. She carefully appraised all the hats inside the broken window. Finally she reached out, selected a small hat covered with purple violets, and fastened it securely on her head.

"Woman's got good sense," a man said.

"Man, oh, man! Let me get in there," said a raw-boned woman who thrust her way forward through the jam of people to seize two hats from the window.

A roar of approval went up from the crowd. From then on when a window was smashed it was bare of merchandise when the people streamed past it. White folks owned these stores. They'd lose and lose and lose, he thought with satisfaction. The words "twenty years" reechoed in his mind. I'll be an old man, he thought. Then: I may be dead before Sam gets out of prison.

The feeling of great power and strength left him. He was so confused by its loss that he decided this thing happening in the street wasn't real. It was so dark there were so many people shouting and running about, that he almost convinced himself he was having a nightmare. He was aware that his hearing had now grown so acute he could pick up the tiniest sounds: the quickened breathing and the soft, gloating laughter of the crowd; even the sound of his own heart beating. He could hear these things under the noise of the breaking glass, under the shouts that were coming from both sides of the street. They forced him to face the fact that this was no dream but a reality from which he couldn't escape. The quivering in his stomach kept increasing as he walked along.

Pink was striding through the crowd just ahead of him. He studied her to see if she, too, were feeling as he did. But the outrage that ran through her had made her younger. She was tireless. Most of the time she was leading the crowd. It was all he could do to keep up with her, and finally he gave up the attempt—it made him too tired.

He stopped to watch a girl who was standing in a store window, clutching a clothes model tightly around the waist. "What's she want that for?" he said aloud. For the model had been stripped of clothing by the passing crowd, and he thought its pinkish torso was faintly obscene in its resemblance to a female figure.

The girl was young and thin. Her back was turned toward him, and there was something so ferocious about the way her dark hands gripped the naked model that he resisted the onward movement of the crowd to stare in fascination. The girl turned around. Her nervous hands were tight around the dummy's waist. It was Annie May.

"Ah, no!" he said, and let his breath come out with a sigh.

Her hands crept around the throat of the model and she sent it hurtling through the air above the heads of the crowd. It landed short of a window across the street. The legs shattered. The head rolled toward the curb. The waist snapped neatly in two. Only the torso remained whole and in one piece.

Annie May stood in the empty window and laughed with the crowd when someone kicked the torso into the street. He stood there, staring at her. He felt that now for the first time he understood her. She had never had anything but badly paying jobs—working for young white women who probably despised her. She was like Sam on that bus in Georgia. She didn't want just the nigger end of things, and here in Harlem there wasn't anything else for her. All along she'd been trying the only way she knew how to squeeze out of life a little something for herself.

He tried to get closer to the window where she was standing. He had to tell her that he understood. And the crowd, tired of the obstruction that he had made by standing still, swept him up and carried him past. He stopped thinking and let himself be carried along on a vast wave of feeling. There was so much plate glass on the sidewalk that it made a grinding noise under the feet of the hurrying crowd. It was a dull, harsh sound that set his teeth on edge and quickened the trembling of his stomach.

Now all the store windows that he passed were broken. The people hurrying by him carried tables, lamps, shoeboxes, clothing. A woman next to him held a wedding cake in her hands—it went up in tiers of white frosting with a small bride and groom mounted at the top. Her hands were bleeding, and he began to look closely at the people nearest him. Most of them, too, had cuts on their hands and legs. Then he saw there was blood on the sidewalk in front of the windows, blood dripping down the jagged edges of the broken windows. And he wanted desperately to go home.

He was conscious that the rhythm of the crowd had changed. It was faster, and it had taken on an ugly note. The cops were using their nightsticks. Police wagons drew up to the curbs. When they pulled away, they were full of men and women who carried loot from the stores in their hands.

The police cars slipping through the streets were joined by other cars with loudspeakers on top. The voices coming through the loudspeakers were harsh. They added to the noise and confusion. He tried to listen to what the voices were saying. But the words had no meaning for him. He caught one phrase over and over: "Good people of Harlem." It made him feel sick.

He repeated the words "of Harlem." We don't belong anywhere, he thought. There ain't no room for us anywhere. There wasn't no room for Sam in a bus in Georgia. There ain't no room for us here in New York. There ain't no place but top floors. The top-floor black people. And he laughed and the sound stuck in his throat.

After that he snatched a suit from the window of a men's clothing store. It was a summer suit. The material felt crisp and cool. He walked away with it under his arm. He'd never owned a suit like that. He simply sweated out the summer in the same dark pants he wore in winter. Even while he stroked the material, a part of his mind sneered—you got summer pants; Sam's got twenty years.

He was surprised to find that he was almost at Lenox Avenue, for he hadn't remembered crossing Seventh. At the corner the cops were shoving a group of young boys and girls into a police wagon. He paused to watch. Annie May was in the middle of the group. She had a yellow fox jacket dangling from one hand.

"Annie May!" he shouted. "Annie May!" The crowd pushed him along faster and faster. She hadn't seen him. He let himself be carried forward by the movement of the crowd. He had to find Pink and tell her that the cops had taken Annie May.

He peered into the dimness of the street ahead of him, looking for her; then he elbowed his way toward the curb so that the people could see the other side of the street. He forgot about finding Pink for directly opposite him was the music store that he passed every night coming home from work. Young boys and girls were always lounging on the sidewalk in front of it. They danced a few steps while they listened to the records being played inside the shop. All the records sounded the same—a terribly magnified woman's voice bleating out a blues song in a voice that sounded to him like that of an animal in heat—an old animal, tired and beaten, but with an insinuating know-how left in her. The white men who went past the store smiled as their eyes lingered on the young girls swaying to the music.

"White folks got us comin' and goin'. Backwards and forwards," he muttered. He fought his way out of the crowd and walked toward a no-parking sign that stood in front of the store. He rolled it up over the curb. It was heavy and the effort made him pant. It took all his strength to send it crashing through the glass on the door.

Almost immediately an old woman and a young man slipped inside the narrow shop. He followed them. He watched them smash the records that lined the shelves. He hadn't thought of actually breaking the records but once he started, he found the crisp, snapping noise pleasant. The feeling of power began to return. He didn't like these records, so they had to be destroyed.

When they left the music store there wasn't a whole record left. The old woman came out of the store last. As he hurried off up the street he could have sworn he smelled the sharp, acrid smell of smoke. He turned and looked back. He was right. A thin wisp of smoke was coming through the store door. The old woman had long since disappeared in the crowd.

Farther up the street he looked back again. The fire in the record shop was burning merrily. It was making a glow that lit up that part of the street. There was a new rhythm now. It was faster and faster. Even the voices coming from the loudspeakers had taken on the urgency of speed.

Fire trucks roared up the street. He threw his head back and laughed when he saw them. That's right, he thought. Burn the whole damn place down. It was wonderful. Then he frowned. "Twenty years at hard labor." The words came back to him. He was a fool. Fire wouldn't wipe that out. There wasn't anything that would wipe it out.

He remembered then that he had to find Pink. To tell her about Annie May. He overtook her in the next block. She's got more stuff, he thought. She had a table lamp in one hand, a large enamel kettle in the other. The lightweight summer coat draped across her shoulders was so small it barely covered her enormous arms. She was watching a group of boys assault the steel gates in front of a liquor store. She frowned at them so ferociously he wondered what she was going to do. Hating liquor the way she did, he half expected her to cuff the boys and send them on their way up the street.

She turned and looked at the crowd in back of her. When she saw him she beckoned to him. "Hold these," she said. He took the lamp, the kettle and the coat she held out to him, and he saw that her face was wet with perspiration. The print dress was darkly stained with it.

She fastened the hat with the purple flowers securely on her head. Then she walked over to the gate. "Git out the way," she said to the boys. Bracing herself in front of the gate, she started tugging at it. The gate resisted. She pulled at it with a sudden access of such furious strength that he was frightened. Watching her, he got the feeling that the resistance of the gate had transformed it in her mind. It was no longer a gate—it had become the world that had taken her son, and she was wreaking vengeance on it.

The gate began to bend and sway under her assault. Then it was down. She stood there for a moment, staring at her hands—big drops of blood oozed slowly over the palms. Then she turned to the crowd that had stopped to watch.

"Come on, you niggers," she said. Her eyes were little and evil and triumphant. "Come on and drink up the white man's liquor." As she strode off up the street, the beflowered hat dangled precariously from the back of her head.

When he caught up with her she was moaning, talking to herself in husky whispers. She stopped when she saw him and put her hand on his arm.

"It's hot, ain't it?" she said, panting.

In the midst of all this violence, the sheer commonplaceness of her question startled him. He looked at her closely. The rage that had been in her was gone, leaving her completely exhausted. She was breathing too fast in uneven gasps that shook her body. Rivulets of sweat streamed down her face. It was as though her triumph over the metal gate had finished her. The gate won anyway, he thought.

"Let's go home, Pink," he said. He had to shout to make his voice carry over the roar of the crowd, the sound of breaking glass.

He realized she didn't have the strength to speak, for she only nodded in reply to his suggestion. Once we get home she'll be all right, he thought. It was suddenly urgent that they get home, where it was quiet, where he could think, where he could take something to still the tremors in his stomach. He tried to get her to walk a little faster, but she kept slowing down until, when they entered their own street, it seemed to him they were barely moving.

In the middle of the block she stood still. "I can't make it," she said. "I'm too tired."

Even as he put his arm around her she started going down. He tried to hold her up, but her great weight was too much for him. She went down slowly, inevitably, like a great ship capsizing. Until all of her huge body was crumpled on the sidewalk. "Pink" he said. "Pink. You gotta get up," he said over and over again.

She didn't answer. He leaned over and touched her gently. Almost immediately afterward he straightened up. All his life, moments of despair and frustration had left him speechless—strangled by the words that rose in his throat. This time the words poured out.

He sent his voice raging into the darkness and the awful confusion of noises. "The sons of bitches," he shouted. "The sons of bitches."

Riveters, *Opportunity*, Spring 1945

The Double Victory Campaign

The predominance of poetry in this section is due in part to the massive wartime output and influence of the poet Langston Hughes, who published regularly in periodicals and who was a member of the Writers' War Board, an organization of writers who used their talents to mobilize the civilian population as best they could. (It is noteworthy that Hughes was investigated by the FBI for alleged subversive activities during the war, as were several African American leaders and the black press in particular, which may have fueled his and their determination to fight segregation.) The African American male soldier is at the center of this poetry, providing an effective tool for deconstructing the racist underpinnings of a society purportedly fighting to preserve democratic principles. He was at the front lines of two battles: the fight against segregation in the armed forces, and the fight against fascist enemies overseas. Airmen at the Tuskegee Army base, the 99th Pursuit Squadron, were a source of particular pride to the black community, for these were the first black pilots to be trained and the first to be sent into combat. Testifying to their symbolic significance is the fact that Gordon Parks, who was the first African American photographer hired by the OWI, tried to accompany the squadron when it first was sent to Europe, but he was prevented from doing so by southern congressmen who did not want the mission publicized, as it would foster ideas of racial equality. Undaunted by the mainstream media white-out, however, black writers and editors put the Tuskegee airmen at the forefront of "Double V" rhetoric, as is evident in the poetry here.

The idea that African American soldiers would demonstrate equality of the races through helping win the war helps explain the attraction of women poets to this subject. African American poets Elsie Mills Holton, Roberta I. Thomas, Ruth Albert Cook, Roberta Thomas, Ruby Berkley Goodwin, Lucia Mae Pitts, Gwendolyn Brooks, Cora Ball Moten, and Margaret Walker all focus on the male subject in this section, and they do so in part to intensify the contradiction between racism at home and the fight for democracy abroad. Unable to go into combat themselves, black women could disrupt a prominent feature of American racism in World War II by putting African Americans into the white-dominated portrait of freedom fighters so central to home-front rhetoric. If dominant-culture media ignored him, these writers testified to the black man's presence in the war. If the War Department stonewalled on using him in combat, then they put the black soldier in the skies, on the sea, or on the battlefield in their imaginations. In this way, black women used male privilege as an opening wedge to pry open racist exclusion of all African Americans from the full benefits of American citizenship.

Central to this effort was the positioning of women as social activists, whether they were entertainers, mothers, domestic workers, or trailblazing WACs and welders. The college students featured in Pauli Murray's piece "A Blueprint for First Class Citizenship" illustrate well the tendency of African American wartime media to laud women for community activism. The most prominent image of female activism, however, was that of the mother, as is evident from the numerous examples of poetry and fiction in this section that center on the maternal gaze or voice. It is worth noting that, in showcasing the African American mother as a figure of angry mourning, these writers subverted dominant-culture stereotypes of the mammy, which not only located the object of black maternal devotion in whiteness but erased the black child altogether. Constructed to emblematize a desexualized motherly persona, the mammy looked after her white charges with complete devotion, her gaze was fixed on the white face, and her voice spoke words of comfort and wisdom to white people. Wartime poetry and fiction, in contrast, places the black child at the center of African American maternal attention, and the black woman's reproductive role symbolizes birth of a new order in which democracy will be achieved for the next generation.

It is this important racial message that lifts traditional gender images out of essentialism in poems like "Mother's Hope," by Valerie Ethelyn Parks, or "Our Love Was a War Baby," by Tomi Carolyn Tinsley. The mothers in these poems articulate an awareness that their babies are vulnerable in a world at war, not just because they're infants in a violent setting but because they're nonwhite in a white supremacist society. Maternal devotion, in other words, carries with it an implicit premise that the black mother's role is to help make the world a less racist place for her children. Similarly, the pregnant women in the fictional stories "So Softly Smiling," by Chester Himes, and "Ante Partum," by Leotha Hackshaw (the war worker whose essay is in Section 1), transcend mere sentimental treatment of women's reproductive capacity by their location in black families struggling for a toehold in what they hope will be a democratic postwar world. In a larger culture that denied them agency as family members as well as individuals, in other words, black women could be empowered and provided dimensionality by such portraits of maternal strength. Pregnant with hope for a better world or left to mourn a fallen child, mothers in African American magazines were foregrounded as compassionate figures who could lead as well as nurture, inspire to action as well as grieve.

NEGRO STORY, JULY–AUGUST 1944

Renunciation

ELSIE MILLS HOLTON

We do not amuse so completely as before.
These dark ones dance no longer with willingness.
Once we lay sullen by the southern river
And raised ourselves from lethargy for another's pleasure.
We warn your audience not to expect comedy much longer.
Those of us who dance today are an elegy to the dancers before us.

Our men are running as rapidly into death as other men,
And death leaves one without identity.
Man's last breath is so close to dying
That were he to reverse the process
He would find in living, too, a sameness.

Goodbye to the days of the jig and the shine boy;
And hello, brother.
We will live with you, work with you,
And sing in your songs your sorrow.
We will weep for your dead as we mourn our own,
and place our blood beside yours upon the altar.

Congresswoman Crystal Bird Fauset, *The Crisis*, July 1943

THE CRISIS, SEPTEMBER 1942

I Believe in Democracy So Much

RHOZA A. WALKER

I believe in democracy, so much
That I want everybody in America,
To have some of it.

The poor white textile workers
    In the mills of Carolina
    Harassed and heckled,
    Sweating and swathed
    With an insatiable desire, to merely,
    Live.
    Peeved,
        Paupered, whites,
They must have some of it.

The defense workers,
    Wide-eyed and starry,
    So engrossed in their task,
    So enveloped in their production
    They forget, that
        It is for them,
    The cogwheels of industry are humming,
    The rivets of machinery are turning,
    Yes, the mills of the gods are grinding.
They must have some of it.

And the refugees . . . . . .
    Bewildered in mind,
    Besmirched in spirit,
    Despondent . . . . destitute . . . debauched,
    Groping . . .
        Hoping mechanically,
        To find . . . . the Light
    Long since . . . . smothered.
They must have some of it.

The capitalists, the magnates . . . . . .
    Lolling in Profits
    Stenched with Greed
    Presumptuous with Power!
    Poor
        Petty
          Plutocrats . . . .
    They must have some of the stuff that their dollars have paid for,
    Though they themselves, are bereft.
    Indeed, they must have some of it.

And the Negroes,
    Digging the ditches in Georgia,
    Playing around the cabins in Mississippi,
    Shoveling coal in Ohio,
        Coal, as dark and pitiless as their Fate.

Negroes,
    Stripped and stilled in Sikeston,
    Unmentioned and forgotten at Pearl Harbor,
    Hounded and herded at Alexandria,[1]
        Herded, as sheep in a strange and borrowed pasture.

Negroes,
    Denounced and deprived of Democracy
    Insulted and inveigled in Industry,
    Shunned and shamed in Society,
    Murdered and mangled,
        On the very land for which they must fight!
    They shall have some of it!

---

1. Sikeston, Missouri, was the site of a lynching in 1942; a black Navy messman, Dorie Miller, machine-gunned Japanese bombers at Pearl Harbor; and three black soldiers were accused of rape in Alexandria, Louisiana, and sentenced to death in 1942.

THE CRISIS, AUGUST 1943

Sunday, December 7, 1941[1]

RUTH ALBERT COOK

Brown, tired man,
All unaware
How envy accents
Your patient stare.
You would give much
To join the crowd,
Hysterical,
And nation-proud.

How great the rage
You could release
If trained upon
Just Japanese.

But in these years,
American,
Your hate—spread from
Idea to man—
Is spent. Fatigue
Alone is left,
And here you stand,
A man bereft
Emotionally.

While passion reigns
In fear-crazed lands—
While seeping blood stains
Blot the world
Where science strives
Now ending, now
Preserving lives.

---

1. This was the date when the Japanese bombed Pearl Harbor, setting off U.S. entry into World War II.

Emergency—
A word to you—
Bonds for sale—
Taxes due.

The shady side
Is where you walk,
Always careful
Because the chalk
Line, parting black
From white, may be
So faint, sometimes
You do not see
That you have strayed—
Before a lash
Has struck you sharp,
And made you dash
Back to the old
Familiar way
You tread in each
Uncertain day.

But maybe this,
Our common fear,
Can make us draw
Together here.

Emergency
may dull the line—
Perhaps, make black
And white combine,
So you can fight,
And, reckless, give
Your life, as you
Could never live—

Caution replaced
With ruthless speed—
Licensed murder
Now for your creed.
No subtlety
Of compromise

To dull your sword—
To dim your eyes.

Brown, tired man,
Take one long breath—
Now, go.
     This is
An easy death.

NEGRO STORY, DECEMBER–JANUARY 1945–1946

Battle for Two

ROBERTA I. THOMAS

If they would surrender the hatred they place
Upon the head of my struggling race
And try to remember that the Negro is Man
E'en though his hue is black and tan,
It would put an end to the mockery
That mars the face of Democracy;
And bring to light so many fine things
That are secretly hidden 'neath Liberty's wings.

Why is it they stress Equality
When it still is ignored by the "powers that be?"
When the hangman's noose still continues to fight
Some poor mother's son through the darkness of night?
It isn't enough to shake a hand, to say a kind word
And then to brand. For prejudice is lowly,
A threat to Mankind—and the ignorance of it
Will tarnish the mind.

Somewhere on the ocean, on the fields tonight,
Black boys are fighting along with the White.
They too, have come to defend Freedom's name
For the color of skin won't falter the aim.
But what shall be offered when the battle is won
And Negro mothers mourn for their sons?
I bid for your answer, O Land of the Free,
A one, or two-sided victory!

NEGRO STORY, MAY–JUNE 1945

The Mistake

ROMA JONES

A soldier on the battlefield lay prone,
His face was drawn and white with stabbing pain.
His life ebbed out with each slow-oozing drop,
His uniform one wet and grisly stain.

The ambulance dashed up, and bore him away,
And tender hands administered to his hurts;
Bound up his wounds, assuaged his agony,
Replaced the blood that 'scaped in crimson spurts.

The gods looked down with mischief in their hearts.
The vials, one marked "A," the other, "B"
By some unknown perversity of Fate,
Were mixed. The soldier's pulse beat steadily.

Such consternation ne'er was seen on earth,
And speculation on "Whose guilt?" ran wild.
The soldier lay, faint color in his face.
The Nordic stirred, and breathed, and, living, smiled.

NEGRO STORY, AUGUST–SEPTEMBER 1945

Poem

EDNA L. ANDERSON

And they shall fight,
Yes, side by side
On battlefields
And oceans wide
With you who dare
To scorn the might
Of God's product
From out the night.

OPPORTUNITY, NOVEMBER 1942

Brown Moon

LUCIA M. PITTS

Dedicated to the 99th Pursuit Squadron, Tuskegee Institute, Alabama

Bright moon
Up yonder in God's skies
Radiant brown, you moon;
For I am brown,
Through eyes of brown
I see you,
And brown is
A soothing, enchanting
Color.

Brown moon,
Up there in the skies,
Look out on our boys
Wherever they be.
Somewhere out there
They are riding the air—
Our brown flyer boys.

Brown moon,
Guide them right;
Be their searchlight.
For in your care
Are they—
Our brown flyer boys
Somewhere
Out there . . .

Dear moon,
Down here
The seasons will move unerringly in—
The lush and vivid autumn days,
The winter—fierce and cold and white;
Spring and summer, with trees blossoming
And the red, red roses
Swaying in the breeze—

The night breeze over the gardens,
Gentle and kind.

But oh, my moon
Out there our boys will be riding,
Piercing the air.
For them no sweet-smelling buds
Nor quiet breezes playing
In the moonlight
Over the tranquil gardens
Of home.
The darkness of night for them,
And, blinding their eyes,
A passionate anger
Against the stalking mob
Which comes to assault our homes
And break our peace.
They may lose the way
And be forever lost
Without God's soft clouds
And you.

So moon, silver-brown moon,
With trembling lips
And torn heart,
On the symphony of the winds
I breathe my prayer—

Light the way
For our boys
Riding the air
Out there . . .

NEGRO STORY, JULY–AUGUST 1944

Dark Men Speak to the Earth

MARGARET WALKER

All we have ever asked of you, O Earth
is a place to sink our feet into soil
our backs against wind
our lips with a prayer to the stars
our hearts on wings of a gull
our eyes on a promise fulfilled.

All we have ever asked of you—
even in hours of dark passage
when our faces were taut
behind masks of suffering
grim yet painfully grinning
sunken in apathy and breathing apology.

All we have ever asked of you
dark earth on which we move
blackness of soil and redness of hills
colors of fire lighting our skin and our blood
hammering life with our toil
brooding darkness over face of a winter stream—

All we have ever asked of you
is a simple thing
only one lovely word to speak and know forever
none of the noble lies
slipping along tongues glibly.

Simple as prayers of pilgrims and deeds of forty-niners
simple as plaintive melody
simple as a spiritual and like a moon-rise
simple as a loaf of bread and like aloof drums.
Give us the simple words to free our hearts from fear
And save our lives with love.

THE CRISIS, SEPTEMBER 1943

Color

MAVIS B. MIXON

I am the color of the Earth.
I have rested on her shoulder.
Wept tears on her bosom,
Sung songs at her heart.
I am the color of the Earth.

I am the color of the Road.
I have shaped tired feet in its dust,
Trod on its rocks,
Stumbled up its hills,
Sped down its straight stretch.
I am the color of the Road.

I am the color of the Sun
I have waked to his lusty call,
Dreamed in his nooning
Toiled in his after-glow.
I am the color of the Sun.

Sun,
Earth,
And shining Road!

Brown
Tan
And golden glow!

God-given
To the Negro.

THE CRISIS, APRIL 1945

Conversation on V

OWEN DODSON

"They got pictures of V stamped on letter stamps;
Miss Eagle wear one in her lapel to her red cross suit;
Mr. Bigful, the bank president, got one in his lapel too;
Some of the people I do laundry with got great big ones in they windows;
Hadley Brothers Department Store uptown
Got pictures of V on they storebought dresses;
Even got a V ice cream dish—girls selling them so fast
Had to run up a sign: NO MORE V SUNDAES;
And bless God, Lucy done gone up North and come back
With one gleaming on her pocketbook.
Now let's get this straight: what do them V's mean?"
"V stands for Victory."
"Now just what is this here Victory?"
"It what we get when we fight for it."
"Ought to be Freedom, God do know that!"

THE CRISIS, MAY 1944

Time Was, Time Is, Time Shall Be

VIVIEN E. LEWIS

Time Was

"Hi there, Black Boy. Tote this bale;
Fetch me my slippers. Bring me that pail;
Strain at barge ropes, cut the corn;
Up from your pallet at the crack of dawn."
"Yas, boss! No, boss!" Grinning and bowing,
No rest for your body when you're done with your plowing.
Whipped by the lash 'til the blood ran like rain,
Salt in your wounds 'til you screamed with pain.

Brown-bodied wenches swinging with grace
Bearing the bastards of the white man's race.
"Nigger do this, and Nigger do that,"
Kicked and cuffed at the drop of a hat.
Crying for freedom in the still of the night
Chanting your songs of deliverance and right.
"Bear with us, Lord, through the weal and the woe."
Over and over—"Let my people go."

Time Is

Broken, black bodies swinging from the trees,
Left in the sun for the buzzards to feed
Slimy with pitch, and feathered like a bird
All he ever wanted was one kind word.
Riding on Jim Crow down through the South:
Dasn't say a word, nor open his mouth.
Dasn't even sleep in a white man's bed—
Unless you are a woman. Yet the river runs red
With the blood of the black boy fighting the wars,
Bayoneted and blasted, score upon score.
Yet, inch by inch and bit by bit,
You've pushed the bars down with patience and grit.
You've come a long way from your shackles and chains;
The tree has born fruit and is budding again.
Doctors, lawyers, writers to please;
Butchers, bakers, laborers—all these
Are but the fledgings of a task half done,
But still you must fight for your place in the sun.
"Bear with us, Lord, through the weal and the woe."
Over and over—"Let my people go."

Time Shall Be

Oh, thou Negro, stand tall and straight;
Get rid of your petty jealousy—the hate
That burns in your bones like a hidden fire.
Let this be your urge—"Your race to inspire."
Yours in the vintage of an African sun
With the sweat and brawn of a job well done.
Time will be when with the white brother
You'll walk side by side in spite of your color.

Rung by rung, heedless of the cry,
"Get back, Negro. You can't get by!"
Rung by rung, 'til your burden you'll drop
Climbing and stretching 'til you've reached the top.
Then the full-throated cry like a voice from the past:
"Thank Gawd amighty! Free at last!"

THE CRISIS, NOVEMBER 1944

A Blueprint for First Class Citizenship

PAULI MURRAY

Howard University traditionally has been called the "Capstone of Negro Education." When 2,000 young Americans, fresh from 45 states and students from 24 foreign countries, arrived there two years ago, their futures uncertain, their draft numbers coming up every day, and their campus surrounded by the dankest kind of degradation, they were tempted to call their alma mater the "keystone" of education. More than half of these students had come from northern or border states or western and middle-western communities. Many of them had never tasted the bitter fruits of jim crow. They were of a generation who tended to think for themselves as Americans without a hyphen.

Thrown rudely into the nation's capital where jim crow rides the American Eagle, if indeed he does not put the poor symbol to flight, these students were psychologically and emotionally unprepared for the insults and indignities visited upon them when they left the campus and went downtown to see the first-run shows, or stopped in a cafe to get a hotdog and a "Coke." The will to be free is strong in the young, and their sensitive souls recoiled with a violence that reverberated throughout the wartime campus.

The revolt against jim crow started with a mutter and a rumble. It was loudest in the Law School where men students, unprotected by any kind of deferment, were being yanked out of their classes and into a G.I. uniform. "I don't want to fight in a jim crow army." "I'd rather die first!" "I'll go to jail first." These were some of the remarks daily. During the first tense days of the wartime conscription, classes were almost entirely disrupted by the feeling of futility and frustration that settled over these young men.

National Youth Administration Leader Mary McLeod Bethune, *The Crisis,* **October 1942**

And then the spirit of revolt took shape. It started in the fall of 1942 with the refusal of Lewis Jones, Morehouse graduate, to be inducted into a jim crow army and the editorial comment of John P. Lewis of *PM* on Jones' stand. Stung into action, a letter signed by 40 Howard University students, supporting the spirit which led Jones to take such action, was sent to editor Lewis. He did not print the letter although he wrote the students a courteous reply.

In January 1943, three women students were arrested in downtown Washington for the simple act of refusing to pay an overcharge for three hot chocolates in a United Cigar store on Pennsylvania avenue. The young women sat down at the counter and ordered hot chocolates. The waitress refused to serve them at first and they asked for the manager. They were told the manager was out, and they replied they would wait, keeping their seats at the counter. After hurried legal consultation the "management" ordered the waitress to serve them, but upon looking at their checks they were charged twenty-five cents each instead of the standard dime charged for a packaged hot drink. The young women laid thirty-five cents on the counter and started for the door where they were met by a half dozen policemen, hauled off to a street corner, held until the arrival of a Black Maria,[1] and landed in prison in a cell with prostitutes and other criminal suspects. It was not until they were searched and scared almost out of their wits that the dean of women at Howard University was notified and they were dismissed in her care without any charge lodged against them.

The flood of resentment against the whole system of segregation broke loose. Conservative administration members frowned upon this "incident" and advised the three young women they should not stage individual demonstrations against jim crow. It was suggested they should work through an organization concerned with such matters.

These young women of Howard were determined. Others joined them. They took the matter to the student chapter of the NAACP. In the meantime from the Law School issued a new trend of thought. The men had spent hours in their "bull sessions" discussing attack and counter-attack upon jim crow. One second-year student, a North Carolinian and former leader in the NAACP, William Raines, had agitated for months for what he called "the stool-sitting technique." "If the white people want to deny us service, let them pay for it," Raines said. "Let's go downtown some lunch hour when they're crowded. They're open to the public. We'll take a seat on a lunch

---

1. Police van.

stool, and if they don't serve us, we'll just sit there and read our books. They lose trade while that seat is out of circulation. If enough people occupy seats they'll lose so much trade they'll start thinking."

While Raines was arguing, another student, Ruth Powell, from Boston, Mass., later chairman of the dynamic Civil Rights Committee, was doing just this. She would sit for hours and stare at the waitress who had refused her service. She reported it disconcerted the management and sometimes she might even be served.

When this point of view percolated the campus, the students went into action. Raines went into the army but his idea went on. A temporary Student Committee on Campus Opinion was formed. A questionnaire was distributed throughout the campus on February 3, 1943, testing student and faculty reactions to an active campaign against segregation in Washington, D.C.

Two hundred ninety-two students answered the questionnaire; 284 or 97.3% of those said they did not believe Negroes should suspend the struggle for equal rights until the end of the war; 256 or 97% of those answering this question said they believed Negro students should actively participate in the struggle for equality during war time; 218 said they would actively join a campaign to break down segregation in Washington; 38 indicated they would not join but would support others who did. Only 6 disapproved of the idea.

A Civil Rights Committee was formed in March under the sponsorship of the Howard Chapter NAACP. The students unearthed an Equal Rights Bill for the District of Columbia, No. 1995, introduced by Congressman Rowan of Illinois and a companion bill introduced in the Senate by the late Senator Barbour from New Jersey.

The Civil Rights Committee undertook a campaign to bring equal accommodations to the District of Columbia. They set up five sub-committees, publicity and speakers' bureau, program and legislative, committee on correspondence, finance, and direct action. They lobbied in groups with the representatives and senators from their states. They made ingenious little collection cans out of hot chocolate cups and collected pennies from their classmates to pay for paper and postage. They held pep rallies around campus and broadcast their campaign from the tower of Founders Library. They sponsored a Town Hall Meeting at Douglass Hall and brought in community speakers to lead a discussion on "Civil Rights" and the techniques by which they were to be attained.

Their most interesting project, and the one to draw the most fire, was the direct action sub-committee. There the "stool sitting" idea combined with the "sit-it-out-in-your-most-dignified-bib-and-tucker" idea to make a fundamental thrust at the heart of jim crow.

A committee of students surveyed the accommodations of the immediate Negro community on northwest U Street. They reported four stores which still excluded Negroes and catered to "White Trade Only." One of these cafes, the Little Palace Cafeteria, run by a Greek-American, was located at 14th and U Streets, NW, in the heart of the Negro section, and the stories told by Negroes of their embarrassment and mortification in this cafeteria were legion.

The direct action sub-committee spent a week studying the disorderly conduct and picketing laws of D.C. They spent hours threshing out the pros and cons of public conduct, anticipating and preparing for the reactions of the white public, the Negro public, white customers and the management. They pledged themselves to exemplary behavior no matter what the provocation. And one rainy Saturday afternoon in April, they started out. In groups of four, with one student acting as an "observer" on the outside, they approached the cafe. Three went inside and requested service. Upon refusal they took their seats and pulled out magazines, books of poetry, or pencils and pads. They sat quietly. Neither the manager's panicky efforts to dismiss them nor the presence of a half dozen policemen outside could dislodge them. Five minutes later another group of three would enter. This pilgrimage continued until the Little Cafeteria was more than half-filled with staring students on the inside, and a staring public grouped in the street. In forty-five minutes the management had closed the cafeteria. The students took up their vigil outside the restaurant with attractive and provocative picket signs, "There's No Segregation Law in D.C."—"What's Your Story Little Palace?"—"We die together—Why Can't We Eat Together?" and so on. The picketing continued on Monday morning when the restaurant reopened its doors. The students had arranged a picketing schedule and gave their free hours to the picket line. In two days the management capitulated and changed its policy.

In the spring of 1944, the Civil Rights Committee decided to carry the fight downtown into the heart of Washington. They selected a Thompson's cafeteria at 14th and Pennsylvania in the shadow of the White House. They took off a Saturday afternoon, dressed in their best, and strolled into Thompson's in two's and three's at intervals of ten minutes. They threw up a small picket line outside. Three white sympathizers polled the customers inside and found that only 3 out of 10 expressed objection to their being served. They scrupulously observed the picketing laws, and neither the jeers of undisciplined white members of the Armed Forces, nor cheers of WACs, WAVEs and other sympathetic members of the public brought any outward response. When 55 of them, including 6 Negro members of the Armed Forces, had taken seats at the tables, and the Thompson's trade had dropped 50 percent in four hours, the management, after frantic calls to its main office in Chicago, was ordered to serve them.

Before the Civil Rights Committee was able to negotiate with the local management of Thompson's with reference to a changed policy, the Howard University Administration, through the office of Dr. Mordecai W. Johnson, requested them to suspend their activities until there was a clarification of Administration policy. A hurried meeting of the Deans and Administrators was called and a directive issued requesting the students to cease all activities "designed to accomplish social reform affecting institutions other than Howard University itself."

The students were quick to take up this challenge. They then directed their efforts at "social reform" toward the Administration itself. They had already requested a discussion with representatives of the faculty and administration. They indicated their unwillingness to give up their direct action program, and appealed the ruling of the Administration to the Board of Directors, which meets in October 1944.

Out of the struggle, however, issued a new level of student responsibility and interest in campus affairs. The students did not win their total battle against Thompson's, but they achieved a moral victory for student-administration-faculty relationships. They learned interesting things about their University—for example, that 60 percent of its income is a grant from the Federal Government, that 22 percent comes from student fees and that 13 percent comes from campus enterprises and that only 9 percent comes from gifts other than governmental aid. They learned that the enemies of Howard University in Congress seek to destroy it every time the voting of appropriations arrives. They also learned that Howard University is a beacon light to the Negro community and a significant contributor to the total community, and that everything done there is watched with intense interest. A Student-Faculty-Administration [committee] has been set up to make recommendations on student affairs.

The question remains to be settled during the coming months whether Howard students shall participate in social action directed against the second-class citizenship to which they have been victimized. There are those who believe the energy and the dynamics of social change must originate in democratic institutions which form test-tubes of democracy and that must be a realistic relation of one's activities in the community to one's studies in the classroom. There are others who believe that education is a static affair and must not be related to the community at large. Between these two points of view Howard University must make a choice.

But whatever the final outcome, Howard may be proud of those students who have led the way toward a new, and perhaps successful technique to achieve first class citizenship in one area of life in these United States.

NEGRO DIGEST, MAY 1945

Dear Dixie...

Dear Sir:

My employer told me of a picture and article appearing in *Life Magazine* showing a night club in New York with colored and white guests. I obtained a copy of the magazine and was utterly amazed to learn the club in question is Cafe Society. At present I am on an important war project. We are practically isolated from all social activity, which I would prefer to walking into a night club, or any place of entertainment, and being subjected to such close contact with Negroes. I sincerely hope Cafe Society is the exception and such practice is prohibited by other clubs.

No doubt you will feel I am prejudiced and a crank. Such is not the case. Negroes, in their right place, are a good race. Here's hoping you can see your way clear to revert to your former restrictions, so we war workers can anticipate more pleasant evenings in Cafe Society in the future.

Sincerely,
Joan B.

Nov. 1, 1944
(79 years after the Civil War)
Dear Miss B:

We are sorry that, being isolated in a barracks so far from New York, you are unable to understand and appreciate the great changes which you are helping to bring about through your efforts as a war worker. Our German enemy has brutally brought to the fore as the main issue of the war the question you raise, that is, the question of "racial superiority." The Negro people have been stirred to demand the rights granted them under Article

14 of our Constitution and under the Civil Rights Law which exists in the State of New York.

Your letter asking us to "revert to our former restrictions" (which, by the way, never existed in Cafe Society—the place, not the sect) in effect asks us to violate the Federal Constitution and the New York State Law. We are sure that you did not intend to be an "accessory before the fact" to the commission of a crime—a crime which is punishable by a fine of $500.

Your letter was very well written and shows that the writer has had quite some schooling and possesses intelligence. But it shows also that there is something radically wrong with our school system and that training was not carried out along truly democratic lines. In spite of your denial, it reeks with race prejudice. You stated that you would not like to be "subjected to such close contact with Negroes," and that Negroes, in their right place, are a good race. What is the right place for any citizen, any human being, in a democracy? We believe in democracy and we are willing to practice it, even if it hurts our business!

And what of our Negro patrons in uniform—some of whom wear medals received for valor performed on the field of battle in the service of our country and in the interest of democracy? Would you have us ban them? Haven't they earned the right to enjoy the benefits of democracy at home?

You complained that you would not want to be subjected to "such close contact with Negroes." As an old customer of Cafe Society, you of course know that we engage Negro talent. Surely you have no objection to sitting close to Hazel Scott[1] where you could watch her talented hands.

No, your objection is not against all contact with Negroes, but is restricted to your prejudices about "social contact" with Negroes.

You have, we are sure, no objection to the most intimate contact of a Negro maid who may wash your most intimate things, cook your meals and drink from your cups. But to allow a cultured Negro to sit in the same room with you? It sends an unprejudiced shiver up your spine.

For your information, and you may so inform your boss and your friends, our place is open to all decent human beings without reservation or restriction. It is our opinion that the color of one's skin is not the determining factor which makes for decency.

Finally, we point out to you that your work in helping the war effort is totally inconsistent with your prejudice against the Negro people. Why fight German Nazism with its hateful racial theory, why fight for the Four Freedoms if you want a section of our population subjected to the same

---

1. African American jazz pianist.

theory, and denied the same freedoms? "There's a new world a-comin'" after this war and one of the things "a-comin'" is the completion of those rights over which a Civil War was fought in this country.

Barney Josephson
Owner, Cafe Society.

THE CRISIS, JANUARY 1944

Interracial

GEORGIA DOUGLAS JOHNSON

Let's build bridges here and there
Or sometimes, just a spiral stair
That we may come somewhat abreast
And sense what cannot be exprest.
And by these measures can be found
A meeting place—a common ground
Nearer the reaches of the heart
Where truth revealed, stands clear, apart;
With understanding come to know
What laughing lips will never show:
How tears and torturing distress
May masquerade as happiness:
Then you will know when my heart's aching
And I, when yours is slowly breaking.

Commune—The altars will reveal . . .
We then shall be impulsed to kneel
And send a prayer upon its way
For those who wear the thorns today.

Oh, let's build bridges everywhere
And span the gulf of challenge there.

NEGRO STORY, AUGUST–SEPTEMBER 1945

Jim Crow Car

EDITH SEGAL

Come sit beside me, sister.
(We won the Civil War).
Why linger in the back-seat?
What are you waiting for?

Your man and mine have said goodbye.
They've left us work to do.
So come and sit beside me.
Let's talk our problems thru.

There are no Jim Crow bullets.
They make all red blood flow.
And under skin both black and white
All blood is red, you know.

And when we sit together
The people all will say:
The blood of my man and of yours
Washed old Jim Crow away.

OPPORTUNITY, APRIL 1943

No Spring for Me

VICTORIA WINFREY[1]

There will be no music or beauty for me in anything—
Until the stench of the battle field has blown away;
And the boom of the war drums is stilled once more:
No birds will sing, no flowers will bloom;

---

1. Victoria Winfrey was an African American worker at Western Electric Kerney works.

Although Spring may come again—and again . . .
I will not hear its songs, nor smell its perfumes—
Unless the fearful dins and cries subside!

THE CRISIS, APRIL 1944

Please, Dear God

RHOZA A. WALKER

A SOLDIER, whispers above the roar
Of cannon fire, smoke and gore
Above the blast that rips the sod,
        "I must not miss! Please, dear God!"
A WOMAN, looks across the miles
Weary . . . aching . . . all the while
Looks over piston, lay and rod
To humbly entreat,
        "Please, Dear God!"

A WEARY WORLD,
    In every tongue . . .
    Vexed with the tune that Aries has sung,—
    Sends up a prayer on trited knees;
    A Prayer for all eternity:
        "This sundered EARTH on which we trod,
    A Psalm of Peace!
        PLEASE, OUR GOD!"

NEGRO STORY, MARCH–APRIL 1945

Gay Chaps at the Bar

GWENDOLYN BROOKS

. . . and guys I knew in the States, young officers, return from the front
crying and trembling. Gay chaps at the bar in Los Angeles, Chicago,
New York . . .

We knew how to order. Just the dash
Necessary. The length of gayety in good taste.
Whether the raillery should be slightly iced
And given green, or served up hot and lush.
And we knew beautifully how to give to women
The summer spread, the tropics, of our love.
When to persist, or hold a hunger off.
Knew white speech. How to make a look an omen.
But nothing ever taught us to be islands.
And smart, athletic language for this hour
Was not in the curriculum. No stout
Lesson showed how to chat with death. We brought
No brass fortissimo, among our talents,
To holler down the lions in this air.

THE CRISIS, JUNE 1943

Colored Mother's Prayer

WALTER G. ARNOLD

Dear Lord,
I've got a boy,
A big, strong, black boy
Who has gone to fight in this
White man's war. . . .

He was a good boy . . . my
Boy was . . . and I'm proud
Of him . . .
For, while he didn't know where
He'd be fighting or what he'd
Be fighting for, he enlisted in the
Army . . .
And I know that he will gladly
Give his life in the
Interest of this
Country.

Father,
I know that You cannot spare
The lives of all us
Innocent black people in this
Calamity which the white man's
Greed has brought upon
This earth . . . so, if You must,
Take my boy home . . . in Your
Keeping. . . .

But most of all Lord,
If my son must fight in
Australia or in other places
Hostile to the Negro . . . keep him
Safe . . . and make those prejudiced
Peoples broad enough to see
That although he is black . . . he is
Unselfish . . . and strong enough to help win
A decision in that great
Battle which they, themselves,
Have proven
Unequal
To.

Amen. . . .

OPPORTUNITY, APRIL 1943

Negro Mother to Her Soldier Son

CORA BALL MOTEN

Your tiny fingers kneaded my dark breast
like wind-stirred petals on the jungle bloom
of my fierce love for you, flesh of my flesh.
My knotted hands, work-calloused thru the years,
Once smoothed the fleecy softness of your hair.
That touch, remembered, thrills my fingers still.
My tortured heart bleeds yet for those deep hurts,

that strewed the bitter way your small feet trod
thru "their" white hate and scorn of your dark skin.

And now, with theirs, who crucified my hope,
your stunted life is staked to free a world;
your life, love's perfect gift, hate-shaped by "them"
to make a clown to hang their jokes upon,
a scapegoat, forfeit for the things "they" prize.

Was it for this I dreamed great dreams for you,
the dreams "they" killed, my son?
        But this—for these,
the born and unborn—every race and creed
on whom the shadow falls of men turned brutes
beneath the crooked cross and Hell-born sun;[1]
I pledge your twisted life to make—for these,
a wick to light a new world's candle flame.
I weave it on the loom of my own grief.

From you, my son, and your dark, outcast breed,
I take a solemn vow, that nevermore
shall manhood's measure be a shade of skin,
nor any race degrade its brother-men.

I charge you by the agony and pain
of mothers, dark and fair, whose sons today,
have sealed the bond of Freedom with their blood,
to lay my gift upon Her altar stone,
and bid the mockers match it *if they dare*—
my one, best, dearest gift, my son, *my—son.*

---

1. Symbols on the German and Japanese flags—the swastika and the rising sun.

THE CRISIS, JULY 1944

I Love Your Eyes

BOOKER T. MEDFORD

I love your eyes;
Not large eyes, yet warm, wise and tender ones;
I've seen them clouded—tearful—misty
And weary from the cares of the day,
Filled with anxiety.
But I have seen them glow
And grow bright
With the love and tenderness of Motherhood,
And with the simple joys of life.—
I would to God I could imprint
My visage in your eyes eternally—
That I may know,
Through storm or calm—
That I am always there,
Even if memory failed you.—
I love your eyes.

NEGRO STORY, DECEMBER–JANUARY 1944–1945

Mother's Hope

VALERIE E. PARKS

Little brown head warm on my breast
Eyes tight-closed in peaceful rest,
Guess it's selfish of me to say,
I wish you could always stay this way;
But maybe some day you'll understand,
When your babe lies tranquil in your arms,
Caressing your cheek with its little hand,
Oblivious of world war alarms
And talk of peace while bullets roar

From man-made birds that swoop and soar.
From God's own clouds their entrails spill
On innocent men, and kill and kill!
Oh, tender babe, so weak, yet strong,
Mother doesn't mean you any wrong
When she squeezes you terribly tight,
And hopelessly hopes with all her might,
That in this greedy world and wild,
You may remain her infant child.

NEGRO STORY, MARCH—APRIL 1945

Our Love Was a War Baby

TOMI CAROLYN TINSLEY

Our love was a war baby—
born shortly after Pearl Harbor,
nurtured on furloughs, and cutting
its teeth on envelopes marked "free."
Despite the label "free," we paid
plenty in the way of absence, lonely
nights, longing, empty arms, and the like.
Its advent was not planned—nor was it
an accident. For Fate had decreed it.

When you went away, the baby seemed such
a small, wee thing; but to me it was already
large, full grown—and with each day has grown
stronger and more beautiful.
And as I watch it mature into a sturdy, fine child,
I wonder—when all the war is done,
when the iron birds' last song is sung,
the steel cobras have spat their last bit of fire,
and you are home again—if you will have
forgot this child . . . Or if recognition
will light your eyes, and you will take
this, which you begot, to your heart?

OPPORTUNITY, APRIL 1943

Letter to the Editor: A Mother's Faith[1]

. . . This is my problem—keeping alive in him that pride and eagerness to help his country win this war. I have read much about the tasks and duties of mothers in wartime. Mine is a big job—much bigger than that of some mothers, for I am a Negro mother; and first, in order to keep that pride and love of his country alive in the heart of my little boy, I've got to fight against the resentment and discouragement that wells up sometimes in my own heart.

The fanatics in my own race almost cause me to waver at times. They say: "What are we fighting for? If we help win the war, we will continue to be kicked around, discriminated against, denied the right to make a decent living." But I don't waver long, for I begin to think about the conquered countries under Hitler's beastly rule, and the atrocities the minority races in these countries have had to suffer.

I have faith in the goodness of America, because I am an American. When my little boy comes to me with a look of bewilderment in his eyes, and says, "I want to do this, or I want to be that, when I grow up, but Joe says I can't because I'm colored. Can't I Mamma?" I point out to him the achievements of the colored artists, musicians, scientists, and champions in the world of sports, and I say: "Where would they be if they had said—'I can't because I'm colored'?"

Yes, I have faith in America, and I love it. I believe in it in spite of the fanatics. I believe that America will eventually wipe out this challenge to her democracy, and that the time will come when no person need fear that he cannot become a truly great American because of race, color or creed. I believe that after we win this war, we will emerge as an even greater nation. I will keep this faith alive in my own heart, and in the heart of my little boy.

---

1. *Opportunity* reprinted this and another woman's letter ("Indiana"), both of which had been published in the "What's on YOUR Mind?" section of *Redbook,* March 1943. *Opportunity* quoted in part this letter from "Georgia," whose nine-year-old son was busy collecting scrap for the war effort.

NEGRO STORY, MAY–JUNE 1944

A Letter to Our Readers

ALICE C. BROWNING AND FERN GAYDEN

For a long time, we, the editors [of *Negro Story*], have been attempting to improve our writing techniques and to express ourselves through the short story. The other day, the idea struck us that among thirteen million Negroes in America, there must be many who were eager to write creatively if they had a market. At this point, *Negro Story* was conceived, and quickly the machinery was started which would bring it to you. There must be thousands of you hungering for stories about Negroes who are real people rather than the types usually seen in print. Our men overseas and in camps have been begging for them, judging from some of their letters.

We feel that, with few exceptions, the Negro creative writer has not yet achieved the same degree of maturity as say the Negro artist in the field of music or in the fine arts or the Negro in other phases of life. However, no one can deny that the Negro writer has an all-important role to play in presenting new characters which are emerging from the scene as well as an interpretation of the scene itself. The Dorie Millers, the Satchel Paiges, and the Hazel Scotts have been untouched as fiction material;[1] in fact, innumerable potentitalities, past and present, have been woefully neglected.

We welcome contributions from young and unknown writers, as well as those from the more distinguished ones. We believe good writing may be entertaining as well as socially enlightening. To agree with this, one need only to look back at many of the best sellers which have molded public opinion and focused attention on social evils. We hope that accumulated copies of *Negro Story* will serve as a valuable record of present-day writing.

We are aware of the increasing number of white fiction writers who portray the Negro sympathetically and honestly. We want stories from these writers. In fact, we do not wish to restrict this magazine to experience seen only through the eyes of Negroes.

In closing we emphasize the belief that the future of the world is at stake during this World War II. But we also believe that Negroes have a great

---

1. Dorie Miller was a black messman in the navy who heroically shot down enemy planes at Pearl Harbor. Satchel Paige was a celebrated ball player in the Negro Baseball League. Hazel Scott was a famous jazz pianist of the period.

oppportunity to achieve integration with the best elements of our society. We, the editors, as Negro women, not only welcome the opportunity to participate in the creation of a better world, but feel that we have an obligation to work and to struggle for it. We sincerely believe that we can make our best contribution in this field.

> Very truly yours,
> Alice C. Browning
> Fern Gayden

OPPORTUNITY, SUMMER 1945

One Blue Star

MAY MILLER

He did not give me a chance to open the door. Even as I hesitated there separating from the ring the right key to fit into the lock, he swung the door vehemently inward and barred the way, waving exultingly in his hand a letter. I knew without questioning its import. Not recognizing one symbol, I read each word as though it had been magnified tenfold.

The President of the United States

To _____ Greetings:

Transfixed, I attempted to utter no sound, to make no movement. His strong arms encircled me and drew me into the hallway. I stood convulsively clutching him, digging frantic fingers into his firm young flesh. And I, who had but once conceived, who had for one brief period only felt life within my womb, knew the stirring of generations within me, suffered the agony of multitudinous birth. Life of dim eras, of far-flung continents swept through and over me, engulfing my entity. I was one with timelessness—I became the black mother of the fighters of the ages.

I was Zipporah, the black wife of Moses, standing amid the alien corn of my mate's new land of adventure, cuddling my wounded dark boy from the taunts of Miriam. I experienced with him the hurt and bewilderment of childhood and held back the puny arms that would have struck at his tormentors, the young of Hazeroth who found his dark skin strange.

"Hush, my beautiful golden boy, your brothers of tomorrow, older and far wiser than you, will fight that your tawny head shall not be bowed in shame."

With Simon of Cyrene, my strong fighter offspring, born to lead insurrectionist slaves, I dreamed a dream of freedom, of freedom snatched through blood and burning. Then by his side climbing the hill to Golgotha, I glimpsed with him for one brief second the light in a doomed man's eyes; and I felt the bitterness and rebellion die in my son's soul as he humbly shouldered the cross and trudged beside his Saviour.

"Don't hear their jeers, Simon—Don't look up to the gaunt cross now fixed against a leaden sky. The crown of thorns is there; the purple robe lies in a crumpled heap on the ground; the torn bleeding form hangs limp now; but we know—you and I—that it has housed the secret of the ages—love of human kind."

In my frail body I have cradled the sperm that came forth dark heroes of distinction. Down the ages, I marched, rode and tented with them—my warrior sons. I call the roll and from the dim corridors of time they answer century after century, from continent to continent:

Antar the Lion—Arabia's black warrior bard, conquering with artful lance and nursing in his soul a poet's vision.

Angelo Soliman—defender of the Holy Roman Empire, snatched from his African hut to be at last courted by Emperor Francis I, himself.

Henrique Diaz—invincible general in the Portuguese army,—on his breast the "Cross of Christ" and in his heart the hope of a free Brazil.

Toussaint L'Ouverture—native governor general of Haiti, whose rule the mighty Napoleon could break only by cheap chicanery.

Chaka—stern military chieftain of the Zulu tribes, building of the uncivilized one of the most effective fighting machines in history and leaving unto his unheeding native land, one rule—"Conquer or die!"

Antonio Maceo—Negro general and hero of Cuba's wars of independence, whose deeds the imposing monument in Havana calls a free people to do honor.

"Stand there in life, my generals, my chieftains, my rulers, robed in your odd vestments and babbling your many tongues, and hear me. Know you that neither time nor space; nor greed, nor prejudice can snatch your prestige nor eradicate from your countries' histories the names you have etched there for immortality."

On these shores of my native Africa I stood when the strange ravishing horde bore down and snatched my strong young sons. With them I traversed an ocean in the stench hole of a slave ship. I huddled near them on the auction block, their great strength bound in irons, their firm gleaming bodies naked for appraisal and barter.

I watched them bend their backs in foreign fields beneath another stretch of sky, toiling to bring the soil to flower. Down to the swamp they crept when stars were hazy and the moon dripped blood—there to nurse a faint hope and seek a God who seemed to have forgot them.

"Make your plans. They will fail, for even your own may prove traitors and bloodhounds have keen scent. But never, never forget that swamp flowers bloom too."

Blood of my blood spattered on the dignified sod of Boston Commons to christen a baby country in its first stretch for liberty. Crispus Attucks,[1] bound though he was by shackles of color, died to bring to liberty a new meaning, a breadth that must eventually encompass a continent and all thereon.

"Crispus, the shot that fell you penetrated to the bowels of a nation. Rest well in your honored grave."

That lank, lank, lean thing that dangles grotesquely on the gallows in yonder clearing—he's mine too. That's Nat Turner—my poor impatient Nat.[2]

Where's the proud army he raised, armed with makeshift weapons, and fired with the promise of freedom? Some captured and punished; others deserted and gone back sniveling to their masters. And now he hangs there alone with only me lurking in the shadows and around him the wise wind howling, "Too soon! Too soon!"

"It's all right, Nat. They have yet to stifle a dream by killing the dreamer. A dream such as yours never ended a broken limb on a skeleton tree."

And here again I am, my dark form silhouetted against a vast white amphitheatre, marble columns rising behind me and below me flowing the lazy Potomac; but I see none of this. The omnipresent thing is the severe white sepulchre,[3] and I claw and claw to scratch my way to the carrion flesh within.

Can he be mine, too? He might; he well might; and I have a message:

---

1. Crispus Attucks was an African American hero of the Revolutionary War, being the first man to fall during the Boston Massacre.

2. Nat Turner was an insurrectionist slave who led a plantation revolt in 1831.

3. A reference to the Tomb of the Unknown Soldier from World War I.

"Son of mine, or son of fairer hue, you are mine, too. Do you not lie here because you believed in a world safe for democracy? That bond at once makes you mine. It mustn't be for naught that you gave up the acrid smell of soil, the feel of soft flesh in the moonlight, the laughter of children at play, even though your brothers returned to a land still shackled by fear, want, and prejudice.

"Time slid rapidly over your alabaster box; and so soon they are at war again, for oppression is a cancer that eats at the vitals of mankind. They are fighting again, mark me, with the word freedom whizzing around them and filling the air.

"Murmuring Potomac, don't drown my whisper; let him hear me."

Dig, dig—I can reach him. Claw, claw—the hard stone softens.

"Hey, Ma, you're scratching me. You're not going to faint, are you?" Gently my son shook me, bringing me back to the stark reality of the present with all my fears and self agony—my yesterdays and todays and all time hereafter bound up possessively in his eighteen-year-old body.

"No, son," I answered steadily, "I don't think I am."

"You were standing there looking queer, staring through me out into space."

"Yes, I know. I saw things; I had a vision."

"Come on, Ma, don't carry on like that. You're not sick, are you? You want me to fight, don't you—fight for those four freedoms we live for, don't you?"

"Yes, son, yes I do." I studied his unlined face marked by the conflict that was tearing him between solicitude for me and the age-old yearning for vindication, for accomplishment. I knew he bore in his young heart the harvest of all those others: their fierce pride, their feel for power and the inward knowledge of their own capabilities and the relentless yearning to realize the world that Simon had envisioned when the scourged Man had spoken.

And he bore their burden too—their burden of frustration and rebellion, for now he was boastfully announcing as if to quiet his own secret misgivings, "And this time there'll be no quibbling. We mean those four freedoms for everybody, everywhere—for Negro boys like me right here in America."

His voice faltered; the grand pronouncement dribbled to a pitiful personal plea; and I felt a gnawing pain for the doubt that clouded his great vision. He must go to battle freed from nagging doubt. He must keep throbbing within him the promise of a better world. His untried youth must nurse a dream, if he is to fight for fulfillment. And eager to quell his inward questioning, I answered quickly, "And that's something well worth fighting for. I shall be proud of you, my son." I had given him up, and spent from the wrenching effort, I sank on the hall seat.

His eyes cleared; the dear swagger returned as he reached in his pocket to draw out a bit of cloth. "Look," he said boyishly, "after I got the letter, I went out and bought this for you to hang in our window."

He tossed in my lap a tiny white silken banner bearing in its center a single blue star.

THE CRISIS, JULY 1942

Living Like a Half Man

PRESS HAWKINS

It was the usual shabby employment agency, and against the wall several women sat on a bench, their neat work bundles and suitcases near them. They were old and young women, tall and short, fat and lean—but they were all colored. One of them was saying in a low steady voice, "He was such a good boy. And Lord, how that woman worked to put him through school!"

"He was a *good* boy—I can't believe it. And I hear they offered him some kind of airplane job at Howard."[1]

Another woman said, "Part I can't understand, she wants him to go. She told him to go! Think now that he could make a little money and she could take it easy. . . . But Nellie always has been a queer one. We been neighbors since twenty-four years ago when I got married and moved into her block. She was a pretty woman then, had a fine husband, big strapping man, ready with a smile and a joke. She was sure crazy about that man."

Somebody said, "Never married again."

"Never even thought of another man. He was a hardworking good man with a job in a factory. They were both so happy when the baby came. And I'll never forget the day they told her Jim—that's her husband—had been killed in the factory. Got caught in some old machine. Never saw anything like it. For two days she didn't cry or carry on. Just sat there, holding her baby tight and saying: 'This one the factory ain't going to get, never going

---

1. Howard University, a historically black institution in Washington, D.C.

to do any of the dirty work, the mean work. My boy is going to be a man! A real man, doing the kind of work he wants—not what they jim-crow him into doing. That dangerous factory work killed my Jim. Dangerous work— so they let our men do it. Who cares if a colored man is killed or hurt? Nobody but his wife. My son, he's going to do a man's work, live the life any man would want, white or black.'

"Yes sir, for two days she sat there shocked, mumbling to herself, watching over that baby every minute, like she thought something was going to happen to it."

A woman cut in with, "He was a cute baby."

"Sure was," the other woman said, continuing, "After the funeral it came out that Jim had left her near four hundred dollars insurance. He was a good man! But she moved back with her mother and started working. I remember asking her, 'Girl, with all that money, why don't you rest yourself for awhile?' And she said, 'I'm not going to touch a cent of that money. It's for my George. In fact I'm going to save and add to it, so he can have an education—so when he gets married his wife won't go near crazy having to worry about him being killed in a factory accident.'

"And that Nellie worked! Worked hard and lived cheap. George was a hard worker as he grew up, too, selling papers after school, doing odd jobs—always doing something. Smart as a whip. She was always watching over him, not spoiling him, but taking care. When he graduated high school she gave him ten dollars—as a present. Said he ought to have a little money on him now. He went out and bought her a dress with that money—and she was as proud as could be of that dress. He was a big, tall, handsome boy of seventeen now. A deep brown boy, big and strong as a man. Played football so good a college let him in for nothing just so he could play on their team. It's the truth. Used to have his picture in the paper some times, and Nellie would carry it around to show everybody. They gave him some easy job around the college—all the players had them—and when he came home for the Christmas holidays, he looked like he stepped out of a magazine. Handsomer than ever, dressed up smart and fine—real clothes—not that sharpie junk the boys wear. All the girls was crazy about him. And he gave Nellie money, near two hundred dollars he had saved."

"I sure remember that," a woman sitting on the end of the bench added. "It was a lean holiday for me and Nellie gave me ten dollars without my even asking."

"It was right after that he went in for airplanes. She expected him to be a doctor or lawyer or something, but he was mad about flying, and anyways there was as much opportunity in that as anything else."

"He was right," a thin woman said suddenly. "There's enough hungry doctors and lawyers in Harlem to prove it!"

The woman who was doing most of the talking nodded and went on. "She showed me pictures of him in a plane and I'd ask her 'Ain't you scared he'll get into an accident?' She just said 'I pray every night for him. But if he has to die, let it be up in the clean, bright air, not in a dirty factory, his body crushed in the dirt and muck.' That's the way she is, understanding everything he does. I guess most of you here was at the party she gave when he graduated. I think the papers said he was the first colored aviation engineer."

"That's what he was," the thin woman said. "I remember cutting the piece out of the paper. And remember the time he took her up in a plane? Glory, Nellie couldn't talk of nothing else for weeks. Said it was like being a king, riding way up there and looking down at the earth. She knew then why he liked flying. Then there was that whole year he kept trying and couldn't get a job. No colored help wanted. They started the defense program and he thought he'd get something sure, but they wanted only white men in them planes. Then just when they started an air school at Howard and . . ."

"Shhhhh! Here's Nellie!"

The tall strong greyhaired woman walked into the office, smiled as she registered with the woman at the desk then sat down with the other women, her handbag at her feet. She said good morning and asked if there had been any jobs and they all talked and suddenly one of the women asked, "Has he gone yet?"

"Sailed yesterday," the mother said quietly smiling.

"Nellie, what you smiling about? Seems to me he could do something beside go away to Russia and fight them old Nazis!"

"But I urged him to go, soon as he said he was thinking about it. This is what I've raised him for."

"To go to Russia?"

Nellie shook her head. "No, but to be a man. Over there, he tells me, they don't care what color a man is—it's what he can do that counts. He wants to get a chance at real flying, show what he can do, and at the same time fight those Nazis . . . those Ku Kluxers."

"But if he stayed here . . . !"

Nellie said, "Yes, he might have got a job, in a jim-crow air school, maybe the Army would have put him in a jim-crow air division. Over there he can live like a man, be what he's capable of being. When he returns, at least he'll know what it means to really live."

"If he returns," a woman whispered.

The mother shrugged. "Then he'll have died like a man, which is better than living like a half man, a second rate human." She forced a smile. "But I think he'll come back; he's very good at this flying."

"I hope so, I sure hope . . ." a woman said and stopped abruptly as the phone rang and the woman at the desk started writing on a pad. "Still I can't see why he had to go over there . . ." The woman at the desk, still talking on the phone, looked over at the women and nodded. The women straightened their dresses, as if they were being inspected.

" . . . I can't see why he had to go. . . . Dear, I hope it's a good paying job, at least twenty dollars a month and not too many kids and laundry."

OPPORTUNITY, SEPTEMBER 1942

Portrait of a Citizen

ZORA L. BARNES

Dear Jane,

At last the day is here—the day I worked for, the day you dreamed of, the day Mom and Pop slaved and sweated for. Yes, sweated is the word for it 'cause the easiest job Mom had during the whole time was that scrubbing job at Sears and Co. I can still smell the lye in that yellow soap as the steamy hot water gushed and slopped over it and you could feel the heat from it a yard away. I can still see Mom flinch every time she'd first stick her hand with the big stiff-bristle brush in that pail of hot water. They advertise lotions for dishpan hands, but I wonder did they ever think of advertising anything to help scrubwoman's hands—yes, scrubwoman's hands, red and rough and riveted with countless callouses and careless splinters, scrubwoman's back knotted about the shoulders with muscles hard as only a stevedore's should be, scrubwoman's shame that her normal school diploma[1] was just a piece of paper yellowed with age and gnawed by mice somewhere down in the bottom of an old trunk.

I used to wonder when I was a kid why Mom would look so queer after some of her old school friends had been to visit. She didn't linger on the porch and watch them out of sight as she did other folks who came.

---

1. Equivalent to a high school diploma.

She'd shake hands if they were men or kiss them on the cheek if they were women, smile kinda gentle like and then go quickly back into the house and mend socks faster than fury. All the time she was mending she'd be whispering to herself "blessed something or other." I never knew exactly what she was saying until one day it came to me she must have been saying the beatitudes. I asked her and she said yes, that if she said it often enough soon she'd believe it and that's all that mattered anyway.

It wasn't easy for Pop either, 'cause the whole time it was up in the morning to go to work and back home in the evening to get ready to go to work the next morning. The only time he had to rest in was on Sunday and that eleven months he was out of work. That eleven months he spent trying to find work and going after surplus commodities. Surplus commodities—that was the only thing I ever saw get next to Pop. He never could understand why they thought he was coming there for food. He wanted a job. He could work as well as the next one; in fact, Pop could put out a day's work better than some fellows my age. And he was one of the best carpenters that ever spit into a sawdust pile. The thing that beat Pop was that he didn't have the "right attitude" for a man on relief. He could speak more than three sentences without saying "yassah, Boss!" so he was one of those "smart niggers" who needed to be shown his place and kept there. Besides, he was clean and had on whole clothes and he owned a house although it was in Mom's name. He didn't even look as if he needed a job, so the "powers that be" decided he needed a dose of the "clients' entrance" in the rear.

"Clients' entrance"—that's a laugh. I always had the idea that a client was someone who was having some professional services done for them. I finally looked it up and I guess they picked the right word because one meaning given is "anyone receiving habitually the protection of a person of influence . . . sometimes, a hanger-on." Pop thought he was under their protective influence, but they cased him as a hanger-on. He sat out there with overripe bananas, squashy oranges, moldy celery leaves and prunes confiscated by millions of gnats.

For eleven months Pop sat back there, damp in the spring, sweltering in the summer and frigid in the winter. He sat back there with a lot of hungry devils who were too hungry to care whose tobacco they shared and too cold to see what color was the man sitting so close to them. I bet Pop found out more about the kind of people they were inside, what they did for fun when they had any, where the biggest blue-gills were caught, why the crippled woman left California. Pop almost proved that winter that hate and bigotry and racial prejudice are digestive disturbances.

For eleven months, Pop would get up every morning, go to the employment office and look around for odd jobs, then come home to stick his old black pipe with the broken stem in the corner of his mouth, rest his chin in his hand and just sit looking into space. Finally, after supper he'd puff a little longer, then knock the ashes out on the heel of his shoe, blow through it a couple of times, get up and say, "Well, Mama, we better go to bed. Imagine I'll get that call to go to work in the morning."

Every night he said it. I thought he was either the dumbest man alive or else the stubbornest. I even teased him about having a one-track mind. He just grinned a little and said, "I s'pect that makes things right simple and easy, Son, 'specially if the track's in the right direction."

Maybe smart folks would say that's the line of least resistance. Maybe clever people depend on knowing that people are like that. The only thing that they don't consider is that sometimes people with one-track minds do get where they are headed for.

Every night he'd polish his work shoes, lay out a clean work shirt and pants. He said there was nothing like clean clothes to prove you'd done a day's work; said you couldn't get very dirty just standing around doing nothing so if at the end of the day you had worked some there'd be some evidence of it. Too, he believed that a thing belonged to you more if you had worked for it because if it had been given to you it always partly belonged to the other person. I remember when I was a kid if I wanted money to buy something or to go somewhere, he'd always say, "I can't give it to you, Son, but I think we can find a job for you to do that's worth that much."

I had everything I wanted but I always worked for it. I never learned any short cuts. I guess that's why it has taken this day so long to come.

Then one day, Pop saw a different man. He must have been new on the staff. Probably he was some kid just out of school, full of ideals of sociology and humanitarianism. He must have talked to Pop in a different way or something 'cause Pop had a livelier step when he came home that evening. His eyes were kinda misty-like and he had that old one-sided grin on his face. At supper he said, "Son, it's the educated young folks in this country what's going to steer this ship of state into home port. We old working men are in it all right, but it's you fellows that are going to give the orders. That's why I wanted you to go to college."

Yes! Pop was a happy man that night. He teased Mom and told me I was just like him—getting uglier every day. Next morning, he couldn't get there quick enough. Went off in a downpour of rain without his rubbers or umbrella and got pulpy wet. Well, this nice young man forgot about him or went to a luncheon and stayed all day or something. Anyway, Pop sat there all day in that mess of wet clothes. Of course, I don't need to tell you about that. I don't need to tell you how sick he was for a while until finally the doctor said that he was fixed for this time and as far as physical and medical laws were concerned he ought to get well. Oh, Jane! What can physical laws do for a man who finds his life's journey is a dead end road? What can physical laws do for a man who has discovered too late that patience is a virtue for animals alone? That virtue is its own reward because that's all you have for being so? The world teaches axioms and proverbs for a man to follow and then forgets to tell him not to depend on them. The big fellows throw an arm of protective benevolence around the little fellow and then lock the door they dare him to try to get in. God, Jane! What can physical laws do for a man whose hope has gone up in smoke before he even gets a good blaze kindled?

What did Pop do? He kinda smiled and said, "Your Mother always said I didn't have sense enough to come in out of the rain."

As for Mom, she never said very much anyway. Now that Pop's gone she says even less.

The day you dreamed of has come. Fellows aren't supposed to know what girls' dreams are like, but Jane, my darling, there's a light in your eyes when you look at me that tells me. It tells me that you're still a little girl dreaming of a knight in shining armor. And to top it off, you think you've found it in me. If it weren't so terribly frightening to me, it would be ridiculous. King Arthur would have thought all the sorcerers in his kingdom had been turned into one awful spirit if they had ever unmasked and found a black knight in the bunch. That crowd was more, if possible, "lily-white" than a certain Southern senator, was worse than the "main liners" in *Kitty Foyle*.[2] (By the way, I lost yours, I'll have to get you another copy.) Too, I guess most of the knights were good-looking and the most that even the kindest people could ever say about my face is that I have a "friendly smile." Yet, you say I'm your dreams come true.

Yes, Jane, you're still a little girl. If you weren't you would not trust me as you do with your every dream of life and happiness. You're still a little girl, Jane. If you weren't you wouldn't believe that people can still "live

---

2. Probably a reference to segregationist Theodore Bilbo of Mississippi. *Kitty Foyle* was a book (1939) by Christopher Morley, made into a film (1940) starring Ginger Rogers as a working-girl heroine. Rogers won an Oscar for the role.

happily ever after." You're still a lithe girl, Jane! If you weren't you'd know that the meek do not inherit the earth because the earth is the Lord's, and most meek people would be scared to death if they ever got a chance to meet anyone as decent to them as that.

Only a very young girl, Jane, would sign a contract to teach in a little back-wash school like yours. Even if they paid you what they promised, it isn't half what the white teachers are getting, yet before the school year is over, the funds run out, the school board looks distressed and apologetic, you feel sorry for the children who don't have half a chance and sign on for another year. Yet, as I sit here looking from my window I see a world of beauty that would make the sorriest heart a gay and gleeful thing, and I am glad from the bottom of my heart that I didn't let you give up that job. I wanted to take you away from a place where you couldn't go to the public library and read or even borrow a book, where you couldn't sit on the benches in the park when you wanted shade and quiet, where you didn't dare try on a hat in a millinery shop or tell the man in the shoe store that the reason the shoes didn't fit was because he wouldn't let you put them on. I'm glad you still have even that job because your three sisters can still go to school in whole clothes; your mother can still have a best dress to go to church in. Yes, at least, she can go to church.

You're a little girl, Jane, but you're a better man than I am. You would have given up that job. You knew you couldn't keep it afterwards. You knew, too, that as the wife of a struggling young colored architect that I'd be building more air-castles than I would low-cost houses. You knew, too, that you'd have to pay for those air-castles of mine with worry, with fear, with maybe, disillusionment—yet, *I looked like a knight in shining armor to you.*

So, Jane, my dear, my darling, I drew my sword, I challenged every foe, I conquered the enemy. I laid the laurel wreath of success at your feet. That firm decided to hire me. Though it was not their policy to hire colored persons to their staff they felt my excellent training and promising work merited their attention. Of course, the salary was lower than was customary because I would not be doing the usual contact work with clients. That was all right, because I don't want to sit at a client's dinner table or drink cocktails with him at his club or take his daughter out to lunch. I was content to know that at last I had what Mom and Pop had planned and worked and sweated for, what you'd dreamed of, what I'd hoped for, but—

This cup of success contains a bitter draught, Jane. I received my first pay check from that job today, but I also received notice to report for selective service duty four days from now.

I'm not a praying man, my darling. It would take a man Pop's size inside to pray after all I've seen and gone through. I'm afraid that circumstances have stunted my inner growth. But I have a faint consolation. Four days from now I'll have on a uniform and *I'll be a citizen!* I'll be one of that vast crowd of young men who are postponing their dreams, their hopes, their loves to join hands and hearts to form a chain of courage and determination for their country. No, I'm not a praying man and now I'll have even less time to learn how, but my darling while you're praying for our little dreams to come true will you say something about hoping that after I get out of that uniform that the "citizen" part will stick?

Lovingly,
Tom.

NEGRO STORY, MARCH–APRIL 1945

Ante Partum

LEOTHA HACKSHAW

The girl was with child. She stood before the mirror gazing at her nakedness. The room was in shadows. Outside, the light was turning into an overcasting grey. She stood before the mirror and looked at her swollen, distorted body, slim limbed, small face with large dark eyes getting darker as she looked. One hand found her cheek. The tip of a small finger found the corner of her parted lips. "God! I'm scared!" The cry, high and shrill, was wrung from her. There was a slight movement, a gentle twitch within her. She straightened with her hand on her belly. Her fingers found a shallow cavity. The navel had almost disappeared into the round mass of stretched skin. She passed her hands over her firm chest. Ed had once called her breasts ripe pears. "Oh, Eddie, come back to me. I need you. I need you now darling." What was it Eddie said about the stirring life within her? "Remember kid, it has to be a girl—with hair that curls like yours. If it isn't, send it back where it came from."

"But Ed," she had said between laughter, "I want a boy."

"Not this round, kid. It's got to be a girl."

The picture of Eddie came before her. Eddie with his quick step and ready laughter. Eddie. . . . Eddie. . . .

The room was now quite dark. Still she stood at the window, her face pressed against the wooden frame. Once more there was a movement, sharp and quick. This time she was startled. One small fist struck quickly again and again. The twitchings increased until it seemed there was only one blurred continuous motion. Her panic grew. She cried out. At last the movements diminished and with one spasmodic jerk ceased. Her panic gradually subsided. She turned slowly away from the window. Her groping fingers found the side of the bed. She stretched upon it, easing herself into the sinking softness of the mattress with a great sigh. The darkness grew, and she slept.

A woman came into the room and stood looking down on the bed. Her forearms were bared to the streak of light streaming in from the street. A man came and stood by her. "It's time to get the doctor, ain't it?" The woman didn't seem to hear. She was still looking down at the girl lying on the bed. Her lips moved, but no sounds came. After a while the man turned and left the room. He went down the squeaky stairs into the kitchen. The potatoes with their skins nearby lay where the woman had left them. A pot was bubbling on the stove. The room was very warm, but the man shivered. He drew the jacket closer over his shoulders. His lips formed a bloodless line across his cheeks. He walked across the room to the telephone. After a wait he heard the doctor's voice. He spoke into the phone with a rasping stream of words. "Doc? I think you'd better come. No. She just screeched a coupla times. Yeah, she's quiet. All right." He bent down and rubbed his hands over his knees. "Christ!" Steps came into the room. He turned to face the woman. Stray wisps of hair hung wearily over her forehead. "You call the doctor?" The man nodded. "He said it ain't time yet." The woman moved about the room. "She's more scared than anything if you ask me." The man nodded again, silently. He wanted to defend the girl, but he didn't know what to say. He thought a while. "Remember how it was with you when Steve was coming?" The woman turned around and faced him. She was big with strong arms. Now they were covered with the dough she was kneading. "Taint the same with me nohow. My babies birthed themselves; I was out working three days after." She went on quietly kneading. "Seem's like it ain't right to make sich a fuss over a natural thing like having a baby." The man fumbled with his fingers. He looked at her and glanced away. "Guess Eddie'd want her to have good treatment." His eyes came back to her face. "He ain't like us. He's city folk." "Then he ought to be here mindin' her now when she needs him." A sudden rage distorted the man's face. "You know where he is. He's doing all he can where he is right now. What do you want from him? You wouldn't mind if the little one were fatherless even before it saw the light of day. You hate him. . . ." He stopped. A scream crashed down from the floor above. He was half-way up the stairs when he heard a car driven into the yard. He stumbled downstairs and flung the door wide. The screams were coming quickly now. Doctor Hilton's massive body filled the doorway. For a moment he stood there chuckling as he stared at the distraught man. "I came just in time, I see." The man nodded. Doctor Hilton laughed. "I've never been TOO late yet. That's a record." His voice changed to hardness as he turned to the man again. "Did you do as I told you? Good! Relax, man! Relax! Your daughter will be all right. She's got youth on her side." He mounted the stairs, but his voice was slow in following him. "Send your wife up here. You go to my car and help yourself to my bottle." Later in the evening, his voice took on more urgency. Once he called down the stairs for more hot water. The man sat in the kitchen kneading his hands between his knees. He watched the woman as she mounted the stairs with slow heavy steps. He went up the stairs treading softly. He bent his head to the closed door but all he could hear were muffled voices. When the woman opened the door he saw the little girl lying on the bed. She was quiet and still, and he thought she was asleep. It seemed to the girl that she was asleep and floating in a grey mist. Eddie was beside her. They were walking along the cow path back of the shed as they used to do when they were first married. They stood on the top of The Knob and looked down on the valley. Below them lay row after row of green growing shoots. To the left of where they stood and a little beyond, the young plants waved gracefully. She felt Ed's arm around her waist. She turned and smiled at him. She saw that the dogwood was in bloom. "Let's pick some dogwood blossoms, Ed." She stood quietly watching him as he filled her arms with the smooth-petaled branches. The sun shone brightly as they dreamed and planned. Something was wrong with the dream. Something was pressing down upon her. She tried to move and found that she could not. Sharp pains were shooting through her. She tried to move again, and cried. "Easy. You'll be all right." Something struck her arm, and the mist gathered around her more densely. This time she fought the mist. Her hands became free and found their way to her hair. The fingers entwined themselves among the strands. The knuckles whitened sharply under the force of her grip. "Oh Ed, I am afraid . . . don't let them do this to me. Please don't let them do this to me." It seemed to her that she was screaming at the top of her voice, but she had made no sound. Dr. Hilton worked swiftly. The cry was shrill in the tense room. Its cadences engulfed the room from corner to ceiling. The girl turned her head at the sound. "What is it?" "It's a girl." Cold, salty tears ran down her cheeks. She turned her head away as if finally rejecting her fears now that they were deposed. "Ed, it's what you wanted." She felt an infinite relief go through her. She bent slightly and glimpsed the red working mouth beside her. She knew that she need not have been afraid and that she would never be afraid again. She murmured as she drifted into sleep. The doctor heard the murmur and bent over her. She was already asleep. He straightened, feeling tired and old. How many times had he seen the struggle for life unfold? Yet it was always new. He looked out into the garden below. The sun was shining now—bright and clear. Another day. The green leaves on the hedge glistened. As he looked, a red cat stalked majestically into his view. She was bedraggled and unkempt. She lay beneath a cluster of shrubbery and began an elaborate toilette. With a pink tongue she carefully licked and stroked each fur. The warmth of the sun finally reached her and she rolled gracefully on the grass. From deep within her came throaty sounds of contentment. She was beginning a new day. In the darkest corner of the barn five new-born kittens were waiting for her to return.

THE CRISIS, OCTOBER 1943

So Softly Smiling

CHESTER B. HIMES

To Roy Johnny Squires, a lieutenant in the U.S. Army, who for six months had seen much of life and too much of death, through the blinding glare of desert heat, it felt unreal being home in Harlem for thirty days. North African warfare had left its mark on him—it kept raging through his brain like a red inferno that would never cease, tautening his muscles and jerking his reflexes and keeping his eyes constantly on the alert. For hours he had been tramping the familiar streets, scanning the familiar faces; and even now, at two in the morning, it did not mean a thing. His nerves were sticking out like wires.

It was too un-dead, un-wounded, bloodless, entire—too human. That was it—too human again after the bombings and the shellings and the snipings, the charges with twenty and the arrivals with twelve; the egg-sized balls of heat that grew like mushrooms at the base of the brain. It was too filled with something, too much like just lying down and crying like a baby. A drink was in line; a drink was most needed.

He pushed into a tony after-hours spot on 125th Street and headed toward the bar.

"Make mine rye," he said to the bartender.

And then, halfway turning, he saw her. He was startled. He had left her in the dull, dawn khamsins[1] where only her face had stood between him and a death that was never two feet off. Those purely feminine features with a tawny skin like an African veld at sunset, so smooth you forever wanted to touch it, crowned by blue-black hair that rolled up from her forehead in great curling billows like low storm clouds. That mouth, wide enough for a man to really kiss, and the color of crushed rosebuds. He could not be mistaken.

She was sitting by herself over against the wall at a low, lounge table, as if waiting for someone. The pianist was playing Chopin's *Fantasie,* and she was lost in listening; maybe trying to catch something that the music promised but never gave. He swung slowly from the bar and sauntered over, magnetized, and stood across the table, looking down at her. Not disrespectfully, not recklessly; but with all the homage in the world.

"You're as beautiful as I knew you'd be," he said.

She turned a widened glance on him, and something new and unexpected, almost unbelievable, came alive in her face, as if she might have seen what the music promised but never gave. Then her long black lashes lowered lacquered fans over the sudden boy-and-girl game in her eyes. After a moment she looked up-from-under into his face and murmured, "I am?" slightly questioning, the corners of her mouth quirking in beginning laughter.

The shaded wall light mellowed her into a painting, life-like and provocative, with eyes like two candles in a darkened church; and perfume came out of her hair and burnt through him like flame. For a long time now there had only been the girl in the clouds; and he could not help himself. He reached out and drew her to him and kissed her with long and steady pressure.

Behind them, some one gasped; a laugh caught, moved, and died.

But he did not hear. Because her lips were smooth and soft and resilient, like the beginning of life, as he had dreamed they would be; and he kept kissing her until the breath had gone from both of them.

Finally she broke away, gasping, "Why did you do that?"

"I don't know," he confessed, his eyes on hers; and after a moment added, as if thinking aloud. "To get something, I guess."

She waited so long that he thought she would not reply, then she asked, "Did you?"

---

1. A hot wind from the Sahara that blows across Egypt.

"Yes."

"I'm glad."

They stood on the brink of something suddenly discovered, something new and big and important, looking at each other until the long, live moment ran out. And then he dropped a bill on the table and took her by the arm and they went outside and turned down Seventh Avenue, silent for the most part, drawing feelings from each other without words, and after a time it began to snow again, but neither of them noticed. Hours later, it seemed, they came to Central Park, and sat on a bench and kissed.

The February daybreak found them still there, two whitened images in the softly sifting snow; and finally she said, "I should have waited for Dorothy, she'll be furious."

"Then—then you're not married?" quickly, as if he had been afraid to ask before.

"No, darling," she teased. "Aren't my kisses adorably inexperienced?"

He kissed her again, then said with an odd solemnity. "They're everything I dreamed that they would be."

They had breakfast at a crowded little lunch counter, but were oblivious of the other people; and when they couldn't stretch the minutes any longer, he said, his intense glance playing over her face, "I have to go back in twenty-nine days, so please don't fall in love with me." Taking a deep breath, he continued, "But don't leave me, please don't leave me; I'm already so much in love with you."

She was looking at him, at his young, gaunt face with too much thinness down the cheeks and too much blankness in the eyes, hiding too much that he had seen that she could now feel hard and constricted inside of him. Looking at him; and at his tall, lithe figure in the jaunty uniform of a commissioned officer, question-marked against the counter and back-grounded against the row of coffee drinking workers, which, without any effort, had she closed her eyes, she could have seen without its litheness, bloated and wormy and unidentifiable as either black or white in the barren heat of an African desert. But her gaze remained steadily on his face, brown and full-lipped and handsome, and once she opened her mouth as if to speak, and then closed it as if she could not find the handle to the words, and finally, when she replied, it was only to say, "Yes," answering in the affirmative to a number of questions he might have found it hard to ask.

Three days later they taxied to Grand Central Station and boarded a train for some little sleepy town somewhere—it did not matter—and they were married. Miss Mona Morrison, successful poet, who had lived alone on Sugar Hill, became the ordinary wife of a U.S. Army officer.

But it did not seem at all strange that this should be happening to her, or to either of them; the strange thing would have been its not happening.

"Sometimes coming back from a raid in the dawn," he told her that night, emotion fingering the edges of his voice, "I'd look up at the reddening sky and feel that all the earth was consuming itself in fire and only heaven would be left; and I'd want so much to be in love, I'd ache with it."

And she whispered in reply, "If I could be that; if I could be heaven and always have you."

After that, nothing was real. It was fantasy, ecstasy, dread and apprehension. It was glory. They went to live in her apartment, and did not need a thing. Neither people nor food nor sleep. Nor the world. Because there was too much of each other within the hours that they would never have.

And the days passed through this enchanted unreality, wired-together and meteoric. There were twenty-six; then there were twenty-five. But each day was filled to overflowing and could not hold it all; and always some spilled into the day following.

In twenty-three days; and then twenty-two.

They barricaded themselves behind illusion and fought against it in the manner of two small children playing house.

They were riding down Fifth Avenue atop a bus, and she was saying, "A month is long enough to stay in Harlem. Next month we'll spend with my folks in Springfield, Ohio. You'll love my mother." Laughing, she added. "She's a Seventh Day Adventist, by way of description."

"I've got some remote relatives in Chicago, too, whom we can visit for a time," he said, catching the spirit of the fantasy, "although my parents are both dead."

"And after that we can wander lazily to the coast. Have you ever been to Los Angeles?" she asked.

He shook his head.

"It's good for a month, too. And I'll introduce you to some of the celebs—Ethel Waters and Rochester and Hall Johnson; you'll enjoy Hall, he's a man of many thoughts; and even Lena Horne, although I'll not promise I won't be jealous if she smiles at you."

"Carmel is a lovely place, too," she went on, "After the war—"

He quickly interrupted, "What war?" and they laughed.

"It's funny how you can grow past things so quickly," she observed, surprised. "Ten days ago I was a rather self-centered poet who prided herself on being remote—and now I feel as if that was another life."

"It was," he said.

And then quickly, almost fearfully, she vowed, "But I'll never grow past you. When you're gone . . ."

She caught herself, but it was too late.

This was it; he was going back, and she was staying here.

"I used to ask myself," he confessed, " 'What have I got in this war? Let the white people fight their own war—I've got nothing to win.' And then I read where some one said, perhaps it was Walter White or Randolph,[2] that America belonged to the Negro as much as it did to anyone. And I got a funny feeling, maybe it was pride, or ownership—I don't know. Anyway I enlisted. And then one day the 'old man' called us in and said, 'We're it.' "

He was silent for a time, looking at the passing sights, and when she did not speak, he went on, trying to explain something:

"I—I don't know just when it started, but I got to feeling that I was fighting for the Four Freedoms. Maybe I had to feel it, maybe I had to feel that it was a bigger fight than just to keep the same old thing we've always had. But it got to be big in my mind—bigger than just fighting a war. It got to be more like building, well, building security and peace and freedom for everyone.

"And—and, what I mean," he stumbled on, "is we don't have to hide from it. It's got to be building for freedom and it's got to be so big and wide there'll be room in it for happiness, too."

She said an odd thing. "We're going to have a son." Because she knew that in these things there was this—which no one could take—this going on of life, which gave to everything else purpose, meaning, a future.

"How do you know?" he asked startled.

"How could we miss?" she countered.

And they were laughing again, so wonderfully happy. But even a song could bring it back, a voice from the radio singing the half-forgotten words: *Leaves are falling and I am recalling. . . .* Because this was so young, so alive, so biological, this was for a togetherness throughout eternity.

It was there the night Bill and Louise threw the party for them, although that was one of the happiest days they ever knew. But for a time they forgot about it; they felt almost as if they had it beaten.

All the old bunch was there, you know their names. Louise made mint

---

2. Walter White was an important leader in the NAACP, serving as its executive secretary from 1931 until his death in 1955. A. Philip Randolph was head of the railroad Brotherhood of Sleeping Car Porters and a key political leader in the 1940s civil rights movement.

juleps and they danced a little and flirted with each others' wives and then began a discussion on political interpretations, which ended with Ted telling the story of *Barker Brown*. Then Henry told the one about the two whales and the "cracker" . . . " 'You mean to say you ain't never seen a *cracker?*' the old whale asked the baby whale . . ." Not to be outdone, Walter told the tale of the ghost of Rufus Jones which came back to earth in the body of a white man and was elected to governor of Mississippi. But the colored folks knew he was old Rufus Jones.

They were having such a wonderful time that Eddie suggested that they do it over again at his flat next month. "How is it with you and Roy, Mona?" he asked.

How was it?

It was on top of them, that is how it was. In thirteen days he was going back to Africa to fight for a democracy he never had; it was reality . . . And then in twelve . . .

The togetherness which was meant to be would be gone . . . In eleven days . . . And then in ten . . . It hung over their heads, staining every moment with a blind, futile desperation, beneath which everything was distorted and magnified out of proportion to its importance, so that now things began to hurt which before would not have mattered, and minor incidents which should have sunk beneath a kiss now grew into catastrophes.

It was that way when he met Earl Henry and Bill Peters who had gone to Chicago University with him. Earl was a cavalry lieutenant, and Pete, sporting the wings of the 99th Pursuit Squadron,[3] said, "I'm an eagle now, sonny."

A reunion was in order, so they found a pleasant little bar on 116th Street.

Roy intended to call Mona from the first, knowing that she would be expecting him home and would worry. But a slightly tipsy celebrant was monopolizing the house telephone, making up with a girl whom, judging from the phrases which drifted Roy's way, he had promised to take some place and hadn't. Roy got change from the barman so as to use the booth telephone; but the barman served the second round of drinks first—you know how those things happen—and then Pete was telling a joke about an Alabama senator and a Negro minister that was good enough to pass on. When he did stand up and start toward the telephone, Earl caught him by the sleeve, and—

---

3. The 99th Pursuit Squadron was the most prestigious branch of the African American military force and was housed at Tuskegee Air Force Base.

" . . . literally forced me to listen," he was telling Mona as the reason he was late.

"And then the third round of drinks was served and I—I proposed a toast to the loveliest woman in all the world."

But in between there had been a moment when he had not thought of her, and this she sensed—this was important.

When she did not smile, he knew that it was there, something pregnant with a hurt, and it was then his words took on the tone of explanation, "I wouldn't, for anything in the world, have stayed if I had thought you would have minded in the least, darling."

Not enough sleep, lack of proper eating, and living each instant on the brink of desperation with the end of their togetherness always there, even on the lips of a kiss, impelled her to say, against her will, "But you could have called, darling, knowing how I would worry—"

"But, sweetheart, I intended to. I had the nickel in my hand—"

"I understand, darling . . ." Pushing from inside of her . . . "I want you to be with your friends . . ." Out of the vacuum left by her relief at seeing him . . . "Sometimes I think we have been together too much . . ." Out of the hours pacing the floor with ragged nerves gouging her like rusted nails . . . "But couldn't you have taken a moment to telephone? If I did not love you so, I would not have been so worried."

He began again, "I wanted to, I intended to—" He spread his hands pleading, "Can't you understand? Won't you believe me? What is it, sweetheart? I—I—"

Pushing and pushing, up through the congested tears in her throat, out between her quivering lips, "If you had wanted to, you would have, Roy, darling. It's because you weren't thinking of me that you didn't; and when you stopped thinking about me, it was not the same anymore. When— when you can forget me in a crowd, it—it isn't what we thought; because it's knowing that l am always in your heart that keeps me p-punching."

They were there, suddenly, a wall of words between them.

"I—I had—" he could not say it again. That live-wire edge of futility building up, and now this wall of words that it had built. But courage was needed, patience, understanding; understanding most of all. And he tried again, smoothing out his exasperation with superhuman will, "Sweetheart, can we talk about it tomorrow? Can we—don't you think we should go to bed tonight? We're both upset. If we could sleep a little in—in—" he paused, and then went on, "I mean, it—it might make a difference, don't you think?"

Without moving, he moved toward her, as if to take her in his arms. And without moving, she moved away.

"Don't you understand what I am saying, Roy?" Pushing and pushing— oh, Dear God, please stop me . . . "Don't you?" . . . Pushing . . .

Her words were like steady shots. Is this how it would feel? A weird relation of thoughts. Could death be worse than this? . . . Echoing in his brain with the shallow faintness of distance: *"Don't you?"*

Now between them the words were gone, engulfing them in unbearable emptiness; and then the upsurge of overwhelming hurt. So tangible he shook great waves of it from his head in a violent reflex gesture, and yet other waves surged over him. They were caught and being carried along, swiftly, blindly; and in her fear, instinctively, she reached out for his hand.

Just that touch, just the touch of hands, and they were safe again; they were in each other's arms and she was crying, "I didn't mean it, darling. Honestly, I didn't mean it."

"I'm a rat," he said hoarsely. "How can you love such a rat as I?"

No, not eventful like the winning of a battle, nor dramatic like the downing of a plane; but to two people in this peopled world, it was a crossing into permanence, a bridging of the gap into immortality which in the final analysis makes the human race the supreme race. For now, togetherness would always be; no matter the war, which had to be fought and won. No matter death, which was but another crossing. There would always be togetherness—always—because they had gotten over.

And suddenly, they began to plan the future.

"We'll buy a farm," he said. "A tiny one just big enough for us. I'll send every cent of my salary home."

"And while you're building us peace and freedom and security, I'll be building our home," she added. "A rambling, old-fashioned, comfortable house out of old stones. I will build it with my hands. And—"

And underneath their rainbow, like planes flying low over the desert, the days moved westward. There were six, and then there were five.

They caught a bus and went upstate and selected a plot of four acres and made a deal with the real estate brokerage; and the next day they consulted an architect in Harlem and pored over blueprints.

"We'll have the nursery here," she said. "It'll catch the sun all day. And out back—"

"We'll plant an orchard," he supplemented. "Pears and peaches—"

"And apples—"

"And we'll have a swing."

"Over here will be your den and when you're a famous attorney you can say—"

"We'll plant flowers," he cut in.

"Of course. Down beside the walk and here in front on both sides. Floral firecrackers and golden stars and hyacinths and—"

"I'll come through Holland on the way home and bring the tulips back," he said. "Pink and white and . . ."

And then there were none . . .

"I'm simply crazy about you, darling," she was telling him. "Remember that most. Remember that I love everything you do, the color of your skin, the way you walk, the way you carry your shoulders so high and bravely; the way you sometimes say 'not particularly so' and 'I mean; well, what I mean,' and the little habit you have of dipping your head and running your hand across your hair when you are thinking . . ."

"And I love the way your eyes look now while you are talking of it," he said. "I'll be seeing them on those days when I take off. I'll always remember your eyes, sweetheart."

"I'll never forget anything about you," she declared. "Never!"

And though they had braced themselves against it from the very first, when the pick-up car pulled to a stop where they awaited at the curb, neither of them were prepared for sight of it. Until the last moment, until the driver said, "I'm sorry, sir," they clung to each other, kissing each other, their eyes locked together, so gallantly, although their lips were trembling and breaking up beneath.

And then he was inside and the driver shifted gears and the motor sounded and he was moving away from her.

She kept biting her lips to hold back screams, and then motion came into her body and she began to wave, wildly, and the words came out in a gasping rush, "Don't forget the tulips, Roy. Don't forget the tulips, darling."

And through the open window, he was yelling back, "I forgot to tell you, set out the apple trees in April. And if it's a girl—" The rest was drowned in motor roar.

The last he saw of her, as the car was merged in traffic, she was standing at the curb, so tiny it seemed from that distance, and so rigid, and finally, so softly smiling.

Singer Lena Horne, *The Crisis*, January 1943

Popular Culture and the Arts

The Office of War Information conducted a campaign to break down racism in the civilian population, but its results were decidedly mixed. Only a handful of films with positive images of African Americans were made, for instance, and from 1942–1945, only sixty-four articles appeared on blacks in national magazines with large circulations according to *The Reader's Guide to Periodical Literature.* So dominant were racist beliefs in mainstream media that even well-intentioned articles on black people could reinforce widespread stereotypes. For example, as late as 1941, a *Life* portrait of an African American soldier refers to him as a "24-year-old colored boy" and the reader is told, "Unlike most Negroes, Raymond does not like dancing." Furthermore, there are photos of him in stereotypical farmer's overalls with a broom and eating watermelon with his girlfriend, a college student.[1] Attention to African American women was virtually nonexistent. Only a handful of magazine articles appeared during the war years with black women as the focus, and these were, tellingly, on entertainers. Most of the progressive films produced in Hollywood placed men, not women, in new roles such as *Bataan* (1943), *Sahara* (1943), and *The Negro Soldier* (1944). The only nonmusical film to depict a black woman in a major role was *Since You Went Away* (1944), which featured Hattie McDaniel as a maid.

The most positive mass-media depictions of African American women were of singers on the stage or in movie musicals. Etta Moten, Anne Wiggins Brown, and others starred in Broadway plays such as *Porgy and Bess* and *Carmen Jones,* while opera stars Marian Anderson and Lillian Evanti toured the world's concert stages. Lena Horne, Ethel Waters, Hazel Scott, and others appeared in all-black musicals such as *Stormy Weather* (1943) and *Cabin in the Sky* (1943) as well as in sophisticated numbers included in white musicals like *Panama Hattie* (1942), *Star Spangled Rhythm* (1942), *Thank Your Lucky Stars* (1943), or *This Is the Army* (1943). Dancers Katherine Dunham and Pearl Primus emerged during this period too and based their choreography on African and Caribbean culture. So important were these new portrayals, as restricted as they were, that theaters in the South commonly cut musical scenes with beautifully gowned, glamorous black stars. Testifying to wartime emphasis on black female beauty are the articles on Hazel Scott, Katherine Dunham, and Lena Horne in this section

---

1. *"Life* Goes on a Weekend Leave," August 11, 1941: 78–80.

that allude pointedly to their sexiness, and stories like Lila Marshall's "The Skater," which features a roller skater whose elegance and attractiveness rivet the attention of all who skate with her.

The groundbreaking success of these singers, dancers, and actresses was featured in black magazines, as were positive visual images of women generally. *The Crisis* ran a series of studio photos portraying African American female entertainers, like Anne Wiggins Brown, Hattie McDaniel, and Etta Moten, all pictured in this section, for several months during the war, while it and *Opportunity* put attractive women on most of their covers, always with captions identifying their career trajectories. The fiction in this section echoes the positive tone of articles praising black artists as it explores the healing dimension of artistic expression and its potential to garner respect, particularly for women. The arts emerge as a site of empowerment for women during the war, much as they did in the Harlem Renaissance, but the arena shifted from literary achievement to success in the performing arts. This is a reflection of the immense popularity of movie musicals after the 1920s as well as of the inroads into Broadway made by black migrants to Harlem.

Although such images made a significant dent on mainstream erasure of black women, there are pieces in this section that illustrate how long real change for African American female artists would take. The brief item on Philippa Duke Schuyler is one of these. With a genius-level IQ, authorship of piano compositions by age four, and celebrated as a virtuoso pianist, Philippa Schuyler became famous for her poise, her precocity, and her amazing talent. Like the film career of Dorothy Dandridge, however, Philippa's promising start fizzled out after the war. Indeed, she died prematurely in a helicopter crash while reporting on the Vietnam War in 1967. Similarly, Hilda Simms's acting career never reached the heights she hoped for after her stunning Broadway debut in *Anna Lucasta,* nor did Anne Wiggins Brown or Etta Moten achieve the postwar fame for which they were positioned. Their stories are sobering reminders that black women faced serious obstacles in artistic endeavors, even when blessed with major talent.

Some of these problems are reflected in this material. For example, black composer William Grant Still's piece "How Do We Stand in Hollywood?" describes Still's frustration over having his suggestions ignored on movie sets as producers and directors operated from stereotypes over how African Americans should be portrayed. He complains about being boxed into narrow categories when he worked on wartime all-black musicals in which his arrangements were considered "too good" or "too polite." Pushed to create erotic scores for the pictures he worked on, Still resented having to stay within the confines of jazz or spirituals. His perception that he was being asked to stay within stereotyped boundaries is confirmed by Fanny McConnell's essay, "A Broadway Taboo Is Lifted," a piece on Hilda Simms, who broke new ground for black actresses when she starred in a dramatic role in *Anna Lucasta* in 1944. Normally allowed only into musical or comic parts, Simms's starring role in a drama intended for a white actress seemed to herald a new era for African American women on the stage. At the same time, the article details the paucity of opportunities for black dramatic art students who faced limited employment in roles that were demeaning caricatures while juggling acting classes with jobs as maids or elevator operators. Similarly, Marjorie Greene's profiles of three young talents in various artistic pursuits in "They Prepare for 'A New Nation' " allude to deadening stereotypes that limit their potential. Penelope Johnson is described as a violinist trained at the prestigious Juilliard School of Music who resists the admonitions of older musicians to "swing" her violin (play it in a jazz style) as did Hazel Scott, a classically trained pianist, who arranged jazz renditions of classical pieces. Johnson was told that in spite of her talent, she would not be accepted as a serious violinist by the white establishment. June McMechen, a young soprano trained in French and German, is said to face a segregated concert stage that threatens to thwart her plans to penetrate the closed worlds of opera and radio, while Mabel Fairbanks, a talented figure skater, shrugs off the warnings of people who tell her African Americans cannot succeed in ice skating. Sadly, it was not until the Olympics of 1988 that an African American figure skater named Debi Thomas was first able to penetrate the color barrier to African American achievement in this sport.

Even celebrities of the stature of Lena Horne, Hazel Scott, Katherine Dunham, and the wartime Broadway musical star Muriel Rahn (a.k.a. Muriel Smith) are portrayed in articles here as having to fight racism in various large and small ways. Rahn's fame as star of the 1944 play *Carmen Jones* could not protect her, for instance, from degrading experiences in Ohio and Indiana hotels described in a *Negro Digest* piece included here, wherein she details being refused service in the Atlanta airport cafeteria. Ironically, Rahn was on a tour selling war bonds for the U.S. Treasury Department at the time. Hazel Scott, wife of New York congressman Adam Clayton Powell Jr. and a film star whose jazz versions of piano classics were world-famous, is shown in another *Negro Digest* article as having to stipulate in her movie contracts that she will not wear a headrag or dirty clothes. The article also mentions she feels compelled to confine herself to one upscale New York nightclub for her performances because it is the only such establishment that admits black customers. Lena Horne, similarly, in "Beautiful but Not Dumb" recounts an unforgettable incident when she was forced to spend a cold winter night with a circus while traveling with her band because they could not find a hotel in the Indiana town where they were playing. Along the same lines, African American writer O'Wendell Shaw creates a fictional story in "Chief Mourner" about a woman dying of cancer in the charity ward of a black hospital who is discovered to be a once-promising dramatic actress whose career was aborted by the dark color of her skin. Racism directed against black actresses is handled in a more empowering but nonetheless pointed way in Elizabeth Walker Reeves's "Monday's Child," in which a class of African American children discusses recent movies based on novels and all the stars mentioned in the story are white.

Despite the fact that racism informs the material in this section, however, the prevailing mood here is positive, and the theme of art overcoming discrimination, or at least alleviating its painful consequences, is pronounced. "Interlude in a Book Shop," by J. F. Powers, for instance, showcases the power of artistic success to challenge racism. In this story a fictionalized famous opera singer disrupts the surveillance of two white bookstore clerks who end up fawning over her when they learn her identity after initially suspecting her of theft. Finally, "Olaf and His Girl Friend" by Ann Petry takes as its main character a dancer modeled after Katherine Dunham. The daughter of an obeah-woman from the West Indies, Belle Rose uses her artistic and spiritual power to heal the man she loves while managing to escape the success that nonetheless imprisons her. Made famous by a white Harlem nightclub owner, Belle Rose is dressed to resemble an exotic feathered creature with her red turban, hoop earrings, and red calico dress supported by stiffly starched white petticoats. Like a bird escaping from its gilded cage, however, she runs off after a performance one night with her West Indian lover, never to return. Tellingly, the falsifying colors this dancer wears at her employer's insistence echo the red and white stripes of the American flag as do the stars of the night into which she flees. This final image of the story captures well the predominant theme in African American magazines that female performers coming to the fore during the war years were challenging in profound ways the racism that for decades had denied their beauty, power, and courage.

THE CRISIS, FEBRUARY 1944

Note on Commercial Art

LANGSTON HUGHES

You've done taken my blues and gone—
You sing 'em in Paris
And you sing 'em in Hollywood Bowl,
And you done mixed 'em up with symphonies
And you done fixed 'em
So they don't sound like me.

Yep, you done taken my blues and gone.

You also done took my spirituals and gone—
And you done put me in Macbeth
And all kinds of Swing Mikados
And in everything but what's about me—
But someday somebody'll
Stand up and talk about me,
And write about me—black and beautiful—
And sing about me,
And put on plays about me!

I reckon it'll be me myself!

POWERFUL LONG LADDER, 1946

Pearl Primus[1]

OWEN DODSON

Who Dances?
Is it the earth, the dark world underneath
Moving up, the goddess and her daughter

---

1. Pearl Primus was an African American modern dancer known for her antiracist and protest themes.

Dancing again, weaving their dance
Through the lines of corn, dancing
Through the vines with the grapes of wrath?
O, the sun is like a shawl on their backs,
The memory of stars halfway in their eyes.

Is it the memory of a lonely black boy lonely on a tree,
The black hope blaring ripeness under the tree,
Trumpeting up a lost and lonely Spring?

Is it Proserpine up again and longing
Or rivers of sweat forming men and growing?
This strangeness is an ease to me,
A refuge in the pop-eyed noon.

Is it Cassandra as she saw the dark wolf
And caught him fast and dug her prophetic fingernails
To below the hair into the flesh
Feeling a dark blood world of hate?

Who dances here?
Surely it is the black girl who has seen the vision,
Who waits, pistoning her feet in the air,
For the new world and the fruit of it.

THE CRISIS, OCTOBER 1945

Marian Anderson

CHARLES ENOCH WHEELER

Your voice is a thrush's call in the still of night,
Notes that remind of stars,
Each note a spiritual star of light—
What memories they bring to my window bars!
The Southland and all it means to me
Sorrow, joy, pain and slavery,
Your voice a star-point that breaks the heart
Of prejudice, keeping us apart.

Contralto Marian Anderson, *The Crisis*, October 1943

OPPORTUNITY, SPRING 1944

They Prepare for "A New Nation"

MARJORIE E. GREENE

The promise of the most brilliant era in American history shows in the post-war world. The demobilization of the American Army, labor turnover, world rehabilitation, reconversion of war industries, international trade complications, political and racial upheaval will whirl in magnificent confusion with helicopters, magic electrons, television sets, and the return of nylons. Americans are eager; they work and wait for the Victory—and the Peace.

None are so eager as the Negro minority, thwarted, segregated, discriminated against for its more than 300 years in America. Its concern is with a re-vitalized post-war *democracy*. Perhaps one of its fondest hopes is that certainly the millions of Americans wading in the blood of World War II, and projecting themselves into every inch of the civilized world as well as into the isolation of the so-called uncivilized portions, cannot withdraw again into narrow, prejudiced lives. A second hope is that absorption with total world readjustment—also pregnant with possibilities of new respect and appreciation for people for their own merits—should leave neither time nor inclination for American citizens to return again to petty persecution of loyal fellow countrymen.

Recent events, particularly the February 1944 report of the National Urban League's Industrial Department, indicate that Negro labor will be given its chance. Several skips around, another group—serious Negro artists—are placing their faith in post-war democracy, seeing optimistically, a healthy rejuvenation of Abraham Lincoln's "new nation."

June McMechen, young soprano, is one of these. She studies hard: long hours with her voice teacher, long hours alone, and other hours with French and German lessons. She has a promising future. Todd Duncan, a former voice teacher, writes: "She has a voice of great distinction; warm and rich—very flexible and of unusual range. The sky is the limit for such a voice and it is left with her." Maizie Browner, under whom she is studying now, says: "She has a fine voice. There is no break at all in it—it flows evenly from the bottom to the top. I wouldn't work with her the way I do if I didn't believe in her voice."

June wants the concert stage, but she wants it as an American—and not as a Negro American. And when she reaches the supreme point of discipline in her art, and brings to song-lovers the perfect product of her years of study, she wants her fingers firmly clasping little silver strings opening new, wonderful "closed" doors: opera, commercial radio—intimate inclusion, as befits a distinguished artist, in America's rich and vital music world. She does not want to face, as a sole recourse, the limited, segregated concert stage.

June has had a nibble at what real democracy can mean. Two years ago, Fred Allen, famous radio comedian, presented her over the Texaco Star Theatre Program in his American College Student Series, as a "talented American student," chosen by the student body of her school, Howard University, "an American college." With admirable poise and in good voice, she sang Gounod's "Ave Maria," and a great many of the 28,000,000 making up the radio audience of the Texaco Star Theatre never knew whether she was Negro or white. To them she was an American college girl with an exceptionally beautiful voice.

Though undoubtedly this event gave June great heart in her ambition to be a singer, she is naturally a conscientious person. In Hannibal, Missouri, her home town, she was an earnest student. Piano lessons, started at the age of six, were well done; elementary and secondary academic work in the interracial schools of Hannibal won honors for her. Her voice was discovered after two years of high school, and from then on that was her point of concentration. In Hannibal she began her voice study under Clara Campbell Stanley. At Howard University she studied under Todd Duncan, was a soloist with the University Choir, sang with the Women's Glee Club, and appeared in the University's production of *Il Travatore*. After Howard University came New York—Juilliard and Maizie Browner. Miss Browner is an American with a German and Viennese music background. She is sincerely enthusiastic about June's voice, and in discussing her work schedule stated: "She has made such remarkable progress that we are working now on heavy coloratura parts."

In the spring June will accompany Todd Duncan on an extended concert tour to sing with him the melodies from *Porgy and Bess*. After this first taste of the "road" she will come back to New York to study again—long and hard.

June is young, in full heart, and eager about her work and believes quite ardently that she will have her chance: "The world is changing so rapidly," she says, "people are getting new ideas and outlooks, and I believe my chances as a singer will be just as good as any American's."

Skater Mabel Fairbanks, *Opportunity,* Spring 1944

Mabel Fairbanks, a chubby, brown Southerner, is crashing a strange, new gate. She is an ice skater who aspires to performance at Centre Theatre, Madison Square Garden and other great ice theatres throughout the country—and she is pointing a pioneering, white, steel-mounted boot, for she is the first of her race to get as far as she has in realizing this astonishing dream.

Mabel came to New York from Jacksonville, Florida, five years ago to "live with her sister and take a business course." But inspired by a Sonja Henie[1] picture, she paid $1.25 for a pair of ice skates and found her way to the Gay Blades, a Broadway ice-skating rink frequented by skating professionals and renowned skating performers. She was assiduous, and her sturdy, flexible body had an almost uncanny sense of balance. She was young, too, but not too young; she was 14 and the white skaters she met at the Gay Blades had been skating for many years by the time they were as old. Tutored at random (she had no money) by champion skaters, she began to master "School Figures"—skating fundamentals. With more studying and a great deal of nerve she switched to "Free Skating," the sensational, showmanship aspect of the art.

Great names in ice skating, and among them Howard Nichollson, who has worked with Sonja Henie, took an interest and gave her pointers. She managed group instruction in ice dancing under the late Joseph Carroll. Lewis Clark, manager of the Gay Blades, was sympathetic and, impressed with her progress, gave her help whenever he could. It was through him that Mabel arranged with her manager, Wally Hunter, to give her first ice show, on March 15, 1942. Although she had been on skates only three seasons, she gave a remarkable performance, with one reporter describing her as "terrific." Now, after five years, she's still studying long hours, catching moments of instruction under name skaters, reading books on ice-skating techniques, and getting tips from her persistent attendance at ice shows. She is now under an intense training period to give a performer's finish to her showmanship and to discipline her in the perfection of her art.

Her progress so far has been miraculous. The November 1943 issue of *Time Magazine* grants: "[this] 19-year-old Harlem girl has turned up to skate figure eights around all but the top white performers . . . she tried on her first pair of skates less than four years ago." Since first putting on her first pair of skates and not even having roller-skated before—Mabel is executing spirals, flying waltz jumps, spins, varied "camel" combinations, and seems

---

1. Norwegian-born figure skater who won ten world championships.

quite capable in quick stops and "axles." . . . She exhibits a mature skater's balance and has an eerie penchant for staying on her feet.

Mabel, shy for her 19 years, shrugs away any mention of serious attention to anything except her skating. She lives it. Wally Hunter, her manager, contrived a portable skating rink with six square feet of ice, and when Radio City, the Brooklyn rink, or any of the other rinks in the city are not available, she repairs to this bit of space calling for every bit of her ingeniousness in her skating maneuvers.

She is anxious, of course, but has no qualms about how far she can go if she is good enough—even in ice skating, a new field for her race. She shrugs her shy shoulders along with the managers of artists and producers of shows who tell her so frequently: "A Negro ice skater? Now what could we do with a Negro ice skater?" She says quietly, "Oh, I'll get there. The war is changing people. They'll be different—"

Penelope Johnson plays a violin. It is a wonderfully toned instrument, used to the brilliance of works such as the Saint-Saens B Minor Concerto, the intricate Bach-Kreisler arrangements, and the moving majesty of Rachmaninoff. She has been studying her violin since she was eight, beginning in Columbus, Ohio, her home, under Otto Kraeuter. Leaving Columbus after graduation from high school, she came to New York to study at Juilliard. After Juilliard came Vera Fonaroff, eminent violin instructor, under whom she is still studying.

From the beginning she has shown unusual talent, of such quality that all of her advanced study has been made possible by scholarship aid, and at present she is in New York under the sponsorship of the Karamu House of Cleveland, Ohio. Once Penelope was in Madame Fonaroff's apartment taking a lesson. One of the residents of the apartment house stopped outside in the hallway to listen. As the remarkable tones of Penelope's violin came through to him, the listener—Maurice Hindus, great Russian author and lecturer—was moved. He asked to come in to listen while Penelope played some more. Later, through him, came a generous gift to help in furthering her plans for study.

Penelope studies at least six hours a day, often more. Madame Fonaroff works with her sometimes as many as four hours because she feels that Penelope "possesses a very unusual talent that is of great intensity. She makes her violin vibrate, and, indeed, penetrates her audience with its warmth!"

As a further musical experience she plays violin in a string quartet and viola in the orchestra of the Mannes Music School. Mr. David Mannes, whose name is one of distinction in the world of great music, said of her in an interview in the charming atmosphere of his school on East 74th Street: "Penelope Johnson is a gifted person. She can become a fine violinist and musician and she is making rapid development in that direction. She is very studious, has a high purpose, and shows the proper humility before this great art."

All of these are reasons why Penelope refuses to believe she is a drug on the music market because she is a Negro playing a serious violin. Outstanding musicians, many of them violinists, and other well-meaning persons have listened, fascinated with her ability, but persistent in the belief that her best bet is to "swing" her violin.[2] Recognition is sure that way, they say to her, easier and quicker. While recognition the other way, they tell her flatly, will probably never come; America and its taste—especially its taste in the color of its serious violinists being what it is.

Penelope can't believe that, and states very frankly: "I believe that America—and the world—will accept me if I am good enough." So she keeps 7:30 A.M. rehearsal engagements followed by 9 o'clock lessons which may run on into the day—so long that she has to "walk around the block" to relax—to follow these up with hours of rehearsal alone. She'll stay buried under that schedule, or another like it, until she is able to emerge one day—not soon—to give the beauty and perfection of her instrument to music lovers the world over.

"After the war?" she muses. "I think the brightest gleam for the American Negro yet is the post-war era."

These are just three young Negro Americans who are turning "crystal balls" in the direction of the post-war world. Somehow they see enough, America's traditional tactics with her Negro minority notwithstanding, to toss a wagering coin on which the solemn face of Lincoln gleams—on both sides.

---

2. To play it is a jazz style.

Piano Virtuoso and Prodigy Philippa Duke Schuyler, *The Crisis,* July 1943

THE CRISIS, JULY 1943

Philippa "Too Good" for Music Competition

The most consistent performer among America's child prodigies, 11-year-old Philippa Duke Schuyler, who has been regularly in the news since her twenty-eighth month, was barred this spring from further participation in the New York Philharmonic Symphony Society's notebook contests after winning eight first prizes, including two medals. According to Rudolf Ganz, conductor of the Philharmonic's children's concerts, Philippa is "too good" to compete with other contestants. Ordinarily contestants are not barred until they have reached their seventeenth year, but Philippa's achievements were held to discourage other children, and she was asked to compete no more.

Winning prizes is an old story for this brilliant youngster. Entering the tournaments of the National Piano Teachers Guild at the age of four with ten original compositions, Philippa has won highest honors for eight consecutive seasons. In addition she has won gold and silver medals from the Music Education League, and a gold medal from the City of New York as a pianist.

Author of more than one hundred piano compositions, she was honored with a silver medallion at the 1939 New York World's Fair, and at the 1940 New York World's Fair as Philippa Schuyler Day was set aside for her at which she played two recitals of classic and original compositions before overflow audiences.

Since December 1933 she has been regularly featured in the press of the nation and such magazines as *Time* (three times), *Look, The New Yorker, Coronet, Calling All Girls, The Crisis, Opportunity* and others too numerous to mention, not only for musical achievement but for general intellectual accomplishment.

Tested psychologically by New York University yearly since the age of four, Philippa has consistently shown an IQ of 185. Last month she was given a freshman aptitude test at Manhattanville College and rated 25 per cent higher than the average freshman. She entered school in 1938 and graduated from grammar school in 1942 with an average of 97 in all studies. She has just completed her first year in high school. In the college textbook

Psychology and Life by Floyd Ruch, she is cited as an example of superior intelligence.

Philippa has given numerous recitals for charity in many cities in all parts of the country. She has often played over the radio and television, and has been featured on such programs as "We, The People," "Hobby Lobby" and "Dr. Pepper." Her hobbies are reading, playing on her gymnasium with her girl friends, and furnishing her doll's house.

OPPORTUNITY, FALL 1944

A Broadway Taboo Is Lifted

FANNY MCCONNELL

So habitually are Negroes portrayed on the stage as servants, insignificant or superfluous to the plot, or in cinema as "ghost bait" in which the whites of their eyes are their biggest asset—that when a serious drama cast with Negro players makes a Broadway appearance and is immediately a hit, theatre history is indeed being made.

Such a drama is *Anna Lucasta,* in which Hilda Simms plays the title role in a sensitively restrained interpretation of the much-tried part of a prostitute.

Anna Lucasta, the story of a girl driven to prostitution by an incestuous father and redeemed by a young man whose evaluation of her goes beyond the immorality of her past, is a drama outstanding for other reasons than that it is a moving play.

It is outstanding first, because although Philip Yordan, a white playwright, did not write his play about Negroes, he nevertheless preferred to have it cast, both for tryout (in the American Negro Theatre—Harlem) and professional opening, with Negro players. And secondly, because nowhere in the play has either playwright or director attempted to burlesque the characters because Negroes were playing the parts.

This is perhaps unique in theatre history.

Anna Lucasta is a play in which any racial group might logically act, and if it is different because of its present Negro cast, that difference is the result of the vitality and imagination that the Negro cast has invested in it.

That the performances turned in by Hilda Simms, Canada Lee, Frederick O'Neal, Alice Childress, Earle Hyman, George Randol and others were substantially good, was evident in the nine curtain calls on opening night and comment of the New York critics in the newspapers the following day.

Hilda Simms has been declared a "find." "*PM* Visits Actress on Her Way Up" was the headline given a recent interview of her by Seymour Peck.[1]

But despite her sensitive acting, her good voice, her good figure and pretty face—attributes that would make any woman a "natural" for a successful acting career—Miss Simms knows and others know that she can "go up" only as high as racial policies controlling the American Theatre prove flexible.

Miss Simms summed up the situation rather well herself in the *PM* interview September 1, when she said, "They [meaning Hollywood] want me to study singing and dancing. But I want to convince them that I'm an intelligent Negro dramatic actress. . . ."

Neither Broadway nor Hollywood has given Negro actors sufficient opportunities in *dramatic* roles to afford them either reputations or livelihoods.

It may be that Philip Yordan, the playwright, and John Wildberg and Harry Wagstaff Gribble, the producers of *Anna Lucasta* (and John Golden who brought another American Negro Theatre production, *Three Is A Family,* to Broadway for a short run this spring), are about to break down the rigid taboo against dramatic roles for Negro actors which are not stereotyped.

Miss Simms's brief but happy dramatic experience since her recent graduation from the University of Minnesota is encouraging in contrast to the situation faced by many Negro dramatic art students in the past.

Many of them on that memorable graduation day in June have been struck by the futility of their own knowledge and talent while listening to white classmates describe the jobs awaiting them in Hollywood, with acting companies, and in radio and schools. Standing in the shadows of the great campus buildings waiting to march to their graduation "ritual," these Negro students felt instead as if it were a march to a dead end. If they had deluded themselves during their four college years, they could no longer do so now as in their minds they wryly juggled their credit hours in acting and stagecraft with jobs as maids or elevator operators.

Some of them did get acting jobs, it is true. But their college degrees were not necessarily recommendations. For it was not dialect they had learned in their voice and diction classes. They had earned no credit hours in the art

---

1. *PM* was a New York newspaper of the era.

of crap-shooting or portrayal of religious "ecstasy." It wasn't to learn these things that their parents' purse was emptied for tuition.

Many of those people now wonder will Hilda Simms, Alice Childress, Earle Hyman, Frank O'Neal and others be forced eventually to join this clown school in order to earn a living at their profession?

The answer is, they won't, if *Anna Lucasta,* together with a few other plays, such as *Decision, Othello,* (and among older ones *Native Son* and *Stevedore*) are indicative of a new trend.

NEGRO DIGEST, JANUARY 1944

Glamour vs. Prejudice[1]

ELSA MAXWELL

The glamorous and great artists of the Negro race are gradually turning the whole race "problem"—which is not, and never was a problem—into a glorious absurdity.

When stiff-necked whites are faced with the beauty and charm of a Katherine Dunham or a Lena Horne, or nettled by the magnificent talent and intellect of Paul Robeson, the idea of "prejudice" seems a matter for concern only in lunatic asylums.

A short while ago, in New York, Katherine Dunham, who is a fine anthropologist, as well as a great beauty and a startling dancer, was to be guest of honor at a dinner arranged by Tim Durant—the producer.

A friend of mine, who is exceptionally wealthy and very sweet, where sweetness is of no matter, was invited. "Would you mind," said Tim, "stopping by in your car and picking up Miss Dunham?"

She had never heard of Katherine Dunham. She was aware neither of the fact that Miss Dunham was a celebrity, nor that her skin has a little more pigmentation to it than, say, the skin of a run-of-the-mill starlet.

When her car stopped at the hotel, and when Katherine stepped in, as gay, delightful and poised as a wood nymph, my friend was flabbergasted. She made what little conversation she could, then relapsed in stony silence.

---

1. This essay is a condensed version of a piece that appeared in the *New York Post,* November 16, 1943. Elsa Maxwell was a columnist for the *Post,* gathering gossip on movie stars, and was a Hollywood celebrity in her own right.

Singer Etta Moten, *The Crisis,* May 1943

My friend sat through the dinner like a frozen statue. Everyone there was uninhibited and relaxed—everyone but my pure little Nordic.

As soon as the coffee was served she ran for her wraps, called her car and bolted into the stygian night. And, I can assure, she was never missed.

The next day she called Tim Durant. "What do you mean," she demanded, "inflicting this on me?"

"You should have been honored," said Tim. "Katherine Dunham is one of the greatest dancers of our time—and you, my dear, can't even rhumba."

"Well," said the society lamb petulantly, "she didn't dance in the car."

For myself, I can say sincerely that I would feel highly honored if Miss Dunham even honored me with an invitation to lunch—and this can be taken as a broad hint.

Let's look this matter of prejudice straight in the eye. I'm sick and tired of all the pussyfooting that's been going on about Jim Crow. Either we are believers in the principles of democracy—as we piously declare, three times a day—or we are a collection of the greatest frauds the world has seen.

For generations the conventional and learned citizens of this republic have stood stolidly silent while the American Negro has been vilified, libeled and denied almost all access to the privileged places of sweetness and light.

The solid south has stood as dumbly as a block of granite. The American Academy of Arts and Letters has not taken up the good fight nor has the sacrosanct Daughters of the American Revolution. Democracy has been wayward in the cause of democracy; and its cultural institutions are all of them suspect.

The myth of "inferiority" has been bandied around like a Tammany Hall political issue. As soon as opportunities for learning were opened up to Negroes—even partially—that myth was exploded. The list of Negro intellectuals, a list which would include such men as George Washington Carver, Richard Wright, Walter White, Countee Cullen and James Weldon Johnson, would be a credit to any national academy.

Such Negro artists as Marian Anderson, Dorothy Maynor, Paul Robeson, Roland Hayes, Duke Ellington and Dean Dixon, the conductor, are outstanding in their respective fields. And at last, in nation-wide lights, we have with the Misses Horne and Dunham, the most powerful of all social weapons: glamour.

I would like to wave this list in the face of every one of those Fascist-minded citizens of Hillburn, N.Y., who are trying to force Jim Crow into the educational life of this state. I would like to wave it in the face of every hill-billy southern Senator.

One of these days the good people of these potentially great United States are going to wake up to the fact that there is one thing much greater than the myths of tradition and pseudosanctities of custom. And that is culture.

NEGRO DIGEST, SEPTEMBER 1945

My Most Humiliating Jim Crow Experience
MURIEL RAHN[1]

If you asked about the ones up north, I might easily have told you about being turned out of the big Auditorium Hotel in Cleveland, Ohio, even though I had a reservation for a room there and a letter to prove it, signed by the manager, on the hotel stationery. I might also tell you that this experience was duplicated at the huge Gibson Hotel in Cincinnati, as well as the English Hotel in Indianapolis, and in each case I had a written letter from the managers, imploring me to please stop at their fine hotels, only to be turned away when they found I was colored.

Or, I might tell you about the kind white people in Lafayette, Indiana, who allowed me to live in the best hotel there but politely requested me to have my meals in my room. You see, I might have contaminated the other diners in the dining room.

But as far as Dixie, I imagine my most humiliating Jim Crow experience happened while I was en route to New Orleans from New York City on a plane trip sponsored by the U.S. Treasury Department during the Sixth War Loan Drive. I boarded the plane at La Guardia Field in New York and the energetic public relations people of the Eastern Airlines and U.S. Treasury Department had the photographers snap my picture together with the captain of the ship, waving a fond "farewell" to New York, which later appeared in the press with the caption, "Carmen Jones off on Bond Tour." The trip was without incident or interest other than the usual niceties exchanged by the passengers until we reached Atlanta, Georgia.

Arriving at the Atlanta Airport, naturally everyone was quick to alight and stretch his legs. The group of passengers, including myself, immediately made for the concessionaire where notions, novelties, coffee and sandwiches were sold.

---

1. Muriel Rahn starred in the Broadway musical *Carmen Jones.*

For a moment I had forgotten I was in Dixie, everything had been so nice "above." I walked into the small concession and purchased a 10-cent comb. Then, innocently, went along with the rest of the passengers toward the lunch counter where coffee and sandwiches were being served.

Imagine my embarrassment when a loud voice with a heavy drawl yelled: "Hey, you can't eat in here!"

Twenty passengers, all white except me, turned around, halted by the remark and stared at the owner of the loud, raucous voice. He repeated, "You can't eat nothin' in here!" and pointed at me. It stunned my fellow travellers as much as it did me but I suddenly realized that now I was back in Dixie.

I lost my appetite, I couldn't have eaten even if I had been starved. I almost lost my temper and started to yell back but I remembered I was in the South. I turned, and walked out of the place.

The rest of the passengers lost their appetites, too, I think, but none of them had the guts to do anything about it, insofar as the owner of the concession was concerned. One kind lady offered to bring some coffee and a sandwich to me on the plane. I thanked her and refused.

A few minutes later the rest of the passengers boarded the plane. There was a sort of strange silence and all seemed to feel guilty. I went on to New Orleans and was instrumental in selling over $1,000,000 worth of War Bonds. I worked during the War Bond meeting with mixed emotion. I wondered whether it was worthwhile. . . . I guess it was!

NEGRO DIGEST, SEPTEMBER 1944

Beautiful but Not Dumb[1]

DAVID HANNA

To be a symbol to one's race and at the same time remain a realist is an uneasy position to maintain—one requiring more than the usual appurtenances of character and a patience that can often become oppressive.

Yet, with a dignity, intelligence, a way of parrying words and a beauty that is dazzling, Lena Horne has managed to accomplish both in the troubled waters of the motion picture industry. And there are no recorded instances

---

1. This essay is a condensed version of a piece that appeared in the *Los Angeles Daily Newspaper,* May 29, 1944.

when the actress has been compelled to squirm uncomfortably in the ticklish chair she occupies.

On meeting Lena Horne at Metro-Goldwyn-Mayer, where she is under contract, one finds a young lady whose low, charming and compelling voice can jump with facility from the technical aspects of the entertainment business to the problems of the Negro in motion pictures. These she knows with a thoroughness and an understanding that have been born, not merely as the result of her present eminent stature, but from a background rich in professional experience.

Her mother, Edna Stockton, was once a prominent member of New York's famed Lafayette players. Until the depression knocked the props out of show business, this group of Negro theatrical craftsmen functioned as artistic, articulate spokesmen for its people.

Organized as a stock company, the Lafayette troupe played New York, Philadelphia and a handful of eastern cities in a repertory of plays ranging from Shakespeare to *Rain* and works aimed primarily at Negro audiences.

Raised, literally, in her mother's wardrobe trunk, it was logical that Lena Horne would turn to the theater for her livelihood. She was barely out of pigtails when she was engaged to sing with Noble Sissle's band—running the booking gamut from one night stands to holdover engagements at the Cotton Club.[2]

She spent night after night sitting up on trains and can recall, with a few shudders, a memorable occasion when she had to park herself in the winter quarters of a circus outside a dismal Indiana town. Not one to minimize the value of any experience, however objectionable, the actress would just as soon skip Indiana in the future.

Miss Horne came to Hollywood at the behest of a night-club operator. Her hit appearance as a chanteuse attracted the attention of MGM's Arthur Freed. Although doubtful that she could duplicate her stage and cabaret success in the movies, she signed a long term contract with the company.

On the screen, her fortunes have advanced rapidly. A unique personality, she has been able to surmount barriers which, heretofore, seemed insurmountable to artists of her race. Consequently, her own people have been lavish in their praise and adulation.

But however strongly Lena Horne may be entrenched in the cinematic firmament, it is obvious that her own success has not affected her viewpoint of the larger issues involved in equalizing artistic and social opportunities for her fellow Negroes.

---

2. The Cotton Club was a prominent Harlem nightclub.

For herself, she would like to play a real part on the screen, rather than be brought in continuously as a specialty performer. Nor does she feel that all Negro films on the order of "Cabin in the Sky" and "Stormy Weather"[3] represent the ultimate in the Negro's artistic expressiveness. For one thing, she wants to sing Julie in "Show Boat"—a role that might have been written especially for her.

In behalf of her fellow artists, Lena Horne visualizes an era in which the Negro will be depicted more realistically and accurately than has been his lot in the past. Admitting that the war has brought some issues into the open and effected an intelligent interpretation of the Negro in occasional instances, she has not acquiesced in the thought that the millennium has been reached.

Indeed, she points out, the ground remaining to be covered is vast. And reactionary forces are strong. Patiently and determinedly posing the point is not the least of Lena Horne's accomplishments in the few years she has been in Hollywood.

However, her verbal ax sharpens when she is faced with those who feel that a Negro depicted on the screen in anything but a menial role automatically implies miscegenation.

There are a thousand ways an accurate picture of Negro life can be achieved on the screen. Lena Horne, for one, feels a responsibility in achieving that objective.

Meanwhile she sings her song in the inimitable Horne manner and with a personality that is impossible to resist; she is making her own quiet and effective contribution.

NEGRO DIGEST, APRIL 1945

She Makes the Wounded Wiggle[1]

MICHAEL CARTER

Some fellows looked at her and wiggled their toes; others wrote her name on an allied bomb and dropped it on or near 10 Wilhelmstrasse, Berlin, Germany.

---

3. Film musicals with all-black casts made in 1943.

1. This essay is a condensed version of a piece that appeared in the *Baltimore Afro-American,* December 30, 1944.

Still others named a Canadian ship after Hazel Scott, $4,000-a-week star of Cafe Society Uptown in New York. It is she who reduced Bach and Chopin to terms Americans can understand.

Miss Scott gets 750 fan letters a week and at least three proposals of marriage, which come from colored and white admirers, judging by the addresses.

Less than eight years ago, this minx-like, provocative young woman was a student at a Harlem girls high school, and not too long ago she was a $65-a-week performer at Cafe Society Downtown.

The Uptown, a considerably classier night club where she now is, was built for and around her. She is the only colored woman so honored.

The moment you enter the place, $3.50 minimum charge, and most drinks a dollar and upwards, you are aware of the fact that this swanky night club in the millionaire's neighborhood was built for her.

Pictures of her abound. Jimmy Savo, comedian, is billed under her. At Cafe Society Hazel Scott is tops.

The difference between Cafe Society Uptown and most other night clubs is similar to the difference between chess and blackjack. Miss Scott contributes to this atmosphere. Men look at her and pant, but they are polite about it.

Miss Scott flits down the aisle to the piano. White spectators lean out to talk to her, but she maneuvers away and sits at the piano.

All the lights dim. Her round, brown face and sensuous shoulders are illumined only by a spotlight. She plays three or four numbers.

As soon as a number is over she floats through the cafe, which she calls a "room" and gets upstairs to her dressing room.

Her parents, both West Indians, were teachers in their islands. Her father, who formerly taught at Fisk,[2] died when she was 14. Her mother, who played the saxophone in an orchestra, taught her to play the piano "because she thought everybody ought to play something."

"I started playing when I was three. I worked my way through school by playing. I guess my first break came after I finished school and started working on the radio. Then I opened at Cafe Society Downtown (in Greenwich Village) at $65 a week. I thought I was really making money, but now? Oh Boy!

"Since then I've worked up to $4,000 a week in pictures and my contract is filled with things saying what I won't do."

---

2. Fisk University is a historically black college in Nashville, Tennessee.

Miss Scott won't wear a handkerchief or dirty clothes in a film; all colored performers in her shows must portray "respectable roles," she must always be presented as an honest, female artist.

Her press agent added, "Hers is the only Hollywood contract like that." He seemed surprised.

Miss Scott cut him off—"I don't like night clubs. But I've turned down four singing maid's roles in movies during the past year or so. Some producers want you to come on the set, dust off a piano and then sit down and play."

"There are plenty of white performers who can play maid's roles and then step out into a pent-house or a school classroom.

"Colored performers represent their people. They must always be on guard against doing anything that will conform to or develop the stereotyped notions about us."

Perhaps that is one reason why Miss Scott does four or five benefit performances a week. Most are for wounded service men and she takes pride in going in wards that other performers avoid. "I have played in many tropical disease wards where the fellows are so badly mangled that screens are kept in front of them.

"I have played in wards where neuro-psychiatric cases are kept. Some of these poor men—colored and white—are paralyzed from head to toe."

It was in one of these that some of the worst cases wriggled their toes to the strains of her boogie-woogie. Hospital authorities took new confidence in music therapy after her performance. "She can make men move muscles that have been still for months," they said.

In one ward, a Greek seaman who had been silent many days, suddenly burst out into an extended conversation in Greek, and hospital authorities considered it an advance.

"I am certain that such performances affect race relations," she said. "I don't play these benefits because I have excess energy, it's a personal thing. I know I'm using what talent I have to do something for America and my people too.

"It's apparent in the Southern boys. At first they are reluctant to accept a colored performer as an artist, but music can soothe the savage beast and they generally act in a human fashion before I'm through."

Miss Scott works 52 weeks a year. "I guess I have unusual contracts even for night clubs. I have a standing engagement here—but I can leave for any picture or any other performance I want to do. I always return to this room and fill out my 52 weeks."

She likes to leave for movies because "I'm not kidding when I say I don't like night clubs. People go to them to get drunk and show other people they're having a good time.

"I like this place because it is agreed that colored people can come here at will." (It is the only upperclass night club where this prevails.)

"This is a place where colored people are first class citizens. I should not ever play a house where we were segregated. I feel badly to know that some have to see my movies from jim-crow stalls."

She has never played a jim-crow theater and her contracts contain a clause prohibiting the segregation of colored people.

Discussing contracts she said: "I held up Columbia's production of *The Heat's On* for three days." In this picture Miss Scott, attired as a WAC officer, appeared in a sequence with eight aproned colored girls.

The producer wanted the girls to wear soiled aprons "to make them look lived in." Miss Scott refused to participate until clean aprons were secured. She timed her refusal to make the company lose three days. The girls appeared in clean aprons.

"There is a type of performer who represents the old school of handker-chief-headed, corn cob pipe-smoking woman and the grinning man. Thank heavens that school is fast disappearing.

"But there are still so few Hilda Simmses, Lena Hornes and Hazel Scotts (she knows she's good) and we need more.

"We go further in acting than in other fields because we are permitted to express ourselves. We could do the same in aviation or anything else if there were fewer obstacles against us.

"But America loves its performers. Those of us who do perform have a distinct duty to accomplish; we must show ourselves to the best advantage."

OPPORTUNITY, SPRING 1945

How Do We Stand in Hollywood?

WILLIAM GRANT STILL

Quick to recognize the fact that films have a tremendous educational value both at home and abroad, allied governments have made excellent use of this medium to an extent that Hollywood itself has boasted of this contribution to the war effort. If we concede that films do educate people in this way, we must also admit that they create lasting impressions in other matters—racial matters, for instance. In this respect, the Negro has been, with a very few exceptions, on the losing end of the deal and, despite the rare gestures of goodwill that have been made, the same old racial stereotypes continue to be perpetuated, the same old clichés abound. . . .

There may come a day when the Negro will have seen so many other sides of Negro life on the screen that he can afford to condone quaint Negro characters and folky acting. At present he cannot do so for the simple reason that many white people are coming to regard those simple characters as typical of an entire race, and that will not aid good race relations in America, nor will it please people in foreign countries whose skins are not white.

For the present, we would like to see ridiculous, criminal, superstitious and immoral characterizations eliminated; Negroes cast in other than servant roles; Negroes' contribution to the war and to American life pictured; Negroes included as extras in background groups; Negroes employed in studios in other positions than those of actor and menial; Negroes employed as authorities on the Negro. We would like to see all-Negro films abolished for, no matter how expensive and glamorous they are, they still glorify segregation. In short, we would like to see the Negro presented to the world and to America as a normal American. If this were done, the films could make a real contribution to inter-racial understanding and to a better world.

When one mentions these things to film people, they invariably say that they are in the entertainment business solely, and that they do not want to put out anything that may be considered a sociological study. That, of course, is logical, but it still does not explain why they are so proud of their educational work in other fields, and why they will not concede that such things can be done simply and without fanfare and the resulting films still be good entertainment. . . .

Supposing, however, that Negroes should be employed as, say, authorities on matters concerning their race. In all probability they would be paid for their time, their names would be advertised and their opinions ignored, for in Hollywood's mind, any white man's opinion is superior to that of any Negro, no matter whether the white man be the office boy and the Negro an eminent author, or vice versa. Even among Hollywood's liberals, who are supposedly friendly to Negroes, this same quirk persists. They wish to use only the Negro's name while they do the work, order the Negro's thoughts and actions, and so on.

To illustrate this point, I might add that when it comes to giving others advice, I have been considered an authority on Negro music in Hollywood. But when it comes to the actual work, most of my opinions and my work have been calmly thrown out as not being "authentic." A little more than two years ago I resigned from an all-colored film when the studio music head told me my arrangements were "too good." Negro bands in the Bert Williams period[1] "didn't play that well," he added. I protested that at that time I was playing in Negro bands and that they played better then than they do now. Then the music director said my arrangements were "too polite." He wanted something more erotic to make it more authentic, he declared. So I, a Negro, who have worked for almost thirty years successfully in both the commercial and symphonic fields, am not authentic? I found it hard to believe, and wondered whence stemmed his superior knowledge. I was officially called the "Supervisor of Music" on that film. After my resignation, the head of the music department accused me of being insubordinate. I am sure that this was the first time in history that a *supervisor* was ever insubordinate.

A similar thing happened when another all-colored film came along and I was asked to do the musical score. I had visions of a magnificent score that would rank along with those written for many European films, for the picture's subject-matter warranted it. Instead, they forbade my using Negro Spirituals and placed so many other useless restrictions on me that I quietly withdrew. The white man who succeeded me on the picture inserted two Spirituals in it and received no condemnation therefore, and he also had some of Beethoven's music in the place where a symphonic work by a Negro composer should have been. He was all set to put the Brahms Fifth Symphony in another spot, but the people around finally convinced him that that was going a little too far. Instead of having a unified score, he had one made up of bits from many different composers.

It goes without saying that we have a problem with some of the Negroes who occasionally work in films too, those compromisers who follow right along in the idea that the white man is always right. Either they are ashamed of their own culture, or they think that by ignoring it they can get farther. It certainly isn't necessary to cheapen one's self in order to be proud of one's own heritage or true to his people and to the ideals he should have in this time of stress. These colored people are so job-hungry that they are willing to follow Hollywood's dictates. All Negroes are not so tempted, and now that they have discovered that they cannot lead all of us by the nose, they have created another dangerous situation, the white "authority" on the Negro. Today the situation is such that among authorities on the Negro there's usually not a Negro in a carload. They do not, unfortunately, balance

---

1. Early twentieth century. Bert Williams was an African American comedian in vaudeville.

this by asking some of us to be authorities on things not connected with the Negro. They simply ignore us.

Not long ago a Hollywood periodical which goes largely to the studios presented an article on Negro music by a white man who has collected Negro tunes from the folk and incorporated them into his own compositions. At the end of this article, the editor added a note to the effect that I endorsed this man and George Gershwin as being the two outstanding exponents of Negro folk music. Immediately I wrote to the editor and requested that he print a simple retraction. I explained that I had never made such a statement, did not consider it true, and while I had no wish to hurt the composer in question, I still did not care to have such an endorsement stand unchallenged. The magazine has never printed a retraction. A few weeks later I read that one of the largest of the film studios was negotiating with this "authority on Negro music" to act as consultant on several pictures, and I happen to know that he considers a typical Negro one who is crude and untutored. He is at the present time actually employed at a studio which is currently making a picture featuring Negroes. The scenarist on the same picture is a Southern white man.

On another occasion, a white composer who had been engaged to write the music for a Negro sequence in a film called to ask me what was a Negro "eppy," what film was it in, and who did it. He didn't mean "epic," he said, he meant "eppy" and he thought that as I was familiar with all aspects of Negro life I would surely know. I didn't. Several hours later he called back and said that what he really wanted was a Calypso singer. He intended to listen to the Calypso singer sing, then he would write the music and get paid for it while the Calypso singer would go his merry way, wondering how to pay his rent with a song.

Fortunately, Hollywood is not one hundred percent full of faults. There are things to be said on the credit side of the ledger too. For many months now, Calvin Jackson, an excellent colored musician, has been employed at M.G.M. Studios as assistant to George Stoll. He arranges, composes, and attends to many technical matters for and with Mr. Stoll. At the same studio, Ralph Vaughn, the colored architect, is one of about thirty senior set designers. So far, the pictures he has worked on have not been Negroid. He designed the tallest building on the M.G.M. lot, the 98 foot high tower that was seen in the film, "Kismet." He also designed the city of Metz as it appeared in "The Seventh Cross" and the longest scenic backing ever made at M.G.M. The latter was the Calshipyard which was used in "Meet the People" and which was portrayed in *Life Magazine*'s display about that film. Both of these young men, I am glad to say, have the personal attributes which make them credits to themselves, to their professions, and to their race. Their successes should make a favorable impression, for the future, on the film executives.

As far as actual films are concerned, we may point with pride to the part played by Kenneth Spencer in "Bataan" (M.G.M.'s film), that played by Rex Ingram in "Sahara" (a Columbia picture), and that in the Warner Brothers' film, "In This Our Life." Significantly enough, the last-named film was adapted from a novel written by a white Southern woman, Ellen Glasgow. Hollywood felt safe in presenting it for that reason, because the moral backing of its distinguished author would not close the Southern market to the film.

So, in the end, it all returns to the most important aspect of this discussion—the financial part of making films. Hollywood is making some concessions, but is still being cautious about the Negro in films, generally speaking. We, on the other hand, are making strong demands for a bettering of conditions, not only for selfish reasons, but because we know, as the members of every minority group know these days, that America's future depends on good inter-racial understanding.

Will our demands be heeded? It all depends on whether we—*thirteen million* of us—have the strength to boycott those films which are not favorable, even to stay away from all motion picture houses if necessary; whether Negro artists have the courage to starve for a little while longer until we can make definite gains; and whether Negro periodicals will back up their splendid editorials and feature stories with a refusal to carry the studio-inspired "news" which, of course, is not news at all.

Can all of us do this? If we can, we have a chance. If we can't, then the sacrifices made by a few of us are made in vain. It is no good for one colored person to take a stand and to have the film executives know all along that they can go to some other colored person who will fix everything up with the Negro race. If we have only a few Quislings[2] we are licked before we start. If we are unified we can be strong.

---

2. A "Quisling" is a traitor who serves as the puppet of the occupying enemy. The term is taken from the name of the head of Norway's government during the Nazi occupation.

Singer Anne Brown, *The Crisis,* **June 1943**

OPPORTUNITY, WINTER 1944

Interlude in a Book Shop

J. F. POWERS

Business was pretty slow. Mr. Flynn, a short man in charge of New Fiction and Biography indulged in desultory conversation with Mr. Mosby, a shorter man in charge of Travel, Garden and Sporting books. Each was what is known in the trade as a bookman. Their eyes, mildly predatory, were on the front door. The wind blew particularly hard and the door squeaked open a few inches in false alarm. They started forward in helpless competition. Then they recovered their poise and resumed conversation.

"Wind's blowing something terrible," Mr. Mosby said.

"Must be coming from the north," Mr. Flynn said.

The door squeaked open again. They were not fooled this time and wisely held their ground. They turned laconic smiles on each other. Mr. Mosby's face gradually became embittered.

"That's the trouble with these doors," he said.

Mr. Flynn changed the subject.

"That new Katherine Coe Smiley book ought to have a good sale," he said.

"Judging from her last one," Mr. Mosby said weightily, "yes."

The door opened and a woman came in, Negro, tall, something more than attractive, beautiful. Mr. Flynn and Mr. Mosby moved toward her at a speed considerably under average for them. When she stopped before a table of 25-cent paper books, they came to a dead halt. Their eyes met and said: "Your customer."

Posthaste they retreated to their former positions. Despair disguised came into their features when she selected one of the 25-cent volumes and browsed in their direction. Mr. Flynn and Mr. Mosby stiffened in the knowledge that one of them must make the sale. Honor forbade actual flight.

She bore down. The front door suddenly opened in salvation for one of them. Like a shot, Mr. Mosby went to welcome his redeemer.

"How do you do, sir! Something in a good book?"

"Say, do you folks handle sporting goods?"

"Sporting goods? No, I'm sorry, no sporting goods."

"That's funny. A fellow was telling me you did."

"No. No sporting goods."

Mr. Mosby shook his head, dismissing the customer, and looked out the corner of his eye. He saw Mr. Flynn reduced to making the paltry transaction. The door opened again and Mr. Mosby charged.

Mr. Flynn returned from the cashier. He was galled to see Mr. Mosby come into another customer, selling a $3.50 biography right off his, Flynn's, table. Mr. Flynn thrust the change into her hand and presented the 25-cent book unwrapped. She looked curiously at it a moment and put it in her handbag.

Guilty, Mr. Flynn explained: "We never wrap small purchases on account of the paper shortage."

"That's all right," she smiled. "I can put it right in my bag. Is it severe?"

"What?"

"The paper shortage?"

"Oh, yes, yes indeed." Mr. Flynn busied himself with straightening books. He slammed them noisily together and put them back where they had been. She walked toward the door, stopping at Current Events.

Mr. Flynn and Mr. Mosby stood together again, ready to serve, waiting, eyes on the door.

"I sold a book off your Biography table," Mr. Mosby confessed. "I saw you were busy with a customer."

"Sure, what's wrong with that?" Mr. Flynn absolved him. "That's what they're there for."

While Mr. Mosby concentrated on the front door, Mr. Flynn gave himself up to higher adventure. His blue eyes, wise in the ways of the world, followed her. She had just left Current Events with a book under her arm and would bear watching. She lingered disturbingly at New Fiction. Mr. Flynn noted her handbag was large enough to conceal a novel. She paged through a book and finally left it on the table with the one she had brought from Current Events. She proceeded to Biography.

Mr. Flynn stepped briskly to New Fiction, restored order there and placed the Current Events book in its proper environment. He then took his stand with Mr. Mosby.

"The nerve of these people," he said.

"I saw it," Mr. Mosby said omnisciently.

Mr. Flynn found no peace. For, carrying a biography, she came back to New Fiction. She looked around on the table and at last turned to them.

"I left two books here," she said.

Very sullen about the whole thing, Mr. Flynn went over to have it out with her.

"Did you want to buy them?" he asked sharply.

"I thought I might, but I've forgotten what they were now."

Mr. Flynn was ripely all smiles and quickly produced the two books.

"Why, yes, these are the ones," she said.

"I never forget a title," Mr. Flynn said. "You can't afford to in this business," he added grimly.

She opened another book. "Is that so?" she inquired. It was not certain whether he was being pampered or ignored. Mr. Flynn could not stand the suspense.

"Now here is a truly great book," he blurted out, picking up the nearest at hand. "An unusual story of settlers at the time of the French and Indian War."

She took the book from him, glanced at the title, the jacket blurb, and put it aside. "I'm afraid that won't do. But I will take this one."

"Yes, I'm so glad you did," Mr. Flynn said warmly. "I was about to recommend it." There was a momentary lapse.

"You were?" she said with rather too much wonder in her voice, disconcerting Mr. Flynn.

But he did not give up. All in all, he was doing splendidly now. She was agreeable to at least a third of the truly great books he recommended. Mr. Mosby became interested and, knifing between her and Mr. Flynn, said:

"How about something in Biography?"

Mr. Flynn took the book from Mr. Mosby and had to reach in front of him for another. "Excuse us, Mosby." Outmaneuvered, though only a little discouraged, Mr. Mosby drew off to a safe distance. It was only a stratagem. He soon returned with just the book for her. To Mr. Flynn's chagrin, she seemed more impressed by Mr. Mosby's recommendations. She would listen to Mr. Mosby where she was curt or indifferent to Mr. Flynn.

The telephone rang in their section of the store. Immediately there ensued a war of nerves. They stood on either side of her, feet planted on the floor, heads slowly revolving like searchlights, their anguished eyes combing the store in exasperation for each other. This failing, they both tried a "Do you mind getting that?" It was a deadlock. The ringing persisted. With a sigh, Mr. Flynn gave way.

"Sporting books!" he announced in restrained glee a moment later. "For you, Mr. Mosby." Reluctantly Mr. Mosby went to the telephone. Mr. Flynn rejoined her with a vengeance.

"Well, well, how are *we* getting on here?" he said.

She said nothing. The sale was assuming tremendous proportions. There were books stacked high in two piles. Other clerks from the hinterlands of Foreign, Art and Technical were estimating at a polite distance. Mr. Flynn bustled ever faster. Mr. Mosby, ostensibly at least, had given up the ghost. The telephone rang again in their section. Mr. Flynn waved a careless hand at it. Mr. Mosby, seemingly tamed, answered dutifully.

"Telephone, Mr. Flynn!" he sang out brightly. "Mrs. Hutchinson in Druid Hills would like a nice English story."

Going to the telephone, Mr. Flynn passed Mr. Mosby and heard him say to her, "One of Mr. Flynn's old customers is on the phone. It always takes ages to satisfy her. Now here's a grand treat in Travel."

Gloomily, Mr. Flynn suggested books to Mrs. Hutchinson. Twice he came over to New Fiction and selected a dozen innocuous titles. Each time, endeavoring to break Mr. Mosby's spell, he assured her he would not be long at the telephone. She did not reply. Mr. Mosby stood confidently at her side, oblivious of Mr. Flynn and rapt in recommending.

Mr. Flynn protested to the telephone. "I *know* you like a nice English story, Mrs. Hutchinson. I'm sorry about *This Passionate Land,* but the reviews were all good. Yes, we'll certainly pick it up tomorrow. I don't for the life of me see how, uh, *what you say* could have been in the book, Mrs. Hutchinson. As I say, the reviews were excellent on the whole. In fact, I don't see how that part escaped the censorship. Right in there, you say, *imagine,* in black and white. . . ."

Mr. Flynn listened to Mrs. Hutchinson and clucked periodically, "You don't say, you don't *mean* to say." He watched them at New Fiction like a wistful hawk. There were three piles of books now. The end could not be far off. He could see Mr. Mosby being jolly, a bad sign, preening himself, preparing for the kill. . . . Mr. Flynn grew frantic.

"One moment, Mrs. Hutchinson, I most certainly did *not* tell you I'd read the book myself! I'm sending you *Blue Banners Flying, Laura Steele* and *O Blessed Day!* Return them at our expense if dissatisfied!" He slammed down the telephone and rushed over to New Fiction.

"Do you deliver?" she was asking Mr. Mosby.

"Thank you, sir!" Mr. Flynn breezed, excluding Mr. Mosby neatly. "I'll just finish waiting on my customer now if you please. Yes, of course, we deliver—anywhere in the city! Much obliged, Mosby."

Mr. Mosby, beaten, walked away and Mr. Flynn became calm. Deliberation flowed into his manner. He scrutinized the piles of books. He showed real concern when he said:

"Don't want any duplications, do we?"

"When will they be delivered?" she asked. "I must have them at once."

"Well, of course, that all depends where they're going."

"The Greystone."

"The Greystone?" Mr. Flynn caught his breath and considered. "Today, if you're sure it's the Greystone *Hotel.*"

"The Greystone Hotel," she repeated evenly.

"I see," Mr. Flynn said blindly.

"Do you have a pen?" she asked. "I want to write a check."

Discreetly, Mr. Flynn fidgeted, playing for time to think over this new development. She regarded him patiently, distantly amused.

"Right over here," Mr. Flynn said with decision and led her to a desk. She asked the amount of the sale and he told her.

"Is there a delivery charge?"

"Oh, no, we assume that."

He took the check from her, glanced at it and walked with it in stiff excitement to the cashier's cage. "Look! Look at the name on that check! She's staying at the *Greystone!*"

The cashier had already spotted her. "At the *Greystone!* Why she's colored!" The cashier seized the check. "The famous opera singer!"

The cashier signaled wildly to Miss Cowan in Juveniles. Miss Cowan came running, stared madly at the check, fingered it in ecstasy and was perfectly amazed. She beckoned to Miss Klein in Periodicals. Even the intellectual Mrs. Kimball in Lending Library, nose in the wind, came along too. All were perfectly amazed.

It was better than a movie star.

Mr. Channing in Poetry, Music and Drama, Humor and Inspiration, a pessimist, scorned them all, telling Mr. Mosby he knew who it was all the time. "But do I go around like a chicken with its head cut off?" It might interest Mr. Mosby to know he had a biography of the singer in his stock.

"You have! Where is it?" Mr. Mosby cried. Coldly, Mr. Channing pointed to it among the music books. Mr. Mosby in delicious frenzy took the biography from the shelf and brought it over to Mr. Flynn at the cashier's cage.

"Look!" he exclaimed. "Get her to sign it!"

Mr. Flynn was too excited. "Do you think I should! Do you think she would!"

"If you don't," Mr. Mosby threatened, "I will!"

Mr. Flynn, holding the biography so that her picture on the jacket was visible, approached her at the desk. Mr. Mosby followed close behind.

"Your book," Mr. Flynn said. "We have your book here." He placed it on the desk before her.

"Yes, I've seen it."

"I wonder if you'd mind signing it for me."

"Not at all." She opened the book and picked up the pen. "By the way, did you read it?" she asked, looking into Mr. Flynn's blue eyes.

Mr. Flynn, taken by surprise, covered up nicely. "Oh, yes. A truly great book! I enjoyed it immensely. Magnificent!"

She laughed disconcertingly. "My!" Mr. Flynn blushed for some reason. She was about to autograph the book when Mr. Mosby spoke:

"Maybe she could be persuaded to write something personal on the flyleaf, Flynn." Her fingers loosened on the pen and, smiling faintly, she contemplated Mr. Flynn's blue eyes. "Since you enjoyed the book so much, as you say, Flynn, she might be willing to do it," Mr. Mosby added. There was a deadly silence.

"Would you?" Mr. Flynn had to say.

"Gladly." She asked him his first name and then inscribed something personal to him. The other clerks, who had gathered in a pious circle, crowded around Mr. Flynn to see what she had written. All except Mr. Channing in Poetry, Music and Drama, Humor and Inspiration who muttered to himself and took down a copy of Bartlett's *Familiar Quotations* and tried to find something about Fame and Gold o'ercoming All. And Mr. Mosby who, smiling now, went over to tell Channing that poor Flynn would have to buy the book now.

NEGRO STORY, MAY–JUNE 1944

Chief Mourner

O'WENDELL SHAW

"Really, Doc," said the youthful intern seriously, "hers is about the strangest case we've ever had in the charity ward. When you consider her color, she's amusing at times. She's as black as the ace of spades, and when she goes off into a delirium, she imagines herself a great actress like—oh, like Rose McClendon, Bernhart, Duse,[1] or some other celebrated actress—" He paused and shook his head. "I tell you, Doc, she's pathetic. Sometimes, the words she utters are strangely beautiful, and she speaks them as if they really mean something to her."

---

1. Sarah Bernhardt, Eleonora Duse, and Rose McClendon were white stage actresses at the turn of the century.

Dr. Benyon slowly laid aside a sheaf of case records on his desk and looked away thoughtfully through a window of his commodious office in Lincoln hospital. In a way, what the intern had just told him of the delirious tantrums of the strange patient was trivial compared with his many greater responsibilities as chief of the Lincoln staff, but it aroused his curiosity nevertheless. Once dramatics had been a dominant interest in his own life. In fact, before he studied medicine, he had been an actor. That had been almost twenty-five years ago, during which period he had traveled the country over as the director of the old Ira Aldridge Players, a group of professional Negro actors. He had never lost interest in the profession, and now, this patient whose deliriums were strange dramatic emotings— well, who was she, if not some person who was crazy even when not in a delirium.

"Is she delirious now?" he asked presently.

The intern nodded. "Yes, at this very moment," he replied. "I think she's now acting the lead role in the old play, 'Hurry the Dusk,' " he added with a snicker of amusement.

" 'Hurry the Dusk,' " repeated Dr. Benyon, ignoring the other's amusement. "We used to play that—I mean the Aldridge Players—we scored our biggest hit in that play. By the way," he digressed, returning to the business of the moment, "did they ever succeed in finding any of her relatives, or any one who knows about her?"

The intern shook his head. "No, Doc," he replied, "and it's sort of ironical that she only has a few more hours to live, and then the potter's field! I'm sure she's known lots of people—important people, too. Yesterday she was mumbling things about Bert Williams, Susie Sutton, Charles Gilpin, Evelyn Preer—"[2] He paused briefly, then went on: "We were thinking, Doc, that maybe you'd take time out and come over and try to talk with her. That damned cancer is taking her away fast, but if you get over to her right away she might still be strong enough to drop a hint as to who she is. As an old stage man, you might recall some of the events she mentions. You may know some of the persons she names, some one who's still living and might be able to contact us with some of her relatives."

The doctor stood up.

"I believe you have something there, Hill. All right, I'll go over and see her. Come along with me."

Intern Hill was saying things as they went along together to the charity ward, but Dr. Benyon was unconscious of what he was saying. The elderly

---

2. African American stage stars of the early twentieth century.

man was deep in thoughtful curiosity. In the charity ward they were met by Dr. Holmes, physician in charge. It was a spacious, airy room, housing more than forty patients, their beds each in a tiny stall formed of immaculate white curtains.

"Today's act is over," smiled Dr. Holmes as he led the way to her stall, which was in a corner of the room, isolated from the others, and lighted by a window above the bed. The three men entered her stall quietly. Dr. Holmes and the intern stopped just inside and watched as their chief stopped at the foot of her bed and looked down upon her.

She was still. Her sunken eyes were closed. Silently, Dr. Benyon studied her face. From illness, her skin was ashen black, but smooth and soft as velvet. He noted the long, silken lashes spanning the lower rims of her deep eye sockets. Her black hair was long, wavy and beautiful, but somewhat tinged with gray. Once a beautiful woman, he thought, but for that awfully flat nose! Something unbelievably grotesque on such a beautiful face. An ex-actress with a nose like that? He shook his head and turned to his two companions.

"I doubt that she's ever been on the stage," he said to them. "You see— that flat nose. Nope. I hardly think she's ever had a chance as an actress."

"I think her nose has been broken," said Dr. Holmes. "I recall now that she once told me it was—in a car accident."

Dr. Benyon looked upon her again, then nodded slowly.

"Yes," he murmured softly, "it's been broken. I should have detected that immediately."

This time he studied her face more closely, imagined it as it must have looked in the flush of her youth, when her nose was higher and more delicately molded. As he continued looking at her, with his mind as well as his eyes, her face began to take on more familiar lines. Presently he recognized it, and in the new realization that dawned upon him, his hand inadvertently gripped the foot of her bed, causing her eyes to flutter and open.

"Princess," he addressed her softly. "Isn't it you, Princess Ebony?"

Slowly she smiled acknowledgment. She was too weak to speak, but the tears that suddenly filled her large, dark eyes told him how happy she was to be called by her old stage name once again.

He moved around to the side of her bed and knelt over her.

"Princess Ebony," he said, "can you recall Bentie—Bentie of the old Aldridge Players? I'm he—I'm Bentie—remember me?"

He saw that his words aroused her, brought a shining light to her face. Slowly, painfully, she smiled and nodded. The sight of her in this condition wrung his heart. It had been years since he last heard of her and many more years since he saw her last. Once he would have married her, if she had been willing. Now, it cut him deeply to think that she, alone in all her misery, was now the only connecting link between him and a past which had been so tremendously exciting and happy.

A weaker man might weep with her now, but not Dr. Howard Benyon. He wanted to talk with her; ask her questions; wanted her to join him in reliving those past days that had been so full of glamour, acclaim and romance. But his medical experience told him that she was now dangerously exhausted; too weak to listen to anything more that he could say. So, he caught her thin hand in his, gripped it understandingly and rose to his feet.

"I'll return when you're stronger, Princess Ebony," he promised.

She managed to smile again, and her eyes followed him as he, with his two companions, left her stall.

"So you once knew her," said Doctor Holmes as the two entered his office.

"I should say I *do* know her," Dr. Benyon relied meditatively. "Why, Lincoln charity ward houses the greatest actress ever produced by the Negro race, Holmes!" he declared. "She didn't get far on the stage. Her color was against her. Black! But it was a beautiful black. Sorta like the blackness of ebony—that's why they called her 'Princess Ebony.' She had a marvelous figure and lovely, long hair, shining like a raven's wing. She was talented, too; cultured and could sing like Black Patti."[3]

"Ah, what an actress she was!" he went on after a pause. "One reading of a part and she was immediately into its mood," he paused again and shrugged. "But she was black! Pretty, but so black no one would take her seriously in dramatic roles—no one but me. Once, I took a gamble and introduced her with a leading role in the then popular play, 'Hurry the Dusk.' I shall never forget that night. It was at the old Park theater in Dallas. She was marvelous in that role, but her audience could not see her art for her color. Many snickered throughout her performance, which was so realistic that it brought tears to my eyes. When the final curtain dropped, she rushed backstage to me and wept bitterly on my shoulder. I tried to console her; convince her that a day would come when our Race would be able to appreciate real art, even when it is portrayed by a black person."

" 'A day will come when they will understand, Princess Ebony,' I told her. 'You will walk out on the stage in a great role—maybe this one again—and

---

3. Black Patti was an African American opera star at the turn of the century.

they will applaud you and acclaim you to the world.' But she remained inconsolable for months."

"Then, one day," Dr. Benyon continued, "she came to me, all smiling and full of determination, just as if a new light had dawned upon her. 'Bentie,' she said, 'I've thought of what you told me, that night, about my possibilities on the stage, and it's true. One of these days, our people *will* appreciate art—my art, too. Listen, Bentie, I'm going to stick to the stage, but from now on, I'm acknowledging facts. They're not yet ready for a jet-black woman in dramatic roles, and until That Day, which you mentioned, I shan't force myself on them again. Hereafter, if you'll permit, I'm going to be the coach and wardrobe woman of this company.' " Dr. Benyon paused and smiled reminiscently, then—

"She became just that," he went on, "our company's coach and wardrobe adviser. All the girls and the fellows loved her. Often they tried to express their sympathy in various ways, but she would have none of it. I knew her only by the name they gave her, 'Princess Ebony.' She liked that title and it fitted her perfectly. A real honest-to-goodness Ethiopian princess could not wear it more regally than she did. I used to look at her and imagine her to be a real Ethiopian princess who had deserted the age-old royalty in her country for the excitement that she had discovered in this country—"

"That's an idea, Doc," Holmes interrupted. "She has no known relatives here, so maybe she *is* an Ethiopian princess in exile."

Dr. Benyon smiled and nodded. "Such a thing is possible. She *could* be an Ethiopian princess in exile. At least we can imagine so, if we enjoy being romantic. She was always a mystery to her friends. None ever knew or heard of any relatives of hers, or where she came from. Another thing: no actress in the company ever attempted a new role until the princess had acted through it for her."

The next morning after a sleepless night of thinking about Princess Ebony and others of those triumphant stage days in the past, Dr. Benyon, sad and wrapped in a mantle of nostalgia for those days, crossed the hospital grounds to the charity ward. He knew that if she had survived the long night before, she couldn't possibly have much longer to live, but he wanted to talk to her once more and, if possible, make her passing a bit more cheery.

"She had a pretty bad night," Dr. Holmes told him. "I don't think she'll make it through the day," he added as the two entered her small room.

Dr. Benyon did not answer him. Silently, he knelt at her bed and gripped her hand, which was cold now, but he saw that she breathed. A lump formed in his throat. His eyes smarted. No, I must not cry, he thought to himself. She lived and loved drama, and I must not let my tears turn her passing into melodrama.

"Princess Ebony," he called to her, almost choking him. "It is I—Bentie. I've come again—to talk to you, if you feel up to it."

As he waited patiently and hopefully, her lashes fluttered, then she slowly opened her eyes and smiled faintly, as if it took her every bit of strength to do so.

"Say," he said cheerily, "you're not trying to bow off the stage just yet, are you?"

From somewhere, she seemed to muster a bit of strength. She stirred weakly and smiled again.

"It's been twenty-five years, Princess," he said, "and 'That Day' we used to talk of has come. Do you recall your vow to stick until the coming of That Day when our race would appreciate your art—remember?"

Tears welled in her eyes. "Yes," she whispered.

"Well," he reassured her, "That Day is here, my dear. If you can stick around and—and get well—"

She winced slightly, cutting him short. He stared at her intently and wondered if this was the end. But presently she smiled again, opened her eyes and looked toward the window into the dim ray of light which sifted through a cloud-hung sky outside.

Then, with a supreme effort, she whispered: "Bentie, That Day *is* here. I hear the curtain rising for me! The stage is bright and beautiful! I hear them applauding for me! The music is divine! I must go out to them now! Wish me luck, Bentie!" She broke off with a deep breath and was suddenly still, as a triumphant smile played about her mouth.

"Princess!" he cried softly, then, realizing that she was gone. "I *do* wish you all the luck—all the luck in heaven!" He bowed his head and was still and silent for a moment. Then he whispered, "Oh, blessed God, give her That Day!"

He felt a gentle hand grasp his arm. Dr. Holmes assisted him to his feet.

Again at his desk in his office, Dr. Howard Benyon blinked several persistent tears down his cheeks and dialed the telephone number of a leading undertaking establishment.

"This is Dr. Benyon of Lincoln hospital," he said to the voice that greeted him. "We have a body for you in the charity ward. No, no, this is not another case for the potter's field. Get a costly bronze casket ready for this body— what? What's that you're asking?"

"I said, who is it?" the voice replied on a note of surprise. "Is it some 'big shot' in your charity ward?"

"Oh," said Dr. Benyon, "why, of course. She's a great actress—unknown to you. Hers is to be an elaborate funeral. There must be loads and loads of flowers. A profound and masterful speaker must deliver her eulogy. There must be plenty of dramatic music. She has no relatives, but once had many friends. I, one of her best friends, will be her chief mourner."

NEGRO STORY, OCTOBER–NOVEMBER 1944

Monday's Child

ELIZABETH WALKER REEVES

I guess lots o' kids hate to see Monday come around 'cause they've had such good times during the weekend. Sure, they'd think I was nuts for saying I can't hardly wait 'til Monday pops up again, 'specially with summer comin' on, but, well, that's the way I see it. No, I never missed but one Monday and that was the time my old man come home and found me reading whilst my sis and brother was scrapping. I guess it's kinda hard for a skinny girl like me to stand up under licks like them, even when he ain't drunk. Anyway, I couldn't get around to make it that Monday morning. But I like Monday mornings 'cause that's the time we go to the English club, and I like that.

Not that I'm the kind that likes all that grammar and poetry stuff they hand you—heck, no, but it's just 'cause I kinda go for the way they talk about literature. Of course, I don't put in much in the discussion, but I'm listening all right. Now since mama ain't 'round no more I don't get no chance to read books much.

Miss Stewart, that's the teacher who's got the club, don't, I mean doesn't (I know the right thing but sometimes I get mixed up) doesn't ask me to contribute nothing. She's real nice about that sort of thing—not bothering folks about telling what they don't know. Besides she's a sweet teacher anyway—not nothing like that Miss Hall I had last year. Take the time Miss Stewart caught me snitching a magazine from the salvage pile. Did she come yanking me down to the principal? 'Deed not. All she said was I must be honor bound to return 'em. And I bring 'em all back. Heck, I don't wanna hold up no war.[1]

---

1. A reference to the paper recycling that went on as part of the war effort.

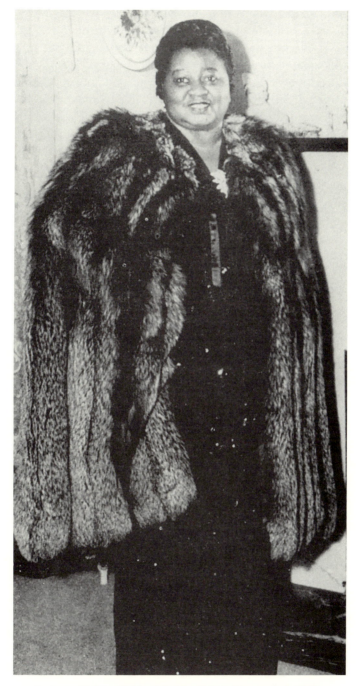

Actress Hattie McDaniel, *The Crisis,* November 1943

Anyhow, what I was getting to, last Monday we had an interesting discussion about all these books they've been turning into pictures. I suppose Miss Stewart had thought it all out beforehand, but anyway it all started when she pops up the question, "How many are going to see 'Jane Eyre'?" Up goes everybody's hand. I look around and stick mine up too, 'cause you get kinda embarrassed when you're left outa things. I guess Miss Stewart was the only one who knew I was lying. Well, she says she's glad to see so many hands 'cause that's a good book. It is, too, she let me read hers last month. Then she gives us a quick gist of it, how Jane Eyre was a governess and wanted to know the mystery of Rochester's castle. That drip, James Jones, wants to know if Jack Benny's in it. Gee, it felt wonderful to be able to laugh in secret with Miss Stewart.

So she goes on to ask if anybody can name another book that's been turned into a picture. Of course, Edith Ryan's hand goes up the highest, so Miss Stewart calls on her to keep her from brushing the ceiling. Edith gets up and, as usual, stands way out in the middle of the aisle so's everybody can see how fine her new dress matches her socks and the ribbons on her plaits. She's one o' them light kids[2] who the teachers like to coddle and always got on something new. Her old man's a doctor and makin' plenty o' money, so she's always got her nose stuck up in the air. Well, anyway, she tells the teacher about "Lassie Come Home." Then everybody's got something to say. I guess all the kids seen it—'cept me. Gosh, that musta been swell! We had a dog once, but one time my old man kicked him out, and he never did come back.

After everybody beefs about that for a while "Fatso" Williams gets up and says he knows about a picture what was made into a book where the people in it had a whole gang o' little dishes and was always lookin' for somethin' in em, and then one night after they'd thrown all the other little dishes away, they looked for it in this last little dish and it wasn't there, and the lady got real mad. Everybody giggles a little 'cause "Fatso" stammers and is always saying something he don't (I mean doesn't) know enough about. But we don't laugh out loud like in Mr. Jackson's room where the kids is always getting put out for cuttin' up, 'cause the kids respect Miss Stewart and don't nobody wanta impose on her.

Miss Stewart looks kinda puzzled and wants to know if anybody has an idea about what "Fatso" is talking about. Then Reginald Wells drawls nonchalantly, "Madame Curie." Now there's a guy for you. He's the kind

---

2. "Light" is a reference to skin color. This character is African American as are all of the children mentioned in the story.

that does things to your heart—one of them smooth browns, you know, with just naturally good hair. No telling when you're goin' 'round a corner in the halls and butt up into him. I 'member the night we had that play and I was running down the hall to get Miss Roberts' keys she'd left in her room when all of a sudden I bumped smack into him. Since it's sorta dark and nobody's nowhere around, he holds me in his arms and kisses me. Then he grins at me and kisses me again. That time I bumps my head against the wall and my back feels kinda sprained, but I cling just the same. After all, look who I'm kissing, the hero in the play. Then he sorta holds onto my hand for a while. It's a hot night and his hand was sweaty and clammy, but I didn't mind, 'cause I'd just as soon kiss it. I'm still mad about that boy, but he ain't said nothing to me since. Well, they don' say much about "Madame Curie" 'cause it seems nobody understood it much.

Grace Young wants to stick her little word in then 'cause she's always gotta be beatin' up her gums after Reggie makes a comment. Everybody knows she's stuck on the fella. Who wouldn't be? She uses bleaching cream and is always piling grease on the back of her head trying to keep her upsweep up. When she explodes for example that she saw "For Whom the Bell Tolls" she's got a voice like an air raid siren starting up.

Then Irma Smith (who's bound to say something to get in good with the teacher) says she thought Greer Garson acted splendid in it. The class shuts her up and sits her down right quick, and she looks kinda foolish. I guess she don't know yet that Ingrid Bergman was in the movie. Bet she didn't have all that money to see it, no how.

Of course, everybody looks at Frances Wright when Miss Stewart says Bergman is a wonderful actress. She "emotes" all over the place and is gonna head straight for Hollywood to be the sepia Bette Davis.

"Re-ally," she says, "it's all a matter of whether or not one is endowed with an innate appreciation for acting. Acting is an art. It is an art that elevates the soul—"

Well, everybody, that's most of us, have heard her quote that speech fifty trillion times, so the kids start to coughing and raising their hands and carrying on. Frances can't talk in all that commotion (I think that's the word) and she looks like she's 'bout ready to burst into tears. Miss Stewart can see what's about to happen, so she sorta tells the class to put a zipper on their mouths and let Frances finish.

She's understanding like that. I told her all about how pop beats us and gets drunk 'cause ma run off with some other guy and how, on account o' that people all avoid us. I never would have said nothing to nobody else, but she just nods her head and all the time I'm talking she's got her arm around my shoulder. That makes me feel kinda good 'cause nobody never hugs me, almost hardly, 'cept the time about Reggie, but that ain't the kind o' hugging I'm talking about.

Well, they keep talking about all the movies they've seen—'bout nothing that bunch ain't seen. (I know better than to say "ain't," but sometimes I slip up.) When it's almost time for the bell to ring, Miss Stewart tells the kids to bring in the money, and she'd take 'em to the theatre at reduced prices. She's swell! While we're packing up books and getting ready to leave, Miss Stewart calls my name and says she wants to see me after class. I guess the kids wondered what she wanted; I wondered too. I didn't know what I'd done 'cept pass a note from Jack to Martha, and I didn't 'spect she'd seen me.

When the club period ends, I go up to her desk to find out what she's got on her mind and she asks, "Are you going to see 'Jane Eyre'?"

I can't imagine her asking such a dumb question like that 'cause she knows I won't get within a mile of the theatre, but I answer just the same.

"No'm. I don't think so."

"Well," she says, "after you've gone to the store for me at noon today, that will be worth ten cents and a ticket to the theatre."

I just got my mouth hung open and couldn't shut it up. I guess I came near blubbering all over and smothering her with "thank you's," but she knows how I feel about literature. The first hour class was filing in and looking at me kinda funny, so I pick up my things and run out so I wouldn't be late for Math. Miss Brown's evil, and she don't like me nohow.

I just can't get over the way there's some nice folks left in the world after all. Miss Stewart's a square shooter. Some day I want to be like her when I grow up and read lots o' literature. I guess there just ain't nobody like her.

Yeah. I like Monday mornings.

NEGRO STORY, MAY–JUNE 1944

The Skater

LILA MARSHALL

Nadine was besieged by an anxious throng of males who pulled her this way and that, in their insistent desires to skate with her, but impatiently she

Bathing Beauty, *The Crisis*, July 1944

shook them off with a regal gesture. One could scarcely read her displeasure in the complacency of her expression, for her calmness seemed that of complete indifference—a sophisticated aloofness. It was not so much a disgust with the attentions of the throng as it was an absence of desire for a partner.

As she skated alone, the eyes of the onlookers followed her graceful movements; no other skater seemed to exist for them. Into her elastic body poured the music. She and the sound were one, sometimes lilting and poetic, sometimes wild and jazzy. Each glide had a natural rhythm; never was there an awkward movement or a misstep to mar the utter perfection of her performance.

The roaring noise from the roller skates was deafening. Masses of Negro skaters were cutting wild capers. Some were lifting their legs high into the air. Some were leaning perilously to one side. Others were dancing. But Nadine held the center of the stage, for all eyes were upon her as she glided past, and comments on her beauty and rhythm could be heard coming from every side.

The rink was a large, bright one. It was painted in salmon and blue tones. Mellow strains from a skillfully played pipe organ could be heard. Some of the songs were waltzes and popular music, while others were the jitterbug songs of the day. The large electric sign above the organ flashed for "Ladies Only" numbers, "Couples Only," and announced races or contests. The atmosphere was gay, and there was a good-natured spirit even when a skater fell. Usually the fallen one jumped up and resumed his stride, but occasionally one had to be carried out. Even in these extreme cases they were soon back skating joyfully with the rest.

You could see all kinds of interesting and amusing sights. One small woman fell and slid halfway through a tall man's legs. Immediately, he reached down, jerked her all the way through and set her upon her wobbly feet. Whereupon, she fell again, piling up several other people on top of her. They all laughed and picked themselves up.

There were racers, beginners, backward skaters, graceful skaters, jitterbugs, and figure skaters all displaying their skill.

But Nadine's pace continued always the same. Gliding smoothly into narrow, impossible places and then out again without touching the struggling masses of flesh, she always emerged looking cool and nonchalant, as if she were alone on the ballroom floor. Sometimes she would dart quickly into a space like a small bright bird as she traveled her purposeless course. She appeared to be skating through life with a glorious, unchangeable rhythm—not a care in the world for anything but the moment.

"Boy! What a picture!"

"What grace!"

"She surely can skate!"

"I'm tell'n you she's the best skater in the rink!"

"And how!"

The nudges and glances of the Negro crowd watching her tireless steps went unnoticed by her, as did their comments. A group of callow brown youth always whistled loudly as she passed them. Even when a bold hand touched her, she floated along unmoved and distant.

A lovely picture she made in her flared, yellow skating dress, which revealed rounded limbs and bosom. Shiny black hair coiled about her head and her olive complexion glowed rosily. She seemed entirely unconscious of her beauty.

"Skate with me."

A deep voice startled her with its resonance, and she was suddenly engulfed by a strong pair of arms, which held her tightly. Experienced with male tactics, she looked up indifferently. She seemed ready for her usual good-natured refusal when the sardonic smile of the young man seemed to startle her, and she almost missed a step. She stared. He was handsome. For a moment she paused, almost imperceptibly, and then, tossing her head, shook herself free from his grasp and continued her flight. Carelessly, he shrugged and skated away. She wavered an instant and went on with her never-changing pace.

To the casual observer, the girl continued to skate as divinely as before, but I could see that her music-laden lethargy had been broken, and that her world had been completely changed. She looked curiously awake—curiously disturbed. No longer was her lightness the froth of the nymph, no longer was her abandon and vigor a gift from the skies; no longer was her relaxation the unconscious beauty of one who dreams. Now she moved with a precise skill. Smiling at those she recognized, the music burst loudly upon her; under its blatant tones, she danced and swayed and swung, entirely aware of her skill. Out of the corner of her eye, she glanced at him, gliding wondrously with all of the best and prettiest girls on the floor, to their evident delight. She looked a little wistful. He suddenly seemed hers. But his indifference matched her own; not once did he look her way.

The music stopped, and as if propelled by the imagination of its tones the skaters continued at the same reckless pace—except one. For as if drawn by a powerful magnet which could not be resisted, the girl glided smoothly off the floor—glided in the direction of an arrogant youth with derisive eyes and an expectant, sardonic smile. There he was waiting for her, tall, brown and handsomer than she expected. He was staring at her strangely. He looked as if he were already in love with her. Never before had she appeared so queer, so dazed. Never before had she seemed so disturbed—bewildered.

He moved toward her. They looked into each other's eyes. His black ones were smouldering; hers were wide and questioning.

"You," he said incoherently, "you."

Sepia Miss America Contestants, *The Crisis*, July 1944

She merely stared at him. It was evident that something had happened to her. She could not speak.

As she stood there and stared, her eyes big and her lips trembling, a slim dark brown girl in a brown sweater and tan skirt skated over to them.

"Bob," she said, and smiled at Nadine benignly, "isn't it time to go home?"

He started. "Yes, dear," he said, and with a last look at Nadine, turned meekly away with the girl, but not before Nadine had seen the flash of diamonds in a platinum band of the fourth finger of her left hand.

THE CRISIS, MAY 1945

Olaf and His Girl Friend

ANN PETRY

This is Olaf's story. I don't pretend to know all of it. I saw parts of it that happened on the dock in Bridgetown, Barbados. And I saw the ending of the story in New York. The rest of it I had to piece together from the things that Olaf's friends told me. As a result I think I'm the only person who actually knows why a pretty little West Indian dancer disappeared very suddenly from the New York nightclub where she sang calypso songs and danced *la conga* and the *beguine*. She was beginning to make the place famous. And she vanished.

It's only if you know Olaf's story that you can understand her disappearance. He was a great big black guy who worked on the docks in Bridgetown. Some two hundred and twenty pounds of muscle and six feet of height. I liked to watch him work. The way his muscles rippled under his skin as he lifted boxes and bags fascinated me. They were those long, smooth muscles you find in perfectly trained athletes.

When the sun shone on him it caught highlights in his skin, so that he looked like an ebony man. I soon discovered that there was a slender native girl who found him even more interesting to watch than I did. I only wanted to paint him against the green water of Carlisle bay. She wanted to marry him.

Her name was Belle Rose. She had that sinuous kind of grace that suggests the born dancer. When she walked she swayed a little as though she were keeping time to a rumba that played somewhere inside her head.

She used to show up at noon time, two or three days a week. She'd sit by him while he ate his lunch. They talked and laughed about nothing at all. His great laugh would boom out the length of the dock and the other dock hands would grin because they couldn't help it.

"Olaf's girl's here," they said.

She couldn't have been more than seventeen years old. The dock boys used to look at her out of the corner of their eyes and flash their white teeth at her but it seemed to be pretty well accepted that she was Olaf's girl.

It was nearly a month before things started going wrong. One day I heard a lot of noise at one end of the dock. I welcomed the interruption for I'd been trying to paint the bay and I was filled with a sense of despair of ever getting that incredible green on canvas. So I left my easel to investigate.

Olaf's girl was standing sort of huddled up. All the laughter gone out of her. She was holding her face as though it hurt. A short, stumpy, dark brown woman was facing Olaf a little way off from the girl.

The woman was neatly dressed even to the inevitable umbrella that the upper class island women carry and she looked for all the world like a bantam rooster. She had one hand on her hip and with the other hand she was gesticulating with the raised umbrella while she berated Olaf in a high, shrill voice.

"I tell you I won't have you seeing her. She's too good for your kind. Belle Rose will marry a teacher," she shook the umbrella under his very nose.

He looked like an abashed great dane. But he stood his ground.

"I do no harm. I love her. I want to marry her."

And that set the old girl off again. "Marry her? You?" she choked on the words. "You think you'll marry her? I'll have you locked up. I'll—" she was overcome with sheer rage.

"I'm honest. I love her. I think she's beautiful. I wouldn't harm her," he pleaded.

She shook her head violently and went off muttering that Belle Rose's father had been a school teacher and Belle Rose wasn't going to marry any dock hand. Her umbrella was still quivering as she hurried away holding the girl firmly by the arm.

She turned around when she was half the length of the dock. "Besides you're a coward. Everybody knows you're scared of the water. Belle Rose will never marry a coward."

Olaf followed them. I don't know how that particular episode ended. But I was curious about him and questioned the dock hands. They told me his father had been a sailor and his grandfather before him. Olaf should have been a sailor but his mother brought him up to be afraid of the water. It seems his father went down with a ship during a violent storm.

Shortly after I learned about Olaf's fear of the sea, he slipped on the dock and went head first into the bay. He managed to stay afloat until the boys fished him out but he was obviously half dead from fright. It was a week before he came back to work.

"You all right, mahn?" the boys asked.

Olaf nodded and kept any feelings he had about it to himself.

It was only because he loved Belle Rose that he came back to work. I overheard them talking about it. They were sitting on the edge of the dock. It seemed to me they were the most paintable pair I'd ever seen. He was stripped to the waist because he'd been working. His wide, cream colored straw hat and faded blue dungarees were a perfect foil for the starched white of her dress and the brilliant red of the turban wound so deftly around her head.

"And we'll have a house not too near the sea," she said in a very soft voice.

"Yes. Not too near the sea," was his answer. "It'll be just near enough to watch the sun on the water in the bay."

"Olaf, you don't like this job. Do you?" she asked.

"Only for you. I like it for you. It means we can get married soon. That's why I came back to work."

I walked away and I asked the boys what became of Olaf's girl friend's aunt. Had she decided they could get married after all? The boys looked sheepish.

"They will have big wedding. Olaf goes every Sunday now to call on Belle Rose. All dressed up in scissors tail coat. With stiff collar. Olaf takes the aunt plantains every Sunday. I don't think she change her mind. Olaf just too big. And she got no man to deal with him," was the answer.

The boys were right in one respect. The marriage banns were posted. But it wasn't to be the big church wedding Belle Rose's aunt had set her heart on. Olaf threatened to elope unless it was a small wedding. And auntie gave in gracefully. I wondered about that. She seemed a domineering kind of old girl to agree to a small wedding when she wanted a large one. The more I thought about it the queerer it seemed that she should have consented to any kind of wedding.

The dock crew quits about five o'clock in Bridgetown. The day I discovered that the girl's aunt had no intentions of allowing any kind of marriage, a big American merchant ship had been loaded with fruit. She was due to sail at seven o'clock. On that particular day Belle Rose's aunt sent Olaf on an errand that took him half way across the island.

I went down to watch the passengers clamber aboard the launch. There were a lot of native women at the dock. They were seeing a couple of passengers off. You could hear their goodbyes and messages half way across the bay.

I stared in amazement. It was Belle Rose and her aunt who were going away. The aunt all officious and confidential at the same time. Ordering Belle Rose to do this and did she have that and where was the small bag. She was fairly bursting with importance.

"My boy in New York sent me the money. The passage fare for both of us," she explained loudly for the benefit of a late comer.

"Belle Rose, do you think you'll like it?" asked one of the younger women.

The aunt didn't give the girl time to answer. "Of course she will," she said firmly. "She's never been off the island. She wants to see the world a bit. Don't you, dear?"

Belle Rose nodded. "Yes, I do. But I wish I could have said good-bye to Olaf. And I did want to stay near him," her voice was wistful.

"You can write to him. You'll see him soon. After all he can come and see you, you know," and with that she hurried the girl into the steamer's launch. She leaned over to whisper to an older woman, "You know it aren't as though he were fit for her," and then turned her attention back to the girl and their bags.

I stood on the deck until the ship had become a mere speck in the distance. New York was a long ways away. A dock hand could hardly hope to get there in a life time. And though the old woman had counted on that, she deliberately sold that girl the idea that New York was some place just around the corner and practically suggested that Olaf could commute back and forth to see her.

I felt like calling the ship back. Because if ever a man loved a woman that man was Olaf and the woman was Belle Rose. He stopped laughing after he discovered the girl was gone. He got very quiet. It wasn't that he brooded or was sullen. He was just quiet and he worked with a grim determination.

When he got letters from her he seemed to come alive again. And I could tell whenever he'd received one. Then the letters stopped coming. I asked him about it. "Have you heard from your girl?"

"No. Not lately. I don't understand it," he said.

A whole year crept around. A year that brought the war a little closer to us. A year in which his letters kept coming back marked, "Moved. Left no address." A year in which the native women came down to the dock to look coyly at Olaf. They walked past him and flirted with him. He ignored them.

I found out later that Belle Rose never received the letters that he wrote her. Auntie saw to that. Finally she intercepted the letters that Belle Rose wrote to him. And then, of course, they moved and auntie gave the post office no forwarding address.

One day out of a clear sky, Olaf signed up on a ship. Olaf who was so afraid of the sea that when he looked out over the bay his eyes would go dead and blank. Olaf who worked with one eye on the sky when the storms came up suddenly. He signed on one of those gray, raffish looking ships that were forever limping into port and disgorging crews of unshaven, desperate looking men. Olaf, who hated the sea, signed on a merchant ship.

It was a long time before I found out how it happened. It seems that he got a message. These days people talk about the underground of the little people in the conquered countries of Europe. But there's always been an underground that could send a message half way round the world.

It happened in Olaf's case. The message travelled in the mouths of ship's stewards and mess boys. It took a good six months for Olaf to get it.

The first boat with the message on it left New York and went to Liverpool. And then to northern Africa. She bummed half way around the world—sneaking from one port to another carrying guns and men and God knows what. And Olaf's message. And everywhere she went the message was transferred to other ships and other men.

The steward on a boat that lumbered back and forth across the Atlantic helped relay it—"tell Olaf"—. The message went to India and the messmen on an English ship learned about it.

Finally it got to Olaf. It was a little, excitable man with just two hours leave who delivered it to him on the dock.

"Belle Rose is dancing in New York in a place that is not good. Not by 'alf. Elmer and Franklin and Stoner sent back word to you. They work in that same place. She dances. And it is not a good dance."

The word had come such a long way and had been such a long time getting to its destination that the little man was breathless from the sheer weight of it. He'd learned it from two sailors in an infamous house on the edge of the water front in Liverpool. His beard fairly quivered with the excitement of it.

"Did you hear me, Olaf?" he asked sharply as though his voice would bring a reaction. "It is not a good dance."

Olaf stared out at the sea. It was a long time before he spoke. "I heard. Yes," he said slowly. "I heard. I will take care of it."

And he walked off the dock and signed up on the same ship that had brought the little man with the message. Just like that. The man who was afraid of the sea signed up on a ship.

I learned afterwards that he worked in the ship's galley—washing dishes and helping with the cooking. He was very quiet. His quietness permeated the stuffy bunk rooms. It made the men uneasy even when they were shooting craps, or singing, or just talking.

He was always in his bunk when he wasn't working. He lay there staring up at the ceiling with an unwinking gaze.

"S'matter with the big guy?" the mate asked nervously. "Guys like that bring bad luck."

"Just quiet," was the usual apologetic answer of the little man who was responsible for Olaf's being aboard.

Olaf hadn't even bothered to find out what port they were heading for. When they docked on a cold, wet night he asked a question for the first time. "New York?"

"This England, mahn," was the answer. "Liverpool."

But they headed for New York on the return trip. If Olaf thought about the danger of the queer, crazy voyage he didn't show it. He was on deck hours before the boat docked, peering into the dark. He would start his search now. At once. In a few minutes.

He asked a black man on the dock, "You know a girl named Belle Rose?"

The man shook his head. "Bud, there's a lot of women here. All kinds of people. You won't find no woman that way. What she look like?" And then he added, "Where does she live?"

"Like—like—" Olaf fumbled for words, his throat working, "like the sun. She's so high," he indicated a spot on his chest. "She's warm like the sun—" his voice broke. "I don't know where she lives."

The man stared at him. "What's your name? Where you from?"

"The Islands. Barbados. To the South. My name is Olaf," and then his voice grew soft as he said again, "Her name is Belle Rose." He seemed to linger over her name.

"Naw," the man returned to his work, "You won't find her, Bud, just knowin' her name."

They were in port just two hours and they were gone again. But the underground had the message. "Olaf from Barbados is looking for Belle Rose."

The dock worker told a friend and the story went into the kitchens, and the freight elevators of great hotels. Doormen knew it and cooks and waiters. It travelled all the way from the water front to Harlem. People who'd never heard of Belle Rose knew that a man named Olaf was looking for her.

The cook in a nightclub told three West Indian drummers who were part of the floor show. Elmer, Franklin and Stoner looked at each other and gesticulated despairingly when they heard it. A message started back to Olaf. It took a long time. Olaf saw the edge of Africa and a port in Australia and Liverpool again before the message reached him.

His silence had grown ominous, portentous. The men never spoke to him. They left him alone—completely alone. They shivered a little when they looked at him.

One of the crew picked the message up in Liverpool and brought it to him. "The name of the place where Belle Rose dances is the Conga."

Olaf went to the mate when he heard it and asked when they'd dock in New York again. The mate stared at him, "I don't know. I never know where we're goin' until we're under way. You got some reason for wantin' to go to New York?"

"Yes. I have to find a girl there," Olaf looked past the man as he spoke.

"You? A girl?" the mate couldn't conceal his amazement. "I didn't know you were interested in girls."

But Olaf had turned away to watch the ship being loaded. They left Liverpool that same night. It was a bad voyage. Stormy and cold. With high seas.

They docked in New York early on a cold bitter morning. They were paid off for the Atlantic voyage and given two days shore leave. The crew disappeared like magic. Only Olaf was left behind.

He asked a policeman on the dock, "Where do black people live in this place?" he gestured towards the city.

"You better take a taxi, boy. Tell the driver you want the YMCA on 135th Street between Lenox and Seventh Avenue. In Harlem."

The man wrote it down for him on the back of an envelope. Olaf looked at the paper frequently while the cab crawled through a city that looked half dead. It was shrouded in gray. It was cold. There were no lights in the buildings and few people on the streets. They snaked their way between tall buildings, over cobblestoned streets, along miles of a highway that ran for awhile along the edge of the river. It was getting lighter and he became aware that all the people on the streets through which they were passing were dark.

He relaxed a little. He was getting near the end of his long journey. "All this place—is all this place New York?" he indicated the sidewalk.

The driver studied him in the mirror and nodded, "Yeah. All of it's New York. Where you from?"

"Barbados," Olaf said simply. He was wondering what could have happened to Belle Rose in this place. And where would he find her?

It was the first thing he asked the man behind the wicket when he paid for his room at the 'Y.'

"I wouldn't know anybody with a name like that," the man said coldly.

"Where is the place called the Conga?" Olaf asked.

"I never heard of it," the man shoved a receipt towards him. "Take the elevator to the fifth floor. Your room is number 563. Next, please."

But the elevator man had heard about the Conga. He told Olaf how to get there. Even told him that eleven o'clock at night was the best time to visit it.

Olaf sat in his room—waiting. He was like a man that had been running in a cross country race and realizes suddenly that the finish line is just a little ways ahead because he can see it.

At eleven o'clock he was in a taxi, on his way to the Conga. The taxi went swiftly.

It was the expression in his eyes that made the doorman at the place try to stop him from going in. He tried to block his way and Olaf brushed him aside, lightly, effortlessly, as though he'd been a fly.

Once inside he was a little confused. There was smoke, and the lights were dim. People were laughing and talking, their voices blurred and loud from liquor. He walked to a table right at the edge of the space used for dancing. A protesting waiter hurried towards him, pointed at the reserved sign on the table. Olaf looked at him and put the sign on the floor. The waiter backed away and didn't return.

I recognized him when he sat down. He folded his arms on the table and sat there perfectly indifferent to the looks and the whispered conversations around him.

I used to go up to the Conga rather often. Barney, the guy who runs it, was a friend of mine. He told me a long time ago that all the dance lovers in town were flocking into his place because of a young West Indian girl who did some extraordinary dancing. Barney knew I'd lived in the Islands and he thought I'd be interested.

I was more than interested, for the girl, of course, was Belle Rose. After the first visit I became a regular customer because I figured that sooner or later Olaf would show up. I wanted to be there when he arrived. The gods were kind to me. As I said before, I saw him when he came in and sat down.

He'd completely lost that friendly look he'd had. He was a dangerous man. It was in his eyes, in the way he carried his head. It was in his tightly closed mouth. A mouth that looked as though laughter were a stranger that had never passed that way. All of the humor had gone out of him. He was like an elastic band that had been stretched too far.

The lights went down and the three West Indian drummers came in—Elmer, and Franklin and Stoner. They filed in carrying the native drums that they played. Drums made of hollowed logs with hide stretched across them. They sat astride them the way the natives do—and drummed.

I couldn't swear to it that they'd actually seen Olaf. After all if you play in one of those places long enough, I imagine you get to know the tricks of lighting and you can see everybody in the place. And yet I don't know. Maybe they had some kind of umpteenth sense. Perhaps they felt some difference in the atmosphere.

When they started to drum it was—well, different. The tempo was faster and there was something subtly alarming about it. It ran through the audience. Men tapped ashes off their cigarettes—and there wasn't any ash there. Women shivered from a draft that didn't exist. The waiters moved ash trays and bottles for no reason at all. The headwaiter kept shooting his shirt cuffs and fingering around the edge of his collar.

Belle Rose came on suddenly. One moment she wasn't there. And the next moment she was bowing to the audience. I wonder if I can make you see her. Half of New York used to go to that dinky little club just to watch her dance. She was a deep reddish brown color and very slender. Her eyes were magnificent. They were black and very large with a curious lack of expression. There's an old obeah woman in Barbados with those same strange eyes.

I think I said that Barney Jones was a showman. He'd gotten her up so that she looked like some gorgeous tropical bird—all life, and color and motion.

She danced in her bare feet. There was a gold anklet around one ankle and a high gold collar around her neck that almost touched her ear lobes. The dress she wore was made of calico and it had a bustle in the back so that every time she moved the red calico flirted with her audience. She had on what looked to be yards of ruffled petticoats. They were starched so stiffly that the dress stood out and the white ruffling showed from underneath the dress. A towering red turban covered her hair completely. There were flowers and fruit and wheat stuck in the turban.

She sang a calypso number first. Something about marrying a woman uglier than you. The nightclub was very quiet. Somebody knocked over a glass and giggled in a high, hysterical fashion. There was a queer stillness afterwards.

I looked at Olaf. He wasn't moving at all. He was staring at Belle Rose. His hands were flat on the table. He looked as though he might spring at any moment. The reflection from the spotlight shone on the beads of sweat on his forehead.

And I thought of that other time when I used to see him, laughing on the dock at Bridgetown with the sun shining on him. Now he was in a nightclub in a cold, alien city watching the girl he had intended to marry. He'd come a long, long way.

The applause that greeted that first number of hers was terrific. She bowed and said, "I weel now do for you the obeahwoman."

Olaf stiffened. His eyes narrowed. The drums started again. And this time I tell you they talked as plainly as though they were alive. Human. They talked danger. They talked hate. They snarled and they sent a chill down my spine. The back of my neck felt cold and I found I was clutching my glass so tightly that my hand hurt.

Belle Rose crouched and walked forwards and started singing. It was an incantation to some far off evil gods. It didn't belong in New York. It didn't belong in any nightclub that has ever existed anywhere under the sun.

"Ah, you get your man," and then the drums. Boom. Boom. "Ah, you want a lover!" Boom. Boom. Boom-de-de-boom. "Ah, I see the spear-et." And the drums again. Louder.

And she walked towards Olaf. She was standing directly in front of him. Hands outstretched. Eyes half shut. Swaying. She stopped singing and the drums kept up their message, their repeated, nerve wracking message. The faces of the drummers were perfectly expressionless. Only their eyes were alive—glittering. Eyes that seemed to have a separate life from their faces.

Belle Rose went on dancing. It's a dance I've never seen done before in a nightclub. It was the devil dance—a dance that's used to exorcise an evil spirit. I don't know exactly what effect it had on Olaf. I could only conjecture. I knew he'd been on boats and ships for months trying to reach New York. The West Indian drummers told me.

He'd been tasting the salt air of the sea. Seeing nothing but water. Gone to sleep at night hearing it slap against the ship. Listened to it cascade over the decks when the seas were high. Living with it morning, noon and night. Even in port it was always there, moving against the sides of the ship.

And he hated the sea. He was afraid of it. He must have gone through hell during those months. Always that craven gnawing fear in the pit of his stomach. Always surrounded by the sea that he loathed.

And then he sees Belle Rose. She's completely unaware of him and more beautiful than ever. With artificial red on her lips and a caste mark between her eyes.[1]

I said Barney was a showman. I suppose he thought it made the girl more exotic. As a final touch he'd had a caste mark painted on her forehead. It was done with something shiny. It may only have been a bit of tinsel—but it caught the light and glowed every time she moved.

I heard Olaf growl deep in his throat when he saw it. He'd been completely silent before. He stood up. All muscle. All brawn. All dangerous, lonely, desperate strength. He walked over the railing. Just stepped over it as though it wasn't there. And confronted her. He had a knife in his hand. I could swear, now, to this day, that he meant to kill her.

She kept right on dancing. She moved nearer to him. I say again that he meant to kill her. And I say, too, that she knew it. And she reached back into that ancient, complicated African past that belonged to both of them and invoked all the gods she knew or that she'd ever heard of.

The drums had stopped. Everything had stopped. There wasn't so much as a glass clinking or the sound of a cork pulled. It seemed to me that I had stopped breathing and that no one in the place was breathing. She began to sing in a high, shrill voice. I couldn't understand any of the words. It was the same kind of chant that a witch doctor uses when he casts a spell; the same one that the conjure women use and the obeah women.

Her voice stopped suddenly. They must have stared at each other for all of five minutes. The knife slipped out of his hand. Clinked on the floor. Suddenly he reached out and grabbed her and shook her like a dog would shake a kitten. She didn't say anything. Neither did he. And then she was in his arms and he was kissing her and putting his very heart into it.

They walked hand and hand the length of the room and out through the street door. A sigh ran around the tables.

I think Barney, the guy who owns the joint, came to first. He ran after them. And I followed him. When I reached the street he was standing at the curb raving, frothing at the mouth as he watched his biggest drawing card disappear up the street in a taxi. I could just see the red tail light turn the corner.

"That black baboon," Barney fumed. "Where in the hell did he come from?"

---

1. This refers to the bindi (dot) placed between the eyes to indicate devotion to one's deity in India. Here it shows the inappropriate way in which this West Indian dancer is being exoticized.

I started laughing and that seemed to infuriate him even more. Finally I said, "Barbados. Where Belle Rose came from. It took a long time for him to find her but I'll guarantee New York will never see her again."

I was right. She disappeared. With Olaf. I worried about Elmer and Franklin and Stoner until I finally heard that they were back in Bridgetown.

You can have your choice as to why Olaf didn't kill her that night in the Conga. I like to think that when he got that close to her he remembered that he loved her and that he'd gone through hell to find her. And all he wanted was to hold her tight in his arms. After all she was very beautiful.

On the other hand, though Belle Rose's father may have been a school teacher, her grandmother was an obeah woman.

Appendix

Edna L. Anderson*
Walter G. Arnold
James Baldwin
Simeon Booker Jr.
Gwendolyn Brooks*
Alice C. Browning*
Elmer Carter
Ida Coker Clark*
Ruth Albert Cook*
William Couch Jr.
Constance H. Curtis*
George E. DeMar
Owen Dodson
Pearl Fisher*
Marie Brown Frazier*
Helen S. Frierson*
Fern Gayden*
Ruby Berkley Goodwin*
Thelma Thurston Gorham*
Shirley Graham*
Leotha Hackshaw*
Chester B. Himes
Elsie Mills Holton*
Langston Hughes
Zora Neale Hurston*
Georgia Douglas Johnson*
Hortense Johnson*
Robert Jones
Roma Jones*
Melissa Linn* (pseudonym; actual
     name unknown)

Frenise Logan
Thurgood Marshall
Booker T. Medford
May Miller*
Mavis B. Mixon*
Cora Ball Moten*
Pauli Murray*
Constance C. Nichols*
Valerie Ethelyn Parks*
Ann Petry*
Lucia Mae Pitts*
Mrs. Charles Puryear*
Muriel Rahn*
Sgt. Aubrey Robinson
O'Wendell Shaw
William Grant Still
Roberta I. Thomas*
Tomi Carolyn Tinsley*
Grace W. Tompkins*
Margaret Walker*
Hazel L. Washington*
Charles Enoch Wheeler
Mae Smith Williams*
Victoria Winfrey*
Octavia B. Wynbush*
*Two anonymous women letter
     writers:*
     a soldier's wife,*
     a mother ("Georgia")*

(*=female writer)

African American ethnicity was determined by general knowledge of the writer, his or her publication in identifiably African American venues such as poetry anthologies of black writers, allusion to the writer's ethnicity in the magazines themselves, biographies, or critical studies, and self-identification within the writer's work.

WRITERS OF UNDETERMINED ETHNICITY

Zora L. Barnes*
Michael Carter
Gloria Clyne*
Marjorie E. Greene*
David Hanna
Vivien E. Lewis*
Lila Marshall*

Fanny McConnell*
Florence McDowell*
Elizabeth Walker Reeves*
Margaret Rodriguez*
Ruby Rohrlich*
Rhoza A. Walker*
Gwendolyn Williams*

NON-AFRICAN AMERICAN WRITERS

Ruth DeCesare*
Esta Diamond*
Zena Dorinson*
Press Hawkins
James Light

Elsa Maxwell*
James F. Powers
Edith Segal*
Andre Spire

_____

(*=female writer)

Bibliography

Allen, Alexander J. "Western Electric's Backward Step." *Opportunity,* summer 1944, 108-43.

Allen, Robert L. "The Port Chicago Disaster and Its Aftermath." *Black Scholar* 13 (1982): 2-29.

Anderson, Karen. *Changing Woman: A History of Racial Ethnic Women in Modern America.* New York: Oxford University Press, 1996.

————. "Last Hired, First Fired: Black Women Workers during World War II." *Journal of American History* 69, no. 1 (June 1982): 82-97.

————. *Wartime Women: Sex Roles, Family Relations, and the Status of Women during World War II.* Westport, Conn.: Greenwood Press, 1981.

Angelou, Maya. *I Know Why the Caged Bird Sings.* New York: Random House, 1970. Reprint, New York: Bantam Books, 1993. [Page citations are to reprint edition.]

Archibald, Katherine. *Wartime Shipyard: A Study in Social Disunity.* Berkeley and Los Angeles: University of California Press, 1947.

Baker, M. Joyce. *Images of Women in Film: The War Years, 1941-1945.* Ann Arbor, Mich.: UMI Research Press, 1980.

Baldwin, James. "Notes of a Native Son." In *Notes of a Native Son.* Boston: Beacon Books, 1955. Reprint, New York: Bantam Books, 1964. [Page citations are to reprint edition.]

Berelson, Bernard, and Patricia Salter. "Majority and Minority Americans: An Analysis of Magazine Fiction." *Public Opinion Quarterly* 10 (1946): 168-97.

Berube, Allan. *Coming Out under Fire: The History of Gay Men and Women in World War II.* New York: Free Press, 1990.

Blood, Kathryn. *Negro Women War Workers.* Women's Bureau Bulletin no. 205. Washington D.C.: U.S. Department of Labor, 1945.

Bogle, Donald. *Brown Sugar: Eighty Years of America's Black Female Superstars.* New York: DaCapo Press, 1990.

————. *Dorothy Dandridge: A Biography.* New York: Amistad Press, 1997.

Branch, Taylor. *Parting the Waters: America in the King Years, 1954-1963.* New York: Touchstone Books, 1989.

Campbell, D'Ann. *Women at War with America: Private Lives in a Patriotic Era.* Cambridge: Harvard University Press, 1984.

Capeci, Dominic J., Jr. "The Lynching of Cleo Wright: Federal Protection of Constitutional Rights during World War II." *Journal of American History* 72 (1986): 859-87.

—. *Race Relations in Wartime Detroit: The Sojourner Truth Housing Controversy of 1942.* Philadelphia: Temple University Press, 1984.

Capeci, Dominic J., Jr., and Martha Wilkerson. *Layered Violence: The Detroit Rioters of 1943.* Jackson: University of Mississippi Press, 1991.

Carby, Hazel. *Reconstructing Womanhood: The Emergence of the Afro-American Woman Novelist.* New York: Oxford University Press, 1987.

Carson, Clayborne. *In Struggle: SNCC and the Black Awakening of the 1960s.* Cambridge: Harvard University Press, 1981.

Chafe, William. *The American Woman: Her Changing Social, Economic, and Political Roles, 1920-1970.* New York: Oxford University Press, 1972.

—. *Women and Equality: Changing Patterns in American Culture.* New York: Oxford University Press, 1977.

Chapman, Abraham, ed. *Black Voices.* New York: New American Library, 1968.

Collins, Patricia Hill. *Black Feminist Thought: Knowledge, Consciousness, and the Politics of Empowerment.* New York: Routledge, 1990.

—. "The Meaning of Motherhood in Black Culture." In *The Black Family: Essays and Studies,* ed. Robert Staples. Belmont, Calif.: Wadsworth, 1991.

Crawford, Vicki, Jacqueline Rouse, and Barbara Woods, eds. *Women in the Civil Rights Movement: Trailblazers and Torchbearers, 1941-1945.* Bloomington: Indiana University Press, 1993.

Cripps, Thomas. *Making Movies Black: The Hollywood Message Movie from World War II to the Civil Rights Era.* New York: Oxford University Press, 1993.

—. *Slow Fade to Black: The Negro in American Film, 1900-1942.* New York: Oxford University Press, 1977.

Dabakis, Melissa. "Gendered Labor: Norman Rockwell's Rosie the Riveter and the Discourses of Wartime Womanhood." In *Gender and American History since 1890,* ed. Barbara Melosh. New York: Routledge, 1993.

Daniel, Walter C. *Black Journals of the United States.* Westport, Conn.: Greenwood Press, 1982.

Doane, Mary Ann. *The Desire to Desire: The Woman's Film of the 1940s.* Bloomington: Indiana University Press, 1987.

Duberman, Martin. "A Giant Denied His Rightful Stature in Film." *New York Times,* March 29, 1998, 38.

Earley, Charity Adams. *One Woman's Army: A Black Officer Remembers the WAC.* College Station: Texas A & M University Press, 1989.

Evans, Sara. *Personal Politics: The Roots of Women's Liberation in the Civil Rights Movement and the New Left.* New York: Vintage Books, 1979.

Faderman, Lillian. *Odd Girls and Twilight Lovers: A History of Lesbian Life in Twentieth-Century America.* New York: Columbia University Press, 1991.

Feldstein, Ruth. " 'I Wanted the Whole World to See': Race, Gender, and Constructions of Motherhood in the Death of Emmett Till." In *Not June Cleaver: Women and Gender in Postwar America, 1945-1960,* ed. Joanne Meyerowitz. New Brunswick: Rutgers University Press, 1996.

Field, Connie, Miriam Frank, and Marilyn Ziebarth. *The Life and Times of Rosie the Riveter: The Story of Three Million Working Women during World War II.* Emeryville, Calif.: Clarity Educational Productions, 1982.

Flexner, Eleanor. *Century of Struggle: The Woman's Rights Movement in the United States.* Cambridge: Harvard University Press, 1975.

Fox, Frank. *Madison Avenue Goes to War: The Strange Military Career of American Advertising, 1941-1945.* Provo: Brigham Young University Press, 1975.

Friedan, Betty. *The Feminine Mystique.* New York: Dell, 1963.

Gabin, Nancy. *Feminism in the Labor Movement: Women and the United Auto Workers, 1935-1975.* Ithaca: Cornell University Press, 1990.

Giddings, Paula. *When and Where I Enter: The Impact of Black Women on Race and Sex in America.* New York: Bantam Books, 1984.

Gluck, Sherna B. *Rosie the Riveter Revisited: Women, the War, and Social Change.* Boston: Twayne Publishers, 1987.

Greenberg, Cheryl. "The Politics of Disorder: Reexamining Harlem's Riots of 1935-1943." *Journal of Urban History* 18 (1992): 395-441.

Gregory, Chester. *Women in Defense Work during World War II.* New York: Exposition Press, 1974.

Harley, Sharon, and Rosalyn Terborg-Penn, eds. *The Afro-American Woman: Struggles and Images.* Port Washington, N.Y.: Kennikat Press, 1978.

Hartmann, Susan. *The Home Front and Beyond: American Women in the 1940s.* Boston: Twayne Publishers, 1982.

———. "Prescriptions for Penelope: Literature on Women's Obligations to Returning World War II Veterans." *Women's Studies* 5, no. 3 (1978): 223-39.

———. "Women's Organizations during World War II: The Interaction of Class, Race, and Feminism." In *Woman's Being, Woman's Place: Female*

Identity and Vocation in American History, ed. Mary Kelley. Boston: G. K. Hall, 1979.

Haskell, Molly. *From Reverence to Rape: The Treatment of Women in the Movies.* New York: Holt, Rinehart, and Winston, 1974.

Higgonet, Margaret Randolph, Jane Jenson, Sonya Michel, and Margaret Collins Weitz, eds. *Behind the Lines: Gender and the Two World Wars.* New Haven: Yale University Press, 1987.

Himes, Chester. *The Collected Stories of Chester Himes.* New York: Thunders Mouth Press, 1990.

———. *The Quality of Hurt: The Autobiography of Chester Himes.* Vol. 1. New York: Doubleday, 1972.

Hine, Darlene Clark. *Hinesight: Black Women and the Re-Construction of American History.* Brooklyn: Carlson Publishing, 1994.

Hine, Darlene Clark, and Kathleen Thompson. *A Shining Thread of Hope: The History of Black Women in America.* New York: Broadway Books, 1998.

Honey, Maureen. *Creating Rosie the Riveter: Class, Gender, and Propaganda during World War II.* Amherst: University of Massachusetts Press, 1984.

Hooks, Bell. *Ain't I A Woman: Black Women and Feminism.* Boston: South End Press, 1981.

———. *Outlaw Culture: Resisting Representation.* New York: Routledge, 1994.

Howell, Robert. "The Writers' War Board: Writers and World War II." Ph.D. diss., Louisiana State Agricultural and Mechanical College, 1971.

Hunter, Tera W. *To 'Joy My Freedom: Southern Black Women's Lives and Labors after the Civil War.* Cambridge: Harvard University Press, 1998.

Ivey, James. "Ann Petry Talks about First Novel." In *Ann Petry: A Bio-Bibliography,* by Hazel Arnett Ervin. New York: G. K. Hall, 1993. [Originally appeared in *The Crisis,* February 1946, 48.]

Johnson, Abby Arthur, and Ronald Maberry Johnson. *Propaganda and Aesthetics: The Literary Politics of Afro-American Magazines in the Twentieth Century.* Amherst: University of Massachusetts Press, 1979.

Jeansonne, Glen. *Women of the Far Right: The Mothers' Movement and World War II.* Chicago: University of Chicago Press, 1996.

Jones, David. "The U.S. Office of War Information and American Public Opinion during World War II, 1939–1945." Ph.D. diss., State University of New York–Binghamton, 1976.

Jones, Jacqueline. *Labor of Love, Labor of Sorrow: Black Women, Work, and the Family from Slavery to the Present.* New York: Basic Books, 1985.

Joseph, Gloria, and Jill Lewis. *Common Differences: Conflicts in Black and White Feminist Perspectives.* New York: Anchor Books, 1981.

Kaldein, Eugenia. *Mothers and More: American Women in the 1950s.* Boston: Twayne Publishers, 1984.

Katzman, David. *Seven Days a Week: Women and Domestic Service in Industrializing America.* New York: Oxford University Press, 1978.

Kesselman, Amy. *Fleeting Opportunities: Women Shipyard Workers in Portland and Vancouver during World War II and Reconversion.* Albany: SUNY Press, 1990.

Kessler-Harris, Alice. "Rosie the Riveter: Who Was She?" *Labor History* 24 (1983): 249–53.

Koppes, Clayton, and Gregory Black. "Blacks, Loyalty, and Motion-Picture Propaganda in World War II." *Journal of American History* 73 (1986): 383–406.

———. *Hollywood Goes to War: How Politics, Profits, and Propaganda Shaped World War II Movies.* New York: Free Press, 1987.

Kossoudji, Sherrie A., and Laura J. Dresser. "The End of a Riveting Experience: Occupational Shifts at Ford after World War II." *American Economic Review* 82 (1992): 519–25.

———. "Working Class Rosies: Women Industrial Workers during World War II." *Journal of Economic History* 52 (1992): 431–36.

Ladner, Joyce. *Tomorrow's Tomorrow: The Black Woman.* New York: Doubleday, 1972.

Langlois, Janet L. "The Belle Isle Bridge Incident: Legend Dialect and Semiotic Systems in the 1943 Detroit Race Riots." *Journal of American Folklore* 96 (1983): 183–99.

Lemke-Santangelo, Gretchen. *Abiding Courage: African American Migrant Women and the East Bay Community.* Chapel Hill: University of North Carolina Press, 1996.

Lerner, Gerda. *Black Women in White America: A Documentary History.* New York: Pantheon Books, 1972.

Lipsitz, George. *Rainbow at Midnight: Labor and Culture in the 1940s.* Champaign: University of Illinois Press, 1994.

Litoff, Judy Barrett, and David C. Smith. " 'Will He Get My Letter?': Popular Portrayals of Mail and Morale during World War II." *Journal of Popular Culture* 23 (1990): 21–43.

Lorde, Audre. *Zami: A New Spelling of My Name.* Trumansburg, N.Y.: Crossing Press, 1982.

Lynn, Susan. *Progressive Women in Conservative Times: Racial Justice, Peace, and Feminism, 1945 to the 1960s.* New Brunswick: Rutgers University Press, 1996.

Marable, Manning. *Race, Reform, and Rebellion: The Second Reconstruction in Black America, 1945-1990.* Jackson: University Press of Mississippi, 1996.

May, Elaine Tyler. *Homeward Bound: American Families in the Cold War.* New York: Basic Books, 1988.

Mazon, Mauricio. *The Zoot-Suit Riots: The Psychology of Symbolic Annihilation.* Austin: University of Texas Press, 1984.

McGuire, Philip. "Desegregation of the Armed Forces: Black Leadership, Protest, and World War II." *Journal of Negro History* 68 (1983): 147-58.

Meier, August, and Elliott Rudwick. *CORE: A Study in the Civil Rights Movement, 1942-1968.* New York: Oxford University Press, 1973.

Meyerowitz, Joanne. "Beyond the Feminine Mystique: A Reassessment of Postwar Mass Culture, 1946-1958." In *Not June Cleaver: Women and Gender in Postwar America, 1945-1960.* Philadelphia: Temple University Press, 1994.

Milkman, Ruth. *The Dynamics of Job Segregation by Sex during World War II.* Champaign: University of Illinois Press, 1986.

Mormino, Gary R. "GI Joe Meets Jim Crow: Racial Violence and Reform in World War II." *Florida Historical Quarterly* 73 (1994): 23-42.

Morrison, Toni. *The Bluest Eye.* New York: Holt, Rinehart, and Winston, 1970.

———. "What the Black Woman Thinks about Women's Lib." *New York Times Magazine,* August 22, 1971, 63.

Mullen, Bill V. *Popular Fronts: Chicago and African-American Cultural Politics, 1935-46.* Bloomington: Indiana University Press, 1999.

Murphy, Beatrice, ed. *Ebony Rhythm.* Freeport, N.Y.: Books for Libraries Press, 1948.

———. *Negro Voices.* New York: Henry Harrison, 1938.

Nelson, Stanley. *The Black Press: Soldiers without Swords.* San Francisco: California Newsreel, 1998.

Newman, Dorothy, et al. *Protest, Politics, and Prosperity: Black Americans and White Institutions, 1940-1975.* New York: Pantheon, 1978.

O'Brien, Kenneth, and Lynn Parsons, eds. *The Home-Front War: World War II and American Society.* Westport, Conn.: Greenwood Press, 1995.

O'Neill, William. *Everyone Was Brave: A History of Feminism in America.* New York: Quadrangle, 1969.

Peterson, Theodore. *Magazines in the Twentieth Century.* Urbana: University of Illinois Press, 1964.

Petry, Ann. *Miss Muriel and Other Stories.* Boston: Houghton Mifflin, 1971. Reprint, Boston: Beacon Press, 1989. [Page citations are to reprint edition.]

———. *The Street.* Boston: Houghton Mifflin, 1946.

Phenix, William. "Eagles Unsung: The Tuskegee Airmen in World War II." *Michigan History* 71 (1987): 24-30.

Polenberg, Richard. *War and Society: The United States, 1941-1945.* Philadelphia: J. B. Lippincott, 1972.

Robnett, Belinda. *How Long? How Long? African American Women in the Struggle for Civil Rights.* New York: Oxford University Press, 1997.

Rollins, Judith. *Between Women: Domestics and Their Employers.* Philadelphia: Temple University Press, 1985.

Roses, Lorraine, and Ruth Randolph. *Harlem's Glory: Black Women Writing, 1900-1950.* Cambridge: Harvard University Press, 1996.

Ross, Joyce B. "Mary McLeod Bethune and the National Youth Administration: A Case Study of Power Relationships in the Black Cabinet of Franklin D. Roosevelt." *Journal of Negro History* (January 1975): 45-60.

Rupp, Leila J. *Mobilizing Women for War: German and American Propaganda, 1939-1945.* Princeton: Princeton University Press, 1978.

Rupp, Leila, and Verta Taylor. *Survival in the Doldrums: The American Women's Rights Movement, 1945 to the 1960s.* New York: Oxford University Press, 1987.

Sandler, Stanley. *Segregated Skies: All-Black Combat Squadrons of World War II.* Washington D.C.: Smithsonian Press, 1998.

Schweik, Susan. *A Gulf So Deeply Cut: American Women Poets and the Second World War.* Madison: University of Wisconsin Press, 1991.

Scott, Lawrence P., and William M. Womack Sr. *Double V: The Civil Rights Struggle of the Tuskegee Airmen.* East Lansing: Michigan State University Press, 1994.

Seaver, Edwin, ed. *Cross Section.* New York, L. B. Fisher, 1947.

Sitkoff, Harvard. "Racial Militancy and Interracial Violence in the Second World War." *Journal of American History* 58 (December 1971): 661-81.

———. *The Struggle for Black Equality, 1954-1980.* New York: Hill and Wang, 1981.

Straub, Eleanor. "U.S. Government Policy toward Civilian Women during World War II." *Prologue* 5 (winter 1973): 240-54.

Talalay, Kathryn. *Composition in Black and White: The Life of Philippa Duke Schuyler.* New York: Oxford University Press, 1995.

Tyler, Bruce. "The Black Double V Campaign for Racial Democracy during World War II." *Journal of Kentucky Studies* 8 (1991): 79–108.

———. "Black Jive and White Repression." *Journal of Ethnic Studies* 16, no. 4 (winter 1989): 31–66.

Walsh, Andrea S. *Women's Films and Female Experience, 1940–1950.* New York: Praeger Press, 1984.

Washburn, Patrick. *A Question of Sedition: The Federal Government's Investigation of the Black Press during World War II.* New York: Oxford University Press, 1986.

Winkler, Allan M. *Home Front U.S.A.: America during World War II.* Arlington Heights, Va.: Harlan Davidson, 1986.

———. *The Politics of Propaganda: The Office of War Information, 1942–1945.* New Haven: Yale University Press, 1978.

Wynn, Neil A. *The Afro-American and the Second World War.* New York: Holmes and Meier, 1993.

Index to Authors

Index to Titles

Credits

The editor wishes to thank the following groups and individuals for authorizing the use of works they have published.

The Crisis Publishing Co., Inc., the magazine of the National Association for the Advancement of Colored People.

The National Urban League, publisher of *Opportunity.*

"Gay Chaps at the Bar," from *Blacks,* by Gwendolyn Brooks, © 1991. Published by Third World Press, Chicago, 1991. Reprinted by permission of Gwendolyn Brooks.

"In Darkness and Confusion," from *Miss Muriel and Other Stories,* by Ann Petry, reprinted by the permission of Russell & Volkening as agents for the author. Copyright © 1947 by Ann Petry, renewed 1975 by Ann Petry. Story originally appeared in the anthology *Cross Section,* 1947.

"Harlem Night" ("Troubled Night"), and "Note on Commercial Theatre" ("Note on Commercial Art"), from *Collected Poems,* by Langston Hughes, copyright © 1994 by the Estate of Langston Hughes, reprinted by permission of Alfred A. Knopf, Inc.

About the Editor

Maureen Honey is Professor of English and Women's Studies at the University of Nebraska. She is the author of several books, including *Creating Rosie the Riveter: Class, Gender, and Propaganda during World War II* and *Shadowed Dreams: Women's Poetry of the Harlem Renaissance*.